Toronto, Montreal
& Québec City

2nd Edition

Herbert Bailey Livesey

Prentice Hall Travel

New York • London • Toronto • Sydney • Tokyo • Singapore

THE AMERICAN EXPRESS ® TRAVEL GUIDES

Published in the United States by
Prentice Hall General Reference
A division of Simon & Schuster, Inc.
15 Columbus Circle
New York, NY 10023

PRENTICE HALL and colophon
are registered trademarks of
Simon & Schuster, Inc.

First published 1991 in the United
Kingdom by Mitchell Beazley, an
imprint of Reed Consumer Books Ltd,
Michelin House, 81 Fulham Road,
London SW3 6RB and Auckland,
Melbourne, Singapore and Toronto as
*The American Express Pocket Guide
to Toronto, Montréal & Québec City.*
This edition, revised, updated and
expanded, published 1993.

Edited, designed and produced by
Castle House Press, Llantrisant
Mid Glamorgan CF7 8EU, Wales

Library of Congress Catalog
Card Number 93-084012

ISBN 0-671-86823-3

The editors thank Neil Hanson of
Lovell Johns, David Haslam, Fred
Midwood, Sally Darlington and Sylvia
Hughes-Williams for their help and
co-operation during the preparation
of this edition. Thanks are also due to
the staff of the London offices of
Québec Tourism UK, the Ontario
Ministry of Tourism and Recreation,
and the Canadian Tourist Office.

FOR THE SERIES:
Series Editor:
   David Townsend Jones
Map Editor: David Haslam
Indexer: Hilary Bird
Gazetteer: Anna Holmes
Cover design: Roger Walton Studio

FOR THIS EDITION:
Edited on desktop by:
   Eileen Townsend Jones
Art editors: Castle House Press
Illustrators: Karen Cochrane,
   Sylvia Hughes-Williams
Cover photo:
   Tony Stone Worldwide

FOR MITCHELL BEAZLEY:
Art Director: Tim Foster
Production: Katy Sawyer
Publisher: Sarah Bennison

PRODUCTION CREDITS:
Maps by Lovell Johns,
   Oxford, England
Typeset in Garamond and
   News Gothic
Desktop layout in Ventura
   Publisher
Reproduction by M & E
   Reproductions, Essex, England
Linotronic output by Tradespools
   Limited, Frome, England

Contents

Ontario and Québec

Toronto

Montréal

Québec City

Maps

How to use this book

Few guidelines are needed to understand how this book works:

- For the general organization of the book, see CONTENTS on the pages preceding this one.
- Wherever appropriate, chapters and sections are arranged alphabetically, with headings appearing in **CAPITALS.**
- Often these headings are followed by location and practical information printed in *italics.*
- As you turn the pages, you will find subject headers, similar to those used in telephone directories, printed in CAPITALS in the top corner of each page.
- If you still cannot find what you need, check in the comprehensive and exhaustively cross-referenced INDEX at the back of the book.
- Following the index, a LIST OF STREET NAMES provides map references for all roads and streets mentioned in the book that fall within the areas covered by the main city maps (the color maps at the back of the book).

CROSS-REFERENCES

These are printed in SMALL CAPITALS, referring you to other sections or alphabetical entries in the book. Care has been taken to ensure that such cross-references are self-explanatory. Often, page references are also given, although their excessive use would be intrusive and ugly.

FLOORS

In Ontario we use the American convention: "first floor" means the floor at ground level. In Québec, to conform with local usage, we adopt the European convention, where this is expressed as "ground floor."

AUTHOR'S ACKNOWLEDGMENTS

The author wishes to thank the Québec Ministère du Tourisme, the Metropolitan Toronto Convention & Visitors Association, Québec City Tourism and Convention Bureau, and Air Canada, for their assistance in the various stages of the preparation of this guide. Thanks are also due to Cherry Kam of the Four Seasons Hotel in Toronto and Jody Goodman of the Hôtel Inter-Continental Montréal, whose help was much appreciated.

Key to symbols

☎	Telephone	▦	Air conditioning
Fx	Facsimile (fax)	▣	Secure garage
★	Recommended sight	▱	Quiet hotel
➤	Parking	▯	Business center
▣	Free entrance	♿	Facilities for disabled
▥	Entrance fee payable		people
▤	Photography forbidden	▨	Dogs not allowed
↗	Guided tour	♣	Garden/terrace
▣	Cafeteria	◀	Good view
✦	Special interest for	↗	Tennis
	children	▦	Swimming pool
◈	Hotel	▼	Gym/fitness facilities
▥	Deluxe hotel	◀	Sauna
♣	Good value	▼	Bar
	(in its class)	▣	Mini-bar
AE	American Express	▬	Restaurant
◆	Diners Club	◢	Deluxe restaurant
◐	MasterCard	♪	Nightclub
VISA	Visa	♫	Live music

PRICE CATEGORIES

▢	Cheap	▥	Expensive
▱	Inexpensive	▦	Very expensive
▥	Moderately priced		

Our price categories for hotels and restaurants are explained in the
WHERE TO STAY and EATING AND DRINKING chapters for each city.

About the author

After an early career in higher education culminating in the post of Director of Admissions at New York University, **Herbert Bailey Livesey** decided that he no longer wanted to get up early and wear suits. An exhibition of his sculptures had proved a modest critical success and a resounding financial flop, so he decided, with greater logic than might be apparent, to leave salaried employment for a full-time career in writing. A native New Yorker, he is the author of nine books on such subjects as education and sociology. *Tournament*, his only published novel, took as its backdrop the world of deep-sea game-fishing.

The descendent of Canadian boatbuilders, and the son of a woman born in Nova Scotia, Livesey has an abiding affection for the people of the land up north. He has written three other books in this series, *New York* (1983), *Barcelona, Madrid & Seville* (1992) and the forthcoming *Boston and New England*. His work appears frequently in a variety of magazines, including *Travel and Leisure* and *Food and Wine*. He and his wife Joanne, a television executive, share four grown children and one very new granddaughter, Juliana. They live in a house north of New York City, overlooking the bay in which explorer Henry Hudson anchored his boat, the *Half Moon,* in 1609.

A message from the editors

Months of concentrated work were dedicated to making this edition accurate and up to date when it went to press. But time and change are forever the enemies, and between editions we are very much assisted when you, our readers, write to tell us about any changes you discover.

Please keep on writing — but please also be aware that we have no control over restaurants, or whatever, that take it into their heads, after we publish, to move, or change their telephone number, or, even worse, close down. Our authors and editors aim to exclude trendy ephemera and to recommend places that give every indication of being stable and durable. Their judgment is rarely wrong. Changes in telephone numbers are something else. We apologise for the world's telephone authorities, who seem to change their numbers like you and I change shirts.

My serious point is that we are striving to tailor the series to the very distinctive tastes and requirements of our discerning international readership, which is why your feedback is so valuable. I particularly want to thank all of you who wrote while we were preparing this edition. Time prevents our responding to most such letters, but they are all welcomed and frequently contribute to the process of preparing the next edition.

Please write to me at **Mitchell Beazley**, an imprint of Reed Illustrated Books, Michelin House, 81 Fulham Road, London SW3 6RB; or, in the US, c/o American Express Travel Guides, **Prentice Hall Travel**, 15 Columbus Circle, New York, NY 10023.

David Townsend Jones, Series Editor, American Express Travel Guides

Toronto, Montréal
& Québec City

Ontario and Québec: discord and empathy

Every nation does battle with perceptions, those assigned to it by outsiders as well as by its own people. Ask an American for a succinct description of Canada, and the response is apt to amount to a vague comparison with the United States, *only quieter.* This image is quite maddening to Canadians, who know better, but must deal with the frustrating knowledge that their society is one of the least well examined and understood in the industrialized world.

Europeans are, if anything, even more ignorant of their loyal ally. Their comprehension of Canada's vastness is scant. Be it known, then, that the single province of Québec is larger in its land area than France, Belgium, Switzerland, Portugal, Spain and unified Germany put together.

Far from being a mere appendage to its rambunctious cousin to the south, Canada boasts an enviable roster of virtues now lost or unattainable by its neighbor. Nowhere is this more evident than in Toronto and Montréal, queen cities of the two most populous of its ten provinces, Ontario and Québec. They are arguably the most liveable and humane of any in the Western hemisphere.

Proof of that claim isn't difficult to find. Both cities enjoy superb public transit systems, an abundance of parks and green spaces, vigorous but unintimidating commercial centers, lively multi-ethnic communities, excellent educational and cultural institutions, and impressive sports facilities featuring roofed stadiums. The last are desirable, if not essential, to foil the long winter. But these cities also boast vast underground shopping and entertainment complexes, making it possible to leave a hotel, have lunch, see a movie, buy a shirt, and quaff a beer in a pub, all without donning a coat or hailing a taxi.

Even the tallest skyscrapers are kept to reasonable heights — they rarely exceed 40 stories and thus retain a human scale. Vehicular traffic is manageable, notwithstanding the complaints of natives, and is far less harrowing than that experienced in London or New York. The streets are well-tended, and, more important, safe, being the beneficiaries of very low crime rates. One result is a thriving nightlife of diverse dining, concerts, clubs and theater.

Nor is that all to commend a visit. Canada is that rarity among nations — an officially bilingual state. That means the privilege of hearing the most melodious of languages in predominantly French-speaking Québec while knowing that assistance in English is never far away. Québec City, in particular, is evocative of a captivating French provincial capital, a walled city with the bonus of a stunning riverside setting. Easy excursions by car can include skiing in Québec's Laurentians, watersports on Lake Huron's Georgian Bay, or a tour of the primordial peaks and beaches of the Gaspé Peninsula.

And should a clincher be necessary, prices for most services and goods are affordable, only partly due to currency exchange rates that have favored American and European visitors for several years.

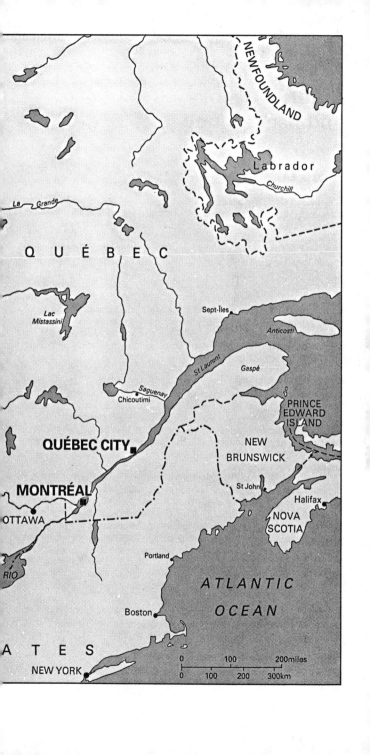

Culture, history and background

A brief history

To a great extent, the history of Canada is that of Québec and Ontario. They were the sites of colonial wars between England, France and the United States. French explorer Jacques Cartier spent the winter of 1535–36 at the site of what became, in 1608 under Samuel de Champlain, the fortress village of Québec. That was only one year after the founding of Jamestown in Virginia. The difference was that Jamestown died while Québec prospered.

The federal capital of Canada is Ottawa, in Ontario Province, to the north of Toronto. It is mirrored by the city of Hull, directly across the Ottawa River in Québec Province. Toronto and Montréal are the financial powerhouses of the nation. Their two provinces contain over 15 million people, more than half the population of the country. And they are on the front lines of the long-festering language dispute, the divisive issue that might yet tear the nation in two.

THE EARLY SETTLERS
Cartier was not the first man to set foot on Canadian soil, nor even the first European. John Cabot established the British claim when he stepped down on the east coast in 1497, and he was preceded five centuries earlier by Norsemen, and, probably, Irish and Iberian fishermen. Even they were latecomers, intruders upon the territories of the Cree and Inuit, the Huron and Iroquois, who began to come from Asia some 40,000 years ago.

The Frenchmen most responsible for opening the huge new continent were fur trappers and traders. An energetic lot, their explorations carried them far to the west, south and north. In 1682, René-Robert Cavalier de LaSalle took a party all the way down the Mississippi to its mouth. After that then-astonishing voyage, the empire of New France swept from the Gulf of Mexico to Hudson Bay. One result was that it barred the westward expansion of the English colonies forming along the Atlantic coast. The circumstances were thus set for nearly a century of war between the French and their Indian allies and the British and their American colonists. Hostilities proceeded with predictable savagery, coming to no decisive conclusion until 1759.

The defeat of an Anglo–American force in frontier Pennsylvania in 1755 marked the start of what was called The French and Indian War. It was an extension of the Seven Years' War in Europe, which pitted Great

Britain and Prussia against France, Austria and Sweden. With England's attention diverted to battlefields as far away as India, New France made a number of sorties into the British colonies, capturing forts in upper New York State, among others.

Then, the 1759 Québec campaign was launched. The Marquis de Montcalm had deployed troops in and near Québec City. The British General James Wolfe sailed up the St Lawrence River and landed on the opposite shore. After several feints and skirmishes, scouts discovered a narrow gap in the rocky cliffs on the French shore. Thinking it impossible to traverse, Montcalm had assigned only a token guard. In the still dark hours of the morning of September 13, Wolfe led his men up through the defile to the Plains of Abraham, a high plateau west of the city.

There the battle was joined, 4,000 French soldiers marching in close-order ranks toward the waiting British force of 4,500. It was over in less than 30 minutes. Wolfe was killed, Montcalm was mortally wounded and died the next day. Québec surrendered. New France was now British Canada. The event is known to this day as "The Conquest," words still uttered with bitterness by many French Canadians.

THE BRITISH "CONQUEST"

The 1763 Treaty of Paris validated the transfer of power. New France became known as Lower Canada, and the new British possession remained overwhelmingly French until the outbreak of the American Revolution in 1775. Persecuted and reviled as "Tories," loyalists to the Crown poured across the border into Canada, settling into the existing English-speaking settlements of Nova Scotia and New Brunswick, but also in Lower Canada along the St Lawrence Valley and as far west as the Niagara Peninsula. Representatives of the American Continental Congress were sent to Lower Canada to attempt to persuade the inhabitants to join them in rebellion against their common master. They were astonished to be rebuffed, failing to appreciate that the royalist Québécois found the American cause as odious as British rule.

When the war began, one of the first offensives of the new Army of the United Colonies was launched against Lower Canada. One contingent took Montréal, then joined General Benedict Arnold downriver in his siege of Québec City. Some French Canadians sold provisions to the Americans and others joined the British defenders at the parapets, but most remained neutral. Stalemate was broken by the arrival of British reinforcements, and the Americans withdrew. It was to be only the first of several American incursions into Canada, the last nearly a century later. That hostile history is understandably ignored when politicians on both sides croon about "the longest unfortified border in the world."

A surge in immigration had begun to populate Lower Canada, and in 1791 the colony was divided in two, creating "Upper" Canada ("Upper" because it was up the St Lawrence, to the west of what became Québec). This was the region eventually called Ontario, in which John Graves Simcoe founded the town of York, later to become Toronto.

The young American republic was again at war with England in 1813, when one of its fleets attacked and burned York. The British, then occupied with Napoleon Bonaparte, waited until after his abdication the following year to retaliate against Washington, DC, where they torched the White House and numerous public buildings.

The war came to its murky conclusion in 1814. The US and Britain did agree to demilitarize the Great Lakes and extend the Canadian–US border along the 49th Parallel to the Pacific Ocean. Relaxation of military tensions, and America's slow-dawning realization that Canada did not wish to merge with her, brought on what came to be called the "Era of Good Feelings."

Immigration from Britain and Europe multiplied. Before long, newcomers to Canada were emboldened to challenge the ruling group known as the Family Compact. When political action failed to bring satisfaction, 1837 saw brief armed revolts against the authoritarian governments of Upper and Lower Canada. While they were quickly suppressed, some of the goals of the protestors were soon realized, including the establishment of elected legislatures.

Canadian wariness of expansionist America was revived with the advent of the war between the states in 1861. In a foretaste of events during the era of the Vietnam War a century later, Union draft dodgers fled into Canada, straining relations between the two countries once again. A foray by Confederate guerrillas into Vermont from their base near Montréal brought American threats of hot pursuit and diplomatic retribution. Cool heads prevailed, but a desire to stiffen the common defense was part of the reason for agreement to Canadian confederation in 1867, through the vehicle of the British North America Act.

Ontario and Québec were two of the first four provinces to sign what amounted to a partial constitution granting them dominion status within the British Commonwealth. Conduct of foreign policy remained in the hands of Imperial London, but the new confederacy was to control its internal affairs.

The first Prime Minister was Sir John A. Macdonald, who served until 1873 and again from 1878–1891. His tenure saw the completion of the Canadian Pacific Railway, an engineering feat that helped unite the ocean-to-ocean country spiritually as well as physically. Four interim prime ministers in the next five years were followed by Sir Wilfrid Laurier, the first prime minister whose background was French. Serving from 1896–1911, he oversaw an era of prosperity and new-found national confidence.

THE EARLY 20TH CENTURY

That optimism was shaken by World War I, in which more than 60,000 Canadian soldiers died, half again as many as were later to perish in World War II. The imposition of military conscription in 1917 was vigorously opposed by French Canadians, who saw it as a form of piecemeal genocide.

After the war, however, Canada emerged as an important industrial power. It did not join the American experiment with Prohibition, and, indeed, fortunes were made in bootlegging liquor to the dry states. It did, however, share in the agony of the Great Depression, which was not relieved until Hitler's rise to power made it necessary to gear up for another European conflagration.

Immigration laws were loosened, and the national population was to double over the next 30 years.

UNITY AND DIVISION

By 1960, a "Quiet Revolution" seized public attention. French Québeckers, chafing under the inherent inequities of living in a predominantly English-speaking country, began to agitate for equal social and legal status. Many felt this was only possible with political autonomy or even complete independence. The separatist *Parti Québécois* came to prominence, and extremists took to bombing Anglo enterprises. In 1968, a bilingual Québecker, Pierre Trudeau succeeded Lester Pearson as Prime Minister.

In 1969, the Official Languages Act provided the mandate for all federal agencies and corporations to provide services in both French and English. It failed to placate the radical separatist group FLQ, which in 1970 kidnapped and murdered a cabinet minister, Pierre Laporte.

The language issue remains the single most volatile and divisive in Canadian life. After Trudeau engineered a Canadian Constitution and Charter of Rights and Freedoms in 1982, which effectively removed the hold of the British North America Act, it was felt necessary to initiate a national conference to address the shortcomings of the constitution. The meeting took place in 1987 and in large measure focused on recognition of Québec as a "distinct society" within the confederation.

Two years later, the resulting Meech Lake Accord (simply "Meech" in political shorthand) drew fire from certain provincial ministers who expressed alarm over what they saw as the special status given Québec.

Since the accord stipulated that all ten provinces must approve its provisions, it foundered and died in 1990. Resurgent Québec separatist sentiments gained momentum. Another constitutional agreement — more complex, yet vague in details of implementation — was hammered together at a meeting of the first ministers in Charlottetown, on Prince Edward Island. In addition to reaffirming Québec's "distinct society" status, its compromises included a proposed new Senate with greater authority, a House of Commons with 25 percent of its seats guaranteed to Québec, a new layer of self-government for aboriginal peoples, and closer provincial authority over funding for infrastructure and social programs.

Although even those ministers who had opposed Meech approved and actively supported this accord, it was defeated in a national referendum in October 1992. That was the final setback for Brian Mulroney, who was by then suffering the lowest approval ratings in national opinion polls of any Prime Minister in this century. He resigned in February 1993, after $8\frac{1}{2}$ years in office.

Again, calls for partial or complete independence gather strength in French Canada, and English Canada seems to care less and less that the shaky union might shatter. The battle that raged on the Plains of Abraham more than 230 years ago has yet to arrive at its final conclusion.

Landmarks in Canadian history

1608 Champlain established an outpost at the site of Québec City.
1642 Founding of the settlement of Ville-Marie by de Maisonneuve, below the hill named by Jacques Cartier as *Mont Réal*.
1670 The Hudson Bay trading company started operations.
1689 Beginning of the French and Indian wars that were to last for 74 years.
1759 British defeat of the French at Québec City.
1763 "New France" ceded to the English in the Treaty of Paris.
1774 Québec Act passed by the British Parliament, granting religious authority to the Catholic Church and colonial observance of the French legal structure.
1837 Dissidents rebelled against the ruling oligarchies of Québec and Ontario but were quickly quelled.
1867 British North America Act created the Canadian Dominion.
1874 First football game pitted McGill University and Harvard.
1896 Wilfrid Laurier became first Francophone Prime Minister.
1891 J.A. Naismith invented the game of basketball.
1893 Professional hockey's Stanley Cup first awarded.
1914 Start of World War I. Conscription caused severe political crisis.
1918 Universal female suffrage enacted for federal elections.
1959 St Lawrence Seaway opened Great Lakes to the Atlantic.
1969 French and English given parity by the Official Languages Act.
1976 *Parti Québécois* wins election in Québec.
1980 People of Québec reject partial independence, in referendum.
1982 Constitution patriated from England, amended by Charter of Rights and Freedoms.
1987 In the Meech Lake Accord, Québec extracted a "notwithstanding" clause that allowed it to override federal decrees.
1990 Meech Lake constitutional accord foundered.
1992 The Charlottetown accord was formulated, but was voted down in a national referendum. 350th anniversary of the founding of Montréal and 125th anniversary of Canadian confederation.
1993 Resignation of Prime Minister Brian Mulroney.

Politics and the US factor

Pierre Trudeau likened sharing a continent with the United States to sleeping with an elephant. The quip speaks volumes, not only about the often bristly relationship between siblings in the same extended family, but also about the national character. Cautiousness is a component of the Canadian makeup, but so is irritation over being taken for granted. Just as the younger brother stands back during episodes of older brother's rage and self-absorbed blundering, so does he also crave equity and recognition of his own distinctiveness. Yet because he is often ignored, he doesn't quite know how to handle attention when it is given him. Canadians seemed almost embarrassed by the outpouring of American gratitude when their diplomats rescued some of their US counterparts during the Iran hostage crisis. They continue to be outraged, on the other hand, over casual US attendance to their concerns about acid rain and free trade.

Their ambivalence breeds both diffidence and defensiveness, a sense of inferiority mingled with a certainty of superiority. They are not, they emphatically want it to be known, carbon-copy Americans, despite surface similarities. Both are children of the lost British Empire, to be sure, the descendants of pioneers and immigrants who share general assumptions about morality and democratic ideals. They eat the same fast foods, follow the same fads, and worry about crime, the environment and the pounds they've been meaning to shed. Most of them, the English-speaking ones, even sound the same, although Canadians give a Scottish *oo* sound to *about* and *house,* and are inclined to append *eh?* to the ends of sentences.

But they differ in nearly as many ways. The population of Canada is slightly more than 10 percent that of the US, but scattered across a land mass that is 10 percent larger. Such geographical separation promotes loyalty to a region, not a country, so most Canadians have only a splintered grasp of the concept of nationhood. That makes all the more alarming to them the paroxysms of chauvinism that periodically seize the people residing below the 49th parallel. Canadians and Americans have fought together in three wars in this century, but they do not always agree on the justice of causes. Thousands of American draft evaders sought refuge in Canada during the Vietnam era and were treated amicably by people who found that particular war repugnant.

While both observe democratic procedures, Canadians vote on a flexible schedule that requires the party in power to expose itself to periodic approval, not merely serve out its term. Its national Parliament is bicameral — the House of Commons elective, the Senate appointive. The Prime Minister, head of the federal government, is only first among nearly equal provincial premiers, and the federal wing of a political party often has different objectives than its provincial versions.

Conversely, the provinces are dependent upon federal support to provide public services and the physical infrastructure, even though they exercise total control over their own educational systems and such natural resources as are found within their territories. A decidedly mixed economy has evolved, part planned, part free market. Forms of cradle-to-grave security, notably in health care, are immovably in place. They are the sort of welfare programs that set wattles aquiver throughout Washington when they are even suggested. That doesn't mean they just happened, for nothing comes easily in Canadian political life. Consensus is elusive at best, with prolonged debate usually required to reach even tentative compromise. It took decades to hammer out the particulars of the Constitution, and that heavily amended document is still under threat.

And always, tossing about "down there," is the wooly American mammoth, all heedless knees and elbows. Canada watches its every move, by turns appalled, amused, bemused, bewitched. Another former superpower was its other immediate neighbor; but the Soviet Union was always over the frozen horizon and what is left of it no longer seems threatening.

The alien political and cultural tremors with which Canada must cope rumble from its south. It has ample advance warning. About 90 percent of its population live within 100 miles of that border, most of it within reach of US television and radio transmitters. The daily dose of situation comedies and game shows may seem benign (or banal) enough, but it is undeniably invasive. Who knows what social viruses — from the Canadian perspective — the nightly onslaught of other influences might carry?

Efforts have been made to dike the flood. "Canadian content" regulations dictate how much of Canadian Broadcasting Corporation programming may be allotted to shows of American origin, and require publishers and film-makers to observe similar formulas. Their effectiveness is debatable. The top-rated US programs weigh heavily on the Canadian charts too.

Because of television, Canadian professional football is withering before the spangled version presented by the National Football League. There are, in all likelihood, more Canadian fans of the Cleveland Browns and Detroit Lions than of the Toronto Argonauts and Calgary Stampeders. Montréal's team faded into total oblivion due to lack of interest. Hockey is a Canadian passion, but the misnamed National Hockey League has only eight teams based in Canadian cities. There are 16 in the US.

Under the circumstances, cross-fertilization is unstoppable. Many of those same film and TV dramas, purportedly situated in Los Angeles or New York, are actually shot in Vancouver or Toronto. (They have to dirty up the streets to make it believable.)

Canadian-born performers are found in every category of American show business. Torontonian Raymond Massey had his most famous role as Abraham Lincoln. Montréaler William Shatner skippered the Starship *Enterprise* through a TV series and five *Star Trek* movies. Comedians and comic actors Alan Thicke, Martin Short, Rich Little, Catherine O'Hara, John Candy, Dan Aykroyd; singers Anne Murray, Robert Goulet, Paul Anka, K.D. Lang; actors Michael J. Fox, Leslie Nielson, Kate Nelligan, Hume Cronyn, Christopher Plummer, Donald Sutherland, and musicians Glenn Gould and Oscar Peterson — all Canadian, and only a few of many.

Celebrated Canadians in other fields include economist John Kenneth Galbraith, fashion-designer Arnold Scaasi, Washington Redskin quarterback Mark Rypien, writer Saul Bellow, real estate developer and publisher Mort Zuckerman, and newscaster Peter Jennings.

So many Canadians — a million a year by some estimates — vacation in the US, in California and Florida in particular, that some local radio stations broadcast daily segments from back home, and newsstands even carry Québec newspapers. In return, American tourists spend nearly $3 billion each year in Canada. In the financial world, investment works both ways, too. More than 70 percent of Canadian imports and exports pass through American hands, and at least that percentage of foreign investment in Canada is American.

On the other side of the ledger, some Canadian firms are highly visible in the US; these include the Four Seasons hotel chain, Odeon Cineplex cinemas, Seagram's Distillers, Peoples Drug Stores, Hardee's Restaurants, Olympia & York land developers, and Harlequin, publishers of paperback romances. Given that degree of interaction, and there is far more than can be described here, it is worthwhile to know who these Canadians are.

The people

They are not what might be expected, especially if one carries only an image of Mounties and Eskimos. For one thing, about one out of every eight Canadians was born somewhere else. Waves of immigration, notably since World War II, have brought millions of Chinese, Greeks, Portuguese, Eastern Europeans, West Indians, Koreans, Thais and Vietnamese. They were greeted with varying degrees of warmth by the already resident Scots, Irish, French, English, Germans and Italians.

Since these newer Canadians only reluctantly relinquish the symbols and ceremonies carried from their former homelands, they have cast a pulsating mosaic of exotic customs and practices upon the often dour foundation laid by their predecessors. The most visible evidence of this is seen along such concentrations of polyglot humanity as Blvd. St Laurent in Montréal and Bloor St. W in Toronto. Between the windows hung with glazed roast ducks and loops of *kielbasa* and greengrocer stands with *bok choy* and *cilantro,* are shops specializing in nothing at all, whose inventories can include videotapes in Cantonese, finger cymbals, memo pads, *cazuelas,* caramel candy, aspirin, incense and earmuffs, all arrayed side by side.

The truly native peoples of Canada are the Inuit and Amerindians. (Names such as "Eskimo" and "Indian" are out of favor, and the innocent British locution of "Red Indian" is regarded as near-racist. Current alternative labels in tentative use are "Original Peoples," "Founding Peoples," and "First Nations."

About 30,000 Inuit live in the far northern precincts of the country, while about 300,000 Amerindians remain in bands (not "tribes") on reserves (not "reservations"), some within walking distance of Montréal and Toronto. Their ancestors were rarely treated as harshly as were their brothers south of the border, but neglect and misguided paternalism thinned their numbers. Genuine concern for their welfare is now apparent, as activists and governments attempt to balance the preservation of traditional native living modes with the relentless pressures of the larger society.

The dominating cultures remain those of the two earliest groups of European settlers, especially in Ontario and Québec. There, Canadians of British Protestant heritage and those of French Catholic background confront each other across historic dividing lines. As is often true of antagonists living on opposite sides of the same street — figuratively and literally — they understand each other better than do those at greater distances from the fray. That prompts more ambivalence. When Québécois nationalism battered its way to power in the 1970s, English-speaking Québeckers left for Ontario by the tens of thousands, but not without regrets.

Although straitlaced Toronto has loosened its corset considerably in recent decades, transplanted Québeckers miss the *joie de vivre* of Montréal, the *croissants* and *café au lait* in sidewalk cafés and the music that thumps on toward dawn every weekend. For their part, clear-eyed Québécois intent on career advancement recognize that English, not French, is the language of business. And since bilingualism is now a marketable commodity, many of them have moved, too. Catholics now outnumber Protestants in Anglican–Presbyterian Toronto.

Given such heterogeneity, generalizations about the reception accorded to visitors are suspect. As a rule, however, courtesy can be expected in most transactions, albeit not always including those with bureaucrats. Social encounters are tentative at first, for Canadians are loath to appear brash or loud, but they soon prove to be open, friendly and curious. Bear in mind that a knowledge of English (or French, for that matter) cannot be assumed, and when a clerk or stranger seems unresponsive to a polite query, he or she may only be thinking who to ask for assistance.

The language issue

There was no event of more profound significance in Canadian history than the British triumph over the French at Québec City in 1759. Although an ecumenical monument now stands in a Québec park honoring the generals of both sides, victor and vanquished, the defeat is still recalled with bitterness by French Canadians. From that day to this, they have felt that they were second-class citizens in their own country, a French island in an English sea.

The official Québec motto has an ominous tone of eventual retribution: *Je me souviens*. Appearing even on automobile license plates, it means "I remember," alluding not only to that historic battle but to every slight since the onset of British sovereignty. By contrast, Ontario plates bear the wan legend "Yours To Discover."

Excesses of zeal and simple insensitivity have been common in both camps, but there is a persuasive case for assertions of anti-French discrimination. Well into the middle of this century, capital and political power were firmly in the hands of merchant princes and bankers of British heritage, and they routinely passed these on to their own kind.

A linguistic racism prevailed, not always overt or even conscious, but nevertheless denying French Canadians access to the executive suite and government ministries. This was especially galling in Québec, where Anglo–Canadians are a decided minority. It should not have been surprising that when the Québécois finally began to organize themselves effectively, they set about getting even. A good deal of petty harassment of the Anglo minority has taken place under the banner of preservation of the French language and culture.

While Canada as a whole is officially bilingual, the Québec government is intent upon making its province unilingually French. Where all exterior signs were until recently required to be in both English and French, now only French is allowed. This was legitimized by a legislative act, Bill 101, and has as its enforcement apparatus the Commission de la Langue Française, a virtual language police. The "tongue troopers" have taken down such unacceptable signs as "Merry Christmas" and confiscated Dunkin' Donuts bags printed only in English. They required Eaton's department store to drop the offending apostrophe and "s" from its name. Sellers of Harris Tweed were instructed to devise an equivalent French label or cease selling the product.

And on, and on. Obviously, this can be prickly terrain, and visitors should tread softly. They will hear unfamiliar words in English as well as French. Anglophones, françophones and allophones are those who respectively speak English, French, or anything else. The local French dialect, called *joal,* is hardly that of the classroom: a *dépanneur* is a corner convenience store, *souper* is the evening meal, and *chiens chauds* are hot dogs, but a *hambourgeois* is not a middle-class actor. (Think about it.) It helps to brush up on highway French, too, for that is how traffic signs read in Québec. When an 18-wheel truck is bearing down from the opposite direction is no time to learn that *reculez* means "Go back!"

Otherwise, the practical effect on visitors is minimal. The telephone operator or waiter gives greeting in French but typically shifts to English upon sensing hesitation. In those cities and smaller towns of interest to most tourists, help is always near.

The creative arts

A rich pool of native talent has cemented Canada's high standing in the performing arts. This is particularly true in classical ballet and modern dance, as exemplified by the Toronto Dance Theatre, Montréal's Les Grands Ballets Canadiens, and the National Ballet of Canada, one of the world's most honored troupes. While they are the elite in the field, other worthy companies vie for attention, among them Montréal's

Entre-Six and Ballets Classiques. They are provided with venues appropriate to their accomplishment, notably the Place des Arts complex in Montréal and the O'Keefe Centre in Toronto. These facilities are shared with such estimable musical organizations as the Toronto Philharmonic, Toronto Symphony and Montréal Symphony. Opera, jazz, choral and chamber music are also well represented.

Film-makers have carved a niche out of the path of the Hollywood juggernaut, frequently winning film festival awards for low-budget features on Canadian themes. Their often understated nature mitigates against the financial success associated with such explosive mega-hits as *Star Wars* and *Home Alone,* but then, they are not attempting to compete in that arena. Since World War II, aid has been given by the National Film Board. This body began as a propaganda arm of the government, moved on to the support of animated short subjects and now underwrites full-length theatrical and TV features. Examples of their quiet artistry are seen in such movies as *My American Cousin, The Grey Fox* and *Leopard in the Snow.*

Much pride is invested in the Group of Seven, a tightly-knit cooperative of painters that enjoyed approbation between the wars. Before them, Canadian painters tended to follow the leads of European portraiture and genre subjects. The ordered, bucolic pictures of the 19thC suggested Flanders and Provence more than they did the palpable silence of the empty prairie and the shriek of winter in the Canadian high country.

That changed with the coming together of a band of young artists at a design firm in Toronto. One of them, Tom Thomson, became enamored of the rugged terrain of Algonquin Park, west of Ottawa. He proceeded to capture it in oils, in distinctive paintings that breathed uniquely Canadian origins. They made converts of his friends Frank Carmichael, Lawren Harris, Alexander Jackson and James MacDonald. Frequently traveling and painting together in the years before World War I, they grew so close that they even worked in the same studio, built by the wealthy Harris.

The war intervened, and Thomson drowned in a lake in his beloved Algonquin Park in 1917; but the others got together again after the Armistice and enlisted Franz Johnston and Arthur Lismer in their movement. They exhibited together for the first time in 1920 at the Art Gallery of Toronto, as it was then called, in a show that won both praise and disapproval. It was the first of many, in Canada, the US and England, where the critical response was enthusiastic. With A.J. Casson and Edwin Holgate, who joined the group later, they were heralded as the creators of an important new school that was to influence Canadian painting into the last third of the 20th century.

The group disbanded in 1932, but its members stayed active, some of them veering into abstractionism in later years. Casson died, at 93, in 1992.

By contrast, a truly native art persists in the works of Inuit sculptors. Working with stone, bone and tusks, they portray what they know best: the work and creatures of their northern habitat — fishermen, polar bears and the musk ox. As admiration and demand for their products have grown, so has their sophistication, and larger pieces can fetch thousands of dollars.

Architecture

There was no significant permanent settlement in Ontario until after New France was ceded to the British in 1763, so the early architectural heritage of the nation's two largest provinces is that of Québec. After establishment of British dominion, however, architectural trends typically followed those prevailing in Europe and the US. Thus, the Georgian style of many late 18thC public buildings flowed into the Classical Revival of the early 19thC, superseded after Confederation by deliriously eclectic flirtations with a blizzard of conceits borrowed from the Italian Renaissance, Gothic, Baroque and French Second Empire, in what can fairly be described as Neo-Everything.

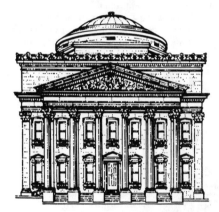

Banque de Montréal

Not surprisingly, the earliest structures reflect the backgrounds of settlers from rural Normandy and Brittany, adapted to the harsh climate and available native materials. They were barn-like buildings of simple, rectangular design, with thick stone walls and roofs steeply pitched to shed snow. Relatively little survives of that century-and-a-half of French rule, and most of it dates from the later decades of the regime.

CHÂTEAU RAMEZAY in Vieux Montréal, now functioning as a small museum, is a prime example from the period. Erected in 1705, it was altered frequently over the years, but retains its essential outlines. Not far away is the **Maison Calvet** (1725), which is an unusually fine example of French–Canadian domestic architecture.

The threat of American invasion during and immediately after the War of 1812 inspired the construction of elaborate fortifications at strategic points along the Great Lakes and the St Lawrence Valley. The extant version of FORT YORK in Toronto dates from 1815, its walls enclosing barracks and blockhouses, as do those of the CITADELLE in Québec City, built by the British in the same period.

At this time, governmental and commercial structures demonstrated an enthusiasm for Greco–Roman themes, with fluted pillars and triangular pediments, as seen in Toronto's **Osgoode Hall**, which was completed in stages between 1829 and 1845. A purer example is the **Banque de Montréal** (see previous page), which bears a Greek temple facade with fewer stylistic intrusions.

A parallel Gothic Revival was preferred for many ecclesiastical buildings, seen nowhere to greater advantage than in Montréal's BASILIQUE NOTRE-DAME. With its twin, squared towers and pointed arch windows, it is reminiscent of London's St Martin's-in-the-Fields.

By the mid-19thC, a wealthy new class of industrialists and financiers was able to indulge itself in any whimsy that it chose. In Toronto, and in Montréal's Golden Square Mile, millionaires commissioned mansions that evoked the Loire château, the Rhineland schloss, the Tuscan villa, the Highlands castle and, not infrequently, elements of all four.

The turreted Scottish baronial look was especially popular, for many of the new rich were of that ancestry. The final expression of this form of excess was Toronto's CASA LOMA, a 98-room mansion that eventually fell victim to the tax collector.

Casa Loma in Toronto

In civic buildings, an interest in the Gothic style resurfaced, but Francophone Montréal gave favor to the French Second-Empire style, which was in vogue from about 1870 to the end of the century. It is exemplified by the steep mansard roofs and tiered pavilions of the **Hôtel de Ville** (1878–1926). The inspiration for Québec City's CHÂTEAU FRONTENAC (1898–1920), which employs green copper roofs and turrets with conical caps, is obvious from both name and appearance.

At the same time, less exalted architecture demonstrated an exuberance of its own. Queen Anne was the name given to the busy admixtures of turrets, bay windows and gables applied to the facades of row houses seen in abundance along the streets of Montréal's Westmount and Toronto's Yorkville. Much of the detailing is crowded up around the eaves and is often of carved and scrolled wood affixed to sandstone walls.

It was not until well into the 20thC that Canadians saw much point in buildings that exceeded five or six stories. Theirs was and still is, after all, a country of underpopulated spaces.

Even by the 1920s, the tallest building in Canada was Montréal's **Sun Life Building**, one wing of which reached 26 stories. But while postwar Europe was rebuilding, Canada was intact. Desirable real estate in the center of cities was increasingly costly, and the obvious virtues of the skyscraper finally became more apparent.

The International Style, promulgated by the minimalist Bauhaus school, took hold in the 1950s. Glass curtain walls were hung on steel skeletons, allowing fewer setbacks, greater height, and therefore maximum square footage. Ornamentation was deplored, right angles and unbroken purity of line exalted. Examples abound in both Toronto's financial district and downtown Montréal, in soaring towers designed by such luminaries as Mies van der Rohe and, more latterly, I.M. Pei.

Every great city needs, or at least wants, a physical symbol of itself. Toronto's CN TOWER, the highest freestanding structure in the world, serves that purpose admirably. At its base is a more recent expression of municipal confidence, the impressive SKYDOME stadium, with its unique retractable roof.

A swelling reaction to the severity of the International Style became apparent during the 1980s, with a Post-Modernist trend that encourages playful uses of

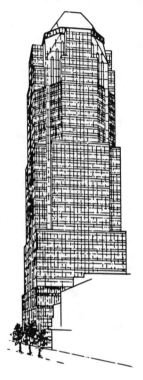

Maison des Coopérants

angled planes, tinted glass and nonessential decorative elements.

One successful example is Montréal's **Maison des Coopérants**, which mirrors the neighboring Christ Church Cathedral in tribute to the city that was and will be.

Perhaps even more delightful, for however long its retains its novelty, is **1000 de la Gauchetière**, which opened in 1992. Its pyramidal copper-and-blue apex rises up behind the cathedral, and it is now the tallest structure in Montréal. It carries its size with impeccable dash and imagination.

Practical information

Before you go

DOCUMENTS REQUIRED

US citizens only need proof of their status: a **passport**, **birth certificate** or **driver's license** will do. Non-citizen permanent residents of the US must present their **Alien Registration Card**. British subjects must show their **ten-year passport** (not a short-term visitor passport), but do not need a visa unless their stay exceeds three months. All visitors, except those permanently resident in the US or in Greenland, will need to have **proof of onward transportation**.

All visitors to Canada may drive for up to three months if they have a full and **valid driver's license**. US citizens driving across the border should bring a **Non-Resident Insurance Card**, and drivers of rental cars from the US must have their **rental contract** with them. You will need a valid driver's license to rent a car.

TRAVEL AND MEDICAL INSURANCE

Medical care is good to excellent, but US citizens should check that their policies provide coverage in Canada. Travelers from Europe and elsewhere are advised to take out separate insurance, as the cost of medical care and prescribed medicines can be very high. Travel agents have the necessary forms, and UK tour operators frequently include medical coverage in their packages. There is no reciprocal medical treatment for UK citizens in Canada.

A traffic accident or the theft of belongings can destroy a long-anticipated vacation, so the moderate costs of short-term riders to homeowner and automobile policies are worthwhile.

MONEY

The Canadian **dollar** is the basic unit, divided into 100 cents and in coins similar to their US counterparts. A gold-colored $1 coin — nicknamed the "loony" after the bird engraved on one side — has replaced the former dollar bill. Other denominations are $2, $5, $10, $20, $50, $100, $500 and $1,000.

US currency is widely accepted, customarily at a premium rate that takes into account the difference in market value. Simplicity and courtesy are better served, however, if visitors from the US exchange their money on arrival. Practically speaking, all travelers from other countries are likely to get more favorable rates at banks or at the currency exchange bureaux to be found in downtown sections of Toronto and Montréal.

Banks and change bureaux typically ask to see some sort of photo ID before cashing travelers checks.

It is always wise to carry cash in small amounts, keeping the remainder in **travelers checks**. Travelers checks issued by American Express, Bank of America, Barclays, Citibank and Thomas Cook are widely recognized, as are those of Visa and Mastercard. Make sure to read the instructions included with the checks, and note separately the serial numbers of your checks and the telephone number to call in case of loss.

Specialist travelers check companies such as American Express provide extensive local refund facilities through their own offices or agents.

Credit and charge cards are welcomed by virtually all hotels and motels, airlines and car rental agencies, most restaurants and many stores. American Express, Diners Club, Visa and Mastercard are those in common use. **Personal checks** drawn on non-local accounts are rarely accepted, although some hotels will cash small amounts in conjunction with a credit card (in effect borrowing against that card).

A relatively new convenience are the **automatic teller machines** (ATMs) now deployed by major banks in the cities of Ontario and Québec. These allow borrowing against credit cards — especially American Express, Visa, and Mastercard — up to the limit of credit assigned to each. Even more useful, visitors whose checking or savings accounts at home are in banks that are members of certain international networks can now make withdrawals against those accounts. At the time of writing, the networks with greatest coverage are CIRRUS and PLUS. Withdrawals are calculated at the exchange rate in effect on the day they are made, and the only obvious cost is the usual small transaction fee.

CUSTOMS

Customs inspections upon entry and exit at US borders are usually brief, involving answers to a few questions and little else. People crossing by car are sometimes asked to open their trunks, but infrequently the luggage itself.

Illegal immigrants and drug smugglers are obvious targets, and penalties can be severe for possession of illicit drugs. Firearms, plants and pets are restricted, if not necessarily prohibited. "Reasonable quantities" of tobacco and a bottle or two of wine or liquor are allowed.

International travelers may bring into Canada, duty-free, either 1.1 liters (40fl.oz) of liquor or wine, or 24 x 355ml (12fl.oz) cans or bottles of beer or ale, as well as 50 cigars, 200 cigarettes and 1kg (2.2lbs) of tobacco. These allowances apply to young people over 18 in Québec and over 19 in Ontario.

TAXES AND REFUNDS

A federal **Goods and Services Tax (GST)** now applies on nearly all merchandise, services, and accommodations in Canada. This tax is levied *in addition to* provincial taxes, on everything from postcards and newspapers to telephone calls and taxi rides.

In the province of **Québec**, the GST is first added to bills for merchandise and services, then an additional 8 percent tax is charged on the total; in effect, taxing the tax as well as the product or service. In **Ontario**, the tax scales vary, from 5 percent on hotel rooms, 8 percent on goods and services to 10 percent for liquor poured in bars and restaurants. At least the two taxes are figured separately, not in combination.

The good news is that many of these taxes, both federal and provincial, are refundable, under certain circumstances.

Keep all receipts for hotel rooms, and goods taken out of the country. (Services and goods consumed in the country are not subject to rebates, nor are tobacco products, alcoholic beverages, rental cars, and meals.) Reimbursement booklets and forms for both federal and provincial taxes are available at border crossings, in airports, and at many duty-free shops. Many hotels and large stores also have supplies on hand.

Make copies of the eligible receipts for your records, and send the originals with the completed form to the **Visitor Rebate Program of Revenue Canada** at the address indicated. If the receipts are from Québec, Revenue Canada will refund the applicable amounts for both the GST and Québec taxes. If the receipts are from Ontario, and you provide the completed provincial application, they will be forwarded to the Ontario Ministry of Revenue for action. The process takes six to eight weeks.

Applications for rebates can be made up to one year after the visit. To obtain the refund immediately, in Canadian currency, submit the application and receipts at a participating duty-free shop. If all is in order, a refund (for up to $500CDN in expenditures each day) is made on the spot. At least $100CDN must be spent to be eligible for refund, but families can pool their purchases.

No doubt changes will occur, so read the instructions in the tax refund booklet carefully. Some confusion and delay are almost inevitable, but these are relatively efficient and responsive bureaucracies. Note that details differ in the eight other Canadian provinces.

TOURIST INFORMATION
Useful free information on visiting the cities and provinces in this book can be obtained from the following addresses. See the PRACTICAL INFORMATION sections for each city, for details of local offices.

Details on Canada:
London   Canadian Tourist Office, Canada House, Trafalgar Square, London SW1Y 5BJ ☎(071)258-6600.
* **New York**   Canadian Consulate — Tourism Department, 1251 Avenue of the Americas, 16th floor, New York NY 10020-1175 ☎(212)768-2400.

Details on Ontario:
* **London**   Ontario Tourism, 21, Knightsbridge, London SW1X 7LY ☎(071)245-1222.
* **New York**   800 Third Ave., New York NY 10022 ☎(212)308-1616.
* **Washington, DC**   Canadian Embassy, Tourism Division, 501 Pennsylvania Ave. NW, Washington, DC, 20001 ☎(202)682-1740.

* **By mail** Write to the Metropolitan Toronto Convention and Visitors Association, P.O. Box 126, 207 Queen's Quay W, Toronto, Ontario M5J 1A7.

Details on Québec province:

* **London** Québec Tourism UK, Québec House, 59, Pall Mall, London SW1Y 5JH ☎(071)930-8314.
* **New York** Délégation Générale du Québec, Rockefeller Center, 17 W 50th St., New York NY 10020-2201 ☎(212)397-0200.
* **Toronto** Bureau du Gouvernement du Québec, 20 Queen St. W, Suite 1504, Box 13, Toronto, ONT M5H 3S3 ☎(416)977-6060.
* **Washington, DC** Bureau du Tourisme du Québec, 1300 19th St NW, Suite 220, Washington, DC 20036 ☎(202)659-8991.
* **By mail** Write to the Greater Québec Area Tourism and Convention Bureau, 60 rue d'Auteuil, Québec (Québec) G1R 4C4.

GETTING THERE

By air Toronto's **Lester B. Pearson** and Montréal's **Dorval** are the region's principal international airports, supplemented by smaller hubs that handle mostly domestic and commuter flights. **Mirabel** airport, N of Montréal, is used for charters and for flights arriving from other continents. Air Canada has extensive daily schedules between major cities in the US and Europe, supplemented by flights by the major carriers of the destination countries.

By train From the US, Amtrak has two scenic routes from Grand Central Terminal in New York to Montréal, and one daily train from Washington and New York to Toronto. VIA Rail connects Toronto, Montréal and Québec City to western Canada. First-class passage on VIA Rail is quite pleasant and not too expensive, with ample leg-room, and meals and drinks served at your seat.

By car Cars have numerous crossing points. Among the busiest are Detroit–Windsor and Niagara Falls, so there can be time savings by crossing elsewhere. The principal N–S routes from New England and New York to Montréal are Interstate Highways 91 and 87; from the Midwest to Toronto, take the I-75 and I-90.

WHAT TO WEAR

Air conditioning and central heating are less often pushed to the extremes they reach in the US, but layering of clothes is still a good idea, peeling off or pulling on to deal with changes in temperature from street to interior and back.

From May through September, a windbreaker with a hood can suffice, if only for cool mornings and boat trips on the St Lawrence. A cotton sweater or wrap is often desirable for evenings or in over-cooled restaurants and theaters.

A raincoat with removable lining is adaptable for the cooler months, but in deepest winter, be prepared to wrap up — caps, scarves, heavy gloves and socks, waterproof shoes or boots.

Informality prevails, especially for sightseeing or dining in sidewalk cafés. Many of the better restaurants prefer men to wear jackets, although relatively few require them, and fewer still expect a tie to be worn. Ask when making a reservation.

Good taste and a sense of decorum dictate the choice of clothing, if only to reduce the visual pollution of unthinking tourists in markedly unbecoming and skimpy outfits. A tanktop and running shorts is not appropriate attire for visiting churches, for example, especially when services are being held.

Dress codes are rarely applied in even the poshest hotels, except for their dining rooms, but mature men and women might well feel out of place in jeans when all about them are in business suits and cocktail dresses. Denim clothing is sometimes barred by smarter discos and clubs.

WHAT TO BRING
Cigarettes and spirits are heavily taxed. Smokers should take along as many packages as are necessary to get through a visit, or expect to pay more than twice as much as at home. Travelers accustomed to a martini before dinner or a bedtime cognac find that bringing the permitted bottle of the favored tipple is a not-insignificant economy.

Adequate supplies of **prescription medicines** and the prescriptions themselves should go on the checklist, along with a spare pair of **eyeglasses**. Most other incidental needs are easily met at the corner convenience store, and prices are comparable to those back home.

A compact **folding umbrella** can prove useful any month of the year.

On-the-spot information

PUBLIC HOLIDAYS
Banks, offices, and schools are closed on: **January 1**; **Good Friday**; Victoria Day, **Monday closest to May 24**; Canada Day, **July 1**; Labour Day, **1st Monday in September**; Thanksgiving Day, **2nd Monday in October**; Remembrance Day, **November 11**; and **December 25**. When any of these fall on a Saturday or Sunday, they are usually observed on the following Monday to make a three-day weekend.

Boxing Day on December 26 is a major shopping day, when stores are open but most other businesses and government offices are closed.

Québec Province also celebrates St John the Baptist Day on **June 24** and Ontario its Civic Holiday on the **1st Monday in August**.

TIME ZONES
Toronto, Montréal, and Québec City are in the **Eastern Time Zone**, even though most of Ontario is directly above that portion of the US in the Central Time Zone, which is one hour later.

The Eastern Time Zone is five hours behind **Greenwich Mean Time**, except during Daylight Saving Time (April to October), when clocks are put forward one hour to take advantage of extra daylight. This coincides with the UK Daylight Saving Time, so the differential for British travelers remains the same throughout the year.

BANKS AND CURRENCY EXCHANGE

Customary banking hours are 10am–3pm (6pm Friday), but there is a recent trend toward opening earlier and closing later.

Banks consistently offer the best currency exchange rates. Remember to have photo identification ready. The better hotels usually convert money or travelers checks for registered guests within a point or two of bank rates. But this is not true of all hotels, so consult a daily newspaper to have an idea of current exchange rates.

There are also private change bureaux and check-cashing stores in the larger cities. Their announced rates sometimes sound more favorable than those of the banks, but the hefty commissions they charge for the service are likely to wipe out the differential. It is best to use them only for small amounts when banks are closed. They also require photo ID.

American Express has a **MoneyGram®** money transfer service that makes it possible to wire money worldwide in just minutes, from any American Express Travel Service Office. This service is available to all customers and is not limited to American Express Card members. For the location nearest you ☎800-543-4080 (in Canada and the US).

COMMUNICATIONS

Mail   Bewilderingly swift technological advances make the use of post office **general delivery** *(poste restante)* services seem almost quaint. American Express and Thomas Cook offices will still hold letters for customers. To collect mail at either agency, be prepared to show the relevant credit card or travelers checks.

The larger and medium-sized hotels routinely make **fax** machines available to guests. Those catering to businesspeople are increasingly providing fax, multi-line telephones and/or computer ports in rooms, either as a standard facility or on request.

Letters and packages mailed from Canada must carry Canadian **postage stamps**, an observation that is less obvious to some Americans than it might seem. While telephone area codes follow the same system in both countries, **postal zip codes** do not. Those in Canada are combinations of letters and numerals, similar to the British system, and must be carefully entered in addresses to ensure delivery.

Telephone   Canadians rely heavily on their telephones, and the system is efficient and bilingual, except during periodic labor disputes.

No international codes are necessary to place long-distance (trunk) **calls between the US and Canada**. Simply enter the long-distance **1** followed by the appropriate 3-digit area code and 7-digit number. The area code for **Toronto** is **416**, for **Montréal** it is **514**, and for **Québec City** it is **418**.

For **international calls**, touch **O** and ask to speak to the international operator.

SHOPPING HOURS

Independent retail shops are usually open 10am to 6pm, Monday–Saturday. Those located in shopping malls and along the corridors of the underground cities of Montréal and Toronto often don't close their doors until 9pm or 10pm, especially on Thursday and Friday. This is also the practice of the large department stores. Variations are common, and even the once-sacrosanct Sabbath prohibition is crumbling. Shopowners in tourist areas are routinely allowed to defy the Sunday closing laws.

Drug and convenience stores (*dépanneurs* in Québec) frequently stay open until 11pm or midnight. A few large food stores are open 24 hours.

PUBLIC REST ROOMS
The availability of public rest rooms is less than ideal, although the situation is better than in most parts of the US and Europe. There are a few in metro or subway stations but they can be messy, although rarely filthy or dangerous.

Museums, department stores and government buildings are other possibilities, as is ducking into the nearest large hotel.

ELECTRIC CURRENT
Standard household current is 110V and outlets accept 2-flat-pronged plugs, as in the US. The 220V current in use in Europe is only used in Canada in industrial situations, and an electrical transformer and universal adaptor is needed, in order to use appliances such as hairdryers. Transformers are available in electrical stores.

SAFETY
Toronto, Montréal and Québec City all enjoy enviably low rates of violent crime. It is likely that not a harsh word, let alone a threat, will be heard on a normal visit. Still, prudence is in order, as in any large city. Walking alone at night through the shabbier districts, or waiting too long at isolated bus stops are to be avoided, especially by women.

When leaving a hotel, take only one or two credit or charge cards and enough cash for the day's planned activities. Use the room safes that are now often available, especially for airline tickets and passports. Otherwise, inquire at the front desk if a safe is available to guests. If your hotel employs the new plastic passcards, do not write the room number on the cardkey itself, but carry it separately.

Leave no articles of value (including clothing) in your car, or at least lock them out of sight in the trunk.

None of these cautions should be taken to imply significant danger, however, for the situation is nowhere near that which inspires the high levels of urban paranoia s of the border. Even panhandlers are diffident and good-humored, although not quite as rare as they once were, given the current harsh economic times.

LAWS AND REGULATIONS
* **Antismoking regulations** are multiplying, in tune with increasing public antipathy to the habit. They are not yet as restrictive as in many parts of the US, but that day approaches. Many restaurants have smoke-free sections, and the larger hotels nearly always set aside one or more floors for nonsmokers. It is polite to ask a cab

driver for permission before lighting up, even if no sign is posted. Smoking in enclosed places, such as elevators, is frowned upon, if not always specifically prohibited.

- **Prostitution** is illegal. It exists, but hardly flourishes.
- The **purchase and possession of illicit street drugs** is illegal, here as elsewhere.
- The **minimum age for drinking alcohol** is 19 years in Ontario and 18 years in Québec.
- If caught behind the wheel of a car while **intoxicated**, a driver risks the suspension of his license for a year.
- **Seat belts** for both driver and passenger are obligatory.
- The **highway speed limit** is 100kph (62mph); elsewhere as posted.
- **Turning right after stopping at a red light** is permitted in Ontario, and exceptions to this rule are displayed. It is *not* permitted in Québec province.
- Cars are supposed to stop to allow the passage of pedestrians in **crosswalks**, but this courtesy is more often observed in Ontario than in Québec.
- Fines can be imposed for unnecessary **use of horns**. Even the ambulances rarely use sirens.
- **Studded tires** are illegal in both provinces.
- **Radar detectors** are illegal, and can be confiscated.

TIPPING

A minimum tip **in a restaurant** is 10 percent, to be left only if the service was sufficiently lax or inept to warrant that small amount. Of course, offensively brusque or rude treatment may deserve less — or nothing at all. If tempted to follow that course, do be certain that the waiter or waitress is at fault, and not the kitchen.

At least 15 percent is more appropriate, as much as 20 percent in luxury establishments or when service was especially attentive. Check bills to see if they include a service charge, a not-infrequent practice. This applies to **hotel room service**, too. Don't tip twice. If the levied charge is 12 percent or less, you might consider leaving a little extra. If staying for two or more nights in a hotel, leave about $1 a night for the **chambermaid**.

Bartenders, **hairdressers** and **barbers** expect 15 percent. **Bellmen** and **porters** should receive something for each piece of luggage carried. A $1 tip is about right, depending upon how heavy the bags are and how far the walk. **Doormen** and **coatroom/rest room attendants** should be tipped, too, usually 50¢–$1.

Taxi drivers are accustomed to 10–15 percent of the fare, the higher amount if they move luggage from curb to trunk or get out to open the door. **Tour guides** expect $1–$2 for their 2 or 3 hours, more if the tour is longer. **Theater and stadium ushers** are not tipped.

DISABLED TRAVELERS

The needs of persons confined to wheelchairs are catered to, but somewhat unevenly. Ramps are provided at major museums and public buildings; many hotels offer lodgings with bathrooms equipped with raised toilets and pull-up bars; downtown corners have curb cuts; special parking spaces are set aside near entrances to stores and shopping malls. Restaurants, however, are often inaccessible, and older structures, especially in Québec City, do not lend themselves to modification.

A free booklet called *Toronto With Ease* discusses services for disabled persons. It is available from the **Metropolitan Toronto Convention and Visitors Association** *(Queen's Quay Terminal, 207 Queen's Quay W, Box 126, Toronto, Ont. M5J 1A7)*.

Also useful is the mid-priced *Handy Travel*, produced by the **Canadian Rehabilitation Council for the Disabled** *(1 Yonge St., Toronto, Ont. M5E 1E5)*.

Emergency information

EMERGENCY SERVICES
Police, fire, ambulance
(Montréal and Toronto areas) ☎911
Police, fire
(Québec) ☎691-6911
No coins are needed for pay phones.

AUTOMOBILE ACCIDENTS
- **Call police** immediately if anyone is injured.
- **If car is rented**, call number in rental agreement.
- **Do not admit liability** or incriminate yourself.
- **Ask witnesses to stay** and give statements.
- **Exchange names**, addresses, driver's license and car registration numbers. A form called the *Constat à l'amiable* is provided for this purpose by car rental firms.

CAR BREAKDOWNS
Call one of the following from the nearest telephone:
- Number indicated in **car rental** agreement.
- The **Canadian Automobile Association** *(☎288-7111 for Montréal area or ☎966-3000 for Toronto area)* if you are a member of an affiliated organization, such as AAA or RAC.
- **Nearest garage** or towing service.

LOST TRAVELERS CHECKS
Notify police immediately, then follow the instructions provided with your travelers checks, or contact the issuing company's nearest office. Contact your consulate or **American Express** *(☎931-4444)* if you are stranded with no money.

See also EMERGENCY INFORMATION in the Toronto, Montréal and Québec City PRACTICAL INFORMATION sections.

Planning your visit

When to go

It is said that Canada has two seasons — winter and July. Not so. Southern Ontario and Québec have a climate very similar to that of the northern tier of the US. Toronto, after all, is actually south of Seattle and Minneapolis. The short, radiant **spring** usually arrives in early April, with the first really warm spell coming in early June. From then until early September, day and night temperatures fluctuate between tee-shirt-hot and sweater-cool.

Nevertheless, in **summer**, anticipate long periods in July and August when the temperature rises above 85° (30° Celsius). Toronto, Montréal and Québec City are all on the water, so high humidity accompanies the heat.

Fall foliage is usually at its most vivid in the last week in September in lower Québec, and a week later in lower Ontario. From mid-September to late October the weather is changeable, but can be surprisingly pleasant for days at a stretch. Winter typically sets in by early November and stays until late March.

Prevailing **winter** winds coming from the NW, though, have often dissipated by the time they pass over Toronto, picking up moisture as they continue over Lake Ontario. The result is that Toronto frequently suffers less snow than Buffalo, NY, to the s.

Montréal, on the other hand, seems perversely proud of its 8 feet of snow each winter. The higher rural regions of Québec and the Gaspé Peninsula rarely get uncomfortably warm, and can be chilly even on July nights.

The entire region is at its best from late May to early September, when café tables spill out onto sidewalks and into backyard courts. Street performers are out in force, the calendar is alive with ethnic and music festivals, and the release from winter's grip visibly raises everyone's spirits. These are the months of the biggest crowds, when the most popular attractions are awash with people. Many of the better restaurants close for vacation, and hotel reservations are harder to come by, even though there is something of a hotel glut in Montréal and Toronto. For those reasons, the shoulder seasons of mid-May to early June or the latter weeks of September may be preferable to those who aren't locked into July and August.

Nor are the winter months to be shunned. Québeckers and Ontarians either ignore the cold and snow or make a virtue of it. Toronto and Montréal have their weatherproof underground cities, and the theater, opera and dance seasons are in full swing. The patrons of clubs and restaurants evince a we're-in-this-together camaraderie, and may, if anything, be even easier to meet.

For the hardy, there are robust winter festivals, including the February extravaganza in Québec City; downhill- and cross-country skiing flourish, and ponds and rinks are aswirl with skaters. In Montréal, carriage-horses are hitched to sleighs *(calèches)* for romantic outings around Mont-Royal. Memories are made of hot buttered rum beside the fire of one of the country inns that abound outside the major cities.

Events for the visitor's calendar

The Tourism and Convention Bureaux are the best sources of information and specific dates for current and forthcoming events in the annual calendar, but the following list provides some of the highlights in the calendar for our three featured cities.

Refer also to RECREATION in Toronto and Montréal, for further events, and PUBLIC HOLIDAYS on page 32.

JANUARY
Three weeks in January, 1st week in February: **Montréal Winter Festival** or **Fête des Neiges**. • Mid-January: **Toronto International Boat Show** at Exhibition Place. • **International Auto Show** at Montréal's Olympic Park. • Late January: **Ice Canoe Race** at Toronto Harbourfront. • Late January: **International Curling Tournament**, held at various locations around Québec Province.

FEBRUARY
First week in February, for about 10 days: **Québec City Winter Carnival** or **Carnavale de Québec**, includes night parades. • Early February: **International Boat Show** at Olympic Park, Montréal.
• Mid-February: **North York Winter Carnival**, Black Creek Pioneer Village, Toronto. • Late February: **Toronto International Auto Show**.

MARCH
Early March: **Outdoors Show** in Montréal. • Late March: **Springtime Craft Show & Sale** at Toronto's Exhibition Place. • Late March: **Festival of Canadian Fashion** in Toronto.

APRIL
Early April: **Springtime Craft Show** and **National Home Show**, Exhibition Place, Toronto. • Mid-April: **opening of baseball season** in Montréal and Toronto • **International Book Fair** in Québec City. • **Stratford Shakespeare Festival Season** opens in Stratford, Ontario. • Late April to early May: **Mozart Festival**, Place des Arts, Montréal. • Late April to early June: **Cirque de Soleil**, a circus without animals, Old Port, Montréal.

MAY
Late May: **International Fireworks Competition**, for 4 weeks in Montréal. • **Québec City International Theatre Fortnight**.

JUNE
Early June: **Le Tour de l'Île de Montréal**, an amateur cycling event. • **Molson Grand Prix**, Formula One race in Montréal. • Mid-June: **Toronto International Caravan**, an ethnic festival at various sites around the city. • **Peoples Comedy Festival**, with international comedians at various Toronto venues. • **International Rock Festival**, various Montréal locations. • Late June: **All That Jazz festival** at sites throughout Toronto. • **Jazz and rock festival**, at various Québec City locations, including free outdoor performances.

JULY
July 1: **Canada Day celebrations** in Québec and Ontario. • July 3: **Commemoration of Champlain's founding of Québec City**. • Early July: **Montréal International Jazz Festival**, lasting 12 days, at various indoor and outdoor locations. • **Québec International Summer Festival**; the largest French-speaking cultural event in North America, with concerts, performances and folkloric events at venues all over Québec City. • Mid-July: **Annual Toronto Outdoor Art Exhibition** at City Hall's Nathan Phillips Square, with more than 500 Canadian and foreign artists competing for prizes. • **Molson Indy auto race** on Lakeshore Boulevard, Toronto. • Late July to early August (for eleven days): **Just For Laughs Festival** in Montréal, with international comedians performing in French and English. • Late July to early August: **Caribana**, a celebration of Caribbean music and culture in Toronto, with parades, pageants and dances at many locations throughout the city.

AUGUST
Early August: **The Americas Cycling Grand Prix**, a World Cup event in Montréal. • Early to mid-August: **Player's International Tennis Championships** in Montréal and Toronto, with top male and female athletes competing in each city in alternate years. • Mid-August to early September: **Canadian National Exhibition**, a major agricultural fair held at Exhibition Place, Toronto. • **Expo–Québec**, a similar event, with rides and entertainment, in Québec City. • Late August: **The Canadian Open golf championship** at Glen Abbey Golf Club in Toronto. • Late August to early September: **World Film Festival** in Montréal.

SEPTEMBER
Early September: **Festival of Festivals**, 250 international films at cinemas throughout Toronto. • **The Molson Export Challenge**, a thoroughbred race, with the largest prize in North America, at Woodbine Race Track in Toronto. • **Québec International Film Festival**, emphasizing French-language films. • Early September: **Montréal**

Marathon, with more than 12,000 runners. • **Montréal Internat-ional Music Festival**, focusing on classical music. • Late September: **Cycling Grand Prix** in Montréal.

OCTOBER
Early October: **opening of professional hockey season** for Toronto Maple Leafs, Montréal Canadiens and Québec Nordiques. Season continues until April. • Late October: **Montréal International Festival of New Cinema and Video.**

NOVEMBER
Early to mid-November: **The Royal Agricultural Winter Fair** at Exhibition Place, Toronto. • **The Annual Santa Claus Parade** in Toronto. • **The Vanier Cup**: Canadian University Football Championship in Toronto.

DECEMBER
Early December: **Québec Crafts Show**. • December 31: **New Year's Eve celebration** in Nathan Phillips Square, Toronto.

Toronto

Toronto: the meeting place

Great cities stimulate epigrammists and myth-makers. Toronto qualified for inclusion in the world's urban elite at least two decades ago. That was a fact certified by the swarms of social scientists and visionaries who tumbled over one other seeking fresh superlatives to describe her. Among them, one Anthony Astrachan came closest when he proclaimed in 1974 that Toronto is "a city that works." That it does, by nearly every legitimate measure.

One of the largest cities in North America, it can claim virtues that may be forever beyond the grasp of its sisters south of the border. Its inhabitants represent every race and major ethnic group on the face of the earth, yet tensions between them are muted, in part because all are alert to the merest twinges of abrasion, and rush to polish them smooth. They can choose to walk across a mile or two of 8,700 acres of parkland at midnight and be virtually assured of returning intact, not having experienced even a harsh word.

Toronto enjoys a singular prosperity brought by the presence of Canada's most aggressive corporations and industries, but growth is controlled, and sensitive to the will of its citizens. For example, few downtown skyscrapers exceed 50 stories, and all new development must incorporate housing as well as office space. The closest it comes to the Hogarthian slums that afflict most cities in the hemisphere are working-class neighborhoods that are merely shabby, not crime-ridden or hopeless.

Toronto is tidy and untroubling, and mindful of the needs of its people and its visitors. The worst thing about it is its tinge of smugness. But then it does have quite a lot to be smug about.

This level of exemplary urbanity was achieved only with the aid of historical accident and twists of fortune. The site was first visited by Champlain's lieutenant, Étienne Brûlé, in 1610–11. "Toronto," aptly enough, was Huron for "meeting place." Few paid much attention to the area, a flat plain on the northern shore of Lake Ontario, until the British sought a more secure location for the capital of their new colony of Upper Canada. The old one was too close to the enemy — the young United States. Governor John Graves Simcoe was hardly enthused about his choice. "The city's site was better calculated for a frog pond than for the residence of human beings," he wrote.

Despite that estimation, he proceeded, with more than a little perverse doggedness, to build a fort and start a settlement, which he named after the Duke of York. Its few dirt streets were a constant quagmire, hence its first unofficial appellation, "Muddy York." In 1834, it was incorporated as a city under its Indian name. One of the earliest industries was livestock slaughtering, leading to the sobriquet "Hogtown," which name was hardly an improvement.

Nor was the overweening English majority as tolerant as they were later to become. Even the Scots had to contend with second-class status. Protestant notions of probity and rectitude clamped a dour morality on the city, which then came to be known as "Toronto the Good." Right up until World War II, 80 percent of the population was Anglo-Saxon. Postwar immigration changed that. Nearly a million immigrants duly arrived — Asians, West Indians, Eastern and Southern Europeans.

By 1977, they and thousands of refugees from ominously separatist Québec had made their new city the largest in Canada. In the process, they imposed a cultural vivacity that was the last ingredient needed to make Toronto the Good downright endearing. Now, the increasingly preferred reference to Toronto, Ontario is writ in fat capital letters — eager and ebullient — "T.O."

The people in Toronto . . . seem healthier and better set-up than those in New York and Boston. Not so driven and not so cramped between big buildings and in narrow streets, they seem to be more good-natured, and they probably enjoy themselves more.

(*Upstate*, 1971, Edmund Wilson, literary critic)

Toronto:
practical information

Getting around

FROM THE AIRPORTS TO THE CITY
Lester B. Pearson International Airport *(map 5 C2)*   Located to
the SW of Toronto, Pearson International Airport accommodates both
domestic and foreign flights of more than 35 airlines. It has three terminals, the newest of which was completed in 1991 and resembles a
shopping mall. When pre-arranging transportation from the airport,
first find out at which terminal your flight is scheduled to arrive.

The 29-km (18-mile) trip to downtown takes 30–60 minutes, depending on traffic, and the least expensive carrier is Grey Coach Lines (☎ *393-
7911).* **Coaches** depart 2 or 3 times an hour between early morning and
midnight, and drop passengers at several downtown hotels. (The list and
number of hotels served changes with some regularity, so inquire before
boarding.) Those who wish to save a few dollars over even this relatively
low fare can take the Grey Coach to the Yorkdale, York Mills or Islington
subway stations and transfer to the **train**, which terminates at Wilson
station. Some hotels provide a shuttle service; ask when booking.

Travelers with heavy luggage or in groups of two or more may prefer
taxis, which are not unusually expensive. **Limousines** cost somewhat
more. If **renting a car** at the airport, obtain a road map and directions
before leaving.
Toronto Island Airport *(map 3 F6)*   This airport handles short commuter flights from other Canadian cities and from several US cities
including Newark. It is reached by a ferry that docks at the foot of
Bathurst St.

PUBLIC TRANSPORTATION
The Mass Transit System   There is no finer mass transit system in
North America. **Subway** trains are swift, quiet, and as brightly polished
as new pennies. Even the platforms are immaculate. There are two
lines, one running from E–W, the other a N–S loop that reaches Union
Station and then bends back. Most of the center city is therefore easily
accessible.

But Greater Toronto sprawls, with many attractions and some hotels
well beyond the reach of the subway. So, the Toronto Transit Commission
fills in the gaps with **bus and trolley** lines.

Transfers between buses and subways are free, but a ticket must be
obtained from the bus driver when boarding, or from the machines near

subway turnstiles. Drivers of buses and streetcars do not carry cash, and fares must be in exact change, token or ticket, on sale at subway entrances and designated stores. Be careful when using tokens, for they are very similar in size, weight, and color to the 10-cent coin.

Fares   Modest discounts are available when purchasing two or more tickets. Passes for unlimited Sunday and holiday travel are available to couples and families.

Times   Trains operate Monday to Saturday 6am to 1.30am, Sunday 9am to 1.30am. Some bus and streetcar lines operate 24 hours, notably those running along King, Queen, and Dundas Sts. Call **TTC** for information (☎ *393-4636, 7am–11.30pm).*

TRAVELING BY CAR

Most streets are wide, and drivers are generally courteous. The only serious congestion is at rush hours and in the downtown commercial district, where parking is difficult and rather expensive. Given the many other viable options, it is best to use a car only for traveling to attractions in outlying districts.

Speed limits   These are posted in kilometers (1 km = $\frac{5}{8}$ mile). See the metric CONVERSION CHART at the back of the book.

Traffic flow   Right turns can be made at red lights after coming to a full stop, unless otherwise indicated. (This is not the case in Québec province.)

Car rental   Renting a car is not prohibitive. There are also weekend discounts to be had, and unlimited mileage plans.

Most large hotels have at least one agency office in or near their lobbies, and the concierge can make arrangements to have cars delivered. The prominent company associated with National Car Rental in the US is **Tilden**, but the other major international firms are also represented.

Laws   See LAWS AND REGULATIONS on page 35. Driving regulations specific to Ontario include the following:

- Cars are expected to yield to pedestrians in marked crosswalks, especially those marked by signs with a black "X" on a yellow sign. Cautious walkers should remain alert to the presence of foreign drivers unfamiliar with that regulation, however.
- When driving behind a streetcar, to ensure the safety of passengers, drivers must come to a complete stop at least two meters ($6\frac{1}{2}$ ft) away from its back door.

TAXIS

As tempting as it is simply to hail a cab when exiting a hotel, it is wise to know in advance the distance to a desired destination. A trip from downtown to, say, the Zoo, takes about an hour — a costly undertaking. A combination of subway and bus can make that trip for far less money. For shorter hauls, cabs are no more expensive than in most large North American or European cities. Many are dispatched by radio and can be summoned fairly quickly by telephone.

Cabstands are found outside large hotels and at subway stations, and taxis can be flagged anywhere. They are of no special color or design, but all have plastic roof lights and electronic meters. When the light is on (only at night), the taxi is available for hire. During the day, the only way to tell is if no passengers can be seen inside.

Useful addresses

TOURIST INFORMATION

- **By telephone or mail**   Contact the **Metropolitan Toronto Convention and Visitors Association** (*P.O. Box 126, 207 Queen's Quay W, Toronto, Ontario M5J 1A7* ☎*203-2500, open Monday to Friday 9am–5pm*). There is also a toll-free visitor information line (☎*800-363-1990, Mon–Fri 8.30am–5pm, Sat, Sun 9.30am–5.30pm*), which can be used from anywhere in the US or Canada.
- **From the US or the UK**   See page 30.
- **In person**   There is a permanent **Visitor Information Centre** outside Eaton Centre, on Yonge St., s of Dundas (*map 4 C8*). Open daily, with slightly shorter hours in winter. Six other seasonal centers (*open late May–early Sept*) are found at various locations around town, including at Nathan Phillips Square, the ferry docks for the Toronto Islands, and the CN Tower.
- **American Express Canada**   The main American Express office and **Travel Service** is at 101 McNab St. (*map 3 D7, general inquiries* ☎*474-8000; Travel Service* ☎*474-8350*). To report lost American Express cards ☎474-9280.

    American Express offers a valuable source of information for any traveler in need of help, advice or emergency services.

MAIN POST OFFICES

595 Bay St. (Dundas)   Map 4C8. Open Monday to Wednesday, Saturday 10am–6pm; Thursday, Friday 10am–9pm
100 King St. (Bay)   Map 4D8. Open Monday to Friday 10am–6pm, Saturday 10am–5pm

TELEPHONE SERVICES

Concerts	☎870-9119	**Road conditions**	☎ 235-1110
Sports	☎964-8655	**Weather**	☎676-3066

TOUR OPERATORS

- **Canadian Lake Express**   Foot of Yonge St. ☎363-4433 or 800-561-5222. High-speed hydrofoil ferries between Toronto and Niagara.
- **Grey Line**   180 Dundas St. W, Suite 1100 ☎351-3311. Bus tours of Toronto and Niagara Falls.
- **Happy Days Tours**   220 Yonge St. ☎593-6220. 4-hour tours twice daily, with pickup at major hotels.
- **Harbour Air**   Toronto Island Airport ☎366-8881. Various

sightseeing flights on fixed-wing aircraft.
- **Just Looking**   51 Alexander St. ☎923-2202. "Step-on" guides using client's car. Tours of Toronto, Ottawa, and Niagara. Bilingual guides available.
- **National Helicopters**   4078 Highway #7 W, Woodbridge ☎851-4815. Helicopter rides.
- **Ontario Black History Society**   10 Adelaide St. E, Suite 202 ☎867-9420. 3-hour tours of 15 sites important in the history of African-Canadians in Toronto.
- **Ryan Helicopters**   Toronto Island Airport ☎362-1010. Sightseeing flights; special charters available.
- **Toronto Architecture Tour**   ☎922-7606. Two to four tours Tuesday to Saturday, June to October, starting at the NE corner of Queen and Bay Sts.
- **Toronto Tours**   134 Jarvis St. ☎869-1372 or 868-0400. Local streetcar tours and day trips to Niagara in mini-buses.
- **Le Tour de Ville**   40 Bay St. ☎693-8556. "Step-on" guides speaking French, English and German.

HARBOR CRUISES
- **Grey Line Harbour & Island Tours**   5 Queen's Quay W ☎364-2412. 1-hour cruises in glass-topped boats.
- **Mariposa Cruise Line**   207 Queen's Quay W ☎366-0178. 1-hour tours and dinner-and-dance cruises on the paddlewheeler *Mariposa Belle,* the *Oriole,* and the *Torontonian.*
- **Toronto Boat Cruises**   At Harbourfront. 283A Queen's Quay W ☎364-4664. Narrated $1\frac{1}{2}$-hour harbor cruises.

LIBRARY
Metropolitan Toronto Reference Library   789 Yonge St. Off map 4A8 ☎393-7000. This library has a collection of 1.3 million volumes. Open daily.

LOCAL PUBLICATIONS
The Globe and Mail emphasizes business and international news, delivered in a tone some think is responsible, others, stuffy. Because it is positioned as a national newspaper, there is only that local news the editors deem to be of wider interest. Its big issue is Saturday, and it is not published on a Sunday. *The Toronto Star,* published daily, has a larger circulation, and although it focuses more heavily on local and provincial matters, its national and international coverage is substantial. The style is lively, with a lingering liberal tinge. For visitors, the Friday "What's On" section is a must.

The Financial Post is the principal weekday business newspaper, similar to *The Wall Street Journal* . Fans of garish right-wing tabloids have *The Toronto Sun,* big on sports and sensation. *NOW* and *eye* are weekly giveaway tabloids about entertainment events. Another source of news and reviews is the slick *Toronto Life,* a plump monthly magazine devoted to the good life.

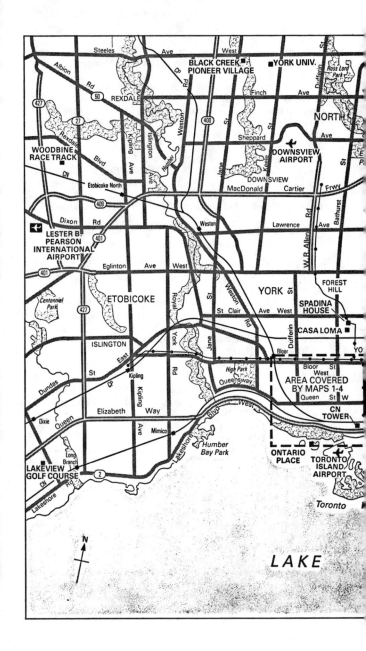

METROPOLITAN TORONTO

Cross streets are referred to as either W or E of Yonge St.

■———■ Railroad and station

●———● Subway and station

0 1 2 3 miles
0 1 2 3 4 5km

ONTARIO

49

Emergency information

Police, fire, ambulance   ☎911
No coins are needed for pay phones.

HOSPITALS WITH EMERGENCY ROOMS
Doctors Hospital   45 Brunswick Ave. (College). Map **3B6** ☎923-5411
Hospital for Sick Children   555 University Ave. (Gerrard W). Map
3C7 ☎597-1500
Mount Sinai Hospital   600 University Ave. (Gerrard W). Map **3C7**
☎596-4200
St Michael's Hospital   30 Bond St. (Queen E). Map **4D8** ☎360-
4000
Toronto General Hospital   200 Elizabeth St. (College). Map **3C7**
☎595-3111
Toronto Western Hospital   399 Bathurst St. (Dundas W). Map **2C5**
☎368-2581
Wellesley Hospital   160 Wellesley St. E (Sherbourne). Map **4B9**
☎966-6600
• **Hospital and Medical Insurance for Visitors**   800 Bay St. Map
  4B8 ☎961-0666. Immediate coverage is available.

DENTAL EMERGENCIES
Toronto General Hospital   150 Gerrard St. W. Map **3C7** ☎340-
3944. Open 24 hours.
Dental referrals help line   ☎967-5649 day ☎924-8041 evening,
weekend and holiday mornings.

PHARMACIES OPEN LATE
Pharma Plus   68 Wellesley St. (Church). Map **4B8** ☎924-7760.
Open daily 8am–midnight.
Shoppers Drug Mart   700 Bay St. (Gerrard). Map **4C8** ☎979-2424.
Open 24 hours.

HELP LINES
AIDS Hotline   ☎392-AIDS
Alcoholics Anonymous   ☎487-5591
Animal emergencies   ☎226-3663 or 222-5409
**Emergency referral Community Services and crisis
intervention**   ☎392-0505
Medical referrals   Ontario Medical Association ☎599-2580 Mon-
day to Friday 9am-4pm.
Poison information centers   ☎598-5900 or 469-6245. Oper-
ational 24 hours.
Rape   ☎597-8808
Suicide/Distress   ☎598-1121 or 486-1456

For advice on **Automobile accidents**, **Car breakdowns**, and **Lost
travelers checks**, refer to EMERGENCY INFORMATION on page 36.

Toronto: sightseeing

An overview of the city

Metropolitan Toronto enjoys an enlightened form of cooperative regional government that incorporates five cities and nine other municipalities. This allows the planning and distribution of such public services as mass transit, roads and water supply, with fewer of the divisive battles over jurisdiction that afflict other metropolitan areas. It is, however, an entity that covers 620 sq. km (240 square miles), which can cause disorientation and a tendency to underestimate distances.

ORIENTATION
The City of Toronto is only one of the constituent parts of Metro Toronto, albeit the most important. At its core, the streets are easy enough to negotiate. With some exceptions, they are laid out in a predictable grid. The lake is on the s, easily located by the landmark CN Tower, and the land slopes upward to the N. Yonge St. is the dividing line between E and W. Signs for streets running E to W are yellow; those N and s are blue. Most, but by no means all, of the hotels and attractions of interest to visitors are within a rectangle starting a few blocks N of Bloor down to the waterfront and from Bathurst St. to Jarvis. This area can easily be covered by combinations of subway and walking.

THE DISTRICTS
THE WATERFRONT *(maps 1–4)*. The waterfront has received much attention in recent years, with ongoing redevelopment intended to enhance access to the lake. A string of barrier islands all but enclose the harbor and provide recreational areas with beaches, boating, picnic areas and cycling paths. To the w of downtown, on or near the water, are the MARINE MUSEUM and ONTARIO PLACE, this last a man-made island with an open-air auditorium, a children's village and a decommissioned navy destroyer. Not far away is the reconstructed FORT YORK. HARBOURFRONT is a series of piers with a growing number of shops, restaurants and marinas, separated from the downtown district by an elevated highway and a swath of cleared land awaiting construction.

THE FINANCIAL DISTRICT *(map 3 E7–4 E8)*. The edge of the Financial District is defined by the highway and the CN TOWER and SKYDOME, a sports stadium with a retractable roof. Nearby is the venerable Union Station, which is backed by a gleaming multistory testimony in glass to the city's commercial clout.

THE CITY HALL DISTRICT *(map3 C7–4 E8)*. Next, a few more blocks N, is the City Hall District, which takes in Eaton Centre, an extremely busy and justly famous enclosed shopping mall. Most of the larger hotels are located in this area. And beneath this entire downtown district lie the concourses of Toronto's own UNDERGROUND CITY, less celebrated but larger than the one in Montréal. To the W of City Hall is the newish ART GALLERY OF ONTARIO and, beyond it, CHINATOWN, one of North America's largest Asian communities.

QUEEN'S PARK *(map3 B7)*. In and around central Queen's Park are the ROYAL ONTARIO MUSEUM, McLAUGHLIN PLANETARIUM, the GARDINER MUSEUM OF CERAMIC ART, the Ontario Legislative Building, and, on the W, the campus of the prestigious UNIVERSITY OF TORONTO.

QUEEN ST. *(map3 D6-7)*. This appealing, semi-bohemian enclave of galleries, bistros and boutiques is blossoming, to the W of University.

YORKVILLE *(off map 3 A7)*. Across Bloor St., with its string of large department stores, is Yorkville, one of the first center-city neighborhoods to be gentrified in the 1960s, its blocks of sandblasted brick row houses now home to upscale shops, restaurants and bars. It also has a number of hotels, including the posh FOUR SEASONS.

ELSEWHERE The superb METRO ZOO, the ONTARIO SCIENCE CENTRE and stately CASA LOMA are all outside the center city, but justify the longer treks.

USING THIS CHAPTER

This chapter on sightseeing in Toronto is arranged in three sections:

- Three detailed **walks** that guide the visitor around **Old Toronto**, the **City Hall area** and **Chinatown**, and **Midtown** and **Yorkville**.
- An alphabetical **A to Z of sights**.
- An excursion to the **Niagara Peninsula**.

Some lesser attractions may be located in the fuller entries below or in WALKS on the following pages: find them through the INDEX.

In the listings below, the indicated **subway stops** are those nearest the attraction, and a long walk or transfer to bus or streetcar may sometimes then be required. If you plan to travel without a car, call ahead to check your transportation route. The closest cross street follows each address (given in parentheses), when applicable.

CROSS REFERENCES

Where a place name appears in SMALL CAPITALS, fuller details can be found in an entry elsewhere in this chapter.

Toronto on foot

Sprawling though it is, Toronto remains a city hospitable to the inveterate walker. Due to citizen insistence on preservation of tradition and maintenance of green spaces, as well as the multiple uses required of new developments, it avoids numbing anonymity, rarely losing its human face.

The following suggested routes pass many recommended sights, and there are ample opportunities for window shopping and resting in parks and cafés.

WALK 1: HIGH FINANCE AND OLD TORONTO
See maps 3 & 4. Subway: Union Station (map 3E7).

Begin a Toronto visit with an exhilarating ascent to the highest vantage point in the city, and end with lunch at a bustling fish house beside the cavernous St Lawrence Market.

Start at the corner of Front St. and John St., two long blocks w of Union Station. Right there is the entrance to **SkyWalk**, a covered passage that leads to the base of the CN TOWER. The needle-like concrete-and-metal structure caused — and still causes — as much controversy as Eiffel's tower, but ungainly as it is, there is no arguing with its claim to the most compelling views in Toronto.

Keeping in mind that it is definitely not an undertaking for the vertiginous, take the glass-sided elevator on a 58-second zoom to the "Space Pod," the bulbous observation platform about two-thirds the way up its 550m (1,815ft) height. That is high enough to see, on the proverbial clear day, the mists of Niagara Falls, 120km (75 miles) SE. For an extra fee, another elevator carries the compulsive 33 stories higher still. The deck is well above the planes taking off at Toronto Island Airport, and provides forever vistas of lake and parklands and, far below, the bristling skyscrapers of the Financial District. The descent is no less electrifying.

Return by the SkyWalk to Front St., turning right (E). In two blocks, the massive Royal York Hotel faces **Union Station**, a Neoclassical terminal completed in 1920. Rail and architecture buffs will want to detour through the columned portico for a look at the restored Great Hall. They don't make them like this any more. The vaulted concourse is 27m (88ft) high, with a frieze up near the ceiling listing the names of destinations of the old Canadian–Pacific Railway. On the far side are two mammoth Neo-Roman columns.

Return outside and continue E on Front to Bay St. Opposite is the **Royal Bank Plaza** building. The pleated glass sides of its two triangular towers have a golden cast, as well they might, given the inclusion of real gold dust in their fabrication. It literally and figuratively outshines its green neighbor, the new **Canada Trust Tower**.

Cross Bay St., then Front St., heading N. A white canopy of ribbed steel beetles out over the sidewalk, connecting the Canada Trust with the even newer **BCE Place**. It provides an arched gallery above a pedestrian mall that is itself cover for an underground shopping concourse. At the far end is **Marché**, a restaurant and food market destined to be as successful as the other enterprises of the prominent Mövenpick company (see WHERE TO EAT on page 101). Return to Bay St., walking N.

In two blocks, turn left (W) on King St. On the left are the bronze slabs of the **Toronto–Dominion Centre**. If it seems reminiscent of the Seagram Building in New York, which is routinely given accolades as the highest expression of minimalist Bauhaus principles, there is a reason: Ludwig Mies van der Rohe was the architect of both. Opposite are the two towers of **First Canadian Place**, a less esthetically pleasing statement, but the home of the new STOCK EXCHANGE and one of the entrances to UNDERGROUND TORONTO.

That subterranean pedestrian mall of shops and restaurants extends several blocks N to City Hall and S to Union Station. Continuing in the same direction, pass a welcome oasis of trees, benches and an artificial waterfall, and turn right (N) on York St. On the right in two blocks is an earlier **Mövenpick**, a busy, mid-priced eatery in which to take refreshment or to remember for a later meal. The **SHERATON CENTRE OF TORONTO** hotel is at the corner of intersecting Queen St.

Across Queen is **Osgoode Hall**, the first wing of which was built in 1832 as home to the Law Society of Upper Canada. A high iron fence surrounds it, erected to keep cows out when that was an annoyance in bucolic Old York. At the near corner is a statue of a pugnacious Winston Churchill. Turn right (E) on Queen.

On the left is **Nathan Phillips Square**, named after Toronto's first Jewish mayor (1955–62). It was during his administration that the design for the new **City Hall** was chosen. That's it beyond his square — two semicircular slabs of uneven height, surrounding a mushroom pod of a structure that serves as a council chamber. In between is a reflecting pool with vertical fountains, which becomes a popular skating rink in winter. Continuing on Queen, the **Old City Hall** looms, with its steeply pitched green copper roofs, conical turrets, campanile and rounded arches of the Romanesque Revival of the late 19thC.

Continuing E, the sandstone building on the right was once **Simpson's**, an old-line department store that recently gave up its ancient rivalry with equally venerable **Eaton's**. Now, it has been taken over by **The Bay**, the contemporary nickname for the even older Hudson Bay Company. It is linked to **Eaton Centre**, a grandiose indoor mall that is said to be Toronto's biggest tourist attraction. Cross at the light under the overhead walkway and enter the Centre.

An impressive, skylit central gallery is lined on several levels with scores of shops and eating places, all vying for consideration. Most are of the familiar middle-brow variety — CDs, jeans, kid's clothing and toys — but there is also a branch of Britain's **Marks & Spencer**. Stroll in a northerly direction. One entrance that might attract the eye is **The Elephant & Castle** (☎ 598-4455), as authentic a reproduction of an Olde English pub as can be found this side of Blighty.

If you are able to resist the acquisitive impulse, continue to the end of the Centre — it takes up three blocks — and through the Eaton store itself. At the N end are escalators climbing up to the intersection of Yonge and Dundas. "The longest street in the world," Yonge goes through many changes along its 1,900-km (1,190-mile) run to Rainy River, up near James Bay, itself an adjunct to Hudson Bay. This particular stretch happens to be especially gaudy, and not especially characteristic. Walk E on Dundas, which angles right for a couple of streets, and turn right (S) on Bond St.

Just after the hotel on the corner is MACKENZIE HOUSE. Born in Scotland in 1795, Mackenzie emigrated to Upper Canada in 1820. A journalist at first, he became the first mayor of the city in 1834 and led a doomed rebellion against the ruling oligarchy three years later. After a period of exile in the US, he returned to Toronto in 1849 and was living in this house at the time of his death.

After a visit, continue s on Bond. At the corner of Shuter St. is the 1848 **St Michael's Roman Catholic Cathedral**, in tidy theological counterpoint to the 1870 Protestant **Metropolitan United Church**, across the street. Turn right (w) on Shuter. At the corner with Victoria St. is **Massey Hall**, built in 1894 for lectures, recitals, and other entertainments. Noted for its glum exterior and fine acoustics, it retained both after its recent rehabilitation.

Continue w and turn left (s) on Yonge St. Down on the left is a unique structure, a single building containing two theaters built prior to the Great War, the **Elgin** and the **Winter Garden** (*☎963-3571 ✗ available Thurs 5pm, Sat 11am ▨*). After a history of use for vaudeville and film, the theaters have been magnificently restored to their former opulence, and again host live theatrical musicals and concerts. Cross Queen St. and turn left (E), then right (s) on Victoria. After an undistinguished two blocks, cross King St. and turn left (E). The dignified limestone and yellow-brick pile at that corner is the KING EDWARD, *grande dame* of Toronto hostelries and reflective of the era for which it was created. Step inside for a peek at the stately, colonnaded lobby. Royalty has walked here.

Continue E on King. Soon, on the left, is the Anglican **Cathedral Church of St James**. It was begun after the conflagration of 1849, which destroyed its predecessor and much of the surrounding area, the old town of York. The 93m (306ft) tower is the highest in Canada. Opposite is a small park called the **Toronto Sculpture Garden**, with a waterfall on the E wall. Because it is used for rotating exhibitions, there often is no sculpture at all. w of the cathedral is the much larger **St James Park**, with picnic tables and colorful gardens. Free concerts are held within, Tuesdays at noon from late June to mid-August.

Soon, on the right, is a pedestrian promenade called Market Lane Park. As you turn down it, the low modern building on the left houses a farmer's market on Saturday, starting at 5am. Emerging on Front St., the large structure on the other side and slightly to the E is the **St Lawrence Market**. Much more active than its neighbor, it certainly deserves a look *(open Tues–Thurs 8am–6pm, Friday 8am–7pm, Sat 5am–5pm)*. If it's time to eat, there are stalls in the market selling snacks. Better still is THE OLD FISH MARKET, a popular restaurant bordering on Market St.

Turn w on Front St., toward the downtown skyscrapers. Up ahead, where Front St. merges with Wellington St., is the unusual **Gooderham Building**, wedge-shaped, with a conical copper tower. Boosters like to brag that the six-story Gooderham predates New York's famous Flatiron Building by a decade, ignoring the fact that the latter is four times as tall. Stay on Front St.

Once past the end of the Gooderham, turn for a look at its rear, flat end. A witty fool-the-eye mural is there, depicting a giant, flapping tarpaulin, with a painting of the side of a building, incorporating four real windows. There is a triangular park next to it in which to rest and consider that this walk has only scratched the surface of surprising Toronto.

WALK 2: NEW CITY HALL TO NEW CHINATOWN

See map 3. Subway: Queen or Osgoode (map 4D8 and 3D7).

A dilapidated but thriving neighborhood of Chinese immigrants was razed in the 1960s to make way for the **New City Hall**. It rose again one mile away, even more vigorous than it was. The route of this walk connects the sparkling, soaring downtown with a growing, bumptious Little Asia.

Start in **Nathan Phillips Square**, the concrete expanse that fronts the new City Hall. There are frequent free concerts and other events here during much of the year *(☎ 392-0456 for information)*. In summer, the reflecting pool near Queen St. has fountain jets; in winter, it becomes a popular skating rink. Ice skates are rented at the counter in the building on the left. Facing the two curving sections of New City Hall, look slightly to the left (w). Over there is a sculpture recognizably by Henry Moore, an artist in particular favor in these parts. Walk in that direction, and then along the walkway beyond the sculpture.

Over beneath the trees to the right is a large playground. Continue past a small sculpture by Maryon Kantaroff (it quite resembles a Moore). This walkway soon ends at University Ave. Turn right (N). On the far side of Armoury St., cross University, heading w. This passes the **Royal Canadian Military Institute**, marked by two 19thC British artillery pieces. Turn left (w) on Dundas St.

In three blocks, another large Moore announces the presence of the ART GALLERY OF ONTARIO, widely known by its acronym, AGO. The museum closed for six months in 1992 for budgetary reasons but re-opened in 1993 with thirty new *and* twenty renovated galleries to house the expanding collections. A wide net is cast, with notable holdings in Egyptiana, Rembrandt, Inuit sculptures, Gainsborough, Van Gogh and many more Moores. Around back, and included in the entrance fee, is THE GRANGE, an 1817 Georgian residence of understated wealth, from the era of the Family Compact. Opposite the AGO entrance *(#326)* is a possible lunch or dinner stop, TALL POPPIES (see page 103).

Continue w on Dundas and it is apparent that this is Toronto's celebrated CHINATOWN. We shall return to it shortly, but for the moment, turn right (N) on Beverly. At the NW corner of Baldwin is the **George Brown House** *(☎ 324-6969 ✗ obligatory, Sun only, 1pm)*. Brown was a father of Canada's Confederation. Born in Scotland, he moved to Toronto in 1843, began publishing *The Globe* newspaper, and was elected to Parliament in 1851. He finished this house in 1877, and died three years later.

Down Baldwin to the right (E) are a surprising number of restaurants in what appears at a glance to be a residential street. Two of the best are the inexpensive Chinese, **The Eating Counter/Ohh Kitchen** *(#23 ☎ 977-7028)* and the accomplished French **La Bodega** *(#30 ☎ 977-1287)*. Clustered around them are Thai, Italian, Malay, and Latin American eateries, and one, **Dessert Sensations** *(corner Henry St.)*, that specializes in exactly what it says. After a bite or a meal, return w along Baldwin as far as Huron St. Turn left (s), and at Dundas, right (w).

This is CHINATOWN with a vengeance, a controlled bedlam of olfactory, aural, and visual stimuli. Ginseng parlors crowd greengrocers selling *bok choy* and ginger root, interspersed by herbalists, and windows hung with roast ducks. Pick among purple eggplants, live crabs, nectarines, dried mudfish, plastic gizmos, the sidewalks narrowed by stands set up by moonlighting entrepreneurs and small farmers. By the evidence of the distinctive Korean script and the numbers of Thai and Vietnamese shops and restaurants, the name of the neighborhood is no longer precise.

The corner of **Dundas and Spadina** is the main intersection of the district. (Spadina, the avenue, is pronounced "spa-DYE-na.") Turn right (N). At the next traffic light, cross Spadina; continue along it, heading N.

Two blocks farther along is Baldwin St. Turn left into **Kensington Market**, a chaotic, pungent jumble of fish stores, cafés, and indoor and outdoor food stalls. It used to have a pronounced Portuguese flavor, but intrusions by merchants of Latin American, West Indian and Asian heritage increasingly dominate. The market area — nearly as residential as it is commercial — is busiest in the mornings and on Friday and Saturday, when stocks are at their freshest and most abundant. Return to Spadina. Dozens of restaurants contend for business, with bargain midday prices. Among the better choices are **Chung King** *(#428)*, **Hunan Palace** *(#412)*, **Kom Jug Yuen** *(#371)*, and **Lee Garden** *(#358)*.

After a few blocks s on Spadina, Chinatown starts to fade, washing against remnants of the long-established fur and leather industry that once ruled this district. Turn left (E) on Queen St. Between Spadina St. and John St., it is a funky, youthful hodgepodge of offbeat shops, bars, and bistros. While there are no architectural landmarks or sights of distinction, a long holiday weekend could be spent along these few blocks, people-watching over coffee and croissants, browsing through bookstalls, slipping into street fashions of the moment, slouching toward midnight in a jumping West Indian reggae joint or afloat on Tex–Mex Margaritas.

WALK 3: MIDTOWN AND YORKVILLE
*See maps **3** & **4**. Subway: Queen's Park (map **3**B7).*

The admirable Torontonian penchant for restraint in the rush to what developers allege to be progress is documented here. It is the city's most compelling argument for that rare form of neighborhood planning that is responsive to the needs of the people living within it. So here there are homes where another metropolis might have dehumanizing high-rises, and shops where the clerks know customers by name, yet all of it with a gloss and panache that is a magnet for suburbanites and tourists.

Begin from the Queen's Park subway station, taking the N exit. Straight ahead is the **Ontario Legislative Building**, a Romanesque pile of red-brown sandstone completed in 1892. University Ave. splits to go round the building on each side. Bear left, past the greenhouses at the edge of the campus of the UNIVERSITY OF TORONTO. The University, founded in 1827, has schools and colleges in every major academic field. It nearly surrounds Queen's Park, in which the Parliament is located, but the larger part of it stretches to the W and N.

Soon, walking N along what is here called Queen's Park Crescent W, is the **Sigmund Samuel Building** *(#14)*. A unit of the ROYAL ONTARIO

MUSEUM, it houses a collection of Canadiana — furniture and domestic accessories — and holds frequent special exhibitions (*☎586-5551, open Mon–Sat 10am–5pm, Sun 1pm–5pm ⊡*).

After a visit, cross the road — carefully — to the **Legislative Building**, taking the sidewalk that leads past the front portico. Assuming restoration work on the roof and facade is completed, a brief detour into the colorful lobby with its grand staircase illustrates the marked contrast to the somber exterior. Back outside, walk between the statues of John A. Macdonald, first premier of Ontario after confederation, and a seated Queen Victoria. Turn left (N) at the end of the building.

The next street on the right is Wellesley. Cross over Wellesley and bear left into the park, an oasis of trees and lawn set with benches and picnic tables. Joggers, sea gulls, lovers, pigeons and Toronto's indigenous fat, black squirrels are peaceful cohabitants. At the equestrian statue of the plump King Edward VII, veer along the northerly path in the direction he faces. This comes, at the far end of the park, to a granite monument to the Canadian dead of many wars.

Cross over Queen's Park Crescent to the w side of what soon becomes Avenue Road (yes, that's the full official name). Shortly, the **McLAUGHLIN PLANETARIUM** appears on the left. An excellent facility, it draws more than 250,000 visitors a year. The next building, adjoining, is the recently expanded **ROYAL ONTARIO MUSEUM**, Toronto's principal showcase of art, archeology, paleontology, and the life sciences. It deserves at least an hour. Upon leaving, the **GEORGE R. GARDINER MUSEUM OF CERAMIC ART** is seen across the street.

For safety's sake, go to the next corner (Bloor St.), cross over, and walk back. Keep the ROM button — it offers same-day admission to the Gardiner, which is far from being simply a collection of plates and vases. It has a most interesting section of figurative Pre-Columbian pottery.

After the Gardiner, turn right (N), cross Bloor and walk along Avenue Road two blocks to Yorkville Ave., marked by the luxury **FOUR SEASONS** hotel. Turn right (E). This is the main street of Yorkville, liveliest when residents have stored overcoats away for the summer. Many of the buildings lining each side are sandblasted 4- or 5-story row houses, salvaged three decades ago when adventurous members of the Love Generation were seeking affordable housing. Rents are no longer cheap, for these are now two of the most expensive blocks in midtown. Many of the cafés and bistros along the way have outdoor terraces or balconies, the better to observe the procession of fit and fashionable young.

On weekends when the weather is good, Yorkville is a corridor of street musicians, caricaturists, mimes, and other performers and hustlers not always easy to classify. There are, as is to be expected in such a milieu, *sushi* bars, unisex hair salons, *shiatsu* massage parlors, cappuccino houses and spas.

Across from the uptown branch of the **Mövenpick** chain is **La Maison de la Presse Internationale**, with abundant Canadian and foreign magazines and newspapers. **Meyer's** delicatessen is there too *(#69)*, an unlikely venue for late-night jazz, and so is **Lovecraft** *(#63)*, a tasteful purveyor of erotic toys and underwear with at least as many women patrons as men. As interesting are **Firehall No.10** *(#34)*, a florid Victorian erected in 1876, and the Neoclassical **Yorkville Public Library** *(#22)*, remodeled in 1978.

Yonge St. is the next important street, heading E. Yorkville can dismay with its rampant consumption, but the antidote lies right across the way. It is the METRO TORONTO REFERENCE LIBRARY. Few libraries are as animated as this one, whose main atrium, with fountains and glass-bubble elevators gliding silently up and down, more closely resembles a rather glitzy hotel lobby. Its message, not the medium, is serious — it has 1.3 million books and about 10,000 audio cassettes.

Outside the library, turn S on Yonge. A restaurant called METROPOLIS *(#838)* gets good notices for its "New Canadian" food, with a menu that sounds suspiciously like a California import. Turn right (W) on Bloor. Through here, it is a spangled canyon of department stores and malls — Holt Renfrew, The Bay, Birks Jewelers — and European boutiques — Chanel, Cartier, Gucci, Charles Jourdan, Georg Jensen. Back at Avenue Road, turn left to pick up the subway near the entrance to the Royal Ontario Museum.

AND ELSEWHERE . . .

Shops, cafés, and restaurants of incredible diversity line the blocks around the intersection of **Bloor St.** and **Bathurst St.** Here is a multi-ethnic rainbow of people and enterprises, among them Poles, Lebanese, Pakistanis, Brazilians, Koreans, Greeks and Egyptians.

And CABBAGETOWN *(map 4 C9)* is an increasingly gentrified neighborhood of once humble 19thC houses not far from Yorkville; start exploring from Parliament and Carlton. While there are some houses of architectural interest, much of the appeal of the area lies in the mingling of bohemian and ethnic lifestyles.

Toronto: sights A to Z

In linguistically bipolar Canada, Toronto occupies the summit of Anglophone culture. It doesn't have the age of Montréal, and its historic buildings rarely predate the 1830s. But it compensates with enticing neighborhoods populated by more than 70 identifiable ethnic groups, and its heritage includes the gifts of two centuries of prosperous individuals of Anglo-Saxon ancestry. Much of this accumulation is on display in its several good-to-excellent museums, at least three of which reward repeat visits.

There are logistics to remember. **Public transportation** is available to virtually every major and secondary attraction, but Metro Toronto is so large that a car is desirable for such worthwhile out-of-the-way destinations as the METRO ZOO, the McMICHAEL COLLECTION and BLACK CREEK PIONEER VILLAGE.

Even those sights that are normally open seven days a week close for Christmas, and Sunday hours usually apply on other holidays.

ART GALLERY OF ONTARIO (AGO)
317 Dundas St. W (McCall). Map 3C7 ☎*977-0414* 📷 *(*📷 *Wed after 5.30pm)*
🚇 📍 *Open June–Sept Tues, Thurs–Sun 11am–5.30pm, Wed 11am–9pm; Mon 11am–5.30pm; Oct–May closed Mon. Hours may vary; call ahead. Subway: St Patrick.*

Few museums are as blessed as this one, with such a large body of work by a single major contemporary artist. British sculptor Henry Moore bequeathed 101 of his sculptures and 57 drawings to AGO, and worked closely with architect John C. Parkin in the design of the stunning pavilion, opened in 1974, that now houses the collection.

A massive sculpture by Moore, *Large Two Forms,* outside at the NE corner of the museum, hints at the riches within. Impressive as these works are, though, there is much more to AGO. Its permanent collection totals more than 12,000 pieces and continues to grow. Nor is it confined to 20thC art, although that is its strength.

Budgetary considerations and new construction conspired to close the museum for six months in 1992. It re-opened in early 1993, with 30 new and 20 renovated galleries, increasing available exhibition space by almost 60 percent. This expansion makes AGO the seventh largest art museum in North America, according to the directors. Continued shuffling and rearranging of the collections make precise cataloging impossible at this point in time.

Among the works generally on view, however, are large Abstract–Expressionist canvases by Ellsworth Kelly, Kenneth Noland, Sam Francis, Larry Poons and Franz Kline. These have been interspersed with bronzes by Rodin, Degas and Matisse — an enlightening juxtaposition. An Old Masters gallery shows paintings by 17th and 18thC artists reminiscent of those of better-known contemporaries. A well-lit Francesco de Mura, for example, could almost be a minor Rubens.

The historical chronology moves forward, with works by such turn-of-the-century innovators as Dufy, Braque, Bonnard, Picasso, Degas and Renoir. Also shown are paintings of the Group of Seven, who were in the vanguard of an important 20thC Canadian movement (see THE CREATIVE ARTS, page 24).

The **Moore Sculpture Centre** still occupies pride of place. Light falls through skylights upon an array of instantly recognizable sculptures that reveal the master's breadth. Those who think of simple, biomorphic shapes in connection with Moore may be surprised to see the remarkable variety of motifs and sizes and the range of materials with which he worked during his career. That exceptional room is linked, by a corridor of more French Post-Impressionists, with a gallery of Inuit prints.

After a tour, keep in mind that AGO's full-service **restaurant** has long enjoyed a reputation superior to those usually operated within museums.

Still another telling contrast is **THE GRANGE**, connected to the museum in back. Built about 1817 for one D'Arcy Boulton Jr., the Georgian mansion is the oldest existing brick dwelling in Toronto. The off-center w wing was added in later decades. After service as the first home of AGO, it was later restored and furnished as a gentleman's residence of 1835. A large park with picnic tables and a playground lies s of the house.

BATA SHOE MUSEUM

The Colonnade, 131 Bloor St. W (Avenue Rd.). Off map 3A7 ☎*924-7463* 📠
Open Tues–Sun 11am–6pm. Subway: Museum or Bay.

Footwear might not seem a sufficiently compelling subject to be the sole focus of a serious museum, but this one changes minds. The collection on display here is temporary, it first must be noted, with a transfer planned for 1994 to a permanent facility at the corner of Bloor St. and St George.

Most of the standard curatorial tricks and techniques are employed to build interest in the subject at hand, including continuous video displays of people jogging and dancing and horse riding, and others asking and answering such questions as "Why is leather the most suitable material for shoemaking?" The tools and products of the craft are well displayed and surprisingly diverse.

An English "musketeer" boot serves as a symbol for the collection, barely holding its own with such exotica as the Ojibwa bear claw slipper, Inuit sealskin *kamiks,* and Pakistani *chappli.* Contemporary fashion isn't ignored, either, with nods to the creations of St-Laurent and Ferragamo. And did you know that shoemakers have their very own patron saint? None other than St Crispin.

THE BEACHES

See the map of METROPOLITAN TORONTO *on page 49. #501 bus.*

Journey E on the Queen St. streetcar and come upon this rakish strand-side community only 15 minutes from the starch and suits of the financial district. A 2-mile boardwalk borders the beach, with cafés, gardens, and volleyball games. One block inland, Queen St. is lined with relentlessly funky boutiques, ice cream parlors, and kick-back bars. The best time to go is a summer weekday.

BLACK CREEK PIONEER VILLAGE ★

Jane St. and Steeles Ave. (1000 Murray Ross Parkway). Map 5B3 ☎*736-1733 or 661-6610 (24-hour recording)* 📠 💺 *Open daily mid-Mar to end Dec; hours vary. Subway: Jane, then #35B bus.*

Sheep graze along the streets, a horsedrawn wagon trundles visitors past the principal sights. Costumed "townspeople" bring this re-created rural 19thC village to life, managing to look as if they actually live and work there. Happily, they keep the standard guide chatter to a minimum, working at their crafts at least as much as talking.

In more than 30 restored buildings (brought here from other sites) they demonstrate the crafts and skills necessary to the good life and simple survival in young Canada — tinsmithing, weaving, cooking, farming, cabinet-making. Blacksmiths fashion tools and horseshoes, women quilt patchwork coverlets, workers grind grains in the authentic grist mill. Some of the results are on sale in the general store.

In summer, a bagpipe-led contingent of the 78th Fraser Highlanders performs military drills and exercises on the village green, and the calendar is dotted with such special events as "sugaring-off" maple trees, an Easter egg-hunt and a Victorian country wedding. The modern visitors' center has a worthwhile gallery of implements and objects of the period, including an appealing collection of toys and dolls. As it is 30–45 minutes from downtown, an excursion might be combined with a visit to the McMICHAEL CANADIAN ART COLLECTION or CANADA'S WONDERLAND, about 10 minutes away.

CABBAGETOWN
Map 4C9. Subway: College, then the #506 streetcar or a 10-min walk E on Carlton St.

The name derives from the 19thC Irish immigrant custom of planting lawns with vegetables rather than grass and flowers. The area was developed initially in the 1850s as clusters of modest stone-and-frame dwellings, but more elaborate architectural styles were later introduced. A tentative gentrification process has taken hold, with more affluent, but often bohemian younger people taking over from some of the older residents. The resulting mix is relatively harmonious in personal interactions, if a trifle jangling in its visual components. Boarding houses, used-furniture stores, and shoestring ethnic cafés stand beside shops selling health foods, expensive bicycles, CD records and cappuccino.

For a quick tour, walk N on Parliament from the intersection with Carlton, turn left on Winchester, left again on Ontario, then left once more at the next unmarked corner, which is Aberdeen St. This route passes some of the more extensive groupings of restored semi-detached and row houses.

A good time to visit is during the September **Cabbagetown Cultural Festival**, with its marching bands, road race, films, and flea market.

Among the restaurants that look as if they might still be in operation next week are **La Mexicana** *(299 Carlton)*, **Tapas Bar** *(226 Carlton)*, and **Novastar** *(458 Parliament)*.

CAMPBELL HOUSE
160 Queen St. W (University). Map 3D7 ☎597-0227 ▨ ✗ available. Open Mon–Fri 9.30–4.30pm, Sat–Sun noon–4.30pm. Subway: Osgoode.

One of the earliest brick houses (1822) when the town was still called York, this was the home of an immigrant Scot, William Campbell, who eventually became a chief justice and was knighted by the Crown. He died in 1834.

Originally located in Old Town, E of the present financial district, the house was moved here in 1972 to save it from demolition. The Ontario Advocate Society of lawyers restored and furnished the building for use as a meeting place. Earnest costumed docents give tours.

A fine example of late Georgian residential architecture, the building looks as if it has always occupied its present site; an iron fence surrounds its plot of trees and grass.

CANADA SPORTS HALL OF FAME
Exhibition Place, just across from the Exhibition Stadium on New Brunswick Way. Map 2E4 ☎260-6789 ▣ Open 10am–4.30pm. Subway: Bathurst, then #511 streetcar.

Canadian heroes in all sports but hockey (see HOCKEY HALL OF FAME) are remembered in rooms crowded with nostalgia. Terry Fox, the disabled athlete who ran across Canada, is among those honored.

CANADA'S WONDERLAND
Highway 400 (Rutherford). Map 5B2 ☎*832-2205* 🖾 💻 ✳ *Open daily end May–Sept 4, Sept and last 2wks in May weekends only. Closed Oct to mid-May.*

To some, it might seem there is a surfeit of amusement and theme parks in the Toronto area. If there is time for only one, this is the choice, and the better part of a day should be allowed. Few possibilities for diversion are left unexploited.

In seven themed areas spread over 370 acres, there are heart-stopping roller coasters — The Bat and SkyRider test the mettle of any *aficionado* — precipitous water-slides, performing dolphins and sea lions, live shows and concerts, restaurants, street performers, fireworks, laser displays, even a 45m-high (150ft) artificial mountain. Two areas are intended specifically for younger children, where they can take rides mild enough not to frighten but exciting enough to be memorable. Smurfs and Yogi Bear and other cartoon characters greet them along the way, and blue ice cream is a favorite treat.

An all-day "Passport" ticket is available to adults and their kids, providing unlimited use of rides and shows at a substantial discount. It covers the charge for everything except food, merchandise, or entrance to the Kingswood Music Theatre (where concerts are held).

CANADIANA COLLECTION/SIGMUND SAMUEL BUILDING
14 Queen's Park Crescent W (College). Map 3B7 ☎*586-5524* 🖾 *Open Mon–Sat 10am–5pm, Sun 1–5pm. Subway: Queen's Park or Museum.*

An annex of the ROYAL ONTARIO MUSEUM on the University of Toronto campus, the collection is an under-appreciated trove of pioneer crafts and furniture, decorative arts, maps, documents, and paintings and sculptures by Canadian artists, mostly from the 19thC. Included are folk-art objects — weather vanes, toys, kitchenware — as well as utilitarian pottery, clocks, miniatures, and pure examples of handmade chairs and storage units.

CASA LOMA
1 Austin Terrace (Spadina). Off map 3A6 ☎*923-1171* 🖾 ◁€ 💻 ✳ *Open daily 10am–4pm except Christmas and New Year's Day. Subway: Dupont, or St Clair West, then the Forest Hill #33A bus.*

Few stately homes, even in Europe, can match this for size, and not many surpass it in grandeur. It was contracted by financier-industrialist Sir Henry Pellatt in 1911 and completed 3 years later. Among its marvels are 98 rooms paneled in oak, walnut, teak and mahogany and lavishly furnished with imports and antiques; 15 bathrooms and 23 fireplaces; hidden passages and staircases; a 100,000-book library; a wine cellar holding 1,800 bottles; an immense pipe organ in a ballroom that could hold 3,000 partygoers; and a 245m (800-foot) tunnel leading to a stable where 20 prize horses were quartered.

The majestically corpulent Sir Henry demanded the best of the 20thC, too, installing Toronto's first electric elevator, and his own switchboard, connecting the castle's 59 telephones with the outside world. There was even a swimming pool, never completed, in the basement. Much of the building was imported from Scotland and reassembled by Scottish masons, part of a crew of 300 workmen. None of that explains the Spanish name, whose origin remains a mystery.

From the outside, Casa Loma (illustrated on page 26) looks very much the baronial residence, with battlements, squared chimneys and medieval conical turrets. Built for $3 million on a hill, its terraces and towers offer views of the downtown skyline, many miles away. The castle couldn't be reproduced today for ten times the price. Even back then, the brutal cost of maintenance of his treasure was Pellatt's undoing.

Recognizing the inevitable, he and Lady Pellatt moved out in 1923. What had proved to be his folly was turned into a hotel two years later. The new owners went bankrupt, too. Casa Loma was eventually taken over by the city in lieu of unpaid taxes in 1934. Sir Henry died in poverty.

On the self-guided audio tour, the tape describes each room. A visit can be combined with one to another mansion, SPADINA HOUSE, a short distance away.

CBC BROADCAST CENTRE
John St. and Wellington St. W. Map 3D7 Subway: St. Andrew.
Lying in the direct shadow of the intimidating CN TOWER, a building has to do something dramatic to get a piece of the spotlight. This undertaking, intended to gather under one roof the far-flung offices and studios of both radio and TV divisions of the Canadian Broadcasting Corporation, did just that.

Its managers enticed Philip Johnson to be the design consultant. Well into his 80s, he did no damage to his controversial international reputation with his contributions to this 14-story headquarters. The architects had about $380 million to spend on expanses of dark glass, formed in cubes and cylinders and set off by thick crimson grids on the facades.

Completed in 1992, parts of the building are open to the public, including a number of the seven TV and 29 radio studios.

CHINATOWN
Map 3C6. Subway: St Patrick, then walk w on Dundas.
There are an estimated 275,000 Chinese and 250,000 Southeast Asians in Toronto. They gather in five distinct neighborhoods around the city, but the best known is this one, centering on the intersection of Dundas and Spadina. This is actually an artificial site: the original Chinatown was displaced more than 25 years ago to allow the building of the new City Hall. (See WALK 2 on page 56).

CN TOWER
301 Front St. W (John). Map 3E7 ☎ *360-8500* ▨ ▭ ▮ *Open June 1–Labour Day Mon–Sat 9am–midnight, Sun 9am–11pm ; Labour Day–end May Sun–Thurs 10am–10pm, Fri and Sat 10am–11pm. Subway: Union Station.*

Touted to exhaustion as "the world's tallest free-standing structure," the Tower's only truly practical function is as a mast for TV and radio transmitters. Otherwise, it is in that category of things that must be discussed because it is there. Certainly the food in the requisite revolving restaurant does nothing to bolster the bleak reputation of such enterprises, and few argue that the Tower makes a significant esthetic contribution to either engineering or architecture.

Such factors had little to do with it. It amounts to a paean to boosterism, an unignorable symbol to distinguish an attractive but not especially arresting skyline.

Constructed of poured concrete and steel, it took 40 months and $57 million to bring it to completion in 1976. At 555m (1,815 feet), the mast dwarfs the 443m (1,454 feet) Sears Tower in Chicago, presently the world's tallest skyscraper. The reason for the CN Tower's "free-standing" qualification is that it has no guy wires. There is a 7-story "Spacepod" two-thirds of the way up, with the restaurant, a nightclub, and indoor and outdoor observation decks.

The elevators are glass on one side, affording continuous views throughout the 58-second ascent. Their young operators are either directed by their supervisors or are merely self-compelled to make such obvious jokes as where the parachutes are stored. From the first observation deck, another elevator carries the willing — or the uninformed — to a second, higher belvedere — the "Space Deck," 446m (1,465 feet) high. Its glass windows bank inward at the bottom, so it is possible to gaze straight down, practically between toes, should one care to do so. This is not — *not* — an adventure to be undertaken by those who suffer even mild vertigo.

All these reservations aside, the panorama is undeniably impressive, spanning more than 100 miles under perfect conditions, across the lake to the s, beyond the northern rim of the city and even down to Niagara Falls on the horizon.

CN Tower and **SkyDome**

THE DANFORTH

See the map of METROPOLITAN TORONTO *on page 49. Subway: Broadview or Chester.*
Greeks are among the most prominent immigrant groups, most visible along Danforth Ave., the extension of Bloor St. to the E of the Don River. Dubbed "The Danforth" by locals, this Greektown is only one of several Greek–Canadian communities, but it is a magnet for lovers of *souvlaki,* spit-roasted lamb, and Aegean-style seafood at moderate prices.

Among the more popular eateries are **Astoria** *(#390* ☎ *463-2838),*

Santorini *(#402* ☎ *462-9431),* **Omonia** *(#426* ☎ *465-2129),* and **Ouzeri** *(#500A* ☎ *778-0500).* Most have live music.

EATON CENTRE
Map 4C8.
The large, enclosed shopping mall reminiscent of Milan's Galleria. See WALK 1 on page 54, UNDERGROUND TORONTO, and SHOPPING on page 112.

EXHIBITION PLACE
Strachan Ave. and Lakeshore Blvd. Map 1E3–2E4 ☎ *393-6000. Ticket prices and hours vary with events scheduled. Subway: Bathurst, then #511 streetcar.*
The location for most of Toronto's major trade shows and expositions, Exhibition Place contains, on 350 acres of waterfront land, a series of large, connected halls dating from the late 19thC.

Exhibition Place is, most famously, home to the **Canadian National Exhibition** in August and early September. The **Royal Agricultural Winter Fair** in November, The **Scottish World Festival Tattoo**, the **Canadian International Air Show**, an annual **Boat Show**, and the **Molson Indy auto race** are also on the schedule (see EVENTS FOR THE VISITOR'S CALENDAR on page 38). Major rock and pop stars, including such unthreatening types as Elton John and Ray Charles appear on stage in the **Exhibition Stadium**.

The **Canadian National Exhibition** is an extravaganza that incorporates horse shows, a midway with food and gambling booths, ferris wheels, roller coasters, fireworks and shows, rides, and a petting zoo for children.

Essentially an old-fashioned carnival on a giant scale, the CNE has its self-consciously edifying elements, principally in featuring the culture of a different nation each year in the International Pavilion. For an overview of the grounds, the harbor, and the downtown skyline, take the **Alpine Way** cable car that leaves from a point just beyond the florid **Prince's Gate**, the main entrance to the grounds.

Even when no such event is taking place, the grounds also contain the MARINE MUSEUM OF UPPER CANADA and the CANADA SPORTS HALL OF FAME. Parking is available but is difficult during major shows and exhibitions, when public transportation is preferable.

FORT YORK
Garrison Rd. (Fleet). Map 2E5 ☎ *392-6907* ▨ *Open May–Sept Mon–Sat 9.30am–5pm, Sun 9.30am–5pm; Oct–Apr noon–5pm. Subway: Bathurst, then #511 streetcar.*
In 1811, when British and American relations were deteriorating, the existing garrison at Fort York was strengthened to withstand an anticipated US invasion of Upper Canada (now Ontario). It was positioned to defend what was then the entrance to Toronto Bay.

The Americans did attack York, on April 27, 1813, landing a force of 1,750 soldiers from a squadron of 14 vessels. They far outnumbered the defenders, a mixed command of British regulars, militia and Indians, who soon retreated. In a rearguard action, the fort's magazine was blown up, killing or wounding more than 300 Americans and about 150 British soldiers. This "Battle of York" ended soon afterwards. During the subsequent 11-day occupation, there was uncontrolled looting and burning by the victors. Hardly an isolated incident for either side in the American Revolution and War of 1812, it nevertheless provided the justification for the greater depredation of the British when they burned and sacked Washington, DC in 1814.

Fort York was rebuilt between 1813 and 1816, and that is what is on view today, restored for the city's centennial in 1934. There are eight barracks, blockhouses and magazines within the star-shaped ramparts.

A 12-minute slide-and-sound presentation skims the history of the site. In the first building of the recommended tour, decidedly Canadian interpretations of history testily describe the battle and American occupations and point out that there were incursions into Canada as late as 1866 and 1870. In those years, an Irish revolutionary organization, the Fenian Brotherhood, led abortive attacks on American and Canadian targets, somehow imagining that this would help pressure England into giving Ireland its independence. The other buildings hint at how the officers, men, and their families lived, in spare, cramped conditions.

GEORGE R. GARDINER MUSEUM OF CERAMIC ART
111 Queen's Park (Bloor). Map 3A7 ☎*586-8080* 💳 *(also gives admission to* McLAUGHLIN PLANETARIUM *and* ROM*). Open Tues–Sun 10am–5pm. Subway: Museum.*
European ceramics and porcelains of the 15th–18thC comprise the nucleus of the collection that consists of more than 2,000 pieces, including 17thC English delftware from the ages of the Stuarts and Oliver Cromwell, Maiolica of the Italian Renaissance, and the popular porcelain harlequins inspired by the Commedia dell'Arte.

At least as impressive is the array of Pre-Columbian pottery on the first floor. The spouted vessels, effigies, funeral urns and pedestal plates date from the earliest Olmec civilization and include objects from the Mexican Toltec, Nayarit, Mixtec and Aztec cultures. The gift shop sells contemporary ceramics of good quality, but expect no bargains.

THE GRANGE
Grange Park, John St. (Dundas). Map 3C7 ☎*977-0414* 💳 *Entrance through Art Gallery of Ontario. Open Tues, Thurs–Sun 11am–5.30pm, Wed 11am–9pm. Subway: St Patrick.*
Said to be the oldest surviving brick residence in Toronto, this relatively modest Georgian house was built in 1817. Connected to the ART GALLERY OF ONTARIO buildings (see main entry on page 60), and for a while its main home, the Grange is now restored to a measure of the 1830s elegance associated with residences of the Family Compact oligarchy. Staff members in costumes of the time provide commentary.

HARBOURFRONT
Map 3F6–4F8. Harbourfront streetcar from Union Station.
A major project of the ongoing effort to make the waterfront more accessible to residents, Harbourfront is a rejuvenated part of a once-di-

lapidated waterside district of warehouses and wharves. The master plan has encouraged mixed-income housing as well as marinas, shops, restaurants and cinemas.

Two superior hotels, the RADISSON PLAZA ADMIRAL and the WESTIN HARBOUR CASTLE, anchor each end of the development, which is still a work in progress. Much of the land backing the waterfront has been cleared of old factories and similar structures, but awaits new construction.

Ferries for the Toronto Islands leave from the dock behind the Westin, and several companies offer lake cruises, especially from **Queen's Quay** (pronounced "key") **Terminal**. That same building also houses the offices of the **Metropolitan Toronto Convention and Visitors Association**.

One seemingly out-of-place attraction is the **Redpath Sugar Museum** *(95 Queen's Quay E (Jarvis), map 4E8* ☎ *366-3561* 🖾 *open Mon–Fri 9am–noon, 1–3.30pm).* Sponsored by the sugar-processing company of the same name, it displays artifacts and informational exhibits about the history of the industry.

Various events and activities are scheduled throughout the year along Harbourfront, including indoor and outdoor concerts by groups spanning every taste in music, dance and theatrical performances, and film festivals — a total of more than 4,000 events annually.

HIGH PARK
See the map of METROPOLITAN TORONTO *on page 48. Subway: High Park* ✦
One of the most fully utilized parks in a city with an abundance of options, it offers its millions of annual visitors a small zoo (🖾), tennis courts, soccer fields, playgrounds, skiing, formal gardens, fishing, a restaurant, boating, and more than 400 acres of shady trees and picnic grounds.

Much of the parkland was bequeathed to the city in 1873 by the engineer and architect John Howard. His Regency house, **Colborne Lodge** (☎ *392-6916* 🖾 *open Apr–Dec Mon–Sat 9.30am–5.30pm, Sun noon–5pm; Jan–Mar Sat, Sun, holidays only)* is near the s entrance of the park, overlooking Lake Ontario. It was built in 1837, and included in the original furnishings are Howard's watercolors of mid-19thC Toronto. The costumed staff demonstrates home crafts of the period.

HOCKEY HALL OF FAME
BCE Place, 161 Bay St. Map 4D8 ☎ *360-7735* 🖾 *Open Mon–Wed 9.30am–6pm, Thurs, Fri 9.30am–9.30pm, Sat 10am–5pm, Sun 12noon–5pm. Subway: Union Station.*
Those who count themselves fans of Canada's violent, graceful national game can revel in memorabilia associated with such past and present legends as Bobby Hull and the Great Gretsky. The first Stanley Cup is among the items on display, as are the jerseys and equipment of notable professional, Olympic, and amateur players. One exhibit is a fully equipped replica of a team locker room.

In addition to interactive games of skill, continuous films of memorable games are shown in two theaters.

KENSINGTON MARKET
Baldwin St. between Spadina and Augusta. Map 3C6.
An enclave of ethnic food shops and stalls surrounded by CHINATOWN.
See WALK 2 on page 57.

MACKENZIE HOUSE
82 Bond St. (nr Dundas). Map 4C8 ☎*392-6915* 📷 *✗ obligatory. Open Mon–Fri 9am–4pm, Sat, Sun and holidays noon–5pm. Subway: Dundas.*
William Lyon Mackenzie was a newspaper publisher and the first mayor of the renamed city of Toronto in 1834. His frustrations in dealing with the powerful Family Compact ruling group drove him into leadership of the 1837 armed rebellion. It lasted only 6 weeks, and Mackenzie lived in exile in the US for the next 11 years, where he continued to agitate for greater democracy both there and in Canada. He was allowed to return after 1849, when governmental reforms were made.

The house, Georgian in style and once one of a block of row houses, is furnished in the Victorian manner that was in vogue when Mackenzie and his family lived there in his later, more peaceful years. Authenticity is manifest in the gas lighting and the middle-class, mid-Victorian furniture. He died in 1861, only three years after moving in, and two of his daughters subsequently ran a boarding school in the house.

Costumed guides more often answer questions than deliver canned lectures. One of them demonstrates kitchen techniques of the period; another shows the use of the kinds of printing presses available in Mackenzie's time. It takes little encouragement for them to reveal the presence of the resident ghost.

MARINE MUSEUM OF UPPER CANADA
Exhibition Place, near Princes Gate. Map 2E4 ☎*392-6827* 📷 ▣ ✸ *Open Tues–Fri 9.30am–5pm, Sat and Sun noon–5pm. Subway: Bathurst, then #511 streetcar.*
The ambitious and very competent Toronto Historical Board operates five properties around the city: FORT YORK, Colborne Lodge in HIGH PARK, MACKENZIE HOUSE, SPADINA HOUSE, and the Marine Museum of Upper Canada, a repository of ships and marine artifacts charting the evolution of leisure and commercial shipping on the Great Lakes from the earliest days of the fur trade.

This museum is situated within a former military barracks that dates from 1841. There are marvelously detailed model ships, nautical equipment on view, and many items salvaged from decommissioned vessels crowd the rooms.

In May, they uncover the ***Ned Hanlan*** *(closed Oct–Apr)*, a restored 1932 harbor tug, and invite visitors to clamber aboard. Children do so without hesitation. The tugboat was named after a celebrated oarsman of the 1870s who became a world champion in his sport. There is a heroic statue of him in front of the museum. A nearby pedestrian bridge crosses Gardiner Expressway to ONTARIO PLACE, and the Canadian National Exhibition is held on the adjacent grounds.

McLAUGHLIN PLANETARIUM

100 Queen's Park (Bloor). Map 3A7 ☎*586-5736 (recorded information)* 🔲
(🔲 *with ROM or GARDINER MUSEUM OF CERAMIC ART ticket, but extra* 🔲 *for some shows)* ✱ *Open daily 10am–6pm, Tues, Thurs 10am–8pm. Subway: Museum.*
This white-towered landmark building was built using funds donated by the philanthropist automobile magnate R.S. McLaughlin.

The **Theatre of the Stars** has a dome more than 18m (60ft) across, employing 80 projectors and hundreds of special effects to simulate shooting stars and black holes and the tapestry of the night sky. Shows, which change each season, last 45 minutes, and take place two or three times daily, with more in summer.

An **Astrocentre** reproduces the solar system in 3-dimension and invites the use of computer terminals and other interactive displays. And the **Laser Theatre** *(additional* 🔲 *Thurs–Sun, varying showtimes)* gets the attention of young people with lightshows featuring music by the likes of Guns N' Roses, Led Zeppelin and Pink Floyd.

McMICHAEL CANADIAN COLLECTION ★

Islington Ave, Kleinburg. Map 5B2 ☎*893-2787* 🔲 ▭ ✗ *available on weekends* ▶ *Open April–Oct, daily 10am–5pm; Nov–Mar, Tues–Sun 11am–4.30pm.*
Highly recommended, if only as an excuse for a country outing, this museum preserves a corner of the Ontario wilderness that inspired the artists whose works are reverentially displayed inside. The collection, and the building in which it resides, are the result of the enthusiasm of the couple whose name they bear. They complement one another, with timbers and masonry as a backdrop for the deeply-felt paintings and sculptures of both Canadians of European background and native Inuit and Amerindians.

The landscape paintings are primarily by the Group of Seven artists (see THE CREATIVE ARTS on page 24). Founders of the first school of uniquely Canadian painting, they were moved primarily by the unspoiled nature preserves and bodies of water of northern Ontario, and were a collective force on the art scene for three decades.

Their work is characterized by distilled lines and shapes, often rendered with limited palettes. Simple overlapping planes are used very effectively to suggest depth. Not that their paintings are interchangeable. At various stages, Tom Thomson worked in bright colors with Impressionistic strokes, Lawren Stewart Harris in sharply stylized forms, Clarence Cagnon in dreamy genre settings — and they were restless, experimental.

Superbly fashioned Inuit sculptures are much on view, as are prints and paintings by members of the Woodlands and Northwest Coast tribal bands. The diversity of native art is shown in carvings of bone, antler, and ivory, as well as the more familiar black and green soapstone. Many break the tidy bounds of expectations, experimenting with concepts and materials while remaining of the culture.

The museum feels warm and cared-for, more like a home (albeit a very large one) than a chilly institution, and few people regret the modest trek required from downtown. A private car is best, taking Highway 400 N to Major Mackenzie Dr., then W to the town of Kleinburg. Public transit is possible, but takes longer and can be confusing. The restaurant is more competent than might be expected, and a lunch on the terrace is a treat, looking out over the trees with not another building in sight.

METRO HALL
55 John St. (King). Map 3D7. Subway: St Andrew.
Opened in 1992, the same year as the CBC BROADCAST CENTRE next door, this fanciful grouping of towers rises W of **Roy Thompson Hall**. Described by some as Post-Modernist in style, as Deconstructivist by others, it outdoes both its neighbors in flair and invention, incorporating pyramidal shapes, cylinders within squared towers, and bulges and opposing indentations that look to have been the result of manipulations by a giant thumb. It is a $211 million fairytale castle, decked in glass of emerald and slate and sea green.

Architecture this playful is doomed to fall into premature dowdiness, so enjoy it while it still outclasses the competition. Housed within are agencies of the Metro Toronto regional government.

METRO TORONTO REFERENCE LIBRARY
789 Yonge St. (nr Bloor). Off map 4A8 ☎393-7196 ▣ Open Mon–Thurs 9am–9pm, Fri 9am–6pm, Sat 9am–5pm, Sun 1.30–5pm; closed Sun May–Oct. Subway: Bloor.
Waterfalls, fountains, pools, and walkways whirl around a 5-story atrium, for this is not just another library. See also WALK 3 on page 59.

METRO TORONTO ZOO
Highway 401 and Meadowvale Rd., Scarborough. Map 6B4 ☎392-5900 ▨ ▣ ✱ ✹ Open daily in summer 9am–7.30pm, in winter 9.30am–4.30pm, with seasonal variations. Subway: Kennedy, then Scarborough #86A bus, or Sheppard, then Sheppard East #85B bus. For public transportation information ☎393-4636.
More than 4,000 creatures are exhibited in simulated natural habitats on a 280-hectare (710-acre) zoological park about one hour from downtown. It's well worth the trip, and most of a day should be planned, to allow a leisurely visit. Obviously the warmer months are preferable, when many of the animals run loose in open areas. But a winter trip is still enjoyable, for almost everything is viewable in the eight large pavilions, each filled with plants, birds, mammals, reptiles, and even fish, characteristic of the regions of the world they represent.

Just inside the gate, mood-setting peacocks stalk imperiously across the path. There are choices as to how to proceed. An air-conditioned **monorail** skims for 25 minutes over the Rouge River valley, where North American animals are quartered.

The **Zoomobile** tram provides a 45-minute overview, in the warmer months. Both rides have commentaries. Or you can walk: blue footprints are painted on the paths, leading past each of the pavilions at the heart of the park. The circuit takes about 3 hours.

At the **Australasia** pavilion, wallabies and kangaroos stare right back from their open pits, and the marine exhibits include lionfish, clown anemone and blue damsel fish from the Great Barrier Reef. **The Americas** are represented by polar bears, whose pools have underwater viewing windows, by flamingos, spider monkeys, jaguars, boa constrictors, armadillos, marmosets, and an aviary of tanagers and toucans.

Lowland gorillas, known to deliver mighty blows against the clear plastic walls of their enclosures, are featured in the **Africa** Pavilion. Look, too, for the Saharan meerkat, a kind of gregarious mongoose that lives in colonies. The patriarch keeps constant watch for predators, from the top of his rock pile, while the family scavenges for food, whining and chattering. Then he changes guard with one of his sons.

Nearby is the largest herd of African elephants in North America. After all that come the **Indo-Malaya** Pavilion, the Lion Trail, the Camel Trail and the Grizzly Bear Trail. Periodically, demonstrations are given of free-flying birds of prey, including bald eagles and great horned owls. Rides are available on two-humped camels.

All along the way, volunteers give directions and enthusiastically discuss the habits and characteristics of the creatures to which they are assigned. Visitors will exhaust themselves before the exhibits run out.

MONTGOMERY'S TAVERN

4709 Dundas St. (Islington); see the map of METROPOLITAN TORONTO *on page 48*
☎*394-8113* ▣ *Open Mon–Fri 9.30am–4.30pm; Sat, Sun 1–5pm. Subway: Islington, then Islington #37 bus.*
The 1837 Rebellion was dispersed by government troops at Montgomery's Tavern, an attractive inn built in the prevalent Georgian style of the period. It has been restored to accept visitors, many of whom arrive expressly for the daily afternoon tea.

MUSEUM OF THE HISTORY OF MEDICINE

288 Bloor St. W (St George). Map 3A7 ☎*922-0564* ▣ *Usually open Mon–Fri 9.30am–4pm, but hours may vary. Subway: St George.*
Four rooms in the Academy of Medicine building are given to displays of the medical arts dating back to the time of leeches and magic potions and beyond.

MUSEUM FOR TEXTILES

55 Centre Ave. (Dundas). Map 3C7 ☎*599-5321* ▣ *Open Mon–Fri 11am–5pm, Sat and Sun noon–5pm. Subway: St Patrick.*
Hidden away on four floors of the CHESTNUT PARK hotel is this worthwhile small repository for textiles from around the world. Both antique and contemporary fabrics are displayed, and there is also an excellent gift shop.

ONTARIO PLACE

955 Lakeshore Blvd. W. Map 1F3 ☎*965-7917* ▬ ▣ ✱ *Open May 30–Sept 7 daily 10am–1am. For transit information* ☎*393-4636.*
These remarkable connected islands, just offshore from Exhibition

Place, defy classification. Part amusement park, part museum, Ontario Place has a movie studio, a stadium that holds everything from concerts to stock car races, elaborate playgrounds, a warship, the **Canadian Baseball Hall of Fame** . . . and that's only half the story.

From Lakeshore Blvd., one of the most arresting structures is a huge geodesic dome, the **Cinesphere**. It presents films in the IMAX format, with images 18m (60 feet) high, and special effects that make participants out of passive viewers. Five elevated "pods" hold a variety of entertainments, including a 3-D cinema and a children's theater. The canopied **Children's Village** has water slides, wading pools, trampolines, swaying bridges, and a treehouse snack bar.

Two yacht marinas are part of the complex, as is the World War II destroyer HMCS *Haida*. Pedal- and bumper-boats are available for rent, and there is an island-to-shore shuttle craft. Up-to-date attractions recently have included parasailing and bungee-jumping, made as safe as innate Canadian caution and ingenuity can contrive.

The several restaurants range from mid-priced waterside cafés to semi-ambitious bistros, and there is an ample number of fast-food stands. Concerts in the **Forum** amphitheater (☎ *870-8000)* have included symphony orchestras, ballet, and pop/rock entertainers of international stature. Live music is usually heard on weekends.

They also lay on such special events as an electrifying fireworks competition, comedy festivals, and stunts by daredevils and highdivers. (See EVENTS FOR THE VISITOR'S CALENDAR on page 38.) And here, beside the lake, the dominant winged moochers are several varieties of sea gulls, both noisier and more handsome than pigeons.

ONTARIO SCIENCE CENTRE

*770 Don Mills Rd. (Eglinton). Map **5**B3 and the map of* METROPOLITAN TORONTO *on page 49* ☎*696-3127* ▨ ▣ =▨ ✱ *Open daily 10am–6pm, Fri 10am–9pm. Subway: Pape, then Don Mills #25 bus or Eglinton, then the Eglinton East bus.*
All stops are pulled to render the world of science both palatable and comprehensible in this quadri-level playground. "Interactive" is a key word, with hundreds of exhibits that invite viewer participation.

The images on a wall of more than 100 TV screens are controlled by the people in the camera's eye. Rainbow trout swim in aerated silos to demonstrate aquaculture. A laser ray burns a hole through a brick. Touch the Van de Graaff generator for a literally hair-raising experience. Step up to any of dozens of computer terminals to ask questions about communications, physics, engines. Operate the kinds of robot arms used in nuclear research. There is a changing program of special exhibitions, focusing on a wealth of everyday subjects.

Movies for senior citizens are shown in the auditorium, and live demonstrations are always on tap. There's even a beer garden.

The four floors of the building step down the slope of a river valley, each unit connected by escalators and elevators. It can be a little confusing to negotiate, so a map is provided at the reception desk. **Level 4** (the top, entry floor) has snack bars, a restaurant, souvenir shops. **Level 3** has a cafeteria, presentation theaters and the temporary exhibition hall.

Level 2 has permanent exhibits on space exploration, molecular structures, earth sciences and food production. **Level 1** (at the bottom) examines technologies, communications, and transportation from steam engines to ships or automobiles. A good strategy is to descend to the lowest level and work up. Even an entire day is not enough to see it all.

QUEEN'S PARK
Map 3B7. Subway: Queen's Park or Museum.
A tranquil greensward below Bloor St. and E of the main campus of the University of Toronto. See WALK 3 on page 57.

ROYAL ONTARIO MUSEUM
100 Queen's Park (Bloor). Map 3A7 ☎*586-5551 (recorded information)* 📷
(also gives admission to McLAUGHLIN PLANETARIUM and GARDINER MUSEUM OF CERAMIC ART) 📷 *(after 4.30pm Thurs)* ✗ *available* ▣ ✵ *Open daily 10am–6pm, Tues, Thurs 10am–8pm; closed Mon from Labour Day (early Sept)–Victoria Day (late May). Subway: Museum.*

As with most major museums in North America, ROM is in a nearly constant state of flux, the latest manifestation of which was a long-term construction program completed in 1990. Even that has not ended ongoing realignment nor delays due to budgetary constraints. The frequent shifts and changes make a room-by-room description difficult, and what follows is intended only as an overview of the nature and content of the several collections.

Art and science combine at ROM, causing sometimes jarring contrasts. Broadly speaking, however, the ground floor concerns itself with art treasures of Imperial China, the 2nd floor with life sciences, and the 3rd with the arts and history of the ancient Mediterranean and Middle East.

This is the largest museum in Canada, so even a cursory visit, passing up some of its parts, will require at least two hours. Since the entrance fee also covers admission to the GEORGE R. GARDINER MUSEUM OF CERAMIC ART, across the street, and the McLAUGHLIN PLANETARIUM is in an adjoining structure, the better part of a day might easily be budgeted for this one block of Avenue Road.

There is a noticeable emphasis on archeology. Up the stairs beyond the gold-domed vestibule is an exhibit plotting the course of the archeological process, from hypothesis and research to fieldwork and analysis. Results of such efforts are seen in the galleries to the right (opposite the ramp leading to the McLaughlin Planetarium). On display are especially fine ceramic sculptures of horsemen, tomb figures, and Tang dynasty mirrors and vases.

Beyond those rooms are architectural elements of the tomb of a 17thC Ming Dynasty general, with its stone camels and guards. In a case in one wall is an arresting gathering of figures representing an official procession of the period, complete with horses and marching bands. Other galleries on this floor are given to temporary exhibitions — "The Art of Chinese Theatre" and a collection of cast-iron penny banks were typical — and to permanent ranks of less-than-electrifying chunks of minerals.

One floor up are rooms likely to be of greatest appeal to younger visitors, with the reassembled fossils of a mastodon and a stegosaurus, mounted rare birds and reptiles, a simulation of a Jamaican bat cave with sound- and light-effects. There are realistically arranged wildlife dioramas, which incorporate the native musk ox, Arctic fox and hare, cougar, and white-tailed deer, as well as African and Asian species.

Certain curatorial decisions might be questioned, as with the valuable space given to a common barnyard chicken, but children run and squeal with delight through these sections. Zoology and fossils are supplemented by galleries given to a potpourri of objects from the permanent collections — Mackintosh furniture, Korean lacquerware, a Japanese palanquin, an Indian chieftain's feathered bonnet.

Highlight of the 3rd floor is the *Caravans and Clippers* exhibit, concentrating on the early civilizations of Egypt, Mesopotamia, the Levant, Greece, and Rome. Many of these artifacts are unexpected, such as the crude but fascinating Egyptian models of farmers and workers that are more than 4,000 years old. Along the way are lovely vessels carved of basalt and alabaster, pottery, sarcophagi, weaponry, a mummy. Worth attention are the videos, in English and French, illuminating the evolution and meanings of hieroglyphs. Hellenic and Etruscan amphoras and jars, in their distinctive black and orange, are seen in considerable number, as are small terracotta figures of the 5th–4thC BC.

Items that don't necessarily fit these broad categories are rotated into view throughout the building, and have included ethnological exhibits illustrating the ways of Canadian Amerindians, rocks and gems, medieval armor, musical instruments. Lack of space keeps many of these from permanent display, a problem expected to be solved over the next few years. Four shops sell jewelry, books, toys, pottery and sculpture reproductions. Audiophones providing descriptions of all the major exhibits are available free at the information desk in the entry hall.

ST ANDREW'S PRESBYTERIAN CHURCH
King St. (Simcoe). Map 3D7 ☎ *593-5600* 🆑 *Subway: St Andrew.*
There it sits, a stolid amalgam of Norman Romanesque and Neo-Gothic ecclesiastical architecture, in stark contrast to the rampant modernity around it. With a bank of contemporary mid-rises as backdrop, and across the street from the glass hatbox that is **Roy Thompson Hall**, the 1875 church gains notice primarily for its squat, largely graceless presence. Its fiscal health was underwritten by selling its air and subterranean rights to developers.

SKYDOME
Front St. (John). Map 3E6 ☎ *341-2770 (tours), 341-3663 (events), 341-2424 (restaurant reservations)* 🆑 ✗ *available. Ticket prices and opening hours vary according to events scheduled* ❤ ➞ 🅿 *Subway: Union Station.*
Domed athletic stadiums are no longer a novelty in North America, but this one advanced the science one step further, with its rigid retractable roof of remarkable design and ingenuity. (The roof of Montréal's OLYMPIC STADIUM is of cloth and takes twice as long to winch into place, even when it is functioning properly.)

Skydome is not to be confused with just any enclosed arena. It is 86m (282 feet) from floor to ceiling, enough to cover a 30-story building. The roof weighs 11 tons, and the field alone could accommodate eight 747 jets. Seating sections move on tracks, to reconfigure for different sports and events. This is the permanent home of the football Argonauts and baseball Blue Jays, and has been used for Aussie Rules football, basketball, cricket, opera, and rock concerts by the mega-brigade (Madonna, Elton John, the Rolling Stones, and so on).

Such projects often provoke superlatives and statistics. SkyDome claims the world's largest scoreboard, and a television replay screen measuring 10.5m x 35m (35ft x 115ft). There are nine restaurants and lounges, 32 fast-food stands, a health club, and a 346-room hotel with 70 (very expensive) rooms and suites overlooking the field. Some 53,000 spectators can be seated for baseball, 50,000 for football and 60,000 for concerts and other events.

When the roof is fully retracted in good weather — a hypnotic process that takes 20 minutes and involves three massive sections sliding into a nest at one end — 91 percent of the audience is exposed to sunlight. Eight miles of zippers hold the Astroturf carpeting together on the stadium floor. The 161 "SkyBoxes," leased by individuals and corporations, cost up to $225,000 a year, and the lessees have spent $100,000 to $400,000 to decorate their spaces. The cost of the entire project had reached $532 million by the time of its completion in 1989.

✘ *Tours are conducted between 9am–6pm daily, when not in conflict with scheduled events. They begin with a slick 20-minute film depicting the planning and construction of the stadium.*

SPADINA HOUSE
285 Spadina Rd. See the map of METROPOLITAN TORONTO on page 48 ☎392-6827 📷 ✘ *obligatory. Open Apr–May Mon–Fri 9.30am–4pm, Sat, Sun and holidays noon–5pm; June–Aug daily 9.30am–5pm. Subway: Dupont or St Clair West, then the Forest Hill #33A bus.*

Overshadowed by its flamboyant neighbor, CASA LOMA, this historic home still has much to commend it, not least a measure of comparative calm. The house was built for financier James Austin in 1866. The furnishings in the $2.5 million collection are original to the mansion, most of them late Victorian, Edwardian and Art Nouveau. They are arranged in rooms restored to their respective periods, remembering that four generations of the family lived in them. Telling glimpses are thus provided into the lives of the wealthy and their large domestic staffs in the days before income taxes.

Laudable preservationist concern for authenticity has led the managers to considerable lengths — the linoleum in the kitchen is a silk-screened custom copy of the covering first laid there. Back then, the estate had more than 200 acres. Now, only six acres of parkland remain, but the garden, restored to the period, has more than 300 varieties of plants and flowers. Hummingbirds whir and dart among the blooms. An informative 15-minute video precedes the 30-minute guided tour.

Unlike the major avenue by the same name — "Spa-DYE-na" — this one is pronounced "Spa-DEE-na." No explanation for the difference seems to be available.

TORONTO ISLANDS

Map 5C3 and 3F6. Harbourfront streetcar from Union Station, then the ferry (☎ 392-8193 ▨) from dock behind the Westin Harbour Castle Hotel (map 4E8).
Opportunities for outdoor recreation in and near the city are almost inexhaustible. Occupying center-stage are the six small islands that nearly enclose the harbor off the downtown waterfront. Public lands are given over to swimming, fishing, sunbathing, picnicking, cycling and boating in summer, cross-country skiing and snowshoeing in winter. About 600 permanent residents live in colonies at the eastern end of the islands.

Centreville *(☎ 363-1112 ▨ ✳ open daily May 20–Sept 4; May, Sept weekends only)* is a genteel amusement park for children. With not a bit of the usual screech-and-flash associated with the genre, it is an intentionally dated place that might have existed at the turn of the century, with a carousel and miniaturized old-time trains and automobiles for kids to ride. A petting zoo is there, and cable cars, bumper boats, a miniature golf course, and swan boats on the lagoon. Fine views of the city, too, with sailboats tacking back and forth in front of that impressive skyline.

Ferries to the islands depart on seasonally staggered schedules to three docks — Hanlan's Point, Centre Island, and Ward's Island. They carry no cars, only passengers and their bicycles, the favored form of transportation over there. Trips take about 10 minutes, with the last at about 10.30 or 11pm. A free tram operates between Hanlan's and Centre, with intermediate stops.

TORONTO STOCK EXCHANGE

2 First Canadian Pl. (King). Map 3D7 ☎ 947-4676 ▨ Open Mon–Fri 9am–4.30pm. Subway: St Andrew.
The nation's busiest exchange admits visitors to a gallery that provides views of the action on the trading floor, although much of it will be understood only by initiates.

UNDERGROUND TORONTO

Maps 3 & 4. Subway: Union Station, Dundas, or Queen.
Toronto's version of a weatherproof city was a byproduct of the downtown construction boom that started in the 1960s, when planners were trying to find ways for people to travel around the area in comfort and safety. Local boosters claim theirs is larger than the one in Montréal, but that is a matter of opinion. It hardly matters, for few people have enough time to browse or dine in all its 1,000 stores and restaurants.

The underground complex began to come to fruition with the 1977 opening of the Eaton Centre, E of the new City Hall. Within a decade, it extended from the Atrium on Bay in the N, under Eaton Centre, Simpson's, the Sheraton Centre Hotel, First Canadian Place, and on to the Royal York Hotel and Union Station on Front St.

There are 3 miles of connecting passageways, with entrances to the hotels and office buildings and access to seven subway stops. In theory, a visitor could arrive by train from other parts of Canada or the US, check into a hotel, make business calls, cash travelers checks, eat every meal of the day, buy gifts for the family, see a movie, drop into a nightclub, check out four days later and get back on the train — all without once setting foot into the cold and slush of a Toronto winter, a humid summer, or an any-season downpour.

There are even trees down there, and the temperature hovers at a year-round 70°. The twists and turns can confuse, however, and making note of landmarks along the way is necessary, to avoid getting lost.

UNIVERSITY OF TORONTO
Map 3B7.

Ontario's most prestigious university and Canada's largest, with more than 55,000 students, occupies prime downtown real estate. The campus lies mostly to the W of Queen's Park, but with some satellite buildings to the N and E. Founded in 1827, it was for decades a collection of essentially autonomous residential colleges, each of them beholden to particular Protestant sects or to the Catholic church.

Those associations no longer pertain, in what is officially a non-denominational institution. Theological training is still one of the courses of study, but among many. In 1921, a team of researchers led by Frederick Banting and Charles Best here discovered insulin and its value in treating diabetes.

✗ Free one-hour tours of the campus are available from **Hart House** *on King's College Circle, June to August, Monday to Friday, three times daily (☎ 978-5000).*

YORKVILLE
Off map 3A7, and see the map of METROPOLITAN TORONTO *on page 49.*
A trendy, upmarket neighborhood N of Bloor St. with scores of shops, restaurants and nightspots. See WALK 3 on page 57.

An excursion to the Niagara Peninsula

In the stillness of the North American wilderness, the earliest European explorers heard the great cataract days before they laid eyes upon it. When they arrived at the precipice, engulfed in clouds of mist thrown up by the eternal crash of tons of water, they must have counted this among the greatest wonders of the Old and New Worlds. They were correct.

On this continent, only the Grand Canyon and the Rocky Mountains compare in grandeur to Niagara Falls, and the best and worst efforts of humans to exploit and defy and humble them have failed to diminish their majesty.

FROM TORONTO TO NIAGARA
See maps 5 & 6.

This suggested excursion from Toronto can be accomplished in one long day, arising before the morning rush hour and returning after nightfall. But the Falls and nearby attractions deserve at least an overnight stay, and a long weekend cannot exhaust the possibilities. Country inns, historic villages, summer theater festivals, wineries and parks, preserved forts and tended battlefields lie along this route. Since the Falls are within easy driving distance of several cities, try not to take this trip on a weekend, when crowds and traffic are at their worst.

There isn't a great deal to be seen in the immediate suburban environs of Toronto, nor in the next 64km (40 miles) or so on the way toward Niagara, so take the Gardiner Expressway W, soon picking up Queen Elizabeth Way (the "QEW" in local shorthand) toward Hamilton and Niagara. It is a conventional superhighway, with little to distract from maintaining the posted speed.

Plans for a leisurely trip might allow time for a detour off the QEW to the **Royal Botanical Gardens** *(680 Plains Rd. W, Burlington, map 5 E2* ☎ *416-527-1158 or 1-800-668-9449* ■ *)*. Take Highway 403 off the QEW in Burlington, following the signs. There are five major garden areas and 48km (30 miles) of nature trails. Most notable are the two-acre display of roses, the Medicinal Garden, and the Laking Garden, with its impressive plantings of iris and peonies. Outdoor gardens, including two teahouses, are open mid-April to late October; the greenhouses October to mid-April. Return to the QEW, now running E, toward Niagara.

Soon, exit onto Highway 55, toward Niagara-on-the-Lake. This flat plain of rich farmland is especially hospitable to the cultivation of fruit, notably peaches, strawberries, cherries, and grapes, as is soon evident in the proliferation of orchards, vineyards, and roadside produce stands. Before long, on the right, is the **Hillebrand Estates Winery** *(* ☎ *416-468-7123)*. Their wines and related gift items are for sale in the winery store; free tastings and tours of the facilities are given 4–5 times daily during the summer.

Continue on Highway 55, which is known as Mississauga St. as it enters Niagara-on-the-Lake. It ends at Queen St.; turn right. This is the main street of one of Ontario's oldest and prettiest villages. There are few harsh modern intrusions, with 19thC houses and their gardens standing well back from the road and an attractive four-block business section of gift and antique shops, restaurants, inns, and churches.

In 1792, it was made the first capital of Upper Canada, a status later given to Toronto (then York) because it was further away from the then-hostile US. Among the prominent buildings are the 1848 courthouse, on the right after Regent St., and the restored 1820 apothecary, on the left at the corner with King St.

❧ ⇛ Easily the most popular and visible hotel in town is the **Prince of Wales** *(6 Picton St., Ontario L0S 1J0* ☎ *416-468-3246 or 1-800-263-2454* ▦ *)*, diagonally across King St. from the apothecary.

Expansions subsequent to the 1864 opening have sustained the mid-Victorian architectural detailing, while providing the up-to-date niceties of a contemporary hotel. These include a reasonably good restaurant, a heated indoor pool, saunas, and a lively lounge with jazz on weekends. Rooms in the older, main building are comfortable but compact; for more space, ask for a room in the newer Prince of Wales Court.

Of the dozen competitors, the clear runner-up is the recently enhanced **Queen's Landing** *(Box 1180, Byron St., Ontario L0S 1J0* ☎ *416-468-2195* ▥), three blocks away. Rooms are spacious, and many have fireplaces. The dining room and terrace overlook the Niagara River. Fitness facilities include a well-equipped gym, an indoor pool, and a separate "Swimex," a small pool with a hidden paddlewheel that creates a strong artificial current for workouts.

If both of these are full, the **Chamber of Commerce** *(King and Prideaux Sts.* ☎ *416-468-4263)* offers a free accommodation service for over 50 local B&Bs and guesthouses.

Wandering along the town's streets is quietly rewarding, and the Chamber of Commerce office provides maps and descriptive materials. There are concerts, garden tours, agricultural fairs, and arts-and-crafts-show weekends throughout the year. The big event, though, is the **Shaw Festival** *(*☎ *416-468-2172 or 800-724-2934 from the US)*, held from late April through October. Accomplished theater companies stage plays by George Bernard Shaw and such contemporaries as Bertolt Brecht and Noel Coward, in three theaters — the modern **Festival** and the older **Court House** and **Royal George**. To broaden the appeal, the program often includes musicals having only remote connections with Shaw.

When ready to leave, proceed E on Picton St. Almost immediately, on the left, is the entrance to **Fort George** *(map 6D5* ☎ *416-468-4257* ▧ *open mid-May (Victoria Day)–end June, daily 9am–5pm, July–Labour Day, daily 10am–6pm, Labour Day–end Oct daily 10am–5pm, remainder of year by appointment)*. Although it is called a "reconstruction," the fort is, more accurately, a re-creation. Constructed by the British in 1800, it was destroyed by American invaders in May 1813. Only the original earthworks and a powder magazine remained, so in the 1930s, replicas of blockhouses and barracks were erected around the old parade ground. From the ramparts, the restored 1817 **Simcoe Navy Hall** can be seen down by the river, as well as the heights on the opposite shore where the American batteries were emplaced. Staff members in period costumes perform drills and tattoos, and guide visitors.

Leaving the fort, continue S on Picton, which soon joins the scenic Niagara Parkway. Signs using grape clusters as symbols indicate that this is part of the Niagara wine route. Soon, on the right, is the **Reif Winery** *(*☎ *416-468-7738)*, which has Saturday tours June to September, and, a little farther on and also on the right, down a road called Line 3, **Inniskillin Wines** *(*☎ *416-468-3554* ✗ *daily June–Oct, Sat Nov–May)*.

The Parkway follows the Niagara River, which can be glimpsed through the nut and fruit trees on the left. It is a lovely road, with small, orderly farms and peach stands and meticulously tended lawns and houses. After a while, the Parkway makes some turns and crosses other roads, but stay with the directional signs that read simply "The Falls."

Up ahead on a ridge is a monument that recalls, at least in silhouette against the morning sun, the one dedicated to Nelson in Trafalgar Square in London. After the Parkway winds up the slope, the monument in

Queenston Heights Park is seen to honor General Isaac Brock, who died trying to capture the hill from American forces in the War of 1812. The General's record includes the conquest of Detroit early in that conflict, and he was in command at Fort George on the occasion of its destruction. Americans of sensitive chauvinistic persuasion may wish to avoid too careful examination of the tablets at these commemorations, by the way. They represent the views of Canadian patriots, after all, and Americans were the enemy at that time.

There is a magnificent view of the river from the base of the monument, and there are picnic grounds and a restaurant in the park. Be careful to take the correct road when leaving the park, following the same signs.

Shortly after the Queenston–Lewiston Bridge to the US side of the river, a turn-off leads to a **floral clock**. It gets more attention than it deserves. Following it is the imposing **Beck Generating Station**, one of two plants resulting from a 1950 US–Canadian treaty to divert parts of the river for conversion to electrical power without destroying the Falls themselves. Other government agencies and a host of private entrepreneurs have done their best to accomplish that desecration on their own, as will be seen.

First, though, on the right is the **Niagara Parks Botanical Gardens** *(open daily in summer, dawn to dusk ✉)*. The 100 acres of gardens, trees, and shrubs are maintained by students who undertake a three-year curriculum at the school of horticulture situated there.

The next attraction is the **Niagara Spanish Aero Car** *(☎ 416-354-5711 ✉ open daily May–Sept, less often Apr–May and Sept–Oct, subject to weather conditions)*. The aerial cable car travels 45m (150ft) above a great whirlpool that twists eternally at this bend in the river 8km (5 miles) below the Falls. Even staunch non-acrophobes might experience a flutter or two on the ten-minute, 1,100m (3,600-ft) round trip from clifftop to clifftop and back. The managers claim a perfect safety record since the ride opened in 1918, for whatever reassurance that might provide. An "Explorer's Pass" can be purchased here, providing discount admission to several attractions around the Falls. It is also a regular stop for "people-movers" that ply this route.

Things start to get a little more unkempt now, with a strip of undistinguished motels, tourist homes, and restaurants. On the right, just before the Rainbow Bridge, is the **Niagara Falls Museum** *(5651 River Rd. ☎ 416-356-2151 ✉)*. Claiming to be the oldest museum in North America, established in 1827, it is a repository of odds and ends undeterred by the constraints of curatorial scholarship. A quick trip round this exhibit will probably suffice.

Egyptian and Indian mummies are on display, as are stuffed birds, fish, two-headed calves, and a collection of the conveyances employed by daredevils who have chosen to plunge over the Falls.

A favorite is one Bobby Leach, a Cockney who went over in a steel barrel in 1911, surviving, but breaking his jaw and both kneecaps. Fifteen years later, on a tour celebrating his exploit, he slipped on an orange peel, broke his leg, got gangrene, died.

Shortly, on the right, is Clifton Hill, a district that embraces more modern, profit-making museums. These and related attractions include a **Guinness World of Records**, **The Haunted House**, an **Elvis Presley Museum**, a **Ripley's Believe It or Not Museum**, and the **Movieland Wax Museum**, along with motels with heart-shaped bathtubs for two, a go-cart track, and fast-food restaurants.

All this is sideshow to the Falls themselves. There are large parking lots on the right. Be prepared to continue some way past the Falls, find a space and then walk back. They are worth it, despite the distractions. Every conceivable means to view and exploit this wonder has been utilized. Helicopters whup-whup overhead. Boats chug back and forth in the roiling waters below. Tunnels burrow behind them, observation decks look down, up, around. Towers and high-rise hotels seem to lean over for a look. Millions of people swarm around them every year.

Yet they remain undiminished. Father Louis Hennepin, the first wide-eyed European to see them, in 1678, grossly overestimated their height at over 200m (660 feet). They are a third of that, but his guess is understandable, so awesome is their power.

There are actually two falls. At this point, the river is divided by Goat Island. On its N side are the **American Falls**, 305m (1,000 feet) wide and plunging over a straight-edged precipice to mammoth boulders 49m (160 feet) below. To the S of the island are the more dramatic **Canadian Horseshoe Falls**, only slightly higher, but over 793m (2,600 feet) across. The combined volume of water flow varies, due to diversion for US and Canadian generating plants, but can reach 37.4 million Imperial gallons *per minute*. At night, the falls are illuminated; in winter, they partially freeze. Both sights are memorable.

Apart from the terrace immediately above the Canadian Falls, the best observation point (◀€) might be the **Skylon** *(5200 Robinson St. ☎ 416-356-2651)*. The 236m (775-foot) tower has lifts scooting up and down the exterior of the structural column to the bulbous knob at the top that contains a deck and two levels of restaurants. As well as the unobstructed view of the Falls, clear weather can reveal the Toronto skyline, about 120km (75 miles) away. Skylon might best be saved for viewing the nighttime illumination.

Probably the best-known visitor "experience" is the **Maid of the Mist** *(5920 River Rd. ☎ 416-358-5781 ▣)*. The double-decked boat steams slowly past the boiling edge of the cataract — unforgettable (and drenching) for its passengers. Hooded raincoats are provided to every passenger, but you should wear clothes that can get wet, anyway.

Continue S on Niagara Parkway, past several parks and viewing areas. On reaching Portage Rd., turn right, following signs toward **Marineland** *(7657 Portage Rd. ☎ 416-356-9565 ▣ open daily)*. The theme park is similar to others by the same name in California and Florida, with bears, bison, elk, a few hundred tame deer, and performing killer whales. Children might regard it as their just reward after looking at scenery and history all day.

Otherwise, continue to McLeod Rd. and turn left (W). After a few miles of strip shopping malls, it joins with the QEW for the drive back to Toronto, which is about 120km (76 miles).

Toronto:
where to stay

Making your choice

The desirability of Toronto as a vacation or business destination is greatly enhanced by the diversity of its lodgings. With more than 30,000 rooms in the metropolitan area, there is truly something for everyone, from grand hotels to clean, no-frills rooms at bedrock prices. For those who have always wanted to splurge on a dream hotel, this is the place to do it.

LOCATIONS

Hotels in all price ranges are concentrated in two central areas of the city. Residents tend to refer to all of the most important parts of the city as "**downtown**." That covers a lot of ground, however. For visitors, it is easier to think of downtown as the Financial District, from the waterfront to City Hall, and **midtown** as the area around Bloor St., Yorkville.

There are a great many motels and hotels scattered over greater Metro Toronto, especially out near Pearson Airport, but they offer no particular price advantage and are often distant from places most people want to visit.

PRICING AND DISCOUNTS

While rates are high at such estimable hostelries as the KING EDWARD and the FOUR SEASONS, they are no worse than at many less desirable hotels in the US and Europe, and prevailing dollar exchange rates make the actual cost 10–15 percent lower than it seems.

Try to arrange part of a trip over a weekend. Every hotel offers substantial discounts for Friday, Saturday and sometimes Sunday nights, at least during the slower months. That means reductions of up to 40 percent for half the nights of an average stay. From January–March, many major hotels are known to slash even weekday prices by as much as 50 percent. When quoted a price for a room, ask for something less expensive. Often, a comparable room will be offered at lower cost.

Children can often share their parents' room for nothing extra. Even a tenuous connection with a recognizable corporation may bring a discount for a weeknight, and senior citizens can routinely get 10 or 15 percent off simply by asking. Snip a few more dollars off the cost by applying for a refund of the 7 percent national Goods and Services Tax and the additional Ontario accommodation tax of 5 percent. Fuller details are given on page 29.

See also BED AND BREAKFAST on page 92.

HOW TO USE THIS CHAPTER

- **Symbols**: Full details of all our suggested hotels are given, and symbols show those that are particularly luxurious (🏨) in style. Other symbols show price categories, and give a résumé of available facilities. See the KEY TO SYMBOLS on page 7 for an explanation of the full list of our symbols.
- **Prices**: The prices corresponding to our price symbols are based on average charges for two people staying in a double room with bathroom/shower. For this purpose, breakfast and tax are not included. Although actual prices will inevitably increase, our relative price categories are likely to remain the same. Prices are given in **Canadian dollars**.

Symbol	Category	**Current price**
▥	very expensive	more than $180
▥	expensive	$140-180
▥	moderate	$100-140
▣	inexpensive	$80-100
▢	cheap	under $80

FACILITIES

The larger downtown and midtown hotels have garage parking. Non-smoking floors are increasingly available, sometimes as many as half of the total. Swimming pools are common, as are simple or elaborate fitness facilities. Cable-connected color TV with pay-per-view movies, elevators, and air conditioning are standard even in economy accommodations, as are private bathrooms (baths *en suite* in local parlance). Conference facilities can be expected at all but the smallest entries, as can access and special rooms for disabled travelers.

At deluxe and first-class hotels, the competition for customers that made common such items as bathrobes and hairdryers, now has managers groping for less ubiquitous extras. This search results in terry slippers, free morning newspapers, two-line telephones, and, in an appeal to ecology-conscious guests, separate recycling bins for discarded paper and cans. Room rates sometimes include complimentary breakfasts. A service charge may be added to checks for snacks and meals brought to the room: don't tip twice.

FINDING A ROOM

Lodging can usually be found on short notice from October–April. The crowded period is May–September, when warm weather attracts large numbers of tourists, as well as visitors to the many trade fairs and conventions. Then it is best to make reservations 2–3 weeks ahead.

When finding a room proves difficult, one source to turn to is **Accommodation Toronto** (☎ 629-3800). They represent more than 100 hotels in all price categories, and will endeavor to match callers with appropriate establishments, at no charge.

Despite the name, **Econo-Lodging Services** (☎ 494-0541) is a competing reservation service for budget to deluxe hotels throughout

Metro Toronto. They also have listings of short-term rental apartments. An active bed-and-breakfast movement vies for attention, offering homey settings and lowish prices. See BED AND BREAKFAST on page 92.

Colleges and universities in the area have dormitory rooms available during summer. Possibilities are **Neill–Wycik College Hotel** (☎ 977-2320), **Victoria University** (☎ 585-4524) and the **University of Toronto, Scarborough Campus** (☎ 287-7369).

Most of the hotels listed below provide **toll-free (800) telephone numbers**. These are intended only for callers wishing to make room reservations, not for private calls to guests. In some cases, these can be called from anywhere in North America; others are restricted to Ontario and Québec or the eastern US. Touch **1** before the rest of the number.

When calling any of the non–800 numbers from outside Toronto, precede them with the Toronto area code (**416**).

Toronto hotels A to Z

CHESTNUT PARK ✿
108 Chestnut St. (Dundas), Toronto M5G 1R3. Map 3C7 ☎ *977-5000 or 800-528-1234* ☒ *977-9513* ▥ *to* ▥ *518 rms and suites* ⬛ � 🆑 ⊕ ⬛ 🆚 ≋ ♈ ⅄ ▣

Location: Near City Hall and AGO. Toronto has an exceptional number of moderately priced, centrally located downtown hotels with every reasonable amenity. Only hopelessly spoiled sybarites can quarrel with the highly favorable value-for-cost equation presented by this new entry. Executives, in particular, appreciate the three phones per room, all with fax and computer ports, the personal safes, and sparkling exercise equipment and indoor lap pool in the health club. Most of the 19 meeting rooms have windows, and some have terraces. Concierge and room waiters are on duty 24 hours. Every important company headquarters in the Financial District is within a short stroll. It even contains, on four of its floors, the neglected but rewarding MUSEUM OF TEXTILES. If standard rates are low for all this, seasonal and weekend discounts are even more attractive.

DELTA CHELSEA
33 Gerrard St, Toronto M5G 1Z4. W (Yonge), ☎ *595-1975 or 800-268-1133* ☒ *585-4362 Map 4C8* ▥ *1,600 rms* ⬛ � 🆑 ⊕ ⬛ 🆚 ≋ ♈ ⅂ ⅄

Location: Near City Hall and Eaton Centre. Very popular with families and tour groups, this isn't for those who prefer a sedate, unhurried pace. Renovations and a new tower have doubled the number of rooms, causing much coming and going in the lobby and an atmosphere that fairly crackles with energy. Its four restaurants are always full. Children have a supervised play center and a pool to permit parents a little adult quality time. They can enjoy their own separate pool, sauna, and health club, away from the tumult and screeches of the little ones. Room service is available 24 hours. The refurbished Pantages Theatre is a short walk away, and tickets to its current entertainment and other plays in town can be arranged when making room reservations. Moderate prices, good location, and the largely successful effort to be all things to all people keep the occupancy rate high.

FOUR SEASONS ▥
21 Avenue Rd. (Bloor), Toronto M5R 2G1. Off map 3A7 ☎ *964-0411 or 800-268-6382 (Canada) or 800-332-3442 (US)* ☒ *964-2301* ▥ *381 rms and suites* ⬛ 🚆 🚆 🆑 ⊕ ⬛ 🆚 ◁ 🛏 ≋ ♈ ⅂ ⅄ ▣ ♫

85

Location: In Yorkville, near Bloor St. shopping and Royal Ontario Museum. From reception to departure, this is an operation as smooth as hot butter on glass. Every link in the Four Seasons chain operates to the highest standards of the hotelier's art, but this one is quite possibly the best of the lot. The fact that younger competitors are closing the gap doesn't tarnish a centimeter of the champ's luster.

Housed in a contemporary highrise at the gateway to Yorkville, it softens the glass and steel exterior with the warmth of Asian floral motifs and reproductions of period furnishings. Mid-to-upper floors tender dazzling views of the city. The chambermaid checks each room twice a day, and food and beverages are available around the clock. Its Business Centre makes available computers and fax machines, cellular phones and Dictaphones, pagers and copiers. They'll even wrap your gifts. Celebrated chef Susan Weaver leads an award-winning kitchen crew that produces memorable meals in the updated **Studio Cafe** and the more formal, oft-honored **Truffles.** And to tone up or come down, there is an indoor–outdoor pool and a fully equipped health club. None of this comes cheap, of course, but if cost is not primary, there isn't a better choice in town.

FOUR SEASONS INN ON THE PARK

1100 Eglinton Ave. E (Leslie), Toronto M3C 1H8. Map 5B3 ☎444-2561 *or 800-268-6282* ⊠446-3308 ▥ *568 rms* ⊷ ⊒ ⒶⒺ ⊕ ⓒ ▨ ⌂ ♨ ⇙ ㏷ ♒ ⚲ ⛾ ⊟ ⟲ ♪
Location: To the ᴇ, one mile from the Ontario Science Centre. It doesn't have the location and cachet of its celebrated downtown sibling, but then, they're riding different ponies. Here is a full-fledged resort in the outlying Don Mills district. The inner court has one pool for lap swimmers, a second deep enough for diving. Inside, next to the fitness center, is still another pool, this one heated. Guests have access to the adjacent **Park View Club**, which has covered tennis courts, squash, racquetball, aerobics classes and a Nautilus

weight circuit. There is a supervised program for children aged 5–12 — games and swimming, all day, and their parents only have to pay for Junior's lunch. More? How about horseback riding or jogging or cross-country skiing on the trails of the adjoining 500 acres? The bedrooms, it must be said, are ordinary, presumably on the assumption that not much time will be spent in them. Still, they offer room service throughout the day and all night.

HILTON INTERNATIONAL

145 Richmond St. W (University), Toronto M5H 2L2. Map 3D7 ☎869-3456 *or 800-268-9275 (Canada) or 800-445-8667 (US)* ⊠869-1478 ▥ *601 rms* ⊷ ⊠ ⊒ ⒶⒺ ⊕ ⓒ ▨ ⌂ ♨ ⚲ ♒ ⛾ ㏷ ⊟ *in some rooms*
Location: In the heart of the Financial District. Clearly oriented to the business traveler, especially in its location. Service standards and fixtures are at the high end of the middle range, short of luxury but more than merely comfortable. For dining, it has the retrograde **Trader Vic's**, as *faux* Polynesian as ever. The blue-suit brigade prevails in the **Barrister's Bar**, while a more relaxed crowd attends to piano music in the **Garden Court Lounge**. They can unwind further in the indoor–outdoor pool. Rooms look pretty much as expected from a Hilton, but are no less satisfying for that. Room service is always available. The Executive Level adds a private lounge and complimentary continental breakfast.

HOLIDAY INN ON KING

370 King St. W (Peter), Toronto M5V 1J9. Map 3D6 ☎599-4000 *or 800-465-4329* ⊠599-7394 ▥ *425 rms* ⊷ ⊠ ⊒ ⒶⒺ ⊕ ⓒ ▨ ⌂ ♨ ⚲ ♒ ⛾
Location: Two blocks w of Royal Alex and Roy Thompson Hall. This is only one — at last count — of eight Holiday Inns in Metro Toronto. It is neither better nor worse than the others, but it *is* handy to the King St. theater district, and charges lower prices than competitors on the other side of University Ave. Several categories of rooms pro-

vide modest-stepped improvements, from slightly more sitting room to views of the lake to suites with balconies. Many rooms have wet bars. The outdoor pool is heated, but not open in colder months. Travellers in Toronto on business may prefer the **Holiday Inn** near City Hall *(89 Chestnut St. ☎977-0707)*. It is pretty much the same as its siblings.

L'HÔTEL

225 Front St. W (University), Toronto M5V 2X3. Map 3E7 ☎597-1400 or 800-268-9411 (Canada) or 800-828-7447 (US) 597-8128 *587 rms and suites* in many rooms

Location: Next to the Metro Convention Centre and the CN Tower. An ideal businessperson's hotel, within a few blocks of every building in the Financial District. Even standard rooms are exceptionally spacious, often with step-down sitting area, high ceilings and banked windows. (Rooms with numbers ending in 02 or 37 are largest.) Telephones with computer ports are on the workdesk, where they should be, and room service brings breakfast as early as 6.30am. As at most Canadian-Pacific city hotels, there are three classes of service. Business class offers express check-in, free breakfast, and nightly turn-down service. Entrée Gold adds its own concierge. The health club has an indoor pool with doors opening onto the patio in summer, a Universal weight circuit, exercycles, rowing machine. Two squash courts, too.

A romantic dinner can be had in **Chanterelles**, but if you must, there is an easy connection to the **Top of Toronto** in the CN Tower. It revolves while you eat. With all this and generous weekend packages, L'Hotel is a good choice for families, as well. When leaving, take advantage of the express check-out service, for the wait at the front desk can drag on.

IBIS ✿

240 Jarvis (Dundas), Toronto M5B 2B8. Map 4C8 ☎593-9400 or 800-221-4542 593-8426 *294 rms*

Location: A short walk from City Hall. Ibis doesn't disguise what it's about. The exterior could not be less ostentatious, guests carry their own bags, and not an unnecessary dollar has been spent on trappings. With that reduced overhead, they can offer comfortable rooms at good prices with either twin- or queen-sized beds. Each has bath, cable TV and radio alarm clock.

Their unnamed restaurant serves workmanlike buffet breakfasts and lunches and *à la carte* dinners. One child under 12 can share its parents' room without charge. The resultant savings can then be blown in Eaton Centre, only three blocks away.

INTER-CONTINENTAL TORONTO 🏨

220 Bloor St. W (Avenue), Toronto M5S 1T8. Map 3A7 ☎960-5200 or 800-327-0200 960-8269 *213 rms*

Location: Near Royal Ontario Museum. It chooses to think of itself as a "boutique" hotel, and while it's a little too large to fit that description, there is a cozily intimate quality to its impeccably decorated halls and parlors. Restrained Edwardian details are blended with Art Deco flourishes and some impressive and thoroughly modern abstract paintings. Room service is available around the clock, and laundry gathered in the morning is back by late afternoon. The fitness center has carpeted locker rooms, 8-station weight machine, treadmill, stepper, steam room and sauna, and an indoor lap pool. Those annoyed by waits at the desk at checkout time can dispose of the task on their interactive room TV — in four languages.

Afternoon tea beside the inner court carries on to unobtrusive piano music. For those who are actually here to work, the dual-line phones have data ports and the business center offers every conceivable service and machine, including pagers and cellular telephones . . . even typewriters, for those who might just prefer working with antiques.

JOURNEY'S END ✿

280 Bloor St. W (St George), Toronto M5S 1T8. Map 3A6 ☎*968-0010 or 800-668-4200* 🖷*968-0010* ▯ *214 rms* ⬤ ═ AE ⊙ ◎ VISA

Location: Overlooking University of Toronto campus. Most few-frills hotels are situated on the fringe of things, but this hotel, from the growing North American Journey's End chain, is a block or so from the Royal Ontario Museum and the heart of the high-rent Bloor St. shopping district. Local phone calls, morning coffee, and the weekday newspaper are free. Rooms are simple, with cable TV and firm beds.

KING EDWARD ⬤

37 King St. (Yonge), Toronto M5C 1E9. Map 4D8 ☎*863-9700 or 800-225-5843* 🖷*367-5515* ▥ *318 rms* ⬤ ═ ▣ AE ⊙ ◎ ▨ ⌂ ♈ ❦ ⅄ ▣

Location: Financial District, near Union Station. The King Eddy was built at the time that its namesake sat upon the British throne (1901–10) and it bears the stamp of that gilded age in all its structural details, rife with rose marble, gold leaf and burnished woods. The ceiling of the stately, colonnaded lobby is nearly lost in shadow, eight stories up, and one can easily conjure the royal party descending the ceremonial staircase. New owners pumped millions of dollars into its renovation, and the hotel now qualifies as a stop on the tourist circuit, even for those who can't afford the steepest prices in town. They can at least stop by for pre-dinner drinks in the lobby, when there is suitably genteel cocktail music.

The dining room, **Café Victoria**, must be the grandest in the city, its ceilings adorned with elaborate plaster moldings. It is only one of several lounges and eating places. Those whose bank accounts can stand the assault have the use of a health club, all-hours room service, and diligent concierges of the Continental school.

NOVOTEL TORONTO CENTRE ✿

45 The Esplanade (Yonge), Toronto M5E 1W2. Map 4E8 ☎*367-8900 or 800-*

221-4542 🖷*360-8285* ▯ *266 rms* ⬤ ═ AE ⊙ ◎ ▨ ⌂ ♈ ❦ ⅄ ▣

Location: Behind O'Keefe Centre. Not all members of this burgeoning French chain offer such good value, nor are they as tastefully turned out. Behind the coolly classic limestone facade with its street-level loggia are spare, comfortable rooms, and a health club with free weights, a rowing machine, indoor pool and whirlpool. Two floors are reserved for non-smokers. Union Station, the Financial District, Eaton Centre, and the St Lawrence Market are all within walking distance, making it a good choice for both leisure and business travelers.

PARK PLAZA ⬤

4 Avenue Rd. (Bloor), Toronto M5R 2E8. Map 3A7 ☎*924-5471 or 800-268-4927* 🖷*924-4933* ▥ *264 rms and 40 suites* ⬤ ═ ▣ AE ⊙ ◎ ▨ ≪ ⌶ ⅄ ▣

Location: Opposite Royal Ontario Museum. Montreal-born author Mordecai Richler is said to have described the rooftop lounge as the only civilized place in Toronto. After its top-to-bottom multi-million-dollar renovation, he probably would affirm that judgement. It has the tone of a patrician's study, with wood-burning fireplace, sofas, and fine views of the city. There are two towers, the "Prince Arthur" and "The Plaza," the latter holding the luxury laurels. Room televisions have an interactive feature that permits electronic checkout and breakfast ordering. Service, however, is comfortingly traditional, with twice-daily maid service, concierge, free shoeshines.

On offer are generous "bed & breakfast" discount packages, available Thursday–Sunday, not just Friday and Saturday. The new business center helps compensate for the lack of a health club and pool. Be sure to use the Avenue Rd. entrance — the old one on Bloor St. is deserted, connected to the new lobby by a narrow, twisting corridor.

RAMADA RENAISSANCE ON BLOOR

90 Bloor St. E (Yonge), Toronto M4W 1A7. Map 4A8 ☎*961-8000 or 800-268-8998*

(Canada) or 800-272-6232 (US) ☒*961-4635* ▥ *256 rms* ━ ▣ ☰ ☒ ▣ ▣ ▥ ⚲ ☙ ⚐ ☸ ♈ ♉ ☐ ♒

Location: In the midst of Bloor–Yonge shopping area. Ramada, an international chain known originally for its motels, has expanded its Renaissance subdivision, and the transformed former Plaza II hotel opened its doors in 1990. It is located next to Yorkville, with all the advantages of Fifth Avenue-style shopping, yet is also geared toward the businessperson of the 1990s, with a full range of conference facilities, business center, private check-in and morning limousine service.

There is direct access to the Bloor Park Club, a fully equipped recreational facility with heated indoor swimming pool, Nautilus gym, squash courts and even aerobics classes. Shoes will be shined overnight and the morning newspaper will be outside the door. The Renaissance Club floor has a private lounge and free breakfast.

RADISSON PLAZA HOTEL ADMIRAL TORONTO–HARBOURFRONT
249 Queen's Quay W (Spadina), Toronto M5J 2N5. Map 3E6 ☎ *364-5444 or 800-333-3333* ☒*364-2975* ▥ *157 rms* ━ ▤ ☰ ☒ ▣ �★ ⚲ ♈ ☸ ♉ ☐ ♒

Location: Harbourfront. Sheathed in blue glass, this relative newcomer is one of only two hotels in the Harbourfront development. The recent change in name and ownership doesn't appear to have altered it much, one way or the other. SkyDome and the CN Tower loom to the N. The Pier 4 complex, of which the hotel is part, has three large restaurants, and a Chinese junk moored alongside, to lend a touch of exoticism. Pretty vistas of the harbor and offshore islands are the backdrop for drinkers seated on the Promenade Deck and in the lounge chairs around the outdoor pool. Nearby are an enclosed whirlpool and a squash court.

Rooms are pleasantly furnished, and minibar and TV with remote control are included. The LRT streetcar provides ready access to Union Station and the Financial District.

ROYAL YORK
100 Front St. W (York), Toronto M5J 1E3. Map 3E7 ☎ *368-2511 or 800-268-9411 (Canada) or 800-828-7447 (US)* ☒*368-2884* ▥ *1,408 rms* ━ ▣ ☰ ☒ ▣ ▣ ▥ ⚲ ♈ ♈ ☞ ☸ ♒ ♉ ♒

Location: Opposite Union Station. As the "largest hotel in the British Commonwealth," warmth and intimacy can hardly be counted among its virtues. After all, if all rooms are occupied, it matches the population of many a small town. Settle instead for its abundant array of shops and services, bedrooms that are entirely satisfactory if not striking, and no less than 12 restaurants and bars. One of the latter, the **Imperial Room**, is a supper club showcase for traveling entertainers, stage shows, and music of the big band era.

A recently completed $95 million renovation program included the addition of a fully-equipped fitness center. There is also a new karaoke bar. This is a place to keep in mind for those occasions when other hotels are full.

SHERATON CENTRE OF TORONTO
123 Queen St. W (Bay), Toronto M5H 2M9. Map 4D8 ☎ *361-1000 or 800-325-3535* ☒*947-4854* ▥ *1,392 rms* ▦ ▣ ☰ ☒ ▣ ▣ ▥ ⚲ ⚲ ⚲ ♈ ♉ ☐ ♒ ♒ ☞

Location: Opposite City Hall and near Eaton Centre. Only a monster of a hotel can underwrite such interior gardens as these, replete with hanging foliage, extensive flower-beds, stands of mature trees . . . and even ducks and a 3-story waterfall. This Sheraton is the second-largest hotel in the city, and it doesn't shrink from its perceived responsibility to manufacture superlatives. A $47 million renovation effort has upgraded both public and private spaces. Apart from the waterfall and gardens, there is a 25m (80ft) pool that is partly inside, mostly out. A California-style hot tub is on hand.

Those who want fancier perks and pampering than found in the standard rooms can upgrade to one of the 150 now allotted to the more luxurious **Towers**. Direct access is had to the Underground.

SKYDOME
45 Peter St. S (Spadina), Toronto M5V 3B4.
Map 3E6 ☎360-7100 or 800-268-9420
(Ontario and Québec) or 800-828-7447 (US)
🖶341-5090 ▥ to ▥ 348 rms ▤ �
▭ ▨ ▣ ⊈ ⅍ ⤨ ⩱ ♈ ⋒ ⅋ ▭ ⊒
*Location: Within walking distance of
the theater and financial districts.* The
youngest of three Canadian Pacific hotels in Toronto (opened late 1989) has
a feature that no other can claim: 70
rooms and suites that overlook the field
of the spectacular SkyDome stadium
itself. They cost a bundle, and obviously
have enormous appeal for rabid sports
fans — the Blue Jays and Argonauts
play there — but the novelty itself is
enough to hold anyone's attention.
Guests assigned to one of the other 280
rooms won't feel deprived, for the
management has loaded them with the
extra touches and electronic doodads
that travelers on expense accounts have
come to expect. They include the morning newspaper with breakfast, 24-hour
food and beverage service, remote control TV, minibars. Many rooms have
VCRs and Jacuzzi baths. The goodies
multiply on the floors set aside for Business and Entrée Gold categories. Just
avoid checking in at game time, when
the throngs clog all the entrances.

SUTTON PLACE KEMPINSKI ▥
955 Bay St. (Wellesley), Toronto M5S 2A2.
Map 4B8 ☎924-9221 or 800-268-3790
🖶924-1778 ▥ 208 rms and 72 suites
▬ � ▭ ▨ ▣ ⊠ ▨ ⌂ ⌸ ⋒ ♈ ⩱
◍ ▭
*Location: Near Queen's Park and
University of Toronto.* Selecting a member establishment of the *Leading Hotels
of the World* is a fail-safe decision. That
prestigious association applies very
high standards, and can be ruthless
when any of their number fall behind
the pace. Certainly no expense nor effort has been spared by the Sutton Place
to remain well above even these lofty
expectations. The multilingual reception is impeccable, fixtures are tastefully opulent, and only the sourest
curmudgeon could find serious fault
with the rooms, many of which have

lawn-deep Oriental carpets on polished
parquet floors. A butler is on call at all
times. Shoe-shines and morning papers
are complimentary. TV, minibar, robes
and hairdryers, of course. An indoor
pool, sauna and massage, naturally.
The **Sanssouci** restaurant is exemplary, especially so at Sunday brunch.
Alexandra's Bar is a welcoming snug-
gery for nightcaps, its entry walls lined
with photos of the celebs who have
sipped within. And a free limousine
whisks guests to the Financial District
every workday morning.

TORONTO MARRIOTT EATON CENTRE
525 Bay St (Dundas), Toronto M5G 2E1.
Map 4C8 ☎597-9200 or 800-228-9290
🖶597-9211 ▥ to ▥ 435 rms and 24
suites ▬ � ▭ ▨ ▣ ⊡ ▨ ⋒ ♈ ⩱
♈
Location: Steps from Eaton Centre. It's
difficult to miss a purple (well, lavender) hotel smack in the middle of downtown. The interior is less gaudy, and the
welcome efficient. Often, the porter at
the door can pick up your key and take
you right to your room. Rooms are
pleasant enough, if nothing out of the
ordinary. For fancier digs, upgrade to
the "Concierge Level," not all that much
more expensive, and boasting a private
lounge for complimentary breakfast
and afternoon *hors d'oeuvres.*

The hotel is as convenient to the
Financial District, shopping, and
theaters as any in downtown. Opened
several years ago, it should have
worked out the final kinks in policy and
service by the time this ink is dry.

VENTURE INN ♨
89 Avenue Rd. (Bloor), Toronto M5R 2G3.
Map 3A7 ☎964-1220 or 800-387-3933
🖶964-8692 ▭ 71 rms ▬ ▤ ▭ ▨ ⊈
⌂ ✿
*Location: Near Yorkville and the Royal
Ontario Museum.* A college-dormitory
air is heightened by the squeaky-clean
young staff. One of several Toronto entries of a growing budget chain, this one
is noteworthy for its proximity to Yorkville. The rooms have firm beds, TV
with pay movies, and not much else,

but the prices are very easy on the bank account. A variety of weekend packages is available.

VICTORIA

56 Yonge St (King), Toronto M5E 1G5. Map 4D8 ☎*363-1666 or 800-668-1562* ☒*363-7327* ▭ *102 rms* ▱ ▭ ▭ ▭ ▭ ▭ ▭ ▭

Location: Three blocks to the s of Eaton Centre. No health club, no pool, no super-heated atmosphere of international commerce. But then, this restored 1908 Edwardian has been around since long before such things were characteristic of city hostelries. Choose it for its low tariffs and its proximity to the Pantages and Elgin Theatres, O'Keefe Centre, Union Station, and downtown offices. Several economical sports and entertainment packages are available.

WESTIN HARBOUR CASTLE

1 Harbour Square (Queen's Quay E and Yonge), Toronto M5J 1A6. Map 4E8 ☎*869- 1600 or 800-228-3000* ☒*869-0573* ▭ *975 rms and suites* ▱ ▭ ▭ ▭ ▭ ▭ ▭ ▭ ▭ ▭ ▭ ▭ ▭ ▭ ▭

Location: At the E end of Harbourfront. Skillful marketing is reorienting this former Hilton from conventioneer warren to in-town resort. There are the necessary ingredients. The health club has free weights, a jogging track, three squash courts, a steam room, whirlpool, Universal machine, and an indoor pool that opens to a terrace in summer. Out there is a new tennis court, too. But what distinguishes this from other hotels is the complete spa facility, which provides loofah-sponge baths, massage clinic, and restaurant menus of low-everything meals. Guests less paranoid about their belt sizes are tempted by the buffet lunch in the revolving **Lighthouse** restaurant, a two-tiered room, 37 stories up. There are two other restaurants and two lounges, one of which has live music. A useful new round-the-clock service allows staff members easier communication with foreign guests — interpreters of more than 140 languages are only a phonecall away. Ferries for the Toronto Islands leave from the dock behind the hotel; a new streetcar loop makes the trip to Union Station in less than 10 minutes.

AND AT THE AIRPORT . . .

The enthusiasm for hotels within shouting distance of the runway and baggage carousel is lost on travelers who don't operate on tight multi-city schedules. Those who do, appreciate the convenience of hotels fully equipped to meet the needs of the businessperson, from conference facilities to health clubs to airport shuttles.

There are at least a dozen of these in sight of the three terminals of Pearson International. The area is utterly void of charm, need it be said, and there is little to distinguish the hotels themselves, but most can handily meet expectations.

Among them, all in the suburb of Mississauga:

- **Celebrity Inn**   6355 Airport Rd. ☎677-1752 or 800-6955 ☒677-1752 ▭ for those on limited expense accounts.
- **Delta Meadowvale**   6750 Mississauga Rd. ☎821-1981 or 800-268-1133 ☒542-4036 ▭ Indoor pool, indoor tennis, health club.
- **Hilton International**   5875 Airport Rd. ☎677-9900 or 800-268-9275 ☒677-5073 ▭ Heated pool, nightclub with live music.
- **Novotel**   3670 Hurontario St. ☎896-1000 or 800-221-4542 ☒896-2521 ▭ New 1991 entry of an expanding French chain; use of health club with racquetball and tennis.
- **Swissôtel Toronto**   6303 Airport Rd. ☎672-700 or 800-637-9477 ☒672-7100 ▭ At Terminal 3; has pool and business center.

BED AND BREAKFAST

The observations about B&B lodgings in Montréal, under that heading on page 169, also apply in Toronto. Please review them before deciding to use the services of the referral agencies listed.

BED AND BREAKFAST HOMES OF TORONTO

PO Box 46093, 444 Yonge St., Toronto M5B 2L8 ☎ *363-6362.*
Full breakfasts at homes throughout Metro Toronto. Send a self-addressed envelope for a descriptive brochure.

DOWNTOWN TORONTO ASSOCIATION OF BED AND BREAKFAST GUEST HOMES

PO Box 190, Station B, Toronto M5T 2W1 ☎ *977-6841 or 408-2666*
🖷 *598-4562.*
Renovated older homes with 50 available rooms. All are handy to subway or bus. Three nights minimum preferred April–October. All homes are nonsmoking.

METROPOLITAN BED AND BREAKFAST REGISTRY OF TORONTO

615 Mt. Pleasant Rd., Suite 269, Toronto M5S 3C5 ☎ *964-2566* 🖷 *537-0233.*
About 30 homes throughout Metro Toronto — descriptions of which are included in the brochure. Credit cards are sometimes accepted.

Smoking is not allowed by most hosts, many of whom may also have pets.

Toronto: eating and drinking

Where and what to eat

Toronto is a culinary free-for-all. The phenomenon of star chefs and cuisines-of-the-week took hold in the self-indulgent Eighties and shows little sign of abating. Restless, impatient, insatiably curious young cooks observe no esthetic restrictions. They borrow ingredients and techniques from scores of national and regional styles and throw them together in multicultural pastiches. A single dish containing Cajun spices, Thai noodles, Chinese mushrooms, Mexican *cilantro* and Canadian venison (with perhaps a rhubarb *coulis* in a phyllo cup on the side) may not have been assembled yet, but it is only a matter of time.

This manic experimentation and its eager acceptance by the public has spawned a global cuisine that may yet get its own name. Much of it can be arch and precious, a collective cleverness gone over the edge. What is surprising are the goodly number of bull's-eyes among all the thudding misfires.

The forum for this race to new frontiers is an updated version of the bistro. It is smaller and more casual than the Old World variety, with no tuxedoed retainers or flaming tableside preparations. Patrons no longer have to take assertiveness training to find out what good food is about. Staffs are not as stratified as they are elsewhere. The sommelier has nearly disappeared, and few places have captains occupying the chain of command between the *maitre d'* and the waiters. If part of the price for experiencing this new looseness is enduring its frequent silliness, no one said life was without flaw.

With all this going on, a favorite buzzword of Toronto restaurant critics is "accessible," as if a plate of food were an exercise in Joycean riddle. In the selections below, we've attempted to give an overview of what is available, from simple to ambitious, cheap to celebratory, from Far Eastern to Middle European, with most of the stops in between. Obviously, this is only a sampling, and a truncated one, at that. Toronto claims somewhere between 4,000 and 5,000 eating places. But the list points the way to fecund neighborhoods, past dozens of restaurants awaiting discovery.

And please remember that, however good, restaurants are a chancy line of business — every year, more than 10 percent of Canadian restaurants fail. Toronto, in particular, has suffered from the recent recession, as indicated by the fact that nine of the 27 restaurants recommended in the first edition of this guide have closed. Always call ahead to make certain your choice is open for the meal you desire, the times for last orders, and, for that matter, whether it is still in business.

WINES AND OTHER DRINKS

The often displayed letters **L.L.B.O.** (Liquor Licencing Board of Ontario) mean that a restaurant is fully licensed to serve wine and spirits. Not all are, so check when booking.

Liquor and wine are expensive, with a 100-percent tax on imports, but Canadian bottlings are less costly and are often quite palatable. To save money in restaurants, consider buying wine by the glass instead of by the carafe or bottle.

Ontario **beers and ales** are excellent and varied. Try Upper Canada, Creemore Springs, Old Jock Bitter, Conners, Sleeman, and Wellington. Espresso and brewed decaffeinated **coffee** is widely available.

Most of the vineyards and wineries of the region are located in the southernmost thumb of Ontario, near Niagara Falls, and in the Windsor area, which is near Detroit. White wines predominate, but there are some reds. Names to look for are Inniskillin, Hillebrand, Château des Charmes, Stonechurch, Reif Estate, London, Pelee Island, and Colio. One unusual speciality of Inniskillin is "icewine." Grapes are left to freeze on the vine into December and January, then picked and pressed at very cold temperatures. The result is a complex dessert wine reminiscent of German *reislings.*

EATING CHEAP

It is possible to eat well on limited funds. In addition to ethnic eateries where prices are generally low, there are ways to try out the pricier emporia without emptying your wallet. Lunch is usually much cheaper than dinner, sometimes by as much as 40 percent.

Restaurants near SKYDOME, or in the theater district, have special menus before a baseball game and after the show. Weekend brunch, an entrenched tradition, usually costs a few dollars less than a weekday meal. Some of the larger restaurants have lower-cost annexes, rooms in the same building with shorter menus and more casual environments. CENTRO and SCARAMOUCHE are two with that arrangement.

EATING FAST

For quick meals and snacks, don't dismiss the carts and vans marked **Shopsy's**. You'll find them parked in busier districts during all but the coldest months. They claim to have the "world's greatest hot dog," and they have a case. The thick, tasty sausage in question is served on a steamed, seeded bun with a choice of several toppings.

A longer menu of better-than-average burgers, sandwiches, and ice cream treats is available at the several locations of the popular **Lick's** chain. There's one near the N exit of Eaton Centre.

Single diners and couples can often avoid a long wait, when arriving at a crowded restaurant without a reservation, by asking to be served meals at the bar. Apart from the convenience, it is an excellent way for a stranger in town to meet people.

USEFUL TO KNOW

- **Opening hours**:   Most of the restaurants listed below are open seven days a week for lunch and dinner, so only deviations from that norm are mentioned.
- **Tipping**:   The standard tip in restaurants is 15 percent, the same as the combined federal and provincial taxes. Since these taxes are now stated separately on the check, as a rule, it is easy to calculate the correct tip.
- **Smoking**:   Restaurants with more than thirty seats are required to have nonsmoking sections.
-

HOW TO USE THIS CHAPTER

- **Location**:   In the listings below, the streets named in parentheses are the nearest *important* cross-streets. Map references are also given for the color maps at the end of the book.
- **Symbols**:   See the KEY TO SYMBOLS on page 7 for an explanation of the full list of our symbols.
- **Prices**:   The prices corresponding to our price symbols are based on the average price of a meal (dinner, not lunch) for one person, inclusive of house wine, tax and gratuity. Although actual prices will inevitably increase after publication, our relative price categories are likely to remain the same.

  Prices are given in **Canadian dollars**.

Symbol	Category	Current price
⬛	very expensive	over $70
⬛	expensive	$50-70
⬛	moderate	$30-50
⬛	inexpensive	$15-30
⬛	cheap	under $15

Toronto restaurants A to Z

ACROBAT *Eclectic*
60 Bloor St. W (Bay). Map 3A7
☎920-2323 ⬛ AE ◉ ⬛ ⬛

It will come as no surprise to anyone dining in Toronto for more than a few days, that this is another rip-roaring enterprise of the hottest restauranteur in town, Franco Prevedello. Canada's own version of California's superchef Wolfgang Puck, he was also the force behind CENTRO, PRONTO, **Splendido**, and **Biffi Bistro**. This one looks like a Barcelona ballroom by Gaudí that took a detour through a Santa Monica watering hole conjured by Frank Gehry. If you have no idea what that might mean, just look: hundreds of bottles imbedded in the wavy carapace that rolls along the wall above the bar. Olive-green tufted banquettes. Tones of sand and terracotta and earth. A silvered upside-down nude acrobat frozen on a high beam in front of the DJ booth. Food is decent Toronto shotgun, on the lines of lamb and gnocchi and mint *aïoli* or salmon with black bean butter sauce. But this isn't about eating, not with a dining space about half the area of the bar. Cruising and mingling are what's on, with a little grazing on the side. Go for the gorgeous people. Seek peace and quiet elsewhere.

AVOCADO CLUB *Eclectic*
165 John St. (Queen). Map 3D7
☎598-4656 ▭ ▭ ▭ ▭

This used to be the once-admired **Beaujolais**. It hasn't changed all that much, just more youthful, friskier, even offhanded. Factory chic still prevails, the warehouse look sustained by exposed ceiling ducts. Decorative overlays are a colorful confusion of inspirations, much like the food. Satays, tandoori dishes, and some Southwestern and Caribbean notions are evidence of a mind more interested in taste and dash than disciplined examinations. This is dining as play, in the prevailing spirit of the gingery Queen St. W neighborhood at its door.

BAMBOO *West Indian*
312 Queen St. W (Spadina). Map 3D7
☎598-4656 ▭ to ▭ ▭ ▭ ▭ ▭

West Indian informality and sensuality rule at this ramshackle club, which grows steamier and even more unpredictable as the night thumps on. It isn't tidy, it isn't tranquil, and anything might happen. Bamboo is a daily party for a crowd that is mostly young, usually hip, and sometimes exceptionally strange. They show up in lace and jeans and Armani and studded leather, but a suit and tie won't arch any eyebrows. There are fake reptiles hanging about, bare plumbing strung with Christmas lights, candles guttering in pots on cast-off 1950s furniture. Bands crank up almost every night around 10pm or whenever they can get themselves together. They go by such names as Culture Shock and Hot Tamales, and their choice of sounds can be jazz, reggae, zydeco, salsa, rock . . . and the unclassifiable. Since the Caribbean food repertoire is limited, the menu shares room with Thai. Noodle dishes are tops; satays and stir-frys are serviceable.

Dinner at sunset on the roof patio is most agreeable. If you're bored at Bamboo, pinch yourself. You may have died in your sleep.

BANGKOK GARDEN *Thai*
18 Elm St. (Yonge). Map 3C7 ☎977-6748
▭ ▭ ▭ ▭ ▭ *Closed Sun.*

Thai is hot! In popularity, that is, and this is the place to see what all the fuss is about. Thai food is also hot in the spicy sense, but not always, and in subtle gradations. The menu ranks the degree of fire in each dish with one to five stars. Level three isn't too much for most people. The teak-and-mirror-lined restaurant, illuminated at night by flickering candles, is a romantic setting in which to partake of lemon shrimp soup, satay or "warrior's curry." The waiters patiently describe and gently coach, even announcing how many chilies there are in each dish. This food is put together with delicacy and balance. Go with someone, preferably several someones, so more dishes can be sampled. Appetizers and seafood are best, the desserts resistible.

BARBERIAN'S *Steak*
7 Elm St. (Yonge). Map 3C7 ☎597-0335
▭ ▭ ▭ ▭ ▭ *Closed Sat lunch, Sun lunch.*

When that urge for a beef booster strikes, there's no better place to mollify it than this old-timey, downtown steakhouse. Buffed wood, dim lighting, and the scattering of squat antiques make it seem older than its three-plus decades. Join its regular coterie of two-fisted carnivores, who like their T-bones and *filet mignons* unadorned and broiled precisely to order, and without *nouvelle* embellishments. Remember beef Wellington? They do, and this version can make one wonder, momentarily, why it went out of fashion. Dark suits and silvered hair are much in evidence — youthful exuberance is not. An after-theater menu is offered from 10pm.

BEMELMANS *Eclectic*
83 Bloor St. (Bay). Map 4A8 ☎960-0306
▭ to ▭ ▭ ▭ ▭

"Now, then, my darling," says one fluttery waitress, "what will you be having?" She sounds about six months out of Liverpool and *very* anxious to please. Everyone on the staff is eager to make you happy. They are proud of their 20 different martinis. Of their unfussy but hardly stodgy Cal-Ital-Asian dishes. Of the half-price pasta happy hour daily 4–7pm. Of the super Sunday brunch. There's a dark and woody bar within, a leafy patio in back, non-smoking sections. Prices are fair. They stay open every night until midnight or later. All this attracts families, young singles and couples, kids, retirees, shoppers, executives. Long may it thrive.

LE BISTINGO *French*
349 Queen St. W (John). Map 3D7
☎598-3490 ▥ to ▥ 🅰🅴 💿 🆅🆂🅰 *Closed Sat lunch, Sun.*

Avid epicures and trend-setters once booked this *haute* bistro to the walls. Those fevered days are gone, and the on-premises owner saw the need to adapt to straitened times. He "re-positioned," as have others who wished to remain in business. They pulled up the carpeting, laid squares of white butcher paper over the tablecloths, simplified the menu and used less expensive ingredients. For all the clear-eyed realism, there remains the sense of a steady, mature presence behind the kitchen doors. Little is seen of former flash and novelty, which was never excessive, but that's not to say that what emerges is staid. Duck is a speciality, arriving smoked or in warm salads or as a *ragoût* with pasta and asparagus. Warm apple tart in a reduced Calvados froth is the signature dessert. The cellar is carefully assembled, and six wines are available by the glass. Suits dominate at lunch, a mixed crowd of Queen Street irregulars and suburban sophisticates at night. They are attended by an efficient staff that could use infusions of warmth.

BISTRO 990 *French*
990 Bay St. (Wellesley). Map 3B7
☎921-9990 ▥ to ▥ 💿 🆅🆂🅰

Take someone with whom there is much to discuss. The rest of the effervescent crowd does, knowing that it will help pass the time awaiting the unpredictable attentions of the sometimes elusive staff. The host is even known to offer single diners a copy of the morning newspaper to pass the time. Relax. This is a bistro, after all, albeit one of the highest order. It's casual enough that the Schwarzenegger lookalike at the next table suffers no embarrassment at drinking Diet Coke with his *pot au feu* while his neighbors rhapsodize over the roast lamb with couscous and the savoury duck *confit*. The food does arrive, eventually, and makes the wait entirely worthwhile. But do take a friend.

BOULEVARD CAFÉ *South American*
161 Harbord St. (Spadina). Map 3B6
☎961-7676 ▥ 💿 🆅🆂🅰

Just about any gustatory need that might be imagined is targeted by this friendly café. It's open 7 days a week, serving sandwiches to 4-course meals. Sunday brunch is bountiful and informal. In summer, a large, covered patio adds to its appeal. A nominal Peruvian identity is announced by South American wallhangings and tables with handmade tile tops, and is carried forth with such dishes from the owners' homeland as garlic shrimp, *empanadas, tamal verde,* and *papas a la Huancaina* (baby shrimp and sliced potatoes in a cheese sauce). They aren't slavish about the connection, though, with burgers and such on the card. Portions are large enough to make appetizer or dessert unnecessary, salsas are tangy but less than torrid. All in all, this is as gratifyingly low-pressure and good-value as dining can get.

BROWNES BISTRO *Eclectic*
1251 Yonge St. (Woodlawn) ☎924-8132
▥ to ▥ 🅰🅴 💿 💿 🆅🆂🅰 *Closed Sat lunch, Sun lunch.*

Maybe this started as a neighborhood place, with people dropping in after work, ties loosened, sleeves rolled up. If so, word got out, and now, on weekends, the line of waiting reservationless diners curls from the bar out into the street. The conventions are there, with white plates on white paper over white tablecloths. The floor is uncovered, the chairs assembly-line bentwood. Wines are sold by the glass, either 3-ounce or 6-ounce, and prices aren't steep, by local standards. Expect no leisurely discussions with the servers about vintages and provenance, though. They move fast, often breaking into trots. Swoop! A pizza. Snatch! A pasta. The cooks in the open kitchen at back remain calm and efficient. They produce nothing a moderately talented home cook can't whip up, but they do it for a hundred or more people a night. Their best efforts are often the daily specials, as with a lima bean and duck *confit* soup and the grilled Arctic char with vegetable salsa. Just don't get too comfortable, or the bill will arrive without asking, an annoying, if understandable, practice

CENTRO *Italian*
2472 Yonge St. (Eglinton). Map 5B3 ☎483-2211 ▥ *(downstairs)* ▥ *(main room)* ▣ ▣ ▣ ▥ *Closed Sun.*

L.A. meets Tuscany in a place still so "in" it almost hurts. There is the room — now with large photos of scenes of Chianti against desert tones with geometric Classical references. There are the trappings — a mesquite grill for designer pizzas and free-range capon. Handsome young waiters in aprons and wing collars ask, "How is the meal so far?" about twice as often as necessary. Why go? Because the food is exceptional, if too chic for its own good. There has been, for example, *tagliatelle* with smoked salmon, roast peppers, cream, vodka and caviar. Cute. Desserts are overblown. Nothing languid about the service — courses arrive too quickly, if anything. Don't go alone. Everyone is celebrating something, be it only their good fortune in being able to afford it. Lower prices, pastas, and piano music pertain in the lively downstairs lounge, which remains full late into the evening.

CHONG STAR HOUSE
Szechuan/Mandarin
418 Spadina Ave. (Dundas). Off map 3A7 ☎598-1325 ▥ ▣ ▣ ▣ ▥
Restaurant critics for *Toronto Life* might

have been a trifle generous in awarding three stars (out of four) to this modest Chinatown eatery. That isn't to say that it isn't equal or superior to most of its welter of competitors along Spadina Ave., though, and it's less chaotic than many. It doesn't hurt that the staff speaks fluent English, not always the case in this precinct. Chef Chong specializes in the Szechuan and Mandarin cuisines, but isn't reluctant to stray into Cantonese, Hunan, and other fields. Among the possibilities are sizzling and snapping lamb in garlicky black bean sauce, and prawns almost any way.

CIBO *Italian*
1055 Yonge St. (St Clair) ☎921-2166 ▥ ▣ ▣ ▥
There are other items on the menu, and some people actually order them. They are missing the point. Pasta is the reason to seek out this understated Rosedale eatery. Start, logically enough, with *antipasti,* a tempting selection. Daily specials — pasta, of course — always represent the kitchen's best thinking of the moment.

Many of the patrons know each other, which makes for a happy clamor. They can't get enough of the place, so even though it's open daily, there is often a line of supplicants on weekend nights. The terrace on Yonge takes some of the overflow on warm evenings.

Another unassuming Italian, closer to midtown, is basement-level **Sisi** *(116A Avenue Rd., off map 3 B7* ☎ *962-0011* ▥*)*. It is small and very popular, and reservations are essential.

ED'S WAREHOUSE *Canadian*
270 King St. W (University). Map 3D7 ☎593-6676 ▥ ▣ ▣ ▣ ▥ *Closed Sat lunch, Sun lunch.*
Kitsch finds its definition here. A warehouse, indeed, it is full of huge fringed Tiffany lamps, massive semi-antiques, stained glass, statuary, and vases almost 2m (6ft) high. Most of the fixtures are the sort that were in brief fashion, never came back, and probably never will. Walls and columns are covered with autographed photos of movie stars of

the first to fifth magnitudes. The food isn't much different from what many of us remember from the days before North America discovered cuisine. Say about 1959, for Parents' Day at the university cafeteria. Waiters are obviously instructed not to linger. An entire meal, appetizer to watery coffee, is served in less than 30 minutes. Go for reasons that have little to do with eating: (a) for a giggle, (b) with kids, or (c) because everyone does, at least once.

Should the experience leave you wanting more, this stretch of King St. also hosts *Ed's Seafood, Ed's Italian Food, Ed's Folly,* and *Old Ed's.* No shrinking violet, Ed Mirvish.

FILET OF SOLE *Fish*
11 Duncan St (Adelaide). Map 3D7
☎598-3256 ▢▢ ▢▢ ▢ ▢▢ ▢▢ *Closed Sat lunch, Sun lunch.*

This theater district fish house fills its seats and cranks up the noise level nightly. The seemingly endless menu has to be handwritten daily, to take into account whatever is available at market. There are more than twenty appetizers, as a rule, not counting fresh-shucked oysters and clams, steamed mussels and made-to-order chowders. Lobster bisque is a favorite, as are the mixed platters. Most Toronto restaurants feel compelled to offer Caesar salad, a local enthusiasm, and this version measures up.

Downstairs is a similar, less formal room, **The Whistling Oyster** (☎598-7707). In the middle is a bar for beer and cocktails surrounded by burbling yuppies, buppies and boomers, single, in couples, or just looking. Over in one corner is a counter where a solemn worker makes chowders and prepares shellfish platters. Up or down, this is the place to try the flinty Ontario white wines. Reserve ahead for Filet of Sole, or settle for a stool down below.

HY'S *Steak*
73 Richmond St. W (Bay). Map 4D8
☎364-3326 ▢▢ to ▢▢ ▢▢ ▢ ▢ ▢▢ *Closed Sat lunch, Sun.*

Fitted out like the library of a Sussex manor house, with ancestral portraits in gilded frames, a carved stone fireplace, and shelves lined with books that actually appear to have been read. This downtown no-bones steakhouse is just the antidote when a few meals of global art food have Real Men climbing the pastel walls of bistros-of-the-moment. Simple chicken and fish dishes are available for any wimps who might venture through the doors, but the point of all this is beef! Seared, succulent, charred prime rib and filet mignon, juices flowing at a covetous look. Guys can chain-smoke and drink hefty Martinis and Manhattans and goblets of hearty clarets and challenge each other about mergers and acquisitions. It shouldn't be necessary to observe that this is not the perfect spot for a first date. By all means, though, stop by for a drink in the fabulously overwrought Victorian bar.

JOSO'S *Seafood*
202 Davenport Rd. (Avenue Rd.)
☎925-1903 or 925-3911 ▢▢ ▢▢ ▢ ▢▢ *Closed Sun.*

"Tasteless," huffed one local critic. She wasn't talking about what arrived on the plate. Paintings and sculptural ceramics crowd the walls upstairs and down. Many of them were created by the owner, and his subject of choice is nudes, mostly female, some male, a few — um — together. Some first-time customers will agree with the critic, and parents will probably want to leave the kiddies at the hotel, but most seem to be amused by or indifferent to the arrays of improbable breasts and related anatomical parts. All that robust ribaldry aside, seafood is the specialty at this Adriatic trattoria — very fresh and prepared with a minimum of trickery. Cephalopods are paramount among the kitchen's concerns, and this is the place to discover that squid and octopus don't have to have the texture of inner tubes. Meat-eaters must seek other refuge.

JULIEN *French*
387 King St. (Spadina). Map 3D6
☎596-6738 ▢▢ ▢▢ ▢ ▢▢ ▢▢ *Closed Sat lunch, Sun.*

This calming retreat is almost as notable for what it doesn't do as for what it does. No effort is made to incorporate elements of seven cuisines on one plate, and the food doesn't look as if it has been pushed and poked to turn it into Cubist collage. Waiters don't swoop, and the host himself isn't above filling a glass. Julien is French, and pretends to nothing else. Each table has white napery and flowers. The grown men and women who comprise the clientele dress discreetly, not like their teenage children. The nightly *table d'hôte* includes soup or salad, a choice of main courses, and coffee or tea all for less than the cost of any *à la carte* item alone. Upstairs is a separate bistro, with a more limited but cheaper menu.

LOTUS *Eclectic*

96 Tecumseth St. (King). Map 2D5
☎ 368-7670 ▥▥ ▣ ▣ ▥▥ *Closed Tues–Sat lunch, Sun, Mon.*

This can't be right, can it? This spare, out-of-the-way storefront restaurant is home to one of Toronto's most gifted chefs? Believe it. Susur Lee began his apprenticeship at age 14, in the kitchen of a fabled Hong Kong hotel, and kept his eyes and ears open every moment of that time. His creations deserve a setting of starched white linens and golden candlesticks and polished teak paneling. They get bare wood floors and blank walls, but what appears on the plain plates makes the surroundings irrelevant. These are nothing less than apotheosis of the pan-Pacific gastronomic creed, rarely matched in these parts and unlikely to be surpassed. Lee's constructions are exquisitely calibrated blendings of flavors, colors, and scents, in compositions of which Miró would be proud. Taste is not sacrificed to esthetics and no one leaves hungry, not with such choices as risotto constituted in fresh celery and carrot juice, topped with barbecued Chinese quail and shavings of Reggiano, ringed with young vegetables and *chanterelles*. Or, the virtual *sushi* of tuna charred on the outside and cool within, touched with ginger and pepper and laid upon a bed

of pickled and saffroned summer vegetables given the unexpected bite of a lemon soya glaze and *wasaba vinaigrette*. Book ahead and arrive with tastebuds at attention. And check the balance on your gold card. It's in for a jolt. You probably won't begrudge a penny.

MASSIMO *Italian*

2459 Yonge St. (Eglinton). Map 5B3
☎ 487-2771 ▥▥ ▣ ▥▥ *Closed lunch.*

On the evidence, it is impossible to offer Canadian urbanites too much pasta. This youthful trattoria made what might seem an enormous blunder by opening directly across the street from the ultimate pasta emporium CENTRO. Yet, it prospers. Prices are lower, the service less arch. The principal product, in whatever form, is properly *al dente*, dressed in sauces that are sometimes spicy enough to pop a few beads of sweat across foreheads. There is occasional relief from noodles, with Tuscan-inspired meats and game, including oxtails with fried *polenta*, and individual pizzas. *Antipasti* and *insalati* are uninspired. While the bare tables and chairs don't necessarily invite lingering, many of the casual clients do just that. They have wine, beer, and a few digestifs, but take pre-dinner cocktails elsewhere.

METROPOLIS *New Canadian*

838 Yonge St. (Bloor). Map 4A8 ☎ 924-4100 ▥ to ▥▥ ▣ ▣ ▥▥ *Closed Sun.*

The elements that constitute "Canadian" cooking aren't easily discerned by foreigners. Judged by this erstwhile diner in Yorkville, it means rabbit, lamb, country sausage, pork, and a predilection for root vegetables and maple syrup. Here, they are put together with flair and an awareness of recent trends. Call it "New Canadian." The kitchen uses domestically raised or gathered provender whenever possible, as with Ontario onion and cider soup, Alberta tenderloin, and Niagara Peninsula baby greens salad. On Monday, you can eat all the mussels you want, all day, for a bargain price. Canadian brews are on tap, as are 23 domestic wines, many of which are sold by the glass. Pastries are baked on the premises. The scruffily informal setting resembles a cartoonish stage set, with goofy murals and a serpentine black Formica bar.

MÖVENPICK *Swiss*
165 York St. (Richmond). Map 3D7
☎ 366-5234 ▥ ▣ ▣ ▣

This New World outpost of a Swiss chain has the requisite Cantonal banners and alpine chalet motifs, the decorative flourishes of a middle-class ski resort. Service is brisk, too rushed by the daily crush of diners to be friendly. The selection of foods is broad and well-prepared, as a rule, served in several distinct sections — a pasta station, buffet tables, an oval dining bar, an outdoor terrace, an inner court, and an omelette counter, not to mention the tantalizing display of guilty treats on the dessert table.

In the heart of the Financial District, it's busy at every meal, even more so at Sunday brunch, when the nonbusiness types show up from all over the city. Reservations are a good idea, although they keep the lineup of eager eaters moving fairly quickly.

There's an equally successful branch in Yorkville *(113 Yorkville Ave.* ☎ *926-9545)* and a newer, larger operation in BCE Place, called **Marché by Mövenpick** *(Yonge and Wellington Sts.* ☎ *369-2300).*

THE OLD FISH MARKET *Seafood*
12 Market St. (Front). Map 4D8
☎ 363-0334 ▥ ▣ ▣ ▣ ▣

Gimmicks abound at this fish house next to St Lawrence Market and up the street from O'Keefe Centre. On Monday, all the mussels you can eat (upstairs only), all the crab legs you want (at dinner only), half-price oysters and clams at the raw bar (lunchtime only). It's a big place, built as a hotel in 1855 and probably not easy to fill. But for all the promotional pizzazz, even regular choices from the long menu are moderately priced. Much depends on what is fresh at market, which may include on

any given day such less familiar aquatic fare as orange roughy, rosefish, and skatewing, as well as cod and halibut. If Arctic char is listed, go for it, since it rarely travels south of the border. Preparations are conventional, and the various combination plates are probably best avoided. Stick to the simple fish dishes of the day.

PALMERSTON *Eclectic*
488 College St. (Bathurst). Map 2B5
☎ 922-9277 ▥ to ▥ ▣ ▣ ▣ Closed lunch.

Jamie Kennedy is a name often uttered when gourmands are asked about Toronto's cadre of celebrity chefs. He left here for a while, and has now returned, to his followers' relief. His arena is surprisingly small, for a reputation so large. The almost ascetic look of the space, and the unobtrusive demeanor of the front staff, have the effect of focusing attention on the maestro in his exhibition kitchen. Fair enough. Food, not the scene, is what's really important here. What emerges is a revelation for the eye as well as the palate, and he handles with élan any type of fowl or fish. Breads are special, including combinations with cheese and veggies that almost constitute meals in themselves.

While the Palmerston doesn't rank very high on the lovability scale, it loosens up markedly in the summer, when the patio is opened. Simple grills are then featured, and Kennedy doesn't regard hamburgers as beneath his dignity. Always reserve ahead.

PEPPINELLO *Italian*
180 Pearl St. (Duncan). Map 3D7
☎ 599-6699 ▥ ▣ ▣ ▣ ▣

A lot is going on in this downtown block in the theater district, with an active cruising saloon on the corner and this busy complex with two large floors of dining, a bar in each. A younger crowd gravitates to the downstairs, while the dressier, somewhat older group goes up above, where reservations are usually required. The fare? What else? Among the more desirable choices are *fettucine* topped with leaves of marinated salmon and a dollop of yellow caviar. A sturdier entry is grilled chicken on spinach and *linguine*. In place of high tea, consider the "La Perla Oyster Hour," when a short, mid-afternoon menu proffers steamed shellfish. A side order of *bruschetta* — slabs of bread piled with roasted peppers — is no less tasty for being this month's cliché.

PINK PEARL *Chinese*

120 Avenue Rd. (Davenport). Off map 3A7 ☎966-3631 ▥ ▣ ◉ ◙ ▨

One of several establishments in a local chain of somewhat self-consciously up-scale Chinese eateries, this entry is the most convenient for visitors, near York-ville. It's also open every day, a fact that's useful to know in a town where the Christian Sabbath is still observed with some rigor. The menu flits through a spectrum of several regional cuisines: Hunan, Szechuan, Pekinese, Cantonese. It is a gracious establishment, with pretty watercolors on the walls and substantial linens on the tables. European methods of service are observed, and there do not seem to be two menus, one for Westerners, one for Chinese. Wines are mostly French and somewhat dear. Beer goes at least as well.

IL PORTO *Italian*

146 Yorkville Ave. (Avenue). Off map 3A7 ☎968-0469 ▥ ▣ ◙ ▨ Closed Sun.

Despite the name, this sedate Yorkville *ristorante* doesn't cleave to prevailing Cal–Ital pyrotechnics. Instead, it takes the daring stance that professionalism is preferable to novelty. The room is calm and soothing, in earth tones and subdued lighting. In the Mediterranean manner, the waiter comes by to present a platter of the fishes of the day prior to cooking, identifying each and inviting close inspection. One of those clear-eyed creatures, simply grilled, with a side order of crisp vegetables, is a safe decision. But choices aren't that easy — not with a menu heavy with such carefully executed classics as *osso bucco* and *scampi*. The well-tailored, polished diners that are to be seen here spend their working days in executive suites.

PRONTO *Italian*

692 Mount Pleasant Rd. (Eglinton) ☎486-1111 ▥ to ▥ ▣ ◙ ▨ Closed lunch.

At this frequent consensus choice for best Italian, the toughest obstacles are getting a table and deciding what to eat. The first is solved by reserving 1–2 days ahead rather than by just showing up. Closing your eyes and just punching a finger at the menu is the easiest way around the second. That way, you may wind up with something composed primarily of goat cheese, *porcini* and sun-dried tomatoes, but just because they're cliches doesn't mean they aren't good. This isn't just another hi-tech Milanese pasta house, either. Veal is special, and most fish and meats are merely grilled and served with minimalist sauces. They do a fresh turn on seafood stew, many of the ingredients grilled prior to incorporation. Quibbles? The din re-sulting from crowds in a room built primarily of steel and glass, and an occasional unevenness of quality.

ROTTERDAM BREWERY PUB *Eclectic*

600 King St. (Bathurst). Map 3D5 ☎868-6882 ▥ to ▥ ◙ ▨

A few steps down from the street is a long room of stone and wooden beams, an opening in the ceiling revealing ranks of copper vats. This is a working brewery, and they take their self-appointed task seriously. The result is a beer-lover's nirvana, with a roster of 300 brands of imported and domestic brews, in addition to those made on the premises. There are daily lunch specials, a popular Sunday brunch, and since it's near the SKYDOME, low-priced dinners before athletic events.

SANTA FE *Tex–Mex*

129 Peter St. (Richmond). Map 3D6 ☎345-9345 ▥ ◙ ▨

Shoes and rubber boots are affixed to the outside of the building in no readily apparent relationship to the inferred theme of the saloon-eatery within. The interior is a visual and auditory tumult, intentionally loud and determinedly messy. Outsize blackboards scream the daily specials. Good-time music on the stereo is all but drowned out by the jolly crowd there. A huge rainbow-colored papier-mâché iguana dangles right above the bar, and rows of baskets are to be seen hanging, higher up. Santa Fe trademarks are acknowledged in the collection of painted wooden snakes and a howling coyote, and with the *nachos, quesadillas* and "kick-ass" *guacamole* on the menu. Ethnic purity is not a goal, however, with such non-Southwestern vittles as Charleston fried scallops and Louisiana blackened catfish also available.

Go. Eat. Ogle. Enjoy.

SCARAMOUCHE *Continental*
1 Benvenuto Pl. (Avenue) ☎ *961-8011* ▥▥▯
to ▥▥▥ Ⓐ Ⓒ ▦ *Closed Sun, lunch.*

Those who seek novelty over substance needn't bother with Scaramouche. This is a classic restaurant, populated in the main by people of a certain age and income that permit them to ignore the side of the menu where prices reside. That isn't to say that the management is indifferent to fashion. They have a sidebar café that specializes in pastas for the younger set. In the main room, the dishes follow restrained *nouvelle* conventions, the fish and meats lying on top of sauces rather than beneath them. Taste sensations are frequent, but using familiar ingredients, not the latest creature to arrive from the Asian Pacific without an English name.

Add to the serenity a panorama of the city beneath a spangle of stars, and it becomes the perfect choice for a last-night farewell to Toronto.

SWITZER'S DELICATESSEN *Deli*
404 Steeles Ave. W (Bathurst) ☎ *882-8100*
▥▯ Ⓒ ▦

Switzer's stayed on Spadina Ave. until long after it had become an anachronism, a Jewish deli in the midst of the noodle shops and the tea houses of Chinatown. Now it has moved to a rather more hospitable neighborhood in North York. Nothing else has changed. Waitresses in those dated hairdos still trundle bounteous platters of Nova Scotia salmon and *pastrami* and gefilte fish and bagels. These edibles are one culture's soul food — as good here as any place w of Montréal and n of New York.

Keep it in mind when off on a visit to Black Creek Pioneer Village.

TALL POPPIES *Eclectic*
326 Dundas St. W (University). Map 3C7
▥▯ ☎ *595-5588* Ⓐ Ⓒ ▦ *Closed Mon dinner, Sat lunch, Sun.*

Creativity reigns behind the skillets of this ever-popular spot, situated just opposite the Art Gallery of Ontario.

Dishes designated as the "Chef's Whim" are always worth a try, at least for nontimid diners. It all arrives looking as pretty as a picture. The decor is attractive, but not distracting, and there is an outdoor court in back.

Toronto: nightlife and entertainment

Toronto after dark

With their pronounced Protestant ethic, Torontonians were long said to be more interested in work than in leisure. It's true that the city turns off its lights early. Bars close at 1am and don't open again until noon. But discos and rock clubs jam on as late as 4am, which should satisfy all but those who need not worry about making a living.

USEFUL TO KNOW

- **Tickets**:   Tickets to most plays and concerts can be bought by phone from **TicketMaster** (☎872-1111). Their lines are open Monday to Friday 9.30am–9pm, Saturday 9.30am–6pm, Sunday noon–6pm. Have a credit card ready.
- **Savings**:   Half-price tickets to most of the same events can be purchased the day of performance at **Five Star Tickets**. Their booth is located either in the lobby of the **Royal Ontario Museum** (winter) or at the corner of Dundas and Yonge near the **Eaton Centre**. Sales are final and must be paid in cash.
- **Cost**:   A cover charge is usually levied wherever live entertainment is on hand. In most cases it isn't confiscatory, although a minimum number of drinks may be stipulated. Supper clubs and dinner theaters allow the option of paying to see the show without having a meal, but with cover charge. Dinner-and-show packages are not especially expensive, but the food is rarely better than passable.
- **Information**:   For information on all forms of performances and nightlife, the most current sources are the Friday edition of *The Toronto Star* and the Saturday issue of *The Globe and Mail*. The weeklies *NOW* and *eye* are also useful, as is the monthly *Toronto Life*.
- **Minimum age**:   The minimum drinking age in Ontario is 19 years.

Nightlife

As in most North American cities born before the automobile, nightlife for the average Torontonian consists of dropping by the neighborhood tavern for an hour or two, to check in with chums or chat up newcomers. Only the very young are likely to go on to a dance club or concert hall early in the work week. Friday and Saturday, their older siblings join them.

BARS

Bars are found in every permutation. There are credible imitations of British pubs, power bars, gay bars, cruising bars, university bars, bohemian bars, theater bars, jazz bars, sports bars, piano bars . . . and even bars in which you might have just a quiet drink.

Pool tables are increasingly standard, and an enthusiasm for karaoke has spread like Asian flu. For those few who are not yet familiar with this diversion of Japanese origin, karaoke is a device that shows the lyrics of songs on a TV screen, with appropriate pictures, and provides musical accompaniment. The soundtrack of the lead singer's voice is removed, allowing brave or exhibitionist customers to get up and perform their versions of Sinatra or Streisand, perhaps even with some air guitar. As often as not, the results suggest a charity event for the terminally tone-deaf. That hasn't dimmed the popularity of karaoke by one wobbly note.

It is most often to be found at what used to be called **singles bars**. These continue to thrive, the habitués proceeding with more caution than a decade ago, for all the well-publicized reasons, but that hasn't seriously derailed the age-old quest.

Two of the first that come to mind are next door to each other — **Scotland Yard** *(56 The Esplanade* ☎ *364-6577)* and **Brandy's** *(58 The Esplanade* ☎ *364-6671).* Near the **O'Keefe Centre**, they are large and busy, relics of a time when fake Tiffany lamps were obligatory decor. They have live entertainment other than karaoke on an irregular schedule. Several similar establishments also occupy the same block.

Up in Yorkville, seekers of companionship favor **Bellair Café** *(100 Cumberland St.* ☎ *964-2222)* for its sleek Manhattan look; food and outdoor tables, a live piano-and-bass duo until 10pm, then disco dancing upstairs. Not far away, **Hemingway's** *(142 Cumberland St.* ☎ *968-2828)* has an extensive following, attired in everything from jeans and tuxes to mink. In good weather, they spill out through the open front, onto sidewalk tables.

PUBS

Pubs, some of which must have been dismantled over there and reassembled over here, are encountered everywhere. Their names are right: **Spotted Dick** *(81 Bloor St.* ☎ *927-0843),* **Toad in the Hole** *(525 King St.* ☎ *593-8623),* the **Duke of Kent** *(2315 Yonge St.* ☎ *485-9507),* and **Duke of Gloucester** *(649 Yonge St.* ☎ *961-9704)* are just four. Inside, with their etched glass, brass chandeliers, flowered carpets, and beer pumps, they do their all to evoke Albion. The **Duke of York** *(39 Prince Arthur Ave.* ☎ *964-2441)* ups its authenticity with bangers and mash and pints of Watney's ale. A loyal neighborhood crowd partakes nightly.

WINE BARS

Wine bars never really caught on. One possibility worth trying, though, is **Raclette** *(361 Queen St. W* ☎ *593-0934).* They keep a score of bottles of white wines in a tub of ice at the front and another dozen or so reds arrayed on the back bar. Tastings are available. Their origins are as diverse as Australia, Argentina, and Bulgaria, with the usual stops in between. A short bar menu features soups, pâtés, fondues. The bar grows livelier as the evening wears on, while the attached dining room is usually near-empty.

Top rooms-with-views are the clubby **Roof Lounge** of the Park Plaza Hotel *(4 Avenue Rd.* ☎ *924-5471)* and the **Aquarius Lounge**, on the 51st floor of the ManuLife Centre *(55 Bloor St.* ☎ *967-5225)*. The former has an open terrace, and the Aquarius is a piano bar with a superb panorama of downtown Toronto. There is no cover charge. Either one is preferable to the frenetic nightclub at the top of the CN TOWER. Two hotel bars with nightly piano music are **Consort** in the KING EDWARD *(37 King St.* ☎ *863-9700)* and **Bosun's** in the RADISSON ADMIRAL *(259 Queen's Quay W* ☎ *364-5444)*, with a pleasing view of the harbor.

CABARETS AND DINNER THEATERS
Cabarets and dinner theaters feature comedy acts, magicians, Broadway musicals, showgirls, and men dressed as showgirls. Most of the following are closed Sunday and/or Monday.

La Cage Dinner Theatre *(279 Yonge St.* ☎ *364-5200)* has dinner and an elaborate revue with female impersonators. Most of the time, scaled-down productions of Broadway and West End musicals are the fare at **Limelight Dinner Theatre** *(2026 Yonge St.* ☎ *482-5200)*, but compilations and revues sometimes tread the boards.

A Little Night Magic is the name of the magic and comedy revue at **Harper's** *(26 Lombard St.* ☎ *863-6223)*, which has two dining rooms. Both grand illusions and up-close table tricks are performed.

At the same address is **The Laugh Resort Comedy Club** *(*☎ *364-5233)*, where single comedians and sketch and improvisational groups take turns. Paula Poundstone and Gilbert Gottfried are among the alumni, for those who follow these things. Tuesday is amateur night, for wannabe comics with steel-clad egos. Dinner-and-show packages are available.

His Majesty's Feast *(1926 Lakeshore Blvd.* ☎ *769-1165)* is one of those "historical" costume cabarets, with the requisite serving wenches, minstrels and mildly bawdy humor. The **Imperial Room** *(Royal York Hotel, 100 Front St. W* ☎ *368-6175)* is a throwback to the glossy supper clubs of a time now glimmering — the kind of place where Fred and Ginger might have twirled and tapped for the swells. Such big-time entertainers as Anne Murray and Tony Bennett have appeared there, although most acts and bands are of lesser wattage.

Martin Short, John Candy, Dan Aykroyd and Rick Moranis, among many, got their start at **Second City** *(110 Lombard St.* ☎ *863-1111)*. The present comedy corps performs its set pieces on weekends, and engages in often riotous improvisations Monday through Thursday. Dinner–show packages are available.

Yuk Yuk's is a comedy club empire with units all over English Canada, and four (at the last count) in Toronto. The two handiest for visitors are downtown *(1280 Bay St.* ☎ *967-6425)* and uptown *(2335 Yonge St.* ☎ *967-6425)*. The mix is of "name" comedians (Robin Williams and George Carlin have appeared) with neophytes, with no predicting what might happen on any given night. There are screamers, misogynists, macho men, man-haters. Some are funny.

Along the Queen St. W nightspot strip, the principal comedy outlet is **Big City** *(534 Queen St. W ☎867-8707)*. Small troupes specialize in parody and improvisation.

DANCE CLUBS AND DISCOS
Dance clubs and discos are no more stable here than in any other city, so always call or check the newspapers to confirm hours and attractions. Entrance policies aren't usually exclusory, but on busy nights there are lines at the doors, and regulars may be waved through before strangers. Most stay open until 2 or 3am, even though they must stop pouring liquor after 1am.

Berlin *(2335 Yonge St. ☎489-7777)* strives to suggest the glittery, prewar debauchery of its eponymous city. Its glossy crowd gladly forks over the steep admission charge, which discourages teenagers and pays for the live bands and professional dancers. The club's advertising asserts that Hollywood stars of the likes of Ann-Margret and Tom Selleck are frequent patrons.

The huge **Copa** *(21 Scollard St. ☎922-6500)* hasn't missed a gimmick, with its banks of TV monitors, laser lights, fashion shows, live bands and free buffets. More than 1,000 people can be accommodated at a time. Anyone who remembers the Moon landing will feel like an antique. **Down Towne Browne's** *(49 Front St. E ☎367-4949)* has dancing seven nights a week to a DJ, with live bands on weekend gigs. Young crowd and young eats — pizzas, burgers.

No ageism at **Studebaker's** *(150 Pearl St. ☎591-7960)*. There are almost as many grayheads as there are youngsters. A real Studebaker takes the place of honor, a relic of the same Fifties epoch that saw the birth of rock 'n' roll. The participants are animated and numerous, no doubt a result of the modest cover charge and uninflated prices. The records spun by the deejay for the central dance floor are less often of the early Elvis era than of the middle Stones. Speaking of whom, Mick Jagger has been known to drop by the **Squeeze Club Café** *(817 Queen St. W ☎365-9020)*, perhaps for the Fifties ambiance, maybe for the billiards and recorded rock.

The Big Bop *(651 Queen St. W ☎366-6699)* has no sign out front, just an inventive paint job. They have four floors to fill, so entrance is rarely a problem, despite the forbidding expressions worn by the doormen/bouncers. It's anti-glitz, almost retro, with its turning mirrored ball straight out of the Twenties. PIB's (People In Black) move themselves to danceable party rock that isn't at the cutting edge and isn't earsplitting. Several bars, pool tables, pinball machines.

JAZZ
There is enough **jazz** to keep enthusiasts happy. Several hotels bring in groups on weekends, and jazz brunch is a staple.

Among the more established rooms is the **Chelsea Bun** *(33 Gerrard St. W ☎595-1975)* in the **Delta Chelsea Inn**. Some bars and clubs irregularly schedule combos, but for jazz most nights of the week, try **Albert's Hall** *(481 Bloor St. W ☎964-0846)* for blues and some Dixie. Every night but Monday, **Bermuda Onion** *(131 Bloor St. W ☎925-1470)* puts on a mixed card of jazz, blues, and pop, by groups large and small.

    George's Spaghetti House *(290 Dundas St. E ☎923-9887)* is the oldest jazz spot in Toronto, featuring traditional chops by the popular Moe Koffman. **Meyers Deli** *(69 Yorkville Ave. ☎960-4780)* is the unlikely venue for trios and quartets, after 10pm on Friday and Saturday. No cover, fully licensed. **Café des Copains** *(48 Wellington St. ☎869-0148)* has a restaurant upstairs, jazz piano downstairs

    Downtown, **Senator** *(249 Victoria St. ☎364-7517)* has a restaurant on the ground floor, a bar featuring guitarists on the top floor, and contemporary jazz in between. Every night but Monday.

ROCK/POP/COUNTRY/FOLK

All the permutations of rock and pop, country and folk are found all over, in cramped cellars, warehouses, above restaurants. For one of the hottest, see the entry for **BAMBOO** (page 96). Similar, at least in heated Caribbean flavor, is **Real Jerk** *(709 Queen St. E ☎463-6906)*, as popular for its Jamaican edibles and Red Stripe beer as for its infectious reggae music. The slapdash decor suggests, rather than replicates, an island beachside music shack. A newer branch by the name of **The Real Jerk Pit** *(240 Richmond St. ☎593-0628)* observes the same fruitful formula. It charges a modest cover for dancing to records after 10pm.

    During the day, the outside of **Chick 'n' Deli** *(744 Mt. Pleasant Rd. ☎489-3363)* looks like just another anonymous takeout joint. At night, it bangs into life as a raunchy roadhouse, with an active dance floor and bands that range from hard-driving rock to blues. They play for a happy, ecumenical crowd of multi-ethnic pseudo-country boys in pointy-toed boots, and young execs that just doff their jackets and loosen their ties. Things are less frenetic, but good times are still to be had at **Chicago's** *(335 Queen St. ☎598-3301)*. Above the bar and restaurant, which has varied entertainers Tuesday and Wednesday, folks drink from long-neck bottles and attend to blues and early rock, Thursday to Sunday.

    Neon palm fronds still shimmer overhead at the old-time rock palace **El Mocambo** *(464 Spadina Ave. ☎922-1570)*. Live acts keep it thumping seven nights a week; many require variable cover charges, some are free. Actor-comedian Dan Aykroyd is the high-profile owner of the restaurant called **X-Ray**. The food is okay, but for alternative rock and funk go upstairs to the **Ultrasound Showbar** *(269 Queen St. W ☎591-7551)*. Not far away, the **Cameron Public House** *(408 Queen St. W ☎364-0811)* moves between alternative and industrial funk by groups called such things as the Nancy Sinatras and Courage of Lassie. Monday, though, is devoted to jazz.

    Club Bluenote *(128 Pears Ave. ☎921-1109)* is the place for top-drawer rhythm 'n' blues. **Spectrum** *(2714 Danforth Ave. ☎699-9913)* has live concerts most nights, with a super lightshow. **Horseshoe Tavern** *(370 Queen St. W ☎598-4753)* charges no admission to the bar in front, but a cover charge applies when live groups appear in the room at back. A sign on the wall reads "No polyester leisure suits after 10pm," a rule that is obviously enforced. A marginally older, more prosperous custom supports **The Devil's Martini** *(136 Simcoe* ☎ *591-7541)*. Open daily from mid-afternoon to 1am, it has good-sized rock bands of a conventional, non-threatening sort later in the evening.

Downtown near the O'Keefe Centre, the new **C'est What?** *(67 Front St. E* ☎ *867-9499)* is a casual basement club featuring self-accompanied folksingers and small pop and rock groups. Sometimes the customers actually listen. There are eight Ontario brews on tap.

Out at CANADA'S WONDERLAND (see page 63), an amusement park open only in summer months, the **Kingswood Music Theatre** presents appearances by an eclectic mix of touring musical acts on the order of B.B. King, James Taylor, and Kris Kross. Discounted combination concert and park tickets are available, but must be purchased in advance of the desired concert date.

Venues for really big names with substantial drawing power are SKYDOME, when the baseball Blue Jays and footballs Argonauts aren't in residence; **Maple Leaf Gardens**, when the hockey team is out of season or out of town; **Exhibition Stadium** on the CNE grounds, used for a variety of lesser sporting events since SkyDome opened; nearby ONTARIO PLACE, a lakeside amusement park of sorts; **Harbourfront**, which sponsors hundreds of free and low-cost concerts and performances; and the **O'Keefe Centre** *(Front and Yonge Sts.* ☎ *872-2262)*, devoted to theatrical and musical events.

The performing arts

Enthusiastic theater- and concert-goers run the risk of being immobilized by the magnitude of choices. Toronto's world-class symphony orchestra, ballet, and opera companies are at the vanguard of about 100 local musical groups, and there is a steady flow of touring organizations from other parts of Canada and abroad. The city by the lake has over 40 theaters, second in number only to New York, in which are mounted both *avant-garde* experiments and mainstream plays of a high professional caliber. Complicated and costly shows such as *The Phantom of the Opera* and *Les Misérables* have received lavish treatment.

Over 125 professional theater and dance companies take advantage of this hospitable climate for the arts, mounting an estimated 10,000 live performances yearly. In addition, long-running theater festivals honoring Shakespeare and George Bernard Shaw take place every summer in the nearby towns of Stratford and Niagara-on-the-Lake.

THEATER
Theater has undergone a remarkable renaissance over the last three decades. In 1962, there existed only two large theaters for live productions. Several grand old theaters were shuttered, dark and moldering

and little thought had been given to new facilities. The city-built **O'Keefe Centre** *(1 Front St. E, map 4E8 ☎393-7474)* opened in 1960, and the rescue soon after of the 1907 **Royal Alexandra** *(260 King St. W, map 3D7 ☎872-3333)* helped to focus the attention of the general public and the business community.

Another opening, in 1970, further consolidated interest — the **St Lawrence Centre for the Arts** *(27 Front St. E, map 4E8 ☎366-1656)*. Its two theaters have hosted such plays as *Crimes of the Heart* and *Kiss of the Spider Woman,* as well as recitals, lectures, and other events. An unusual pair of theaters stacked one atop the other, the 1913 **Elgin** and 1914 **Winter Garden** *(189 Yonge St., map 4D8 ☎594-0755),* were originally intended as vaudeville houses. With the growth in popularity of film, the Elgin was converted to a cinema and the Winter Garden was boarded up and forgotten for over half a century. In the 1980s, they were restored to their past glory, as was the similar **Pantages** *(244 Victoria St., map 4C8 ☎362-3218).* All three are now devoted to the production of mainstream musicals, comedies, and occasional dramas.

All this successful activity inspired others to look around for alternative venues. Performance spaces have been created out of factories, warehouses, stables, firehouses, deconsecrated churches, mansions. Among the more active are:

- **Alumnae Theatre**   70 Berkeley St. Map 4D9 ☎364-4170
- **Annex Theatre**   730 Bathurst St. Map 2A5 ☎537-4193
- **Factory Theatre**   125 Bathurst St. Map 3D5 ☎864-9971
- **du Maurier Theatre Centre**   231 Queen's Quay W. Map 3E7 ☎973-4000
- **Poor Alex**   296 Brunswick Ave. Map 3A6 ☎927-8998
- **Tarragon**   30 Bridgman Ave., off map 2A5 ☎531-1827
- **Theatre Passe Muraille**   16 Ryerson Ave. Map 3C5 ☎363-2416

These, and many of the thirty or more additional venues, specialize in offbeat or innovative performances that often defy categorization.

For current offerings, consult the entertainment weekly *NOW,* the Friday "What's On" section of *The Toronto Star,* or call the **Toronto Theatre Alliance** *(☎ 536-6468).*

CINEMA

Film has its major celebration during ten days each September, with the annual **Festival of Festivals** *(information ☎968-3456),* at which more than 250 new movies from around the world have their showcase. Coupon books and passes to specific blocks of films go on sale well in advance, and are often cheaper when purchased before August.

As attendance at the festival demonstrates, this is a city of serious film buffs. Toronto is, after all, the third-largest major film production center in North America and there is support for even the most obscure, camp, and/or inaccessible films from every corner of the world.

There are a number of repertory and art houses from which to choose. Programs often include series of movies on a particular theme, be it a genre or the work of a single director or actor. Features are changed frequently.

Venues include the following:

- **Bloor**   506 Bloor St. W. Map **2**B5   ☎532-6677
- **Cineforum**   463 Bathurst St.   ☎777-2022
- **Fox**   2236 Queen St. E   ☎691-7330
- **Kingsway**   3030 Bloor St. W   ☎236-1411
- **Nostalgic**   3030 Bloor St. W   ☎236-1411
- **Paradise**   1006 Bloor St. W   ☎537-7040
- **Revue**   400 Roncesvalles Ave. Off map **1**C1   ☎531-9959

For commercial films out of Hollywood and Europe, the giant Canadian cinema chain **Cinéplex Odeon** has its flagship facility in **Eaton Centre** (☎593-4535), with 17 screens and the ability to shuffle programs according to demand. On Tuesday, Cinéplex tickets are half-price.

DANCE

Toronto's dance companies perform in a number of venues, both indoors and out. The **National Ballet of Canada** (☎872-2262), with some 70 dancers, is the third-largest in North America. It has a classical foundation, but tackles modern works as well. In summer, it appears at Ontario Place; in winter, at the O'Keefe Centre. Contemporary forms are explored by the **Toronto Dance Theatre** (☎967-1365).

The **Première Dance Theatre** at Harbourfront (*Queen's Quay Terminal, map 3F7* ☎973-4000) enjoys the company's presence most of the year, and **Dancemakers** (☎535-8880) performs there too.

CLASSICAL MUSIC AND OPERA

Lovers of classical music and opera are abundantly served by as many as 100 local companies and musical organizations. Blessed with a mighty reputation, the **Canadian Opera Company** (☎872-2262) is also one of the largest in North America. Most of its performances are in the original language of the composer, but the company was one of the first to project librettos in English on a screen above the stage. Seven operas are staged each year at the **O'Keefe Centre** or the **Elgin Theatre**.

Of equal stature is the **Toronto Symphony Orchestra** (☎593-4828), which appears about ten months a year at **Roy Thomson Hall** (*60 Simcoe St., map 3D7* ☎598-4822), opened in 1981 and noted for its superb acoustics and unimpeded sightlines. In summer, the orchestra moves to Ontario Place. The orchestra often teams with the **Toronto Mendelssohn Choir** (☎598-0422), which has close on 200 singers, producing a heavenly sound that brings it into considerable demand around the world.

The recently restored 1894 **Massey Hall** (*178 Victoria St., map 3D8* ☎363-7301) serves as home to the **Toronto Philharmonic Orchestra** (☎971-9111).

Among other classical groups to look out for are **The Canadian Brass** (☎967-1421), the **Orford String Quartet** (☎861-8600), **The Chamber Players of Toronto** (☎862-8311) and the **Tafelmusik Baroque Orchestra** (☎964-6337), which plays on original period instruments.

Toronto:
shopping

Every human need

Even the most aggressively acquisitive shopper could not exhaust the possibilities here. Every reasonable need, and most frivolous ones, can be met in a retailing environment that takes every step from deepest discounts in 3rd-floor walkups to hushed emporia so rarefied that it's boorish to inquire about prices.

WHERE TO GO
Shops are found everywhere, of course. But there are several highly attractive concentrations along particular streets and in enclosed malls where almost every want can be satisfied.

Eaton Centre *(map 4C8)* is said to be the number one tourist attraction in Toronto, a claim proved by the throngs that course through it 12 hours a day. The enclosed 4-tiered mall contains more than 300 shops and eating places, a 17-screen cinema, and the mother Eaton's department store *(open Mon–Fri 9am–9pm, Sat 9am–6pm, closed Sun)*, which occupies nine floors. The complex runs three full blocks between Dundas in the N and Queen to the S, and is connected to Underground Toronto and **The Bay** department store (formerly Simpson's), opposite on Queen. Goods are primarily mid-priced popular brands, with some luxury items, and names include **Marks & Spencer**, **Bally**, and **Jaeger**.

Bloor St. *(map 3A7–4A8)*, W of Yonge to a little beyond Avenue Rd., is home to two major department stores and many famous international retailers. The **Holt Renfrew Centre** incorporates the eponymous department store and 37 satellite shops on three levels. Among the latter are **Bally Shoes** and **William Ashley China**. It connects with the subway and **The Bay**, across the street.

Walking W, dozens of stores offer the products of such leading names as Burberrys and Ralph Lauren. Men's clothiers **Harry Rosen** *(#80)* and **Stollery's** *(#1)* are two to look for, as is **Liptons** *(#50)*, representing a number of Canadian designers for women. **European Jewelry** *(#111)* carries Rolex and Cartier. High-profile single-brand stores are numerous, including **Gucci**, **Tiffany**, **Cartier**, **Louis Vuitton**, **Chanel**, **Hermès**, **Georg Jensen**; there is also a **Marks & Spencer**.

Yorkville *(off map 3A7)* is bounded on the S by Bloor St., but has a different identity. Its stores are no less upscale, but they are a bit less glittery, more iconoclastic. A good place to start is **Hazelton Lanes** *(55 Avenue Rd.)*, a relatively small 2-story mall that contains a number of "name" boutiques (including **Hermès** and **Yves St-Laurent**) and many fine Canadian clothiers. Look for **Andrew's** and **Alan Cherry** for high fashion for women from such European designers as Armani and Mugler. Afterward, it can be rewarding to browse along Yorkville Ave. E to Yonge and then (one block S) W on Cumberland St., as much for the lively street scene as for the shops.

Queen St. W *(map 3D6)* follows a different drummer, at least between John St. and Spadina Ave. The street signs are subtitled "Fashion District," and there are clothing options, from studded suede minidresses to vintage cloche hats to those filmy blouses that only the most confident or oblivious women can wear in public.

But the street is hardly single-minded. It has affinities with New York's SoHo and London's King's Road — youthful, arty, quirky — and along its bumptious way can be found laptop computers, saxophones, chess sets, penguin pull-toys, military prints, compact discs, tofu burgers, and 53 of the 55 volumes of the complete works of Balzac. Many shops feature Canadian designers, including **Club Monaco** *(#403)*, **Ms. Emma** *(#275)*, **Le Château** *(#336)* and **Emily Zarb** *(#276)*. For furs and leathers often at near-wholesale prices, continue W and turn right (N) on Spadina. There are more than a dozen furriers between there and Sullivan St.

Harbourfront *(map 3E7)* has many shops spaced between its restaurants and marinas, and nearly all are open on Sunday. Two buildings in particular deserve attention. **Queen's Quay Terminal** *(☎363-4411)*, near the middle of the waterfront strip, is a converted warehouse that now shelters over 100 boutiques, crafts booths, a theater and restaurants. At the W end of Queen's Quay W is the **Harbourfront Antique Market** *(☎340-8377; closed Mon)*, with more than 100 permanent dealers selling every imaginable object and collectible from the last 150 years. Find estate jewelry, duck decoys, country furniture, silverware, art glass, and, as they say, "much, much more." Most accept credit cards. On Sunday, at least 100 more exhibitors set up shop on the pier across the street.

Several **museums** have excellent shops, with art reproductions, books, crafts, gift ideas, cards, calendars, and souvenirs, usually of high quality, if not low price. In particular, seek out those at BLACK CREEK PIONEER VILLAGE, GARDINER MUSEUM OF CERAMIC ART, and the ROYAL ONTARIO MUSEUM.

Finally, there is **Honest Ed's Emporium**, at the corner of Bloor St. W and Markham St. Ed Mirvish, Toronto's most visible millionaire merchant, is a presence impossible to ignore. His empire includes the Royal Alexandra Theatre and several restaurants, as well as his retail enterprises, and Ed won't let anyone forget it. The fount of his fortune is this sprawling store, covered with signs and racing lights only slightly less gaudy than downtown Las Vegas. There, he peddles low-end housewares and related products. Signs on the walls reflect the founder's idea of wit: "Please don't bother our help. They have their own problems." Nearby is **Mirvish Village**, a block of houses between Bloor and Lennox, leased by Ed to private retailers. Most exercise more restraint than their landlord, selling books, antiques, discount clothes.

A walk W on Bloor is a plunge into ethnic Toronto, with seemingly a restaurant for every one of its 70 national groups.

USEFUL TO KNOW

- **Making payments**: Credit cards are widely accepted; personal checks drawn on out-of-town banks are not.
- **Obtaining tax refunds**: Keep receipts for all purchases. Both a provincial sales tax and a 7 percent federal Goods and Services Tax are charged on nearly every item, but foreign visitors can apply for refunds for much, if not all of it. See PRACTICAL INFORMATION on page 29 for fuller details.
- **Opening hours**: Despite continued resistance, much of it from the provincial government, Toronto's blue laws forbidding Sunday shopping are crumbling. Stores in such tourist areas as Harbourfront are allowed to be open, and larger stores are either defying the ban or rallying support to have it repealed.

    As a rule, though, store hours are 9 or 10am–6pm Monday to Saturday, with one late night until 8 or 9pm, usually Thursday. Eaton Centre and the stores of Underground Toronto stay open until 9pm Monday to Friday.

WHAT TO BUY

All the major international names are represented — Ralph Lauren, Hermès, St-Laurent, Turnbull & Asser, Bulgari, Jaeger, Charles Jourdan, Cartier and Vuitton, to drop a few. There is no particular advantage to buying a $600 sweater or $250 shoes here, however. Better buys, not for their cheapness but for their generally excellent quality, are **Canadian crafts**, **antique country furniture**, and **clothes** by native designers and bespoke tailors. **Mennonite quilts**, **Inuit sculptures** and **Amerindian weavings** are delightful.

Toronto shares leadership in the Canadian fashion industry with Montréal, resulting in wide selections of both men's and women's clothing as stylishly conservative or as head-turningly visionary as might be desired.

Every human need can be satisfied in at least one of Toronto's malls and shopping districts, but here follows a brief selection of stores that might fill your special requirements.

Antiques

- **Allery**   322 Queen St. W ☎593-0853. Maps and prints, most more than a century old, and authenticated. Good prices.
- **Atelier Art and Antiques**   588 Markham St. ☎532-9244. Vintage folk art — wood carvings, weather vanes, duck decoys.
- **Journey's End**   612 Markham St. ☎536-2226. Part of the Mirvish Village complex around the corner from Ed's main store. Selling china, silver, and oddments for nearly 30 years.
- **R.A. O'Neil Antiques**   100 Avenue Rd. ☎968-2806. Pine furniture and accessories of mostly Canadian origin.
- **Primrose Lane**   1258 Yonge St. ☎969-8855. Specialist in Victoriana, including furniture, silver and china.
- **Sandy's Antiques**   3130 Bathurst St. ☎787-5230. Substantial discounts on silver, much of it pre-1900.

Arts and crafts

- **Algonquians**   670 Queen St. W ☎368-1336. Amerindian masks, carvings, handknit sweaters, quill boxes and other indigenous crafts.
- **Clay Design Studio**   170 Brunswick Ave. ☎964-3330. Contemporary Canadian ceramicists, potters, custom jewelers.
- **Dexterity**   173 King St. E ☎367-4775. Ceramics, furniture, glass and clothing.
- **The Guild Shop**   140 Cumberland St. ☎921-1721. Canadian crafts in all materials, and a selection of Inuit sculptures, and native crafts. Run by the Ontario Crafts Council. Another branch in Terminal 3 at Pearson Airport.
- **The Isaacs/Inuit Gallery** 9 Prince Arthur Ave. ☎921-9985. Antique and contemporary Inuit and Amerindian carvings, prints and wall-hangings.
- **Prime Canadian Crafts**   229 Queen St. W ☎593-5750. Vintage and contemporary Canadiana, including pottery and folk art.

Books and magazines

- **Bakka Science Fiction**   282 Queen St. W ☎596-8161. Claims to be Canada's largest seller of new and used sci-fi.
- **The Book Cellar**   142 Yorkville Ave. ☎925-9955, open Sunday. Across from the Four Seasons Hotel. International newspapers and magazines as well as books.
- **Albert Britnell Book Shop**   765 Yonge St. ☎924-3321. Nirvana for bibliophiles is this cozy retreat dating from 1893.
- **Can-Do Bookstore**   311 Queen St. W ☎977-2351. Everything for the hobbyist and do-it-yourselfer: woodworking, cooking, crafts, plumbing, modelmaking, and much more.
- **The Children's Book Store**   604 and 597 Markham St. ☎535-7011. Author appearances and readings. Audio and video cassettes.
- **The Cookbook Store**   850 Yonge St. ☎920-2665. Every cuisine, every taste, the books supplemented with videos and magazines.
- **Edwards Book and Art**   170 Bloor St. W ☎961-2428 and 356 Queen St. W ☎593-0126. Two locations of a small chain emphasizing art books, but not ignoring other categories.
- **Lichtman's**   144 Yonge St. ☎368-7390 and 595 Bay St. ☎591-1617. These are two of several branches, all carrying expansive selections of magazines and foreign newspapers, as well as current books. Open daily, including Sunday.
- **World's Biggest Bookstore**   20 Edward St. ☎977-7009. Near Eaton Centre; open 7 days. Perhaps the claim is hyperbole, but with 1 million volumes, there's little point in disputing it.

Toronto: recreation

Toronto for children

For all its recent press as Canada's first world city and the glossy cosmopolitanism that implies, Toronto remains, as it has always been, a family town. With its marvelous zoo, exciting theme parks and entertainments geared to the young set, no child ever need be bored. Some of the best of these are outlined here.

Refer to entries in SIGHTS A TO Z, NIGHTLIFE AND ENTERTAINMENT and SPORTS, and look for the ✿ symbol, indicating things especially suitable for children.

AMUSEMENT PARKS AND ZOOS
At the very top of any list for parents with kids in tow must be the METRO ZOO and CANADA'S WONDERLAND. Each should be allotted the better part of a day because they have much to offer and are both at some distance from downtown. In addition, there is the **African Lion Safari** (☎ 519-623-2620). About an hour's drive w of Toronto, it is a drive-through game park where lions, zebras, giraffes and many other species roam freely, some of them approaching to put their noses against car windows.

Downtown, ONTARIO PLACE has rides and activities in its Children's Village, including an area where, if parents allow, they can get deliriously soaked with hoses and water pistols. **Centre Island** has an intentionally old-fashioned amusement park and a petting zoo. HIGH PARK also has a small zoo. The ONTARIO SCIENCE CENTRE, with its array of razzle-dazzle hands-on exhibits, is as entertaining as an amusement park, and is educational, to boot.

BOAT TRIPS AND RIDES
The **ferry** to the Toronto Islands has an unobstructed view of the skyline. The glass **elevators** that shoot up the outsides of the WESTIN HARBOUR CASTLE hotel and the HILTON INTERNATIONAL are free. There is a fee for the ride to the top of the CN TOWER, but kids will never get higher off the ground without boarding an airplane. The very young may find it frightening.

Boats providing narrated 1–1½-hour harbor cruises depart from several piers along Harbourfront. The **Wilderness Adventure Ride** at ONTARIO PLACE is a treat. And kids who have never seen one are bound to get a kick out of riding the **subway**.

EVENTS AND ENTERTAINMENTS

HARBOURFRONT celebrates an **International Children's Festival** and has **fireworks** on Victoria Day. Both happen in May. There are more pyrotechnics on Canada Day (July 1st) at ONTARIO PLACE and HARBOUR-FRONT. In late July arrives the colorful **Caribana West Indian Festival**, with parades, music, and dancing in the streets, which take place at various locations (☎ 925-5435). Mid-August sees the opening of the **Canadian National Exhibition** at Exhibition Place, with a carnival midway, rides, big-name rock concerts and an air show.

A stop at the big windows of the **City TV** building at the corner of Queen St. W and John St. might energize children bored with people-watching in Toronto's bohemia. Depending on the time of day, they can see functioning studios, live shows, and interviews with rock musicians. For a small fee, they can record their opinions on almost any subject on an outdoor "VideoBooth."

SHOWS AND THEATER

In a category all its own is the **Tour of the Universe** (☎ 364-2019; *hours may vary, so call ahead),* at the base of the CN TOWER. It simulates a 21stC spaceport, with the employees acting as futuristic "commanders" and "pilots." There is a lot of hokum involved, which can prove irritating to adults who aren't in a playful mood, but the climax takes the form of a very effective "voyage" into space, fraught with danger and close calls.

The **Laser Theatre** and **Theatre of the Stars** at the MCLAUGHLIN PLANETARIUM provide a great spectacle for older children. **Young People's Theatre** *(165 Front St. E, map 4D9* ☎ *864-9732)* and the **Puppet Centre** *(171 Avondale Rd.* ☎ *222-9029)* offer a variety of winning productions. Reservations are usually required.

Sports in Toronto

Canadians are intensely involved in their games, both as spectators and participants. While hockey is the undisputed national sport, enthusiasm is nearly as great for baseball and football, and cycling and skiing consume active leisure hours.

AUTO RACING

The grounds of the Canadian National Exhibition and nearby streets *(map 1 E3)* are the site in mid-July of the **Molson Indy** (☎ *595-5445).* Cars are of the Indianapolis 500 variety, rather than Formula One, and they reach speeds approaching 200mph. Tickets are available, at varying prices, for the several segments of the 3-day event.

BASEBALL

Apart from the bleats of purists who think baseball should be played on grass rather than carpet, there is no better facility in which to watch baseball than the splendid new SKYDOME *(map 3E6, tickets and information* ☎ *341-1111).* Sightlines are exceptional, and the retractable roof ensures that no games are called on account of rain. Not that poor weather and the considerably less desirable old Exhibition Stadium ever discouraged the fans of the Toronto Blue Jays. They are one of only two Canadian teams in Major League Baseball, and were the first non-US club to reach and win the so-called World Series in 1992, setting new attendance records along the way. Only hockey holds a higher place in the hearts of Torontonians.

BOATING
Rowboats, canoes and/or pedalboats are available for rent at ONTARIO PLACE, at the pond in HIGH PARK, and on Centre Island, in the harbor. See also SAILING AND SAILBOARDING.

BOWLING
A Canadian version of the game employs five pins. Several establishments offer both this and the more familiar ten-pin version, including **Plantation Bowlerama** *(5837 Yonge St.* ☎ *222-4657)* and **Thorncliffe Bowlerama** *(45 Overlea Blvd.* ☎ *421-2211).* They are at some distance from the downtown district, however.

CYCLING
Toronto is an enthusiastic cycling city, with many miles of carefully laid-out routes in the city and its parks. One of the most popular is the 19-km (12-mile) **Martin Goodman Trail**, which runs along the waterfront past Ontario Place and Harbourfront. HIGH PARK and the TORONTO ISLANDS are easily accessible. Make a call to the **Toronto Bicycling Network** *(* ☎ *766-1985)* for updates on cycling news and special events. The Parks Department *(* ☎ *392-8186)* provides maps of its trails, and free street guides and newsletters are available in bicycle stores.

From May to September, bicycles are available for rental on **Centre Island** *(* ☎ *365-7901)* and also at **McBride's** *(180 Queen's Quay W, map 3E7* ☎ *367-5651).*

Bicycles are allowed on subway trains except during rush hours, and on the Toronto Islands ferries, with some weekend restrictions. Most riders wear helmets, and a law requiring them is pending. Cyclists are expected to observe the same traffic laws as motor vehicles.

FISHING
Lake Ontario has a substantial trout-and-salmon fishery, courtesy of diligent stocking by wildlife management departments. Scores of charter boats are available in and near the city for half- and full-day expeditions. Call **Ontario Travel** *(900 Bay St.* ☎ *965-4008),* or stop by their office for information on regulations and licenses. Unfortunately, Lake Ontario is badly polluted and caution must be exercised in eating any fish caught in it.

The cheapest fishing is at the ponds in HIGH PARK and on the TORONTO ISLANDS, both of which are open to casual anglers.

FITNESS CENTERS

Finding a place to work out isn't easy in a strange city, if the hotel doesn't have its own fitness center. Many in Toronto do, or have arrangements for their guests with nearby health clubs. Three that have especially good facilities, with exercycles, weight circuits, pools and saunas are the WESTIN HARBOUR CASTLE, the SHERATON CENTRE, and the FOUR SEASONS INN ON THE PARK. Look for the ♥ symbol in WHERE TO STAY on pages 83–92 or ask when making hotel reservations.

Otherwise, the **YMCA** *(20 Grosvenor St.* ☎ *921-5171 and 2532 Yonge St.* ☎ *487-7151)* allows use of its facilities for a low daily fee. At Grosvenor St., there are weight rooms, running track, pool, and squash and racquetball courts; the one at Yonge St. has only workout classes.

Pay-as-you-sweat arrangements can also be made at the **Downtown Tennis Club** *(21 Eastern Ave.* ☎ *362-2439),* the **Adelaide Club** *(King and Bay Sts.* ☎ *367-9957),* and at the **Premier Health and Fitness Club** *(675 Yonge St.* ☎ *323-9259).*

FOOTBALL

Canadian football looks and plays very much like the American version, with minor variations in scoring, the number of downs (three instead of four), and the dimensions of the field. The local professional team is the up-and-down **Toronto Argonauts**, which plays at the SKYDOME *(* ☎ *595-1131).* Two of the team's owners are hockey superstar Wayne Gretzky and comic actor John Candy.

Attendance at Canadian Football League games is dwindling and there are repeated rumors of impending collapse. Montréal has already abandoned the sport. Part of the cause is the growing appeal of the gaudier American university and professional game, beamed across the border on television and radio from mid-summer to late January. The CFL season ends in November with the Grey Cup championship.

GOLF

The **Canadian Open** is held at **Glen Abbey Golf Club** in Oakville *(map 5 D2* ☎ *844-1800).* Municipal courses within Metro Toronto are **Don Valley Golf Course** *(4200 Yonge St.* ☎ *392-2465),* **Humber Valley Golf Course** *(40 Beattie Ave.* ☎ *392-2488),* and **Lakeview Golf Course** *(Lakeshore Blvd. W, map 5 C3* ☎ *278-4411).* All are 18-hole courses with inexpensive green fees. Glen Abbey is a par 73, Don Valley is a par 71, the others, par 70. Some of the courses are located on the map of METROPOLITAN TORONTO on pages 48–49.

For information about other area courses open to the public, call **Ontario Travel** *(* ☎ *965-4008).*

HOCKEY

The **Toronto Maple Leafs** haven't been contenders for the hallowed Stanley Cup trophy for more than two decades. That doesn't deter their rabidly loyal fans from buying all the seats for every face-off at the **Maple Leaf Gardens** venue *(60 Carlton St., map 4 B8* ☎ *977-1641).* This, after all, may be *the* year. The hotel concierge may be able to get tickets.

HORSE-RACING

Followers of both thoroughbreds and trotters are well-served. **Woodbine Race Track** *(Highway 27 and Rexdale Blvd., map 5 C2* ☎*675-6110)* hosts the legendary Queen's Plate in July. Its seasons are late April to early August and September to October. **Harness-racing**, with both pacers and trotters, meets three times a year at the venerable **Greenwood Race Track** *(1669 Queen St. E, map 6 B4* ☎*698-3131)*. **Mohawk Raceway** *(Highway 401 W, off map 5 D1* ☎*854-2255)* has an enclosed grandstand for comfortable viewing of standard-bred harness races in fall and spring meetings. For locations, see also the map of METROPOLITAN TORONTO on pages 48–49.

RUNNING

Many of the same trails used for cycling (see CYCLING above) are excellent for runners. The boardwalk of the community known as THE BEACHES, E of downtown on Queen St., is another possibility. For advice, call the Parks Department *(☎392-8186)*.

SAILING AND SAILBOARDING

Boats and windsurfers dance across the harbor every warm day of summer and into gray October. A favored push-off point is THE BEACHES community, E of downtown. Sailboards can be rented from **Wind Promotions** *(☎694-6881)*, who are located at the W end of the boardwalk. A good source of information about both sailing and sailboarding (or windsurfing) is the **Ontario Sailing Association** *(☎495-4240)*.

SKATING

Toronto makes the most (or the best) of its winters, with more than 125 artificial and natural rinks. All are free. Perhaps the most popular is the frozen reflecting pool in **Nathan Phillips Square**, in front of the new City Hall, while the largest is at HARBOURFRONT. Skate rentals are available at both. There is at least one rink in every neighborhood, and many more in the parks *(for information on locations* ☎*392-7251)*. Most are open from 9 or 10am until 10pm Monday to Saturday, and until 6pm Sunday. For indoor skating, there is a rink at the **Hazelton Lanes** shopping mall in Yorkville.

SKIING

While there are a number of good slopes for downhill skiing, equipped with lifts, within 2 hours of downtown, there are also slopes in town that can be satisfying and also reduce expenditure of time and money. **Earl Bales Park** *(☎224-6411)* is one option, with four short runs and it offers rentals; **Centennial Park Ski Hill** *(☎394-8750)* is another, offering T-bar lifts and rentals.

Those who demand greater challenges and have the time, can call **Ontario Travel** *(☎965-4008)* for suggestions.

One delightful possibility for some cross-country skiing is the METRO ZOO *(☎392-5900)*, where the whimsically named Zooski Trails curl around the animals. A fee is charged; they have rentals. **HIGH PARK, Tommy Thomson Park**, and the TORONTO ISLANDS are free and closer.

Call the Parks Department *(☎ 392-8186)* for advice. For ski conditions ☎963-2992.

SOCCER

There's no telling how long the latest attempt at a professional soccer league will last, but the game known as football on every other continent can be seen at **Varsity Stadium** *(Bloor St. W and Bedford, map 3A7 ☎ 979-2186)*.

SWIMMING

Lake Ontario, sadly, is polluted, and its beaches are often closed as a result. The water is quite cold, too. Even so, there are many popular beaches, if only for spending a day in the sun. To the E of downtown is the aptly named BEACHES community, with a boardwalk and sailboard rentals. For great views of the city while taking a dose of vitamin D in its most palatable form, the beaches of the TORONTO ISLANDS can't be bettered.

In addition, the Parks Department operates 50 indoor and outdoor pools in various venues *(for locations ☎ 392-7259)*. Visitors might have little need for these, since most of the larger hotels have their own pools, which are usually much less crowded.

TENNIS

The **National Tennis Centre** *(☎ 665-9777)* on the York University campus is the setting every summer for the Player's Canadian Championship. For amateurs, there are free courts in several city parks and on the TORONTO ISLANDS, many of them illuminated for night play.

The **Ontario Tennis Association** *(☎ 495-4215)* is also a useful source of information. Call the Parks Department *(☎392-7291)* for locations and hours.

Montréal

Montréal: foreign yet familiar

To call Montréal a city possessed of a dual personality is a willful act of understatement. It is much more. Just when it seems to have arranged itself tidily under the aphoristic banners routinely assigned to it — "the Old Country next door" that is "big on life" — Montréal rears up and reveals yet another of its many aspects. Contrast and contradiction are the real rewards it grants to explorers of its variegated *quartiers*. True, it melds the comfort of the familiar with the tang of the foreign.

At first look, the glass-and-steel towers of its commercial district may seem interchangeable with any middle-sized metropolis on the American continent. Yet this is the second-largest French-speaking city in the world, a mighty distinction from Boston or Cincinnati. Hundreds of miles from the ocean, it is nevertheless a major port, gateway to the inland seas called the Great Lakes. In the very shadow of the pronounced modernity of its thriving downtown is a living remnant of the frontier settlement of three centuries ago. As New World Gallic as it undeniably is, with its French signs and names and *pâtisseries* serving bowls of *café au lait,* the city retains decidedly Anglophile neighborhoods and makes room for enclaves that live and breathe the Eastern European and Asian origins of their inhabitants. The only course is to settle back and revel in Montréal's diversity.

Montréal is an island, too, the whole of which constitutes a metropolitan area of 29 towns and cities and 2.8 million people. Over 65 percent are Francophone, 20 percent Anglophone, and the rest command some other first language. The ubiquitous city emblem seen hanging from lampposts reflects the origins of its first residents. The design combines a French *fleur-de-lis,* an English rose, a Scottish thistle and an Irish shamrock. In the classic pattern of immigration, those settlers were soon joined by Germans, Poles, Slavs and Italians, and followed in more recent decades by West Indians, Chinese, Greeks, Latin Americans, and refugees from south and southeast Asia. Given the inherent possible tensions, they show a remarkably high level of inter-ethnic tolerance.

A form of regional government extends train lines and public services well into the suburbs, so municipal boundaries blur. The part of the city that is of most interest to visitors, however, is relatively compact, and an enthusiastic walker can cover most of it in three days. It is dominated by Mont-Royal, simply "The Mountain" to residents. It looks taller than it is, due to the flat river plain from which it rises, and the illuminated cross at its peak is a landmark seen from every part of the city.

The British came, saw — and conquered — in 1760. Blvd. St-Laurent came eventually to be the north–south dividing line between French Montréal to the east and English Montréal to the west. There are still two school systems, one Catholic, one Protestant, as well as French and English universities.

So, while geographical demarcations have been overwhelmed by events, the Anglophone culture prevails in its traditional redoubts, despite streets now called rue Crescent and rue Mackay, while the Latin Quarter of St-Denis is as French as the Parisian Left Bank.

Montréal: practical information

Getting around

FROM THE AIRPORTS TO THE CITY

There are two principal airports serving Montréal.

Dorval *(map 11 D3)*   Flights from the US and other parts of Canada are handled at Dorval, which is 22km (14 miles) w of downtown. The **Autobus Aéro Plus** *(☎ 514-633-1100)* makes the trip in about 30 minutes. It leaves Dorval every 20 minutes and stops at four large downtown hotels before reaching its final destination, the **Voyageur Terminal** *(505 blvd. de Maisonneuve E, map 8 C4 ☎ 514-842-2281)*, where there is the Berri-UQAM Metro station. The fare for this journey is moderate.

Metered taxis from the airport cost twice as much, before tip, and limousines still more.

Mirabel *(map 11 B1)*   Most international flights from countries other than the US land at Mirabel airport, 55km (34 miles) NW of the city.

The **Autobus** operates on a similar schedule from there, and its fare is about the same as for Dorval, despite the greater distance. **Taxis and limousines** are considerably more expensive, however.

Cars can be rented at both airports.

PUBLIC TRANSPORTATION

Metro and bus   The integrated bus and Metro transit system is superb. The **Metro** is clean, safe, and swift and its routes are easy to understand. There are four lines in operation, with a fifth nearing completion. Where the routes intersect, transfer to another line is free, as is transfer between connecting buses and Metro trains. Ask the bus driver for a transfer ticket upon debarking; in Metro stations, transfer tickets are dispensed from machines to be found just beyond the turnstiles.

Fares   The fare is for a trip of any length, and is not graduated according to distance. Buying a book of six tickets reduces the cost of each trip. Bus fares must be paid in exact change, but Metro tickets are accepted.

Times   The trains run between 5.30am and about 12.30am, although bus schedules vary.

Trains   **Amtrak** trains *(☎ 800-426-8725)* coming from the US, and **Via Rail** trains *(☎ 514-871-1331)* from other parts of Canada, arrive at the downtown **Gare Central** *(935 de la Gauchetière, map 10 F4 ☎ 800-361-5390)*.

TRAVELING BY CAR

Stories of the devil-may-care habits of Québec drivers are somewhat overdrawn. In the main, they are courteous and orderly, apart from a propensity for tire-screeching starts and stops. They are, however, less likely than drivers in Toronto to heed the rights of pedestrians in crosswalks.

Traffic flow   Except during the morning and evening rush hours, traffic flows at tolerable levels. Major arteries are broad and well-marked, and only the streets of the historic district of Vieux Montréal are uncomfortably narrow.

Parking   Many of the downtown shopping complexes have their own underground parking lots. There are also plenty of parking lots and garages, and these are not too expensive. Much downtown street parking is metered, and street signs show where and when parking is permitted. Note that the meters are positioned several feet back from the curb so that they are not covered by the banks of snow thrown up by plows after winter storms.

Car rental   Renting a car is fairly expensive, but discounted weekend packages are available. Most large hotels have at least one agency office in or near their lobbies, and the concierge can make arrangements to have cars delivered. The prominent company associated with National Car Rental in the US is **Tilden**, but the other major international firms are also represented.

Laws   See LAWS AND REGULATIONS on page 35.

TAXIS

For short distances, walk; for long trips, take the bus or Metro. In between, use cabs. While taxi fares are not exorbitant by current international standards, neither are they a bargain. A trip from downtown to such outlying attractions as the Olympic Stadium looks deceptively short on maps, but the meter clicks merrily away and the final bite can easily equal that of a good meal.

Taxis are sedans of no particular type or color, but with plastic roof lights that are illuminated at night if they are available for hire. They can be hailed in the streets or found at stands outside hotels and other important sites. Many are radio-dispatched, so they arrive fairly quickly if called from a restaurant or theater.

CALÈCHES

Horsedrawn open carriages are an anachronism in most modern cities, but somehow less so in Montréal, especially in the old quarter. They gather there at **Place Jacques-Cartier** and, less often, at **Dorchester Square** in downtown. The season depends on the weather. In winter, horses wait at Beaver Lake to pull sleighs around the parklands of Mont-Royal, as romantic an enterprise as might be imagined. Prices are steep, but sometimes negotiable.

Useful addresses

TOURIST INFORMATION
Useful free information on Montréal and Québec province can be obtained in the UK, the US and Canada. See TOURIST INFORMATION on page 30 for addresses.

- **By telephone or mail**   For all postal and telephone inquiries, contact **Greater Montréal Convention and Tourism Bureau** *(1555 Peel St., Suite 600, Montréal, Québec H3A 1X6)* ☎ *514-873-2015 in Montréal or* ☎ *800-363-7777 from other parts of Canada and the US).*
- **From the US or the UK**   See page 31.
- **In person**   Visit the main tourist office, **Infotouriste** *(1001 rue du Square-Dorchester, near Peel, map 10 F4; open daily except Dec 25 and Jan 1).* There is also a branch office in Vieux Montréal on Place Jacques-Cartier *(174 Notre-Dame E, map 8 D5),* and others at Dorval and Mirabel airports.
- **American Express Travel Service**   Offices of American Express Travel Service are located in the downtown Bay department store *(map 8 E4* ☎ *281-4777)* and also at 1141 de Maisonneuve W *(map 9 F3* ☎ *284-3300).*

  American Express offers a valuable source of information for any traveler in need of help, advice or emergency services.

TELEPHONE SERVICES
Daily events   ☎352-2500 (English) ☎353-2000 (French)
Sports and recreation   ☎872-6211
Road conditions outside Montréal   ☎873-4121
Travel information (Québec)   ☎873-2015
Weather   ☎636-3026

TOUR OPERATORS
- **Amphi-Tour**   ☎386-1298. An amphibious bus tours the city on land, then waddles into the river and cruises around the harbor.
- **Delco Aviation**   ☎663-4311. At Laval — seaplane rides.
- **Grey Line**   ☎934-1222. Variety of bus tours departing from Square Dorchester and major downtown hotels.
- **Guidatour**   ☎844-4021. Walking tours for groups and individuals and "step-on" guides using client's vehicle.
- **Heritage Montréal**   ☎842-8678. Several tours with preservationist architectural slant.
- **Hertz Tourist Guides**   ☎937-6690 or 739-3844. Walks, and multilingual "step-on" guides.
- **Step-on Guides**   ☎935-5131. Walking tours of Old Montréal and the Underground City; 3 hour tours in your car.
- **Les Tours Diamant**   ☎744-3009. Walking tours for large groups, car tours for small groups.
- **Tours Guidés de Montréal**   ☎484-0104. Walks, step-on guides, and bus tours in Montréal, Québec City and the Laurentians.

RIVER TRIPS

- **Le Bateau-Mouche** Jacques-Cartier Pier in the Old Port, map **8D6** ☎849-9952. Daytime and 3-hour dinner cruises for up to 160 passengers, in glass-enclosed boats.
- **Croisières du Port de Montréal** Victoria Pier in the Old Port map **8C6** ☎842-3871. Variety of cruises featuring brunch, supper, night excursions and day trips; mid-May to mid-October.
- **Lachine Rapids Tours** Victoria Pier, 105 de la Commune St. W, map **8C6** ☎284-9607. White-water trip over the upriver rapids, end of April to October 1.
- **Croisière Louisiane** Alexandra Pier in the Old Port, map **8E6** ☎397-1001. Cruises of varying lengths, in a replica of a 19thC steamboat. April 19–November 1, 4 times daily.

MAIN POST OFFICE
1025 St-Jacques Map **10F4** ☎283-2567.

LIBRARIES
Bibliothèque Nationale du Québec Three locations: 1700 St-Denis, map **8C4** ☎873-4553; 125 Sherbrooke W, map **7D3** ☎873-0270; 449 de l'Esplanade, map **8D4** ☎873-3065. Closed Sunday, Monday.
Montréal Central Library 1210 Sherbrooke E, map **7B3** ☎872-5923. Largest of 24 branches, with collections on history of French Canada. Open daily.

LOCAL PUBLICATIONS
The *Montréal Gazette* is the primary English-language newspaper. Its Thursday and Friday editions carry useful entertainment sections listing the week's concerts, theatrical performances and club schedules. *En Ville* is a free magazine distributed by hotels and is more complete than most examples of the breed. Hotel newsstands often sell major US and European newspapers and periodicals, but a generally better source is the **Maison de la Presse Internationale** *(550 Ste-Catherine, map 8E4* ☎*842-3857 and other branches).* French-language papers are *La Presse, Le Devoir* and *Le Journal de Montréal.*

Emergency information

Police, fire, ambulance ☎911
No coins are needed for pay phones.

HOSPITALS WITH EMERGENCY ROOMS
Hôpital général de Montréal 1650 Cedar, map **9G2** ☎937-6011
Hôpital Royal Victoria 687 Av. des Pins O, map **7E2** ☎842-1231
Hôpital St-Luc 1058 St-Denis, map **8C5** ☎285-1525

HOSPITALS WITH POISON CENTERS
Hôpital de Montréal pour enfants (children's hospital) 2300 Tupper. Map **9H3** ☎934-4400
Hôpital Ste-Justine 3175 Côte Ste-Catherine ☎731-4931

DENTAL EMERGENCIES
3546 Van Horne ☎342-4444. Open 24 hours.

PHARMACY OPEN 24 HOURS
Jean Coutu Drug Store 1370 Mont-Royal E ☎527-8827

HELP LINES
Alcoholics Anonymous ☎376-9230 (9am–11pm daily)
Animal emergencies ☎731-9442
Distress Centre (personal counseling) ☎842-7557
Referral Centre ☎931-2292 (for questions about health, social services, welfare; open Mon–Fri 8.30am–4.45pm)
Sexual assault ☎934-4504
Suicide-Action ☎522-5777
Traffic police (Sureté de Québec) ☎598-4141

For advice on **Automobile Accidents**, **Car Breakdowns**, and **Lost Travelers Checks**, refer to EMERGENCY INFORMATION on page 36.

Montréal: sightseeing

An overview of the city

The Island of Montréal has nearly 30 townships, with a number of parks scattered around its perimeter. Its major sights and attractions, however, are concentrated in the city itself. Most of Montréal is oriented toward the St Lawrence River, which forms the lower shore of the island.

ORIENTATION

With the exception of some of the residential areas around Mont-Royal, the streets follow a more-or-less regular grid plan. That is where some initial confusion may set in. Montréalers — and *most* published maps — consider the river to be due s. By that reckoning, Blvd. St-Laurent, which divides the city in half, is a N–S street, while rue Sherbrooke and Blvd. René-Lévesque are primary arteries running E–W. In geographical fact, though, the river at that point runs more nearly on a N–S course, so Blvd. St-Laurent actually runs almost E to W. No wonder the sun seems to be rising in the south!

Don't fight it. Stand downtown and face the harbor. That's "south." Turn around. That's "north." Otherwise, not a single direction you receive will make any sense. However, to make the best use of space, our maps **7–10** and on pages 132–3 show true north at the top of the page.

Boulevard St-Laurent is the dividing line between E and W.

THE DISTRICTS

Most business and leisure activities take place in six distinctive districts.

VIEUX MONTRÉAL *(map 8)*. This is where the city began. Neglected and run-down for much of the present century, it began to be restored in the 1960s, partly in anticipation of the Expo World Fair in 1967. At that time, it was declared an official historic district, covering about 95 acres. Warehouses were converted to residential, office, and retail purposes, and 18thC houses were coaxed back to life as restaurants and dwellings. Work continues, but the narrow streets invite strolling.

DOWNTOWN *(maps 7–10)*. Downtown is the central business and shopping district, bristling with skyscrapers that give way, here and there to churches and leafy pocket plazas. There is more than is immediately apparent, for beneath those shiny monuments to corporate enterprise is *la ville souterraine,* the famous underground city. It began in the 1950s, when developers were inspired to add subterranean concourses beneath new buildings and to fill them with shops, movie theaters and restaurants. The idea took hold. One set of concourses linked up with another, and another. Hotels and Metro stations added entrances. Now it is possible to stay a climate-controlled week beneath the ground and never open an umbrella.

GOLDEN SQUARE MILE and **RUE CRESCENT DISTRICT** *(map 9 F3–G3)*. The Golden Square Mile and adjoining Rue Crescent district are the core of Anglophone Montréal. Some of the mansions of 19thC British industrialists and bankers survive along rue Sherbrooke, several as galleries. Instruction is in English at highly regarded McGill University, and grand hotels sibilate with the echoes of former British privilege. Anglophone yuppies besport themselves nightly in the lively bars and eateries along Crescent and MacKay.

PLATEAU MONT-ROYAL *(see ORIENTATION MAP on page 132)*. Truly, this is the other side of the coin. The presence of the Université du Québec à Montréal nourishes a Latin Quarter atmosphere of youthful exuberance, the cafés and bistros of St-Denis alive with experiments in rebellion. Farther N, Blvd. St-Laurent (a.k.a. "The Main") and Av. du Parc pulse with ethnicity, a groaning table of diverse foods and exotica.

PARC DU MONT-ROYAL *(maps 7 & 9)*. Mont-Royal Park thrusts above the skyline, its green spaces crossed with trails for jogging and cycling, its meadows set with sculpture and skating ponds and even a short ski run.

ÎLE STE-HÉLÈNE *(see ORIENTATION MAP on page 133)*. Out in the St Lawrence is the island of Sainte-Hélène. Accessible by bus, Metro and ferry, the island has extensive picnic grounds, pools, an aquarium, an early-18thC fort, an amusement park, and active exhibition pavilions that remained after Expo '67.

USING THIS CHAPTER

This chapter on sightseeing in Montréal is arranged in two sections:

- Three detailed **walks** that guide the visitor around **The City Center**, **Old Montréal** and **Parc du Mont-Royal**.
- An alphabetical **A to Z of sights**.

Some lesser attractions may be located in the fuller entries below or in WALKS on the following pages: find them through the INDEX.

In the listings below, the indicated **metro stops** are those nearest the attraction, and a long walk or transfer to bus or streetcar may sometimes then be required. If you plan to travel without a car, call ahead to check your transportation route. The closest cross street follows each address (given in parentheses), when applicable.

CROSS REFERENCES

Where a place name appears in SMALL CAPITALS, fuller details can be found in an entry elsewhere in this chapter.

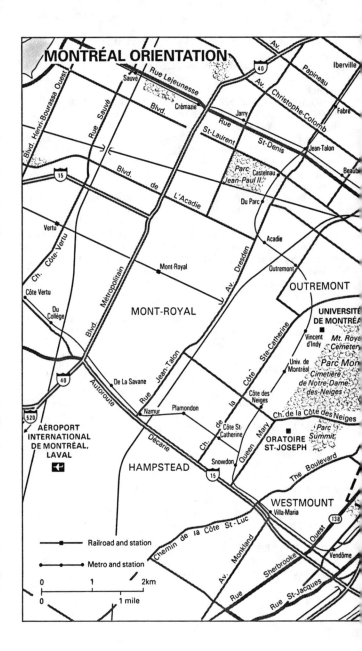

MONTRÉAL ORIENTATION

Av.
Papineau
Iberville
Rue Lejeunesse
Sauvé
40
Christophe-Colomb
Crémazie
Fabre
Blvd.
Jarry
Rue
St-Laurent
St-Denis
Jean-Talon
Blvd. Henri-Bourassa Ouest
Rue Sauvé
Beaubi
Castelnau
Parc
Jean-Paul II
Blvd.
de
15
L'Acadie
Du Parc
Vertu
Acadie
Côte-Vertu
Av. Dresden
Mont-Royal
Outremont
Ch.
OUTREMONT
Côte Vertu
Blvd. Métropolitain
UNIVERSITÉ
DE MONTRÉA
Du
Collège
MONT-ROYAL
Vincent
d'Indy
Mt. Roya
Cemeter
Côte Ste-Catherine
Univ. de
Montréal
Parc Mon
40
Jean-Talon
Cimetière
de Notre-Dame
des-Neiges
Autoroute
Rue
De La Savane
Côte des
Neiges
520
Décarie
Namur
Plamondon
Ch. de la Côte des Neiges
AÉROPORT
INTERNATIONAL
DE MONTRÉAL,
LAVAL
de
la
Côte St-
Catherine
Parc
Summit
Queen Mary
ORATOIRE
ST-JOSEPH
HAMPSTEAD
Ch.
Snowdon
15
The Boulevard
WESTMOUNT
Villa-Maria
138
Chemin de la Côte St-Luc
Av. Monkland
Ouest
Vendôme
Sherbrooke
Rue
Rue St-Jacques

Railroad and station

Metro and station

0   1   2km

0   1 mile

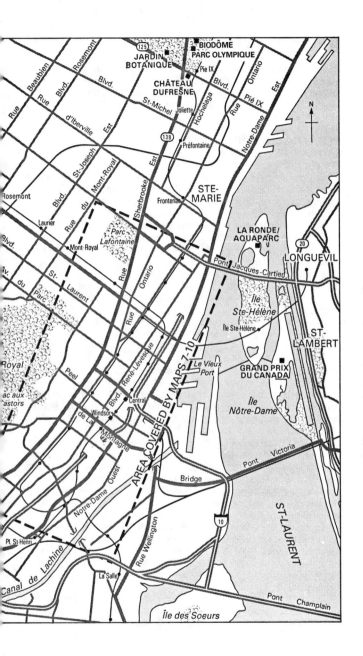

Montréal on foot

Few North American cities are as amenable to walkers, at least in the warmer months, and the evening hours hold no terrors. The tours outlined below pass most of the major sites, but also provide the observant visitor with the telling details and tableaux that underscore Montréal's rich diversity.

WALK 1: THE CITY CENTER
See maps 7–10. Metro: McGill.

The heart of the district now commonly known as the West End bore various names over preceding generations — New Town, St-Antoine Ward, the Golden Square Mile. It was, from 1860 until World War I, the exclusive enclave of the largely Scottish financial barons who once controlled nearly 70 percent of the Canadian economy. They built mansions that incorporated European styles as diverse as Tudor and Tuscan, Greco-Roman and Gothic. Although some of those Victorian and Edwardian architectural fancies survive, most of that heritage was sacrificed to the erection of commercial buildings, a trend that accelerated with the skyscraper boom that began in the 1960s and has yet to abate. The district still contains streets of recycled row houses, however, as well as parks, museums, cathedrals, universities and multileveled shopping complexes.

To begin this tour, take the Union exit from the McGill Metro station. Directly opposite is the CHRIST CHURCH ANGLICAN CATHEDRAL, a noteworthy Gothic Revival structure completed in 1857. Its backdrop is the **Maison des Coopérants**, a playful Post-Modernist office tower (pictured on page 27) that incorporates angular Gothic conceits in its facades and twin "steeples" echoing those of the church. Its usually pinkish glass changes tone with the weather, slipping from cornflower blue in bright sunlight to steel-gray under stormy skies. Beneath both buildings is a new subterranean shopping gallery, and the church is flanked by two venerable department stores, **La Baie** (The Bay) and **Eaton**. The entrance to Christ Church is on rue Ste-Catherine. Its limestone interior and high wooden roof deserve a look, and organ recitals are scheduled some afternoons.

After leaving the church, angle across Ste-Catherine toward Carré Phillips, a square containing a statue of Edward VII, and, usually, a farm stand selling apple and maple products. Walk s on Union past **Henry Burkes et Fils**, the long-established purveyor of gold and silver jewelry and household objects.

Turn right (w) on Blvd. René-Lévesque (which remains Blvd. Dorchester in the minds of Anglophones). René Lévesque was the leader of the separatist-minded *Parti Québécois* in the turbulent 1970s, and a hero to most Francophones. The 1st Baron Dorchester was Sir Guy Carleton, the British governor of Québec province during the time of the American Revolution.

At the far corner of University, on the right, is **Place Ville-Marie**, a massive 45-story skyscraper in a cruciform configuration intended to echo the cross placed on Mont-Royal by Jacques Cartier. Opened in 1959, it was the first structure to incorporate a large underground shopping mall, providing sheltered access as well to movie theaters, cafés, two rail stations and three hotels. Its success prompted later builders to construct similar facilities, which, when linked together, resulted in the creation of the Underground City. Just past Place Ville-Marie is an esplanade with a fountain and four peaked glass roofs over the concourse below. To the N are seen Mont-Royal and part of the McGill University campus, and across the street is the hotel **REINE ELIZABETH**.

Next to the hotel, on the same side, is the **CATHÉDRALE MARIE-REINE-DU-MONDE**, completed in 1894. This basilica is a replica (more or less) of St Peter's in Rome, but about a quarter the size of the original. The new skyscraper with the pyramidal copper-and-blue top that rises behind the cathedral is **1000 de la Gauchetière**. Central to its abundant attractions are the lobby atrium, which has 18 live trees, and in back, a giant indoor ice-skating rink ringed by cafés and with seating for 1,600 spectators. At 51 stories, "Le Mille" is the tallest in the city, dwarfing the odd building next to it, the hotel **CHÂTEAU CHAMPLAIN**. Known as the "cheese grater," the hotel's resemblance to that kitchen implement is created by its rows of upturned semicircular windows. It stands behind the open green space of **Place du Canada**.

On the right, across from the cathedral, is Dorchester Sq., rechristened from Dominion Sq. in a bit of political juggling to compensate the loss of the Baron's boulevard to René Lévesque. An inviting oasis in summer, with its old trees and benches, the square is also the starting point for bus tours of the city.

On the right side of Dorchester Sq. (while facing N) is the **Sun Life Building**, a wedding-cake structure built in successive layers during the 1920s, and the tallest building in the province until well into the post-World War II era. On the ground floor of the building at the NE corner of the square is an **Infotouriste** office, with a helpful staff, hotel and rental car reservation services, souvenirs, and many free brochures about Montréal attractions. Walk across the square to bordering rue Peel and continue N, past the Belgian restaurant **L'ACTUEL** and several currency exchanges that compete with each other to offer the most attractive rates, occasionally better than those observed by banks. Turn left (W) on Ste-Catherine.

Near the next corner, at #1128, is a branch of the Maison de la Presse Internationale chain, which carries periodicals and newspapers from around the world. In this direction lies the trendy **rue Crescent** district, full of tiny boutiques and art galleries and the cafés and pubs favored by Montréal's younger Anglophones.

Turn right (N) on rue Bishop, at the Church of St James the Apostle. The large, unsightly building next encountered on the left belongs to Concordia University. In two blocks, across rue Sherbrooke, is the Neoclassical marble facade of the **MUSÉE DES BEAUX-ARTS**, the city's most important art museum. Opposite is a large new annex, which takes up the whole block, including the interior of the graceful older building at this corner.

After visiting the museum, turn E along Sherbrooke past its concentration of expensive antique stores and galleries. The RITZ-CARLTON hotel, Montréal's epitome of Establishment luxe, lays on a correct British tea each afternoon in its summer garden, or in the wintertime Café de Paris. Proper dress is required to join its society custom.

A little farther on, **Maison Alcan** has won prizes for its skillful blending of a modern office building with the 19thC residences fronting on Sherbrooke. Concerts and exhibitions are frequently mounted in the atrium there.

Continuing on Sherbrooke, on the other side, is the entrance to MCGILL UNIVERSITY. Its grounds are open to the public. At #690 is the MUSÉE McCORD, which specializes in Canada's ethnology. It has reopened (in 1992) after a long period of renovation and expansion. Turn right (S) on University for McGill Metro station.

WALK 2: VIEUX MONTRÉAL (Old Montréal)
See map on next page and map 8C5–E5. Metro: Square Victoria.

The evolution from trading post to commercial metropolis took place in this historic quarter beside the St Lawrence River, but by the 20thC, Old Montréal was in danger of total disintegration. Corporations moved away, residential neighborhoods sprang up to the N, and demolitions and major fires accelerated its decline. That trend was slowed in the 1960s, when the entire area was declared a landmark district, and strict regulations controlled proposals to either raze or build. Although much remains to be done, deterioration has been arrested and continuing private and public restoration efforts now make a visit to the quarter virtually obligatory. Shops, cafés and taverns brighten its narrow streets, and the buildings constitute a living museum of 18th and 19thC native architecture.

Three Metro stations serve Old Montréal, but for this tour, start from the Square Victoria station, taking the McGill/St-Jacques exit. The plaza, initially known for the statue of the long-lived monarch for which it was named, has recently been re-landscaped and given a fountain. The statue was exiled to a smaller square, on the other side of rue St-Antoine, one block N. The modern tower on the W side, erected in 1966, houses the **Bourse** (Stock Exchange). Visits to the 41st floor are permitted to those wishing to witness the largely incomprehensible activity on the exchange floor. Across McGill, to the E, note the new arcade entrance between two older buildings. Marked 747 Square Victoria, it leads to the new World Trade Centre and Inter-Continental Hotel.

Walk S, toward the river, on the right side of McGill. On the right are several examples of 19thC commercial and civic architecture, including, at #360, the former headquarters of the Grand Trunk railroad company. Cross over to the left side of McGill at rue St-Paul. The next open space on the left is the **Place d'Youville**, one of the first public squares in Montréal. At this end, it is used as a parking lot. Walk to the far side and turn left. In one short block, at rue Normand, is seen the restored, obviously very old **Hôpital général des Soeurs Grises**. Begun in 1694, the hospital was home to Mother Marie-Marguerite d'Youville, founder of the Sisters of Charity, or Grey Nuns. They ministered to the sick poor, and the former hospital is still an active convent. Mother d'Youville was canonized by Pope John Paul in 1990.

Turn right on rue St-Pierre for a look at the front of the ancient structure. The warehouses on the opposite side date from the 1870s, and now contain shops and luxury apartments. At #118 is the **MUSÉE MARC-AURÈLE FORTIN**, devoted to the career of the French Canadian landscape watercolorist who died in 1970. Return to Place d'Youville. Directly ahead is a 1903 firehouse, identified by its three arched doorways and the *Caserne Centrale de Pompiers* sign. Restored, it is now the **Centre d'histoire de Montréal** *(#335* ☎ *872-3207* 📷 *open daily in summer; closed Mon late Sept–early May)*. The museum's 14 rooms contain displays and audiovisual records of the city's development. Descriptive labels on the exhibits are in French, but a brochure in English is available at the front desk. Presentations of stages of the port's history employ sound-and-light activated by sensors. They simulate a factory, a characteristic brick triplex residence, even a tram. After a look, turn left from the front door, past the front of the museum, then left again.

A few strides along are the **d'Youville Stables**. First erected c.1740 and restored c. 1825, they were actually used to store potash, not horses. A low portal gives access to the tranquil inner courtyard, and on the left is the popular **GIBBYS** restaurant, decorated in appropriate period style. It sets out tables in the court on warm days.

Continuing E on the elongated Place d'Youville, walkers encounter an obelisk marking the spot where French colonists founded Montréal in 1642. Led by the zealous missionary Paul de Chomedey, Sieur de Maisonneuve, they named their new town Ville-Marie. From there, the immediate area is called **Pointe-à-Callières**, commemorating a governor who negotiated a peace treaty with the Iroquois Indians in 1701, ending a 14-year war. It is the oldest place of European habitation in Montréal, the point at which the small river St-Pierre entered the much larger St-Laurent (St Lawrence). The new **MUSÉE D'ARCHÉOLOGIE ET D'HISTOIRE**, now stands there, protecting the *in-situ* remains of Amerindian and French settlers.

Bearing left, the next square along this route is **Place Royale**, which was once a military parade ground and later the city market. Now it is raised above archeological digs connected with the museum. Turn left into Place Royale, beside the old **Custom House** (1837), then left again, on rue St-Paul.

At the next corner, by the L'Air du Temps jazz club, turn into rue St-François-Xavier. At #453 is the 1903 Stock Exchange, now the **Centaur Theatre**, where English-language productions are mounted. Shortly, on the left, is the **Ponton Costumier**, its windows full of rubber masks and costumed mannequins. The shop has been in business since 1865. Also note, at #443, the capable French restaurant, **BONAPARTE**.

Continue to rue Notre-Dame, the first named street in Ville-Marie, laid out in 1672. Turn right (E). Soon, on the right, is the outer wall of the **Vieux Séminaire des Sulpiciens** (Sulpician Seminary). Begun in 1680, it is Montréal's oldest existing structure. The mechanism of the clock, which can be seen through the seminary's iron gate, was originally made

of wood and is said to be the oldest of its kind in North America (c.1700).

Next to the seminary is the presbytery of the **BASILIQUE NOTRE-DAME**, which lies just beyond. This Neo-Gothic church was completed in 1829 and seats 4,000 worshipers. Ornately carved woods and 14 stained-glass windows form the impressive interior, and a 5,772-pipe organ takes full advantage of the superb acoustics.

The **Place d'Armes** fronts the Basilica, with a statue of Paul de Chomedey de Maisonneuve, the founder of Montréal, looking rather like a Musketeer. Amidst the somewhat glum institutional buildings that contain the square on three sides is the domed **Banque de Montréal** on the N side, an 1847 Greco-Roman structure featuring a portico with six massive columns (see picture on page 25). A museum inside the bank *(open Mon–Fri 10am–4pm)* celebrates the expectable with a collection

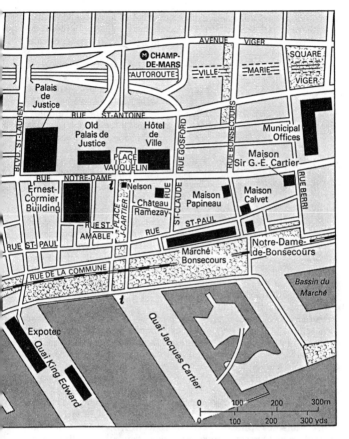

of currencies and piggy-banks. The grandiose vestibule has massive pillars of black marble. At this point, the tour can be broken off by walking N along the E side of the square, then down Côte de la Place d'Armes to the Place d'Armes Metro station. Otherwise, turn right (E) from the front of the basilica along rue Notre-Dame.

The next intersection is Blvd. St-Laurent, which divides Montréal into E and W. Cross over. On the left is the new courthouse, a bleak contemporary intrusion that looms over the 1849 **Palais de Justice** it supplanted. The top floor and dome of the Palais date from 1891, the painted white stone of the addition in obvious contrast with the gray of the original lower floors. It now houses city offices.

Opposite the old Palais is the **Ernest-Cormier Building**, built in 1926, notable for its Art Deco lanterns and majestic copper doors. Next on the left is the small square with a statue honoring Jean Vauquelin, a naval hero who defended New France in engagements with the British in 1758–59. In warmer months, a fountain splashes before him.

Hôtel de Ville

The park is overshadowed by the quarter's most august structure, the 1878 **Hôtel de Ville** (City Hall). In best Second Empire manner, it employs mansard roofs, squared turrets and robust Neoclassical detailing in the facade, which are all seen to great advantage when it is illuminated at night.

Charles de Gaulle, never one to let slip an opportunity to tweak Anglo-Saxon noses, delivered his "Long live free Québec" speech from the balcony over the front entrance in 1967. (He neglected to observe that he had several active separatist movements in his own country, and would have been outraged if a visiting Canadian statesman had ever shouted, "Long live the free Basques!" from, say, the Arc de Triomphe.)

Sloping down to the right is Place Jacques-Cartier (to which this tour soon returns). Continue along rue Notre-Dame. Near the next corner is the handsome CHÂTEAU RAMEZAY, erected in 1705 as the home of the 11th French governor of Montréal and later the official residence of British Governors General. It was occupied by commanders of an invading American army in 1775–1776. Fully restored, it serves now as a showcase of domestic life among the privileged in the early 18thC. One block more is rue Bonsecours. Turn right and walk down the inclining street, lined with houses from the colonial period.

The **Maison Papineau** *(#440)* was built in 1785 and was the birthplace of Henri Bourassa, founder of a Québec family that is still influential today. The exterior siding is of wood, fashioned to imitate stone. On the left is one of Montréal's best-known restaurants, LES FILLES DU ROI. The name refers to young women recruited by the French king in the 1660s to help populate the fledgling colony. On the corner is the **Maison Calvet** (c.1725). A superb example of a traditional French dwelling, it was restored in 1964 through the largesse of the owners of the Ogilvy department store. Fittingly, the ground floor is now an appealing bakery and café, with an antique fireplace in its far wall.

Across the street is the ÉGLISE DE NOTRE-DAME-DE-BONSECOURS. The founder of the sailor's church was Marguerite Bourgeoys, who led an order of noncloistered nuns in the 17thC. A statue of the Virgin stands atop the roof, behind the steeple, her arms outstretched to welcome returning ships. It can be seen as you turn right at the corner. On the site of two earlier churches destroyed by fire, the present chapel was completed in 1772. A tower with about 100 steps offers a good harbor view.

Turning right on rue St-Paul, the long Neoclassical building with the prominent dome is the **Marché Bonsecours**. It was used by the Canadian Parliament in the mid-19thC, but soon became a public market, which it remained for a century. It was then occupied by municipal offices, and casual visitors were not permitted entry for many years. In 1992, in celebration of the city's 350th anniversary, the bottom two floors were opened to the public. They have been used for mixed programs of exhibits and musical performances. It is uncertain how long that policy will continue.

At #295 was once a hotel that counted Charles Dickens among its guests. Continue another block to Place Jacques-Cartier and turn right, up the hill toward the **Hôtel de Ville**. The long plaza was a market place in the early 19thC, and remained so until the 1960s. Several of the buildings along the sides are good, if abridged, examples of Québec architecture, which blended memories of the architects' French homeland with a pragmatic recognition of Canada's harsh winters. Steeply sloped roofs were designed to shed snow, and the thick walls helped keep out the cold.

The square comes to life every spring with a flower market, sidewalk cafés and the lively atmosphere created by street entertainers and throngs of natives and tourists. Amid all the eateries of lesser ambition is **LA MARÉE** *(#404),* an accomplished French restaurant in a carefully restored stone house. In summer, artists and craftspeople set out their wares (nothing out-of-the-ordinary) in rue St-Amable, off the w side, and hours can be easily spent among the cabarets, boutiques, bars and restaurants in the immediate vicinity.

At the top of the square is **Nelson's column**, erected in honor of the British victory at Trafalgar several years before the much larger monument in London. It has provided a convenient target for ideological vandals during heightened periods of French separatist sentiment. As a result, the statue of Nelson has been replaced by an inexpensive, and obvious, fake. The ersatz English admiral gazes across rue Notre-Dame at the statue of French navigator Vauquelin, the two being enduring juxtaposed symbols of Montréal's duality. The Champ-de-Mars Metro station is down rue Gosford, to the right of the City Hall.

WALK 3: PARC DU MONT-ROYAL
*See map **9**F2–G2.*

The 20thC has penetrated the heights of Jacques Cartier's *Mont Réal* in the shape of a huge metal cross, lit at night by hundreds of bulbs. Erected in 1924, it commemorates the wooden crucifix planted there by de Maisonneuve in 1643. The hilltop has been preserved as parkland and much of it remains true to the original 1870 concept of landscape architect Frederick Law Olmsted, designer of New York's Central Park, which achieved an entirely natural look through careful planning. On the far side are two vast cemeteries — one French, one English — and a somber basilica with one of the largest domes in the world.

141

The park can be seen by taking a *calèche* from Dorchester Sq. or bus #165 from the Guy-Concordia Metro station, changing to the #11 bus, which has a stop at Beaver Lake. In winter, the horses that are attached to *calèches* in summer, pull sleighs from the lake. But the park is best experienced on foot, if one *caveat* is observed. Only the reasonably fit will want to undertake the first phase of this suggested trek, that of hiking from the downtown district to the crest. Others are wise to take a taxi to the **Châlet de la Montagne** and pick up the walk from there.

At the N end of rue Peel is a flight of steps leading to a path that soon joins a marked jogging trail, rising toward the left and doubling back to the right. Shortly, on the left of the trail, are wooden stairs climbing into the trees. Take them. They seem unlikely ever to end, but they do, and the reward is a partial vista of the city below. Continue up the paved path, the Chalet de la Montagne coming into view on the right. At the chalet, bear left to the esplanade and its sweeping panorama — the city hemmed in the distance by the river, and it, in turn, by the Eastern Townships of the S bank. Still farther, on clear days, is the Adirondack range of neighboring New York State, and off to the left are the beginnings of the Laurentian Mountains. Muggers are not a common threat in the park, so this is also a good vantage at sunset or after dark, when the city is a jewel box of winking necklaces of light.

Circle around the far side of the chalet, taking the left (paved) fork at the next intersection. The way is shared with serious runners, amblers, cyclists and an occasional horse and rider. Slowly descending in a roughly NW direction, it soon comes to a stone building beside a large parking lot. This is the **Musée de la Chasse et de la Nature** (Museum of Hunting and Wildlife) *(open Tues–Sun 10am–5pm; closed Mon and Sept–May)*. After a brief visit, continue in the same direction along the central path that crosses an open, rolling field serving as an outdoor sculpture garden.

Down the hill is the **Lac aux Castors** (Beaver Lake), a name referring to the fur-trapping history of the region rather than to the actual presence of those once highly profitable animals. In summer, ducks paddle among the remote-controlled model boats and sailing ships, young lovers find themselves quiet shaded places, and families tend charcoal grills beside picnic tables. In winter, a rope-tow carries skiers up to the top of the gentle slope, and skaters twirl on the frozen lake.

Follow along its near shore to the pavilion, where refreshments and rest rooms are available. Walk on past the pavilion to the edge of the double road called the Chemin de la Remembrance. A forest of headstones begins on the other side, the **Notre-Dame-des-Neiges Catholic cemetery**. The entrance is 50 yards up on the right. Still farther in the same direction is the **Protestant cemetery**, notable for the splendor of its monuments and memorials that stand as proof of the greater economic power of its 19th and early 20thC occupants. Montréal's Anglophones and Francophones rest thus in their eternal peace, separate and slightly unequal even in death. The graveyards are open daily *(8am–5pm in winter, 8am–7pm in summer)*. If the French cemetery is open (and after a visit to the English one), enter and follow the paths downhill. If it is closed, turn left and take the sidewalk bordering the road, in either case heading toward the pointed green dome now visible in the distance. Just beyond the high wrought-iron main gate is a bus stop.

Those who still have energy to spare can continue along Chemin de la Côte-des-Neiges to the intersection with Chemin de la Reine-Marie. Turn left across Côte-des-Neiges and shortly arrive at the entrance to the grounds of the **ORATOIRE ST-JOSEPH** (St Joseph's Oratory), a fittingly imposing end to the walk. There is another bus stop near the entrance. The #166 bus can be taken from there to the Guy-Concordia Metro station, or, with luck, an infrequent cruising taxi can be snared.

Montréal: sights A to Z

Montréal has no repositories of art and history to compare with those of New York, London or Paris. Only a handful of the largest historic buildings and museums require more than an hour of any but a specialist's attention. That is not a fact to be mourned, and won't be by those who would rather spend their time shopping, strolling, or observing the rhythms of the city from a table in a pleasant sidewalk café.

Still, in anticipation of the 350th anniversary of the founding of the city in 1992, two of the most important museums were expanded — the McCORD and the BEAUX-ARTS — and a third, the MUSÉE D'ART CONTEMPORAIN, was moved to a new, central facility. And even without these, Montréal has easily enough sights to occupy a week's vacation.

BASILIQUE NOTRE-DAME ★

Place d'Armes and St-Sulpice. Map 8E5 ☎*849-1070* 🖼 *𝒳 available. Open early Sept–late June 7am–6pm, rest of year 7am–8pm. Metro: Place d'Armes.*

Québec's finest testament to the potential of ecclesiastical architecture, this Catholic church was the masterwork of an Irish-American Protestant, James O'Donnell. Certainly it is surpassed by none of the 375 churches on the island of Montréal. O'Donnell is credited by many for the Gothic Revival of the early 19thC, a movement that veered sharply away from the Georgian and Greco-Roman Classicism of the preceding century. The style persisted for 75 years in the face of a welter of revivalist and eclectic architectural notions.

The exterior was completed in only 6 years, in 1829, and the experience so moved O'Donnell that he converted to Catholicism, and was eventually buried here. The interior was another story, requiring a full 40 years before completion. It was worth the wait. Wherever the eye falls is a wealth of detail, most of it intricately carved wood and exquisite joinery, often gilded and painted with a precision to challenge that of medieval artisans.

Yet while the credit rests with its European progenitors, these walls are distinctively Québécois, robust in execution and resonant of their frontier Canadian roots. The project must have been a joy for Victor Bourgeau, the architect who was forced during the same period to execute a design for the Cathedral of Marie-Reine-du-Monde that he reportedly deplored.

143

Of particular interest are the high altar, a commission of the French artist Bourich, and the pulpit statues by Philippe Hébert. The stained-glass windows, from Limoges, were installed in 1929.

Prized for its acoustic clarity, the church is often the scene of jazz and classical concerts, including the famous Christmas recital of Luciano Pavarotti. Up to 4,000 people can be accommodated at worship or performance, washed by the majestic chords of an organ with five keyboards and 5,772 pipes. On special occasions, the 12-ton bell in the w tower peals over Vieux Montréal.

A small **museum** (🖾 *open Sat, Sun 9.30am–4pm)* contains religious objects, art works and embroidered vestments.

BIODÔME ★
4777 Pierre-de-Coubertin (Bennett). Map 12C5 ☎872-3034 🖾 🖭 Open daily, hours vary. Metro: Pié-IX.

Shuffling and recycling a number of pre-existing attractions has resulted in this remarkable, possibly unique, facility. The building, adjacent to the Olympic Stadium, was originally erected as a velodrome for the 1976 Games. Its new inhabitants were gathered, in part, from the zoos at LaFontaine and Angrignon parks and the now-closed aquarium near La Ronde amusement park on Ile Ste-Hélène. Since it is truly a new concept, Biodôme cannot be readily compared to other institutions. Think of it as a living museum of natural history with subtle lessons about ecology.

The designers have created four distinct ecosystems under this one roof, representing the Amazon jungle, the Laurentian forest, the St Lawrence valley, and Antarctica. Enter the **Amazon jungle** environment first and find waterfalls, fish swimming in pools, lush plants, even columns made to resemble banyan trees, with real monkeys and parrots in their upper branches. The air is steamy, heavy with moisture. Visitors stroll through as if they had just stepped off the weekly mail packet on an Amazonian tributary. A corridor to the next encapsulated world contains tanks of red-bellied piranha, angelfish, neon tetras, and exotic frogs, followed by a bat cave.

Next, the cooler, more familiar *Forêt Laurentienne*, with live birch and fir and maple trees. Brook trout and mallard ducks swim in the ponds beneath the beaver dam, playful otters swoop and dive in their own pool.

In the **St Lawrence** capsule, depicting marshlands, starfish cling to the bottoms of tidal pools. Gulls shriek, unseen whales keen. And the **Antarctic** replication has platoons of puffins and penguins doing bellyflops in the icy water. It is all brilliantly conceived and executed, illustrating the interplay and interdependence of every plant and organism and climatic imperative. Rarely has pedagogy been so palatable. Biodôme's chief deficiency? Simply that there isn't more.

BOULEVARD ST-LAURENT
Maps 7C1–8D5. Metro: Sherbrooke or Mont-Royal.

Known to both Francophones and Anglophones as "The Main," this N–S avenue was the historic dividing line between the French East End and the English West End of the elongated metropolis. It remains the pulsing central artery of Montréal's best-known immigrant neighborhood. Novelist Mordecai Richler's rapacious Duddy Kravitz served his apprenticeship here among Greeks, Germans, Poles, Italians and Eastern Europeans. When the newcomers made their fortunes, or at least salaries adequate to move up to Outremont or the suburbs, their places were taken by newer waves of Portuguese, Indians, Thais, West Indians and Vietnamese.

Their children return as predictably as puffins for their weekly ingestion of smoked meat, bagels, *borscht, bigos, pikilía* and *pla lad plik.* Nothing but a *bona fide* blizzard keeps them from their Saturday treks along what many consider to be the soul of the city. The nickname may have arisen from the fact that immigrants once tumbled off ships at the wharves in what is now Vieux Montréal and walked up this main street until they found lodging, work, and pockets of others of similar background. Some peeled off to establish the city's compact Chinatown, but most continued N, beyond Sherbrooke.

Between there and Av. Laurier is the most engaging stretch. St-Laurent isn't included on architectural tours, for its loft buildings and tenements are of largely shabby aspect. But it bristles with life, 24 hours a day, and the only danger is sensory overload. All-night clubs and avant-garde boutiques have staked their claims among the ethnic groceries, fish stores, discount clothiers and houseware stores.

Purveyors of high-style furs and low-cost leathers insinuate themselves betwixt bakeries, delicatessens, jazz bars and hyper-trendy *boîtes* and galleries. Yet despite the presence of hipper-than-thou designers and periodic invasions of suburbanites and tourists, gentrification has yet to afflict The Main with the cute and predictable.

CATHÉDRALE–BASILIQUE MARIE-REINE-DU-MONDE
*Blvd. René-Lévesque and rue de la Cathédrale. Map **10**F4* ☎*866-1661 (rectory)* ☒ *Open summer daily 7am–7.30pm, other months Sun 9.30am–7.30pm, Sat 8am–8.30pm. Metro: Bonaventure.*

The first Catholic cathedral was on rue St-Denis, in the heart of French Montréal. When it burned down in 1852, then-Bishop Bourget determined that the site of its replacement should be in the western part of the city. Presumably his intent was to serve his city-wide congregation more efficiently, although the opportunity to insert a bastion of the Roman faith in the very midst of the Protestant West End must have added a certain piquancy to his decision. His overwhelmingly Francophone flock protested the relocation to alien territory, delaying implementation until 1875, when construction finally was begun.

Bourget had in mind a scaled-down replica of St Peter's in Rome. Church architect Victor Bourgeau resisted that plan with the understandable reluctance of an artist of integrity asked to reproduce the work of others. His replacement so botched the job, however, that he agreed to join the effort after it had begun.

The cathedral did not commence its liturgical life until 1894, a decade after Bourget died. The result is less a replication of St Peter's than an echo, only partly because it covers less than one quarter the area. Unlike the original, it is overwhelmed by nearby skyscrapers, and there is no sweeping colonnade embracing a great plaza at its approach, as there is in Rome. The facade is nonetheless impressive, with its Neoclassical columns and triangular pediment forming the portico. The dome, or cupola, is 77m (252 feet) high, compared to the 152m (500 feet) of St Peter's, and is slightly more than half the diameter of its model. The row of statues standing along the cornice are of local patron saints, rather than the Apostles.

The most compelling feature of the interior is the copper-and-gold-leaf copy of Bernini's *baldachin*, the canopy above the altar.

CENTRE CANADIEN D'ARCHITECTURE

1920 rue Baile. Map 9G3 ☎ *939-7000* 📷 📶 *Open Wed, Fri 11am–6pm, Thurs 11am–8pm, Sat, Sun 11am–5pm. Closed Mon, Tues. Metro: Guy-Concordia.*

This ambitious new museum and research center opened in 1989, its primary concern being the preservation and exhibition of drawings, photographs and other materials related to architecture. That mission admittedly makes it of specialized interest, and there are none of the whizz-bang, hands-on, interactive exhibits that other museums employ to engage visitors.

The Centre is the result of a single woman's vision and drive. Phyllis Lambert had the advantage of being the daughter of the founder of the Seagram distillery empire, and the energy to see her project to its conclusion. That meant the commissioning of the dignified contemporary building that embraces the 19thC Second Empire manse known as the Shaughnessy House.

Situated in the w part of the city, it presents its best face to Blvd. René-Lévesque, but the entrance is around back. The collection includes more than 45,000 photos and 135,000 books.

CHÂTEAU DUFRESNE — MUSÉE DES ARTS DÉCORATIFS

Sherbrooke E and Pié-IX. Map 12D5 ☎ *259-2575* 📷 *Open Wed–Sun 11am–5pm. Closed Mon, Tues. Metro: Pié-IX.*

Said to have 44 rooms, although it looks smaller, the undeniably luxurious residence was erected between 1915 and 1918 at the behest of brothers Oscar and Marius Dufresne. Prosperous citizens of what was then the independent municipality of Maisonneuve, they chose a muted Beaux-Arts design, but had it executed in the emerging technology of reinforced concrete, not chiseled stone.

Still only partially restored and largely empty of furnishings, it is now the home of the **Museum of Decorative Arts**. A handful of rooms are open, with only hints of former opulence, mostly in carved paneling and architectural elements. The library, for example, is of decidedly Gothic inspiration, while the smoking-room shows mock-Arabic traceries. A top-floor gallery displays a somewhat incongruous collection of modern furniture dating from the 1930s. Works by Marcel Breuer and Frank Lloyd Wright are included.

While it may perhaps not be worth a special trip, a visit to the château can be combined with one to the nearby JARDIN BOTANIQUE or PARC OLYMPIQUE.

CHÂTEAU RAMEZAY

280 Notre-Dame E (Place Jacques-Cartier). Map 8D5 ☎*861-3708* ▨
✗ *available* ♿ *Open Tues–Sun 10am–4.30pm. Closed Mon, except mid–June to early Sept. Metro: Champ-de-Mars.*

When Governor Claude de Ramezay commissioned this house in 1705, Montréal had only 1,200 inhabitants living in 152 dwellings. Given the often harsh and straitened circumstances in which most of them lived, his new mansion must have seemed very grand indeed. It does so even now, at least in some of the larger rooms furnished with imported tapestries and mahogany *boiseries* (carved panels) that provide an intriguing peek into the domestic life of the 18thC aristocrats living in New France.

From 1764–1849, it was the residence of the Governors General of British North America, interrupted by a brief occupation by American officers during the 1775–76 military occupation.

Prints, paintings and useful signs trace the history of the house and the city for which it was a focal point. The main floor has 12 rooms, and Ramezay needed them all, since he had 16 children. A stuffed beaver beside a richly embroidered greatcoat are emblematic of his participation in the lucrative fur trade. The subterranean floor has displays of housekeeping crafts and Amerindian artifacts.

CHINATOWN

Map 8D4. Metro: Place d'Armes.

The Asian enclave hunched around the intersection of Blvd. St-Laurent and rue de la Gauchetière seems to grow smaller, unlike those in New York and San Francisco. It is tidier than its counterparts, too, with the usual pagoda facades, neon Chinese characters, and roast ducks in its windows, but with far less refuse underfoot. Threatened by encroaching development, it survives for now as a refreshingly exotic oasis in an enveloping sea of modernity.

CHRIST CHURCH CATHEDRAL

Ste-Catherine W and University. Map 8E4 ☎*288-6421* ▨ *Open daily 8am–6pm. Metro: McGill.*

Called the "flying church" and the "floating cathedral" because of the vast network of underground corridors and galleries beneath it, the Anglican cathedral was opened in 1859. Its design is understated, not flamboyant, Gothic, executed by Frank Wills of Salisbury, England. The original stone steeple was taken down in 1927 when it appeared to be threatening the structure of the building. A lighter aluminum replica was put in place in 1940.

The most notable feature of the interior is the *reredos* behind the altar, carved stone depictions of seven scenes from the life of Christ. Organ recitals take place throughout the year.

DOW PLANETARIUM

1000 St-Jacques W (near Peel). Map 10F5 ☎*872-4530* 📷 *Free show Mon night. Schedules vary; call ahead. Metro: Bonaventure.*

A splendid spectacle is provided by 100 projectors casting images on a dome more than 60ft across, hushed "oohs" and "aahs" attending the changing depictions of planets, nebulae and quasars. Presentations change periodically, and narrations alternate in French and English. Monday evenings, this "Theater of the Stars" displays the sky as it appears that very night.

ÉGLISE DE NOTRE-DAME-DE-BONSECOURS

400 St-Paul E (Vieux Montréal). Map 8C5 ☎*845-9991* 📷 ◀€ *Open Nov–Apr 10am–5pm, May–Oct 9am–5pm. Metro: Champ-de-Mars.*

Marguerite Bourgeoys arrived with de Maisonneuve in the 17thC to become Ville-Marie's first teacher. Soon after, she founded Canada's first religious order, the Congregation of Notre-Dame. The existing 1772 church was built upon the foundations of the earlier 1657 version. Both have sheltered a wooden Madonna that gained a reputation for miracles, especially to mariners and fishermen who came to give it honor for saving them from accidents at sea; thus its name, the "Sailor's Church." Following its recovery after a theft, the original Madonna was locked away, and a replica was substituted.

A small basement **museum** contains 58 miniature stage sets charting the life of Bourgeoys. An **observatory** above the apse is open to the public, with views of the old town, port and river.

ÉGLISE DE ST-ENFANT-JÉSUS

5039 St-Dominique. Map 7C1 ☎*271-0943. Metro: Mont-Royal.*

The Main's only contribution to significant city architecture was begun in 1857 but achieved notability with the later addition of its richly sculptured Neo-Baroque facade. Cherubim, angels and biblical figures gaze down upon quiet **LaHaie Park**.

ÎLE STE-HÉLÈNE

Map 12D5. Metro: Île Ste-Hélène.

As part of Montréal's epic efforts in preparation for the 1967 Expo world fair, this island in the middle of the St Lawrence was doubled in size. That was not enough, so a second island was created from scratch with landfill — the **Île Notre-Dame**. Since then, the two have become prime recreational centers. Connected to the city by the Metro and the Jacques-Cartier Bridge, the Île Ste-Hélène has a thrill-happy amusement park, LA RONDE, an 1824 fort, swimming pools (and an old-fashioned swimming hole), restaurants and *pique-nique* grounds. In May and June it is the site of the **International Festival of Fireworks**; in winter, cross-country skiers and snowshoers brave the chill.

Parts of the Expo exhibition remain, marked by Buckminster Fuller's **geodesic dome**. The skin of that unusual monument was burned off by fire, leaving only its skeletal frame.

Île Notre-Dame has a lovely **floral park** *(open mid-June to Sept),* a track for Formula One races, and a gigantic rectangular lake made for the '76 Olympics. The basin is a winter skating rink and a summer site for windsurfing and sailing.

The island's newest attraction is the **Palais de la Civilisation** (☎ *872-4560*) 🔲 🔲 *open early May–end Sept daily 10am–8pm*). Billed as an international exhibition center, its first show was an ambitious survey of the Roman Empire, with artworks and historical artifacts.

For the exhibition and picnic grounds on Île Ste-Hélène and Île Notre-Dame, take the Metro to the Île Ste-Hélène stop, at the w end of the island. For La Ronde, take the Metro to Papineau, then the shuttle bus outside.

JARDIN BOTANIQUE (Botanical Garden)
4101 Sherbrooke E (Pié-IX). Map 12D5 ☎872-1400 🔲 *𝑘 available* 🔲
Open June 24–early Sept 8am–8pm; late May–June 23 and mid-Sept to mid-Oct Mon–Fri 9am–6pm, Sat and Sun 9am–8pm; mid-Oct to early May 9am–6pm. Greenhouses open daily 9am–6pm (7pm in summer). Metro: Pié-IX.

No one appreciates flowers more than those living in regions with short growing seasons, and Montréal's superb Botanical Garden satisfies that need. Founded in 1931, it is among the largest in the world, at 73 hectares (180 acres). It boasts over 26,000 species of plants and trees, arranged in outdoor beds and groves and in nine greenhouses heavy with the scent of tropical blooms.

An open-sided sightseeing tram (🔲) provides a good overview of the exhibits. A recorded bilingual narration describes each section, from the rose garden with its signature "Montréal Rose" to the aquatic gardens afloat with lotus and hyacinth to the Japanese gardens that opened in 1988. Audio cassettes can also be rented for self-guided walking tours.

One unmissable highlight is the **Japanese Pavilion**. The building displays works of art, and has periodic, shortened versions of the traditional tea ceremony (the real thing can take hours). Outside is a fascinating *bonsai* collection — artificially dwarfed trees more than 20 years old and barely 1ft high. A particularly arresting specimen of this ancient horticultural art is a spectacular American Larch growing from a rock. It is over 150 years old.

One of the greenhouses features a waterfall that feeds a series of ponds displaying giant Amazon waterlilies. Another showcases *penjing,* the Chinese version of *bonsai,* and a third has more than 1,200 varieties of orchid. Special displays are arranged for Christmas and Easter. An **Insectarium** occupies a new pavilion, near the entrance gate at the Sherbrooke E side. Children squeal delightedly at the tanks of live creepy-crawlies — scorpions, tarantulas, and their kin. Otherwise, the panels and cases of mounted butterflies and other bugs constitute an exhibit of somewhat specialized interest.

A **Chinese Garden** was opened in 1991, designed in a style known as Meng Hu Yuan, deriving from the 14th–17th Ming dynasty. It incorporates a skillful arrangement of bubbling water courses, wood carvings, and hillocks. More than 2,300 tons of stones were required, 300 of them imported from China.

The PARC OLYMPIQUE is a short walk from the front gate, giving an opportunity to take in the two major attractions in this eastern sector of the City. A free shuttle bus to the Olympic stadium and BIODÔME is available at the gate near the Insectarium.

LACHINE CANAL
Map 10J4–G6 ☎283-6054 ▣ Open daily sunrise–midnight.
Early in the history of European Canada, it was believed that if a detour could be made around the turbulent Lachine Rapids of the St Lawrence River, a passage to the Orient might be discovered. The digging of a canal was first proposed in 1680, as a way for the fur brigades traveling to the NW to bypass the rapids. However, construction of a canal didn't begin until 1821. When work was completed four years later, the waterway opened shipping between Montréal and the Great Lakes.

Completed in its final form in 1925, the St Lawrence Seaway made the canal redundant only three decades later, and it was closed to navigation more than 25 years ago. Now it is being transformed into a recreational resource, with lighted 11km (7-mile) cycling and cross-country skiing tracks along its banks.

An **interpretation center** *(open mid-May to early Sept)* at 7th Ave. and Blvd. St-Joseph in Lachine explains the history of the canal's development.

MAISON SIR GEORGE-ÉTIENNE CARTIER
458 Notre-Dame E. Map 8C5 ☎283-2282 ▣ ✗ with reservations. Open May, June 9am–5pm; July, Aug 10am–6pm; Sept–Apr Wed–Sun 10am–noon, 1–5pm. Metro: Champ-de-Mars.
Following his service from 1857–1862 as co-premier of Canada, with Sir John A. MacDonald, Sir George-Étienne Cartier reached his highest achievement as one of the fathers of the Canadian Confederation. He lived in both parts of this double house between 1848 and 1871, until two years before his death.

Restored by the Canadian Parks Service, the two buildings are now a museum of middle-class Victorian domestic life. An audio-visual presentation describes the era.

McGILL UNIVERSITY
805 Sherbrooke W. Map 7E3 ☎398-6555 ▣ ✗ by appointment. Metro: McGill.
Canada's most prestigious and best-known university was founded in 1821 on royal decree by George IV, on 18 hectares (46 acres) of land bequeathed by James McGill, a wealthy fur merchant. Classes began in 1829. The campus has since expanded to 32 hectares (80 acres) on the slopes of Mont-Royal. It incorporates the site of the Amerindian village of Hochelaga, established before the first Europeans arrived. Courses are conducted in English for the more than 30,000 students; medicine is most often judged the strongest program.

Members of the family who established an important sugar-refining company named after them, underwrote the **Redpath Museum** *(☎398-*

4086 📷 *open Sept–June Mon–Fri 9am–5pm, June 24–Labour Day Mon–Thurs 9am–5pm).* It's the august structure just left of the road leading from the main gate.

Included in its compact collection are prehistoric fossils, crystals and geological samples, and Egyptian antiquities.

MUSÉE D'ARCHÉOLOGIE ET D'HISTOIRE ★
359 Place Royale. Map 8E5 ☎*872-9150* 📷 ✗ *available. Open late June–Labour Day Tues–Sun 10am–8pm; Sept–late June, Tues–Sun 10am–5pm. Closed Mon. Metro: Place d'Armes.*

What more logical site for a museum of the city's archeology and history than the Pointe-à-Callières? It was, after all, at the juncture of the St-Laurent and St-Pierre rivers that Montréal began more than 350 years ago. When excavations at the edge of Vieux Montréal unearthed centuries-old coins, bones, and shards, it was decided to erect this startling new building. It links underground crypts and ancient building foundations with the Old Custom House at the back of Place Royale.

Try to catch the start of the multi-media show, which takes a masterful spin through history in an arena set above the actual ruins of the old city. With headphone narrations in both French and English, it deploys magically appearing screens, lights, and images with a stupendous special effect at the end that won't be revealed here. A self-guided tour then descends into a subterranean network of four centuries of habitations, sewers, streets, even a 17thC graveyard. Along the way are displayed relics unearthed during the digs — pre-historic arrowheads and French colonial hatchets, teacups, buttons.

After passing through a remnant of the channelized river St-Pierre, the visitor reaches galleries containing interactive games and devices encourage visitors to "talk" with a holographic Indian chief and a French colonist. The exit passes through the gift shop in the Custom House.

MUSÉE D'ART CONTEMPORAIN (Museum of Contemporary Art)
185 Ste-Catherine W. Map 8D4 ☎*873-2878* 📷 ✗ *available. Open Tues–Sun 11am–6pm, (Wed until 9pm). Closed Mon. Metro: Place-des-Arts.*

The museum and its post-1940 paintings and sculptures celebrated more than 25 years of existence with the move to this new facility in Place des Arts in 1991. That got it away from its former location in a remote waterfront district that had never developed as the planners had hoped.

A deservedly larger audience can now discover its admirable collection, which is dominated by Québec artists and other Canadians working in a wide variety of styles and media. They have not been outdistanced by colleagues in larger art centers. Their creations are as daring, as provocative, as outrageous as anything to be found in New York or Paris.

Here, for example, is an assemblage of stacked SONY television sets, with haunting images changing to a French commentary that makes itself understood even to Anglophones. Some are giant installations, others attract the eye because they aren't -- the three glass piggy banks on pedestals, for example. Inevitably, there are works by those artists who choose to heap things on the floor, including seashells, dried beans, and in one case, dust bunnies (as North Americans engagingly call those clouds of dust that gather under beds...).

There are some pieces on the ground floor, but most are one story up. Climbing the stairs, the *collection permanente* is to the left, the *exposition temporaire* to the right. In the former, art works are usually grouped stylistically, rather than by chronology or nationality. (Watch for Charles Gagnon, who has both photos and a painting on view.) While Canadian artists are featured, there are many other familiar names, including Larry Poons, Antoni Tàpies, Jean Dubuffet, Max Ernst, and Kenneth Noland. A busy schedule in the auditorium presents performance artists, dance, and music, as well as events not so easily classified.

MUSÉE DES BEAUX-ARTS (Museum of Fine Arts) ★

1379 and 1380 Sherbrooke W (Crescent). Map 9F3 ☎285-1600 ▨
✗ *available* ▣ *Open Tues–Sun 11am–6pm (Wed, Sat 9pm). Closed Mon. Metro: Peel, Guy-Concordia.*

Montréal's largest museum, erected in 1912 and expanded in 1975, has now added a striking annex on the opposite side of Sherbrooke. This extension has brought about a significant improvement in the exhibits. Where the old arrangement, lacking space to do itself justice, had seemed marred by a fuzzy curatorial focus, the permanent collection has fleshed out the exhibits in each department. What were merely tantalizing tastes of the arts of many cultures can now be taken in big, satisfying gulps.

Enter the museum through the new white marble-faced pavilion on the s side of Sherbrooke (*#1380, corner of Crescent*). The adjacent building was a 1905 apartment house. The facade was retained, but its interior was scooped out to house the museum shop and offices. The main entrance is 12m (40ft) high, opening out into an atrium that rises all the way to the 5th-floor skylight. The gallery space has been tripled, with the above-ground floors in the annex, two more below street level, and still more rooms beneath Sherbrooke that connect with the original museum.

A good way to proceed is to take the elevator to the top floor and work down to the last subterranean level. From there, a tunnel incorporating more galleries leads across to the old building, and to yet more exhibits.

In the new pavilion, which was designed by Montréal architect Moshe Safdie, the galleries contain diverse selections that don't necessarily flow logically from one to the next. A small version of Rodin's *The Thinker*, for example, introduces rooms of Irish and English 18th and 19thC crystal, Shropshire and Staffordshire porcelains, Italian ceramics. Elsewhere, furniture designs by Eero Saarinen and Charles Eames are followed by paintings by Matisse and Picasso and sculptures by Lipshitz and Barbara Hepworth.

On the 4th level are some of the museum's prizes — paintings in oils by Hogarth, Reynolds, Bruegel the Elder, Van Dyck, and, almost hidden, El Greco's *Portrait of a Man*. Also here is Daumier's familiar *Nymphs Pursued by Satyrs,* Renoir's *Young Girl With a Hat,* a Monet seascape, and a young Cézanne. A glass-sided sculpture court still at this level offers a panoramic view of the city (👁). If there is only time for a short visit, make it this floor.

The lowest level (**S2**) has canvases by Josef Albers and Hans Hofmann standing near contemporary works; they seem as daring today as they once were. Many 20thC artists have drawn inspiration from the primitive arts of Africa and Oceania, so the next juxtaposition makes more sense than some others. The new galleries under the street are devoted to impressive masks and carvings from such places as Mali, the Ivory Coast, Nigeria, and New Guinea.

Then follow Chinese ceramics and garments 600 to 900 years old, some Egyptian sculptures and Greek vases. The rooms lead to the sub-lobby under the light-giving glass pyramid that can be seen at street level, to the right of the steps to the old building.

Take the elevator to the main floor of the original building, saving energy for the Pre-Columbian ceramic figures and ceremonial vessels of the Mexican Inca and Maya civilizations. Alaskan Inuit carvings dated as early as 300BC are revelations, crude though they are. More polished in execution are the 19th and early 20thC pieces by their descendants, wrought from walrus tusk and stone.

The remaining floors of the old building are used primarily for temporary exhibitions, numbering a dozen or more a year. A large museum shop offers books, games, crafts, reproductions, and a number of Inuit carvings for fair prices. A research library, for use by certified students, holds more than 50,000 works, and lectures and educational programs are given in the auditorium.

MUSÉE MARC-AURÈLE FORTIN

118 St-Pierre (near Pl. d'Youville). Map 8E6 ☎845-6108 📷 *✗ available.*
Open Tues–Sun 11am–5pm. Closed Mon. Metro: Square-Victoria.

Temporary exhibitions of other artists are periodically mounted, but the permanent collection of this unusual museum is composed solely of works by Marc-Aurèle Fortin (1888–1970). A prolific watercolorist, he sought to do nothing less than initiate a native Canadian school of landscape painting divorced from the dictates of European forerunners. Some think he succeeded.

MUSÉE McCORD (McCord Museum of Canadian History)

690 Sherbrooke W (University). Map 7E3 ☎398-7100 📷 *✗ available* 📖
Open Tues, Wed, Fri 10am–6pm, Thurs 10am–9pm, Sat, Sun 10am–5pm.
Closed Mon. Metro: McGill.

The province's main ethnographical collection has long been housed in this 1905 building situated across the street from the campus of McGill University, of which it is part. A major part of the museum's collection preserves elements of the arts and cultures of the four main aboriginal societies — the Inuit of the Arctic regions and the Amerindians of the west coast, central prairies and eastern woodlands.

Major renovations completed in 1992 gutted and rebuilt the interior and added a large new wing. The new atrium connecting the old and new wings is curiously affecting, even though all it displays is a large map of Canada and the legend, by Wordsworth, "What we have loved, others will love, and we will teach them how . . . . "

The rooms beyond the atrium are primarily for temporary exhibits. A large gallery then focuses on the "First Nations," with Inuit parkas, kayak models, and ivory carvings, Huron pottery, and Micmac quillwork and birchbark designs. The upstairs galleries have narrower appeal, dealing with the building of the 1860 Victoria Bridge and domestic life in Quebec at the turn of the century.

The Musée McCord concentrates on a fairly specialized field of interest. The exhibits are sensibly mounted and are organized with clarity.

OLD FORT AND DAVID M. STEWART MUSEUM

Île Ste-Hélène. Map 12D5 ☎861-6701 ▧ ↝ Open daily in summer 10am–6pm; Sept–May Wed–Mon 10am–5pm. Parades take place in summer at 11am, 2.30pm, 5pm. Metro: Île Ste-Hélène, then a 15-min walk, following signs for Vieux Fort.

Shortly after the war of 1812, a legitimate British fear of another American invasion prompted the Duke of Wellington to order the building of this moated fortress. It was completed in 1824 and became one of a string of St Lawrence fortifications.

The arsenal, barracks and blockhouses have low profiles, nestling behind high walls. A number of rooms, occupied by the David M. Stewart Museum, show an intriguing collection of maps, navigation equipment, furniture, and kitchen implements of the era, as well as the expected antique weaponry and uniforms. There is a copy of the first book printed in 1776 in Montréal, by Fleury Mesplet, later the founder of the *Montréal Gazette*. In summer, on the parade ground in front, young people costumed as soldiers of the Fraser Highlanders and the *Compagnie Franche de la Marine* periodically perform drills to the skirl of bagpipes and pretend to repel attackers. The presence of the "French" force is still another smoothing of French–Canadian feathers, since the fort did not exist until long after New France had become English Canada, the real British army having withdrawn from the island in 1870.

A popular restaurant, LE FESTIN DU GOUVERNEUR, is in a restored building in the grounds.

OLYMPIC PARK   See PARC OLYMPIQUE.

ORATOIRE ST-JOSEPH

3800 Chemin de la Reine-Marie. Map 12D4 ☎733-8211 ▧ ◃⵪ Open daily summer 6.30am–10pm, winter 6.30am–5pm. Metro: Côte-des-Neiges.

Few people are undecided about this immense basilica positioned on the flank of the highest point in Montréal. For the faithful, its grandeur is suitably humbling for entry into the presence of their Maker. For others, its awesomely bulky dimensions are merely gloomy and ponderous. Large, it certainly is. The huge dome is said to surpass in size all but those of St Peter's in Rome and St Paul's in London, although that feature, and the hilltop location, more often remind viewers of the

**Oratoire
St-Joseph**

Sacré Coeur in the Paris quarter of Montmartre. One Brother André, a lay brother in the Holy Cross order, was responsible for initiating the sanctuary project, starting with the small surviving chapel he erected in 1904. That accomplishment and his reputedly miraculous healing powers eventually led to his beatification, one level below sainthood. (St Joseph is the patron saint of Canada and of healers.) He died in 1937 at the age of 91, never to see the completion of his vision, which took another 12 years.

The basilica was begun in 1924 to the plans of architects Dalbe Viau and Alphonse Venne, while the interior was the commission of the French master Henri Charlier, who was responsible for the altar, crucifix, and sculptures of the Twelve Apostles. The result is primarily of Italian Renaissance inspiration, similar in outline if not in grace to the Duomo in Florence. A carillon with 56 bells, originally intended for the Eiffel Tower, was installed in 1955. With an elevation of 263m (863 feet) above sea level, the shrine has compelling views of the northern part of the island of Montréal.

PARC ANGRIGNON

*3400 Blvd. des Trinitaires. Map **12**E4* ☎*872-2815* 📷 *Metro: Angrignon.*
An important green space near downtown, the park has picnic grounds and a 4-mile cycling and ski trail. A winter wonderland of a snow festival — the **Fête des Neiges** — is held from mid-December to mid-February, when the trees twinkle with lights and decorations and there is an ice-skating trail for adults and an illuminated ice slide for children.

PARC LAFONTAINE

*4000 Av. Calixa-Lavallée. Map **7**A3 ☎872-2644 ▢ except ▨ for tennis courts. Open daily 9am–10pm. Metro: Sherbrooke.*

This is one of Montréal's oldest parks. In recognition of the city's cultural duality, half the park is landscaped in the English manner, the other in the more formal French style. Picnic areas border its several ponds and lakes, and there are seven tennis courts. In winter, there are skating rinks and snowshoeing and skiing trails.

PARC OLYMPIQUE (Olympic Park)

*4141 Pierre-de-Coubertin (Bennett). Map **12**D5 ☎252-8687 for general information ☎253-3434 for baseball tickets ◄ ▢ ✗ (charge payable) ◄ ▣ Open daily 9am–6pm. Metro: Pié-IX or Viau.*

When the 1976 Summer Olympics were awarded to Montréal, there were relatively few existing facilities in which to hold its many events. Olympic Park was the solution. Just 15 minutes E of downtown, it contained a velodrome (now the new BIODÔME), stadium, and natatorium with several swimming pools. A retractable roof was deemed desirable for the flying-saucer-shaped central area, so an inclined tower now rears over it, from which 26 heavy cables winch back the heavy fabric covering. It is an ungainly structure, and the resulting effect is not unlike that of a giant stork leaning over a birdbath. The esthetic controversy that ensued was compounded by a decision to impose very stiff taxes, especially on cigarettes and on property owners, to pay for the billion-dollar enterprise. In many minds, "The Big O" became "The Big Owe."

Roger Taillibert designed the entire facility. Movable seating sections can be adjusted to accommodate 60,000–80,000 spectators. This allows for the very different configurations required for a baseball diamond (the Montréal Expos play here) or a soccer field, as well as for concerts, conferences and exhibitions.

The roof, made of Kevlar cloth, measures more than 16,700 sq.m (20,000sq. yards) and weighs nearly 50 tons. When first installed, it could be retracted or deployed in 45 minutes, when all was in working order.

Olympic stadium

Increasingly, that has not been the case, and the Kevlar suffered a major tear in a 1991 windstorm. Those problems forced a decision to replace it with a rigid roof of Plexiglas or aluminum, at an estimated cost of $20 million. A decision by the municipal authorities to seek the Super Bowl for 1997 is expected to provide the incentive.

The signature tower, or mast, is 168m high and slopes at a 45° angle. (Compare that to the 5.5° incline of the Leaning Tower of Pisa.) A funicular along the spine of the mast carries 90 passengers in 95 seconds to the observation deck at the top, and there is a 56-km (35-mile) view on a clear day (👁).

At the base of the tower is the **natatorium**, with a curved roof over its six pools on three levels. The general public can take a swim in the pool (☎ *252-4737 for information*). In summer, a shuttle bus service is provided between BIODÔME, the Olympic Park and the nearby JARDIN BOTANIQUE.

A few blocks to the N are the double pyramids of OLYMPIC VILLAGE, where the athletes stayed in 1976. These are now private apartments and are regarded as highly desirable.

PLACE DES ARTS

175 Ste-Catherine W (between Jeanne-Mance and St-Urbain). Map 8D4
☎285-4200 for information ☎842-2112 for tickets ☎844-1211 for tours
📷 ✗ available. Metro: Place-des-Arts.

Montréal's already impressive center for the performing arts has undergone further expansion, now including the visual arts. The sprawling main building has four theaters and concert halls, ranging in size from the 2,982-seat **Salle Wilfrid-Pelletier** to the 138-seat **Café de la Place**. A new home for the MUSÉE D'ART CONTEMPORAIN was completed in 1992, along with another small theater. As the prime venue for symphony concerts, dance, opera, drama and lectures, the center supplements its offerings with lunchtime events, which are often free.

In winter, there is an outdoor skating rink.

PLACE MONTRÉAL TRUST

McGill and Ste-Catherine W. Map 8E4 ☎843-8000 📷 ═ 🛒 Open daily
8am–9pm. Metro: McGill or Peel.

Successful esthetically and commercially, this squat mid-rise building in the heart of the downtown shopping district does almost everything right. Polished brown granite and gray-green glass and trim comprise the exterior, while the several atrium floors enclose more than 120 shops and eating places. Among these are Bally, Marks & Spencer, Abercrombie, and Crabtree & Evelyn. Try to ignore the fact that most of the plantings are fake.

LA RONDE AMUSEMENT PARK

Île Ste-Hélène. Map 12D5 ☎872-6222 📷 🛒 ✱ Open May weekends
11am–1am; May 26–Sept 4 Mon–Thurs 11am–midnight, Fri, Sat 11am–1am.
Closed Sept 5–April. Metro: Papineau, then shuttle bus.

Full of music, fireworks, parades and the kinds of hair-raising rides that tear endless shrieks from willing participants, this permanent fair-ground was another project of Expo '67. The double-tracked roller-coaster is said to be the highest in the world.

It competes with the 20 water slides of the satellite **Aqua-Parc** in producing satisfying adrenalin rushes, as merrymakers allow themselves to be dropped from dizzying heights. (One slide is more than 23m (75ft) high and seems nearly vertical; tamer chutes also exist.) On Wednesday and Saturday, $\frac{1}{2}$-hour musical revues from eight countries are presented, and there are also daily performances by the resident circus, including animal and trapeze acts. Youngsters are entertained in a fairyland children's village populated with a host of fanciful animals and animated wooden soldiers.

During the **International Fireworks competition** in May to June, the pyrotechnics synchronize with stirring amplified music. All this, plus numerous snack bars and restaurants, and fairly high admission fees, suggest that a visit be scheduled for the better part of a day.

RUE PRINCE ARTHUR
Map 7C3. Metro: Sherbrooke.
A cross-street between Blvd. St-Laurent and the handsome residential Carré St-Louis, this was transformed into a pedestrian mall some years ago. Unabashedly touristy, most of the commercial tenants are restaurants, many of them Greek *brochette* factories bearing such imaginative names as *La Casa Grecque, La Caverne Grecque, La Cabane Grecque* . . . . In summer they set out white resin tables and chairs, the better to sip *sangria* and to watch the inevitable collection of street musicians, puppeteers, jewelry-makers and caricaturists drawn by the promise of all those plump tourist wallets. Few natives admit to coming here, but the low prices are difficult to resist.

RUE ST-DENIS
Map 7B1–8C5. Metro: Sherbrooke.
The blocks around the intersection of rue St-Denis and Ste-Catherine are as French as Montréal gets, especially for those who spent even a few of their salad days on Paris' Left Bank. The presence of the large Francophone Université du Québec sets the tone. Thousands of students, professional and temporary, ensure the profitability of jazz clubs and student cafés that crowd the sidewalks. Youthful insights and revelations crackle in the air they share with the smell of *espresso* and the unmistakable fumes of *Gitanes* cigarettes.

This is the *Quartier Latin,* scruffy and vibrant, as transitory as its New Age bookstores and holistic herbalists and as enduring as the eternal process of self-discovery.

As you progress farther N, up the hill, the street, too, is traveling up the economic and maturation scale. Scores of boutiques, storefront restaurants and yuppie bars crowd the way to **Carré St-Louis**, the city's most harmonious square of late 19thC row houses. Unfortunately, the square has latterly become a gathering place of derelicts and drug abusers, most of them more distasteful than dangerous.

ST LAMBERT LOCK

Rt. 132 at E end of Victoria Bridge. Map 12D5 ☎*672-4110* 📷 ◀€ *Observation tower open daily May–Oct 9am–8pm.*

Access for ships to the Great Lakes, in the heart of the continent, was desired from the earliest colonial days. Canals were dug to avoid the rapids and waterfalls along the way, but it was not until the middle of the 20thC that deep-draft ships were able to make the 3,700km (2,300-mile) voyage from the Atlantic Ocean to Lake Superior. Construction of the St Lawrence Seaway, a cooperative venture between Canada and the US, was completed in 1959. The entire project took just 5 years and, along its route, includes 15 locks, which lift ships eventually to more than 183m (600 feet) above the Atlantic sea level.

This lock is accessible from downtown Montréal, but only by car. Drive to the E end of Pont Victoria and take the exit marked "Écluses." Park in the "Observatory" lot. It's a short walk from there to the observation tower. Massive gates weighing 190 tons each rise and fall, the water in the lock draining and filling and draining again. Sometimes, it is only to allow a small pleasure craft through; at others, to raise or lower the huge ships (called "lakers") especially designed to ply this route. Often more than 213m (700 feet) long, to carry maximum cargoes of grain and ore, they are still narrow enough to fit through the locks.

A video monitor in the tower shows a short film in French or English describing the history and operation of the Seaway.

UNDERGROUND CITY

Map 10F4.

Given Montréal's humid summers and frigid winters, the development of a weatherproof city *beneath* the city was a logical by-product of the downtown construction boom that began in the 1960s. It began with the first major skyscraper complex, Place Ville-Marie. While they were about it, the owners decided to install arcades for retail outlets beneath their building — a canny use of valuable ground and air space. Soon, other builders were doing the same thing, and passageways were punched through to connect them. Now, there are nearly 27km (17 miles) of covered corridors and arcades, air-conditioned or heated according to season.

The expanding Metro Toronto subway system, also begun in the 1960s, linked this hidden second city to outlying attractions, such as PLACE DES ARTS and the ÎLE STE-HÉLÈNE. The largest components of the "city" are below Place Bonaventure, Place du Canada and the originator, Place Ville-Marie. The present totals include 200 restaurants, 1,600 shops, 30 bars, 40 banks and 34 cinemas and theaters wholly contained within the growing supermall. In addition, ten hotels, two department stores, 10 Metro stops, and rail stations have entrances to its underground walkways. It is therefore possible to leave a hotel, have lunch, see a movie, and even take a train to Toronto and back without once stepping outdoors.

This was an amoeba-like growth, however, created by private entrepreneurs and following no master plan; so the maze of promenades and atriums can bewilder even natives who turn off their regular routes, and it is necessary to make careful note of landmarks along the way. There are plans afoot to give some order to the complicated layout. In the meantime, there are worse things than getting lost down here — things such as driving rain . . . blizzards . . . sweltering temperatures . . . .

UNIVERSITÉ DE MONTRÉAL

2900 Blvd. Édouard-Montpetit ☎ *343-6111* 📷 *✗ by appointment. Metro: Université-de-Montréal*

This is the largest French-language university outside Paris, with nearly 58,000 students in more than 400 undergraduate and graduate programs. The campus is on the opposite (N) slope of Mont-Royal from McGill University, continuing the separations, intended or accidental, between the city's two main cultural groups.

Ernest Cormier, an influential pre-war architect, designed the main building in 1924. After a long period of construction, and the onset of World War II, classes did not begin until 1943.

VIEUX-PORT (Old Port)

On the waterfront, between McGill and Berri. Map 8D5 ☎ *496-7678* ◀ *Metro: Champ-de-Mars or Square-Victoria.*

Repair and recycling of the old piers at the edge of Vieux Montréal is approaching completion. In the process of transforming the area from shipping to recreational use, a linear park has been carved from the once desolate space that lies between the still-functional railway line and the water's edge.

From the promenade, it is possible to reach out and touch the freighters, tankers, and occasional cruise ships that still put in there. Most of the docks and surviving storage sheds have been cleaned up, the buildings now used as exhibition spaces, or, in two cases, as a super-screen IMAX cinema and a flea market.

Walking E, the most imposing architectural presence is the **Marché Bonsecours**, its silvery dome glinting in the sun. It has the kind of grandeur associated with Paris. Next to it is the ÉGLISE DE NOTRE-DAME-DE-BONSECOURS, with a statue of the sainted Marguerite Bourgeoys, her arms outstretched to returning ships and sailors. The port is liveliest in summer, with puppet shows, street theater and arts and crafts exhibitions. Bicycles, rollerbladers, joggers, trains, and *calèches* stream by.

One focal point is the **Clock Tower** on Quai de l'Horloge, at the E end of the development, with 200 stairs up to an observation deck. Information about the harbor is displayed there. On summer weekends, there are free guided tours of the port by tram.

Cycles built for one, two, and even four riders are available for rent. Cruises of the river and over the Lachine rapids depart and return here. Pedestrian entrances to the harbor are at the ends of Blvd. St-Laurent and Place Jacques-Cartier.

Montréal:
where to stay

Making your choice

Fevered hotel construction over the last two decades has created a buyer's market in which visitors can nearly always obtain rooms in the price range and location they desire. Moreover, those accommodations represent bargains compared to their counterparts in the larger cities of the US and Europe, especially when taking into account the favorable exchange rates of major currencies against the Canadian dollar. Montréal's **LE QUATRE SAISONS** and the **RITZ-CARLTON**, for example, maintain standards equal to those of their opposite numbers in London and New York, yet their rooms cost up to a third less. And those pacesetters now also have powerful competition from the very new **INTER-CONTINENTAL** and **VOGUE** hotels.

In addition, a remarkable number of mid-priced downtown hotels offer such enticements as swimming pools and health clubs. Away from the central core, tariffs are still lower, at no significant loss in convenience, and a strong bed and breakfast movement is present.

PRICING AND DISCOUNTS
Costs can be shaved still further. To fill their beds Friday through Sunday, even the most opulent hotels offer weekend discounts. Most sweeten the package with free cocktails, breakfasts, parking, or sightseeing tours, a roster limited only by the imaginations of marketing directors. Many hotels allow children to stay free in their parents' rooms, or at a small supplement. During the week, businesspeople should inquire about corporate rates, and senior citizens are often eligible for discounts. Obviously, a little shopping is in order.

Room rates do not include meals, and the combined provincial/ federal tax adds another 15 percent. A service charge is sometimes added for room service. Be certain not to tip a waiter twice.

See also BED AND BREAKFAST on page 169.

FACILITIES
Virtually all downtown hotels have garage parking, for which an extra charge is usually made. Increases in the corps of the health-conscious have inspired the installation of fitness rooms, which can range from bare spaces with a few exercise mats and a stationary bicycle, to full-scale complexes with racquetball courts, weight circuits, jogging tracks and aerobics classes. Swimming pools are surprisingly common, and

most are indoors. Complimentary morning newspapers in the guest's choice of French or English typically accompany room service breakfast or are left outside the door.

Color TV is found even in moderately-priced hotels, often with cable and/or closed-circuit movies. All the lodgings listed here have private bathrooms, and unless otherwise noted, all have air conditioning and elevators. Most have eased access for disabled persons, and many have added ramps and specially modified rooms.

HOW TO USE THIS CHAPTER

- **Location**:   In the listings below, the streets named in parentheses are the nearest *important* cross-streets. Map references are also given for the color maps at the end of the book.
- **Symbols**:   Full details of all our suggested hotels are given, and symbols show those that are particularly luxurious (🏨) in style. Other symbols show price categories, and give a résumé of available facilities. See the KEY TO SYMBOLS on page 7 for an explanation of the full list of our symbols.
- **Prices**:   The prices corresponding to our price symbols are based on average charges for two people staying in a double room with bathroom/shower. For this purpose, breakfast and tax are not included. Although actual prices will inevitably increase, our relative price categories are likely to remain the same.

    Prices are given in **Canadian dollars**.

Symbol	Category	Current price
▥	very expensive	more than $180
▥	expensive	$140-180
▥	moderate	$100-140
▯	inexpensive	$80-100
▢	cheap	under $80

FINDING A ROOM

If arriving without a room reservation, a possibility for assistance is **Centre de Réservation de Montréal** (☎ *932-9121 or 800-567-8687* 🗐 *932-7070*). They may try to sell packages of tours and theater and sports tickets, however. The majority of the desirable hotels are located in the heart of the downtown district, along **rue Sherbrooke** or in the **rue Crescent** district. A few are found in the **St-Denis Latin Quarter**, on the slopes of **Mont-Royal**, or near the airports.

Toll-free (**800**) numbers are provided by many hotels. In some cases, these can be used only within Canada, while others connect with the US telephone network. If an 800 call does not get through, use the regular number, preceded by the Montréal area code, **514**.

Montréal hotels A to Z

AUBERGE DE LA FONTAINE
*1301 Rachel E (Parc LaFontaine), Montréal
H2J 2K1. Map 7B2* ☎597-0166
🅵597-0496 ▥ to ▥ *21 rms* 🖼 ▦
🆎 ▣ ▥

*Location: Opposite the Parc LaFon-
taine.* European-style inns are as rare as
frog feathers in North American cities.
Montréal is an exception, and this
smart, intimate inn is exemplary. A
handsome stone structure with a shiny,
pressed-tin roof, it stands a few strides
away from one of the prettiest parks in
the city. The staff is helpful and friendly,
even before you sign in. When booking
a room, indicate your leisure interests
and they'll send a list of events occur-
ring during your stay. Breakfasts are
included in the already low rates, an
important saving.

BONAVENTURE HILTON
*1 Pl. Bonaventure (Mansfield), Montréal H5A
1E4. Map 10F4* ☎878-2332 or 800-
268-9275 (Canada) or 800-445-8667 (US)
🅵878-3881 ▥ *393 rms* ▦ 🖼 🆎 ▣
▣ ▥ ♿ ♨ ⤳ ☂ ☏ ♪

*Location: Atop Pl. Bonaventure and the
Central Railway Station.* They like to
think of it as a downtown resort hotel,
and they almost have a case. From the
street, the building looks like just another skyscraper, the lower floors composed of stores, restaurants, offices and
a convention hall. From the air, however, the top six floors form a hollow
square around a garden terrace with
brooks stocked with goldfish. For a
memorable sensation, enter the indoor
passageway and swim out into the
heated pool — in a snowfall.

Rooms either look out upon the city-
scape or down into the garden, with its
trees and patios. The restaurant **Le Cas-
tillon** receives high marks from local
gourmands.

LE CENTRE SHERATON MONTRÉAL
*1201 Blvd. René-Lévesque W (Stanley),
Montréal H3B 2L7. Map 10F4* ☎878-
2000 or 800-325-3535 🅵878-3958 ▥
827 rms ▦ 🖼 🆎 ▣ ▣ ▥ ♿ ♨ ⤳

☂ ⤳ ☂ ▣ ♪
*Location: Downtown, near Dorchester
Sq.* No stinting on *this* lobby: It's an
atrium 5 stories high, full of towering
palms and other plantings, awash in
light from the wall of glass facing the
boulevard. A pianist plays and cocktail
waitresses circulate beneath the green-
ery. The hotel-within-the-hotel concept
employed in many big-city Sheratons
reserves the five top floors for fancier
rooms and suites with their own check-
in and a lounge serving free breakfast
and afternoon tea. Given the full-
fledged health club, five bars and three
restaurants, there is no need to leave,
but the lively Rue Crescent district is
nearby.

LE CHÂTEAU CHAMPLAIN
*1 Pl. du Canada (Peel), Montréal H3B 4C9.
Map 10F4* ☎878-9000 or 800-268-9411
(Canada) or 800-828-7447 (US)
🅵878-6761 ▥ *606 rms* 🖼 ▦ 🆎 ▣
▣ ▥ ♿ ♨ ⤳ ☂ ☂ ⤳ ♪ ☒ ▣ *in
some rooms.*
*Location: Between the Windsor and
Central Railway stations.* Inverted
semicircular windows cover the sides of
the slender 36-story tower, making it
instantly recognizable by its nickname,
"The Cheese-Grater." Nurse a drink in
its penthouse lounge for one of the
city's most arresting vistas. Those who
stay for more than the view find com-
modious rooms equipped with in-
house movie channels and minibars.
Many are reserved for nonsmokers.
Children under 17 are allowed free in
their parents' rooms. They can pass
time in the indoor pool, always a delight
for youngsters, while the grownups
have **Le Caf' Conc'** nightclub.

CHÂTEAU VERSAILLES
*1659 Sherbrooke W (St-Mathieu), Montréal
H3H 1E3. Map 9F3* ☎933-3611 or 800-
361-7199 (Canada) or 800-361-3664 (US)
🅵933-7102 ▥ *177 rms* ▦ 🆎 ▣ ▣
▥ ♿ ✂ ☂ ▣ ⌕
*Location: Rue Crescent area, near the
Musée des Beaux-Arts.* Beginning as a

small European-style *pension* in the 1950s and expanding over the years into three adjacent houses, this is Montréal's most publicized in-city inn. Knockout decor is not to be expected in its 70 rooms, although a few antiques and artworks are scattered about the lobby area. Bedrooms are clean, plain, comfortable.

After the success of the first enterprise, the owners decided to expand into a modern tower across the street, the **Tour Versailles** (*1808 Sherbrooke W, Montréal H3H 1E3; same ☎ and* ☒ *)*. Geared to the business traveler, the modern annex has 107 rooms with large work tables and security boxes. Laptop computers and secretarial services are available. Respectful notices have been given to the **Champs-Élysées** restaurant in the tower. The desk staffs are eager to help with restaurant and theater reservations. Room-service breakfast arrives promptly.

LA CITADELLE
410 Sherbrooke W (Durocher), Montréal H3A 1B3. Map 7D3 ☎*844-8851 or 800-363-0363* ☒*844-0912* ▥ *199 rms* ☲ ▣ ▧ ◉ ▣ ▨ ⌂ ६ ✿ ⇌ ♪♯ ♈ ⇌ ▣
Location: Near Place des Arts and shops. One of La Citadelle's virtues is that a suite can be had for the same price as a plain double at competitors of its class. There's nothing grand about the facility, yet few standard amenities are neglected. Food and beverages are available at all hours, and each room has minibar and closed-circuit TV. (The remote control is tethered to the bed table.) In addition to the heated indoor pool, guests can work out on Nautilus devices in the compact gym, and wind down with sauna, steam room, or massage. Continental breakfast is included when taken in the **C'est La Vie** café, another saving, and the morning newspaper awaits outside the door. All this constitutes one of the better deals for business travelers on a tight budget.

DELTA MONTRÉAL
450 Sherbrooke W (City Councillors), Montréal H3A 2T4. Map 7D3 ☎*286-1986*

or 800-268-1133 ☒*284-4342* ▥ *465 rms* ☲ ▣ ▧ ◉ ▣ ▨ ⌂ ६ ✿ ⇌ ♈ ⅋ ▣ ⇌ ♪♯ ♨

Location: Near downtown shopping and Place des Arts. Although it has been on the scene since 1986, the paint barely looks dry. That can be counted as a measure of the management's commitment to proper maintenance and attention to detail. Businesspeople are the obvious target clientele, with a center that provides copiers, computer modems, secretarial services and telecommunications. The executive on the go can pump up for the day's challenges in a large health club with exercycles and Universal weight circuit, an indoor lap pool and two squash courts, or mellow down in the outdoor pool, whirlpool, sauna or massage room.

Families aren't neglected. A supervised game-and-crafts center keeps children busy for hours. Two restaurants, a jazz lounge and two Signature Service floors round out the attractions.

LE GRAND
777 University (St-Jacques), Montréal H3C 3Z7. Map 8E5 ☎*879-1370 or 800-361-8155* ☒*879-1761* ▥ *to* ▥ *737 rms* ☲ ▣ ◉ ▣ ▨ ⌂ ६ ⇌ ♈ ⅋
Location: Next to the Stock Exchange, a walk to Old Montréal. Once a Hyatt Regency, it retains that chain's flair for the dramatic, right up to the requisite revolving rooftop restaurant. Although the location is less than beguiling — adjacent to highway exit ramps and elevated train lines — it's well placed for access to downtown offices and the respite of Old Montréal. Available to guests are a full-service spa and pool, features common, but not universal, in the city's first-class and luxury hotels. The posh 25th floor is reserved for those willing to pay for private reception and free breakfasts and cocktails.

HOLIDAY INN CROWNE PLAZA
420 Sherbrooke W (Bleury), Montréal H3A 1B4. Map 7E3 ☎*842-6111 or 800-465-4329* ☒*842-9381* ▥ *489 rms* ▣ ☲ ▣ ◉ ▣ ▨ ६ ⇌ ♈ ⅋ ♪♯ ⇌

Location: Near Place des Arts. A multimillion-dollar infusion upgraded the once dowdy vertical motel to first-class, if not luxury, stature. That was necessary to compete with the cluster of upper-middle hostelries in the vicinity, and it succeeded. The pool is indoors, supplemented by exercise equipment, whirlpool, and sauna. Two executive floors with such extra perks as complimentary continental breakfast and private lounge with afternoon hors d'oeuvres are available at modest surcharges.

There are seven Holiday Inns to be found in the Montréal area, including the **Holiday Inn Richelieu** *(505 Sherbrooke* ☎*842-8581 or 800-465-4329),* near Carré St-Louis.

HOWARD JOHNSON PLAZA

475 Sherbrooke W (Aylmer), Montréal H3A 2L9. Map 7E3 ☎*842-3961 or 800-361-4973* ▥ *194 rms* ⚑ ▨ ◉ ◖ ▨ ▭ ▦ ▯ ⌇ ⌂ ▭ *in some rms.*

Location: Near Place des Arts and McGill University. Renovations a few years back elevated this hotel from the pack of competitors that cluster along this section of Sherbrooke. The glassed-over front terrace, open for drinks and meals in warm months, lends an elegant, animated note. Lobby and bedrooms could use some of that quality, but considering the reasonable prices and excellent location, this is a near-bargain.

L'INSTITUT

3535 St-Denis (Rigaud), Montréal H2X 3P1. Map 7C3 ☎*282-5120 or 800-361-5111* ▥ *42 rms* ▭ ▨ ◉ ▨ ▯

Location: On Carré St-Louis. A satisfying possibility in the Prince Arthur–St-Laurent area is this unusual hotel, operated by earnest undergraduates of the Québec Institute of Tourism and the Hotel Trade. Even though it is, in effect, a laboratory for young people intending to make their careers in the hospitality business, guests give up little in comparison to conventional hotels, and they gain a level of care and attention rarely encountered elsewhere. Room

rates include breakfast. It's a short walk to either the Latin Quarter or Blvd. St-Laurent.

INTER-CONTINENTAL ▱

360 St-Antoine W (St-Pierre), Montréal H2Y 3X4. Map 8E5 ☎*987-9900* ▤*987-9904* ▥ *to* ▥ *359 rms* ▭ ▨ ◉ ◖ ▨ ⌂ ⌇ ⌇ ⚑ ▭ ▯ ⌂ ▭

Location: At edge of financial district and Vieux Montréal. The latest contender for the laurels shared by the RITZ-CARLTON and LE QUATRE SAISONS stakes its claim in another, equally interesting, part of town. Old Montréal is out one door, the World Trade Centre out another. Bedrooms are bounteously proportioned, and since they are on the 10th floor or higher, most have fine views of either the river or Mont-Royal. Their large marble bathrooms have both tubs and shower stalls. Laundry is returned in hours, not days, shoes are polished overnight for free, complimentary newspapers in the correct language appear outside the door. Guests can choose messages through voice mail or operator.

Since the Inter-Continental chain is owned by a Japanese company, the 24-hour room service menu includes what it describes as a traditional Japanese breakfast. Adding to the hotel's visual interest is its connection — over a pedestrian bridge above a grassed-in concourse — to the 1889 Nordheimer Building. Once burnt-out and its status uncertain, the elegant building was thoroughly refurbished with a superbly restored lobby and bar. Stone vaults down below may date from the 18thC. Their use, and those on the floors above, are primarily as function rooms, not sleeping quarters.

JARDIN SINOMONDE

99 Viger W (St-Urbain), Montréal H2Z 1E9. Map 8D5 ☎*878-9888 or 800-465-4329* ▤*878-6341* ▥ *235 rms* ▭ ▨ ◉ ▨ ▯ ⚑ ⌇ *some rms.*

Location: Adjacent to Chinatown. Perhaps because the company already has many hotels in the city, the owners downplay the fact that this is yet another Holiday Inn. Hence the name. Its schizophrenia is amplified by the two restaurants, one of which serves Chinese food, the other, Western. While there is nothing startling or new about the decor, do seek out the authentic Chinese garden.

An excellent location for guests on business or at leisure, the hotel has, virtually at its doorstep, the Place d'Armes Metro station, the Palais des Congrès (convention center), the World Trade Centre, Vieux Montréal, and Chinatown.

MANOIR LEMOYNE

2100 Blvd. de Maisonneuve W (Atwater), Montréal H3H 1K6. Map 9H3 ☎*931-8861 or 800-361-7191* ⊠*931-7726* ▥ *286 rms* ═ 🆎 ▣ ▥ ▥ ♿ 💅 ⇌ ⛵ 🍷 ☞ ♈ ♪ 🔲

Location: Near The Forum sports and concert arena. Hockey and rock fans couldn't be better placed; others will think it a little too far w of downtown. That's the only drawback, and it does much to compensate. For the price of a single in one of the first-class hotels, get a duplex suite complete with dining room, kitchenette and balcony. Cable TV with closed-circuit movies and stocked refrigerators are included. Facilities include indoor swimming pool and garden, two saunas, bar and restaurant. There can't be a better choice for families or those planning a long stay who prefer not to spend it in a standard boxy room.

LE MERIDIEN MONTRÉAL

4 Complexe Desjardins (Jeanne-Mance), Montréal H5B 1E5. Map 8D4 ☎*285-1450 or 800-361-8234 (Québec) or 800-543-4300 (rest of Canada and US)* ⊠*285-1243* ▥ *626 rms* 🖼 ═ 🆎 ▣ ▥ ▥ ♿ 💅 ⛵ ⇌ ☞ ♈ 🔲 *(most rms)* ♪

Location: Across the street from Place des Arts. Roughly equidistant from the Latin Quarter, rue Crescent and Old Montréal, this east-downtown area is within easy walking or Metro distance of all that Montréal offers. The concert halls and theaters of Place des Arts are a few steps away, and the hotel is often

used as the headquarters of the International Jazz Festival. A glass tower erected in 1972, it is an integral part of a block-square complex of office buildings and subterranean shopping malls. An indoor pool hovers above the catacombs and beneath the rambling lobby. For something rarely found among everyday hotel inducements, play a round on their indoor golf course. A nonsmoking floor is available, as is a special "Le Club Président" executive level with its own lounge and check-in.

MONTAGNE

1430 de la Montagne (Ste-Catherine), Montréal H3G 1Z5. Map 9F3 ☎*288-5656 or 800-361-6262* ⊠*288-9658* ▥ *132 rms* 🆎 ▣ ▥ ▥ ═ 🖼 ♿ ⇌ ☀ ♪

Location: Rue Crescent district. The management shows an almost bewildering number of faces to its public. The lobby has a pronounced Belle Époque/Art Nouveau character, exemplified by a fountain surmounted by a brass, female nude butterfly with stained-glass wings. Businesspeople with a Continental flair populate the flamboyant **Crocodile**, while their younger, up-and-coming cousins cruise **Thursday's** singles bar. Drinks and light lunches are also taken beside the rooftop pool, but excellent French cuisine and service are the attractions at the mezzanine **Le Lutétia**. And then there's the piano bar, the discotheque, the tea room, the boutiques . . . all this in a hotel with only 132 rooms and suites, many of them as eclectic as the rest of the place.

NOVOTEL

1180 de la Montagne (René-Lévesque), Montréal H3G 1Z1. Map 10F4 ☎*861-6000 or 800-221-4542* ⊠*861-0992* ▥ *200 rms* ═ 🆎 ▣ ▥ ▥ ♿ 🖼 🍷 ♈ ☞ 🔲

Location: In rue Crescent nightlife and dining district. The European chain specializes in sensibly-priced rooms equipped as middle-management executives expect. This includes wide work tables with twin-line phones with data ports for PC modem. "Workmanlike" describes the fitness center, too, and that word can be applied to the entire operation. Nothing glamorous, but nothing to impede work or play, either, unless you insist on room service at 3am.

LE QUATRE SAISONS 🏨

1050 Sherbrooke W (Peel), Montréal H3A 2R6. Map 9F3 ☎ *284-1110 or 800-268-6282 (Canada) or 800-332-3442 (outside Canada)* ☎ *845-3025* 🎞 *300 rms* ▬ 🆎 🎫 🎴 📺 🖼 ♿ ✉ ♈ ☿ 🎵 ☎ ◻

Location: Near McGill University. This estimable Canadian-owned chain has more than 20 hotels in North America, with more on the drawing boards. They are routinely accorded the highest rank, and this one does full justice to that lofty reputation. This is contemporary luxe in a glass high-rise, not the Old World variety, but little is left to chance. Rooms are spacious and fully appointed, including complimentary closed-circuit movies, terry robes, minibar, bathroom hair dryer and scale. They'll provide a room facsimile machine, on request. Nonsmoking floors are available.

The 3rd-floor health club has a Keiser weight circuit. For an exhilarating change-of-winter-pace, plunge into the indoor pool, swim outside, then back, without leaving the water. Sauna, whirlpool and steam room are also available. Room service is on call round the clock. **Le Restaurant** is *the* site for power breakfasts, and power dinners, for that matter. Health-conscious diners can choose from an "alternative cuisine" card. In the piano bar, a table of bite-sized sushi treats and seafood nibbles awaits imbibers.

RAMADA RENAISSANCE DU PARC

3625 Av. du Parc (Prince-Arthur), Montréal H2X 3P8. Map 7D3 ☎ *288-6666 or 800-268-8998 (Canada) or 800-228-9898 (US)* ☎ *288-2469* 🎞 *467 rms* ◻ ▬ 🆎 🎫 🎴 📺 🖼 ♿ ✉ ☿ 🎵 ⚡ ♈

Location: Near Place des Arts and McGill University. Comparable in all ways to competitors closer to the city center, yet with significantly lower tariffs, this hotel deserves careful consideration. Part of the La Cité complex,

it has access to better sports and fitness facilities than any of them. The roster includes indoor and outdoor pools, squash courts, indoor running track, weight rooms, saunas, Turkish baths and whirlpools. There's even tennis, in summer. After a pressurized coat-and-tie day in the conference rooms of downtown towers, slip into jeans and relax in the funky *boîtes* and bars of St-Denis and St-Laurent.

LA REINE ELIZABETH 🏨

900 Blvd. René-Lévesque W (Mansfield), Montréal H3B 4A5. Map 10F4 ☎ *861-3511 or 800-268-9420 (Québec and Ontario) or 800-828-7447 (US)* ☎ *514-861-3536* 🎞 *to* 🎞 *1,016 rms* ◻ 🆎 🎫 🎴 📺 ♿ ▬ ◻ ♿ ◻

Location: Downtown, above the main railroad station. Royalty and heads of state choose the "QE" (Queen Elizabeth) as a matter of course. True, there are three or four hostelries boasting higher overall levels of luxury. None has a more central location, however, and the management endeavors to satisfy all but lowest-budget travelers. It has three classes of accommodations: Entrée Première has comfortable rooms at relatively moderate tariffs; Entrée Silver and Gold lay on such extras as private concierge, separate elevator, bathrobes, free breakfasts, lounges, and special check-in service. The **Beaver Club** is the most celebrated of its several restaurants, a haunt of the power elite.

RITZ-CARLTON 🏨

1228 Sherbrooke W (Drummond), Montréal H3G 1H6. Map 9F3 ☎ *842-4212 or 800-363-0366* ☎ *842-4907* 🎞 *240 rms* ▬ ◻ 🆎 🎫 🎴 📺 ♿ ☘ ☿ ◻ ♈ 🃏

Location: Near the Musée des Beaux-Arts and rue Crescent district. The famous black-and-white *porte-cochère* has sheltered members of royalty and the Establishment since 1912. They expect the ultimate in polished treatment, and get it. The international survey of the respected *Institutional Investor* magazine routinely ranks it among the top five hotels in North America. Nothing is overlooked at the Ritz, no caprice unattended. They once delivered pots and utensils to Sophia Loren's suite so she could cook her own pasta; a staff member officially witnessed the first marriage of Elizabeth Taylor and Richard Burton. Every room has remote-control TV, stereo, clock radio, electronic safe, umbrella, robes, minibar, lighted makeup mirror, hairdryer, bath telephone, and bathroom TV speaker to keep track of the morning news. All are of ample proportion, so about the only thing that suites have is still more room and the extra furniture to fill it.

The ground-floor **Café de Paris** is not only a prime power breakfast site, but one of the city's best eateries. In summer, business is moved out into the meticulously landscaped garden, where afternoon tea is an obligatory event. Ducks paddle about in the pond in the center, squawking decorously. This is still a bastion of dignity in an all-too-casual world.

VOGUE 🏨
1425 de la Montagne (Ste-Catherine), Montréal H3G 1Z3. Map 9F3 ☎285-5555 *or 800-363-0363* 🖃849-8903 ▥▥▥ *142* rms ⬛⬛⬛⬛⬛⬛⬛⬛⬛⬛⬛⬛
Location: In rue Crescent nightlife and

dining district. If the walk through the tasteful lobby and spruce halls doesn't signal the management's intent, check the items in the minibar. Yes, down there at the end of the list are caviar and foie gras. These people are serious about challenging the hegemony of the RITZ-CARLTON, just a few blocks away. Peek into the bathroom: large marble tub with whirlpool, fat thirsty towels and robes, separate shower stall, digital scale, and of course, a TV on an adjustable pedestal.

What is more, even standard rooms have four telephones, a fax machine, and computer port. On the beds are puffy duvets — in the closets, umbrellas and electronic safes. Fresh flowers dress the table. For an extra touch of glamor, request one of the 25 baldaquin beds. Room service throughout the day and night, of course, as well as free shoeshine and daily newspaper.

Crowning all is the **Société Café**, which almost immediately gained a reputation as glossy as any hotel dining room in the city. If the Vogue has a deficiency, it lies in the modest equipment and dimensions of the exercise room. For those who require more demanding fitness machines and graduated weights, guest passes to a nearby club are available.

AND AT THE AIRPORTS . . .

Likely to be of interest primarily to strictly-business sorts or people with early flights, airport hotels do their job with no more fuss than is strictly necessary.

Montréal has two airports, and there are possibilities for satisfactory accommodation at either.

At **Mirabel,** they include **Le Château de l'Aéroport** *(Box 60, Montréal J7N 1A2* ☎476-1611 🖃476-0873 ▥▥▥ *).* No room service or bellhops, but there is an indoor pool and sauna.

Within easy reach of **Dorval** Airport and downtown are the **Holiday Inn Pointe Claire** *(6700 Trans-Canada Highway, Pointe-Claire, Montréal H9R 1C2* ☎697-7110 *or* 800-465-4329 ▥▥▥*)* and the **Holiday Inn Aéroport** *(6500 Côte-de-Liesse, Montréal H4T 1E3* ☎ *739-3391 or 800-361-5430* ▥▥▥*).* In both, residents have access to fitness centers and indoor pools.

Also near Dorval Airport is the **Aéroport Hilton International** *(12505 Côte-de-Liesse, Montréal H9P 1B7* ☎*631-2411 or 800-268-9275* ▥▥▥*).*

BED AND BREAKFAST

As the term is employed here, "bed and breakfast" refers to rooms in private homes, not inns or *pensions* in the European sense. Reservations are made through referral agencies, which attempt to match each client's needs with an appropriate lodging. Accommodations range from spare, utilitarian rooms with the bath down the hall, to housekeeping apartments of engaging design and every hotel comfort except room service. Their primary appeal is their low prices. Even the most handsomely appointed rarely reach the top of our moderate (▥) price band.

But price is not all. Many guests could easily afford the fancy downtown hotels, but prefer the homey environment of a B&B, the opportunity to spend time with their Canadian hosts and their often international guests. The owner-hosts are an invariably gregarious, energetic lot, knowledgeable boosters of their city and storehouses of information and opinion.

A modest sense of adventure is required, if only because matchups between guests and hosts are made by telephone or mail. There is no guarantee that the resulting fit will be smooth, for there is not the relative certainty of expectation that one carries into a Hilton or a Holiday Inn. For that reason, it is important to be as precise as possible about requirements. Private bathrooms, for example, are available, but cannot be assumed. TV sets in bedrooms are the exception, not the rule, although there might be one in the front parlor. Hosts may forbid smoking, or pets, or children under a certain age. Some impose curfews. Most locations are within easy reach of public transit, but some outlying areas can be as distant as an hour from major attractions.

Reserving well in advance is always wise, especially in summer. As a rule, a deposit equal to one night's stay is required, the balance payable upon arrival. Credit cards are often accepted, if only for the deposit, but not always and not all types. Given the inherent quirks and volatility of the business, the agencies listed below should be regarded only as a first source.

A BED AND BREAKFAST DOWNTOWN NETWORK

3485 Laval, Montréal H2X 3C8 ☎*289-9749* 🄵*287-7386* 🄰🄴 🄾 🄥🄸🄴
Many homes handled here are located near the rue Crescent and Prince Arthur/St-Laurent districts. Parking is often available.

BED & BREAKFAST DE CHEZ NOUS

5386 Brodeur, Montréal H4A 1J3 ☎*485-1252 or 488-3149* 🄾
About 30 residences, situated mostly in the residential quarters on the slopes of Mont-Royal rather than in the city center. Some efficiency apartments (self-catering) are available on a weekly basis.

MONTRÉAL BED & BREAKFAST

4921 Victoria, Montréal H3W 2N1 ☎*738-9410* 🄰🄴 🄾 🄥🄸🄴
Said to be the first of the B&B networks, with a wide range of accommodations in about 50 houses in all parts of the city.

RELAIS MONTRÉAL HOSPITALITÉ

3977 Laval, Montréal H2W 2H9 ☎*287-9653* 🄾 🄥🄸🄴
Full breakfasts, not just coffee and *croissant*, they say. Some accommodations are close to luxurious. Parking available.

Montréal: eating and drinking

Where and what to eat

Trenchermen and gourmands rejoice, for Montréal has few peers in North America for quality, value and diversity of dining. With an avidity bordering on obsession, TV and the print media chart the comings and goings of favored chefs, the opening of new restaurants and the decline of culinary reputations.

All this concern is undoubtedly due to the French heritage of a populace that cares deeply about food and its preparation. That cultural inclination stokes the desire to eat out often, despite economic uncertainties, which may explain why Montréal restaurants did not suffer as much in the latest recession as they did in Ontario. Nearly a third of the Toronto restaurants listed in the last edition of this book went out of business, compared to only three of those listed in Montréal.

WHAT IT COSTS
The tab for a taste of this good life can be surprisingly low. A grand 4-course repast in one of the city's most expensive restaurants handily matches a similar spread in New York for taste and presentation, yet costs as little as half as much. More good news: lunch in that same place is 25 to 60 percent less than dinner, due to the widespread practice of offering steep discounts at midday to attract businesspeople and shoppers. Those visitors who can bring themselves to have their main meal in the early afternoon, in the Latin manner, can sample the wares of establishments that might prove otherwise out of reach. This entails little sacrifice. Lunch menus are shorter, but with many of the same dishes as on the dinner menu, and the animated 2-hour lunch is very much alive. See also PRICES on page 172.

WHAT TO EAT
Given Montréal's prevailing cultural and linguistic demographics, any food other than French can be regarded as ethnic. That doesn't mean the rest of the world is neglected. Immigration has brought able practitioners of many national kitchens to join the feeding frenzy. Italian and Chinese restaurants are especially favored, but many others, typically at much lower prices, purvey Greek, Korean, Japanese, Middle Eastern, Thai, Indian and Portuguese edibles.

There is an indigenous French–Canadian repertoire, too — a home-cooking with roots in the colonial past and incorporating such quintessential New World products as maple syrup. Many of these distinctive Québécois recipes involve lard and beans, hardly the light touch many diners now prefer. Among the more enticing traditional staples are a ground-pork pâté, pork pie, and the ultimate regression to childhood, sugar pie. Discussions of the last achingly high-calorie dessert narrow over whether it should have nuts or not, a single crust or two, or be made of brown sugar or maple syrup. No exploration of Québec is complete without a sample.

EATING FAST
Natives love their lowbrow fast foods as much as their turbot and *entrecôte au poivre,* and arguments can arise over where to find the best *chien chaud* (hot dog), pizza, or *hambourgeois.* At the top of this pecking order is a taste treat that expatriate Québeckers yearn for above all others. It's smoked meat, a delicatessen specialty that falls somewhere between corned beef and *pastrami,* but is less fatty, and distinctively flavored according to inevitably "secret" recipes. It is often served in a do-it-yourself heap of slices, with a stack of rye bread and a plate of delectably greasy *pommes frites.*

Another, fortunately unique fabrication is something called *poutine,* a lumpy assemblage of cheese curds, french fries, and brown gravy. A recent invention of uncertain provenance, it can easily be avoided.

WINE AND FOOD
When selecting a wine with dinner, the bottle is usually not opened until the main course arrives, unless specifically requested earlier. Most restaurants serve decent wines by the glass, which reduces waste and the final reckoning, especially since wine and liquor are heavily taxed.

About a quarter of all Montréal restaurants allow patrons to bring their own wine, and nearby convenience stores cater to the practice. Look for the symbol in store and restaurant windows of a red hand holding a bottle, or the words *Apportez votre vin* (bring your own wine).

CAFÉS AND SNACK BARS
Cafés are resting places as much as anything. The most obvious are the many branches of **A.L. Van Houtte**, reliable serve-yourself operations featuring *croissants,* quiches, sandwiches and the founder's coffee. More traditional cafés, in tone if not in decor, typically offer a limited range of *croissants,* fruit tarts, quiches, and the like. Often notable for their excellent *espresso* and *café filtre,* they invite lingering and have loyal patrons of all ages and persuasions. They are found in greatest numbers in the **St-Denis/St-Laurent** area and in **Vieux Montréal.** Most are open every day, from early morning to late at night.

At the lower end of the food chain is the snack bar called a *casse-croûte.* The name translates, more or less, as "break bread," with hot dogs and baked beans or French fries the usual offering. They are scattered around the city, even in the tonier neighborhoods and tourist districts. To assuage pangs in anticipation of a grander meal later on, or when there isn't time to dawdle at a table, they're just the ticket.

USEFUL TO KNOW

- **Tipping**: Provincial laws require the posting of menus with prices outside every eating place. Tips of 10 percent are regarded as adequate in humbler establishments; 15 percent is the standard in those in the mid-to-upper range. Gratuities are easy to calculate, as you need only copy the separately listed combined federal and provincial tax, which is $15\frac{1}{2}$ percent of the total. Only extreme satisfaction with all aspects of a meal prompts the average Québécois to leave as much as 20 percent.
- **Reservations**: Montréalers live for the weekend, not the workplace. That means reservations are essential Thursday through Saturday for dinner at any restaurant of even middling achievement. For "hot" restaurants, the rule applies any time. Ordinarily, a call a few hours in advance suffices. Heaviest demand is between 8-9pm.
- **Opening hours**: Most of our restaurants are open seven days a week for lunch and dinner, so only variations from that norm are given.

HOW TO USE THIS CHAPTER

- **Location**: In the listings below, the streets named in parentheses are the nearest *important* cross-streets, provided as an aid to locating them. Map references are also given for the color maps at the end of the book. :
- **Symbols**: See the KEY TO SYMBOLS on page 7 for an explanation of the full list.
- **Prices**: The prices corresponding to our price symbols are based on the average price of a meal (dinner, not lunch) for one person, inclusive of house wine, tax and gratuity. Although actual prices will inevitably increase after publication, our relative price categories are likely to stay the same. **Canadian dollars** are quoted here.

Symbol	Category	Current price
⬜	very expensive	over $70
⬜	expensive	$50-70
⬜	moderate	$30-50
⬜	inexpensive	$15-30
⬜	cheap	under $15

Montréal restaurants A to Z

L'ACTUEL *Belgian*
1194 Peel (Ste-Catherine). Map 9F3 ⬝
☎866-1537 ⬜ ⬛ ⬛ ⬛ ⬛ *Closed Sat lunch, Sun.*

Downstairs is a lively bar, upstairs the restaurant, crisp and uncluttered, with bare parquet floors and bentwood chairs. Ask for a window table overlooking Square Dorchester.

The house specialty is mussels. They come in several guises, inevitably accompanied by double-fried potatoes that approach perfection. Bountiful second helpings are also traditional.

The waitress asks if you like your food spicy, as with the steak tartare, which is as tasty a version as can be found anywhere.

BAGEL ETC. *Eclectic*
4320 St-Laurent (Marie-Anne). Off map **7C1**
☎845-9462 ⬜ to ⬜ 💳 💳 Open till
3.30am. Closed Mon.

Montréal bagels are thinner, crisper and better than the New York variety, which have the consistency of setting cement, and here is the living proof. The menu ranges beyond bagels to goulash and burgers, served by artistes who obviously have better things to do with their valuable time.

BEAUTY'S *Deli*
93 Mont-Royal W (St-Urbain). Off map **7C1**
☎849-8883 ⬜ No cards. Closed Sun in
July-Aug.

On every native's list of musts for visitors is breakfast at Beauty's — the delicatessen as institution. No-one mentions that the food can easily be duplicated in any of a thousand places across North America. Never mind. Bacon and eggs sound so much more exotic in French. Everything is fresh, including the orange juice.

Arrive by 9am to be reasonably sure of a seat on Sunday morning, when the faithful are as likely to arrive by bike as by Jaguar.

BONAPARTE *Eclectic*
443 St-Francois Xavier (Notre-Dame). Map
8E5 ☎844-4368 ⬜ 💳 💳 💳 💳
Closed Sat lunch, Sun lunch.

No bells and whistles here, no gastronomic pyrotechnics, just reassuring professionalism. Fish and game are special, but beef is done to order and chicken cooked to that fleeting moment halfway between underdone and rubbery. Expect no lemon grass nor serrano chilies, but that doesn't mean what appears is pedestrian. There is that unexpected *lasagna*, a little wonder, sandwiching thin slices of halibut spread with earthy puréed mushrooms and red peppers between disks of spinach pasta.

À la carte prices are moderately high, offset by the special *déjeuner d'affaire* (business lunch) and the nightly *table d'hôte*. The several busy rooms are nearly always full, and drop-ins can expect a wait.

LA BRASSERIE HOLDER *Brasserie*
3616 St-Laurent (Sherbrooke). Map **7D3**
☎842-6383 ⬜ 💳 💳 Closed Sat lunch,
Sun lunch.

A space that has been, in its recent past, a plain guzzler's tavern and a hip tapas design bar is now an updated brasserie (at this writing, it must be hastened). By definition, a brasserie is a bistro that pushes beer and dishes like sausage and sauerkraut. Beer is featured here, true, but most patrons choose wine, and the food is lighter. Steamed salmon, for example, is cool at the center, enclosed with boiled new potatoes and a decorative fan of undercooked snow-peas. Service can be swift, even a little pushy, as if they can't always wait to turn the table over to waiting customers.

CASA PINO *Italian*
1472 Crescent (Maisonneuve). Map **9F3**
☎844-4477 ⬜ 💳 💳 💳 💳
All of young Montréal must pass this corner of rue Crescent and de Maisonneuve sooner or later. They drop in here as late as 3am for pastas, salads, or any of the 24 different types of individual pizza. Many insist that the pizzas are the best in town, although they are less robust than most American versions.

CATHAY *Chinese*
73 de la Gauchetière W (St-Urbain). Map
8D4 ⬜ ☎866-3131 💳 💳 💳 Open
daily.

When one popular Chinatown eatery dies — the lamented *Kam Fung*, in this case — there is always another ready to step forward, and with hardly a missed beat. *Dim sum* is the reason for Cathay, too, and lunch is the time. Chinese families from all over the metropolitan area flood back on weekends to this displaced fragment of Hong Kong. That's the fun time to be here, crowds and all. The drill is simple. They don't take reservations on weekends, so walk up to the podium on the second floor and obtain a numbered ticket, then return to the end of the line snaking down the stairs.

Once called and seated, attend to the women pushing trolleys between the tables. Each cart has two or three different *dim sum,* perhaps curried shrimp balls or boneless chicken feet or balls of rice and chicken strips steamed in a water-lily pad, among three-score irresistible goodies. They are identified by the waitresses, who serve them up and add the cost to the bill left on each table. Diners eat until full — or, commonly, more than they should. To be seated sooner, couples or single diners can volunteer to share their table.

LES CHENÊTS ⌂ *French*
2075 Bishop (Sherbrooke). Map 9F3
☎844-1842 ▥ ᴀᴇ ⊕ ⊙ ᴠɪsᴀ
One reason why this is one of Montréal's priciest restaurants is apparent upon entering. Every wall is hung with phalanxes of expensive copper pans, and even the bar has a copper top. The setting of banquettes amid tones of warm brown is as classic as the entirely French menu. Specials are recited in either French or English by faintly bored waiters who look to have been around for years. Judicious seasonings and attractive presentations draw an older crowd that doesn't care to be startled. It's a suave, calming venue for special-event dinners, not daily bread.

CHEZ DELMO *Seafood*
211 Notre-Dame W (St-François). Map 8E5
☎849-4061 ▥ to ▥ ᴀᴇ ⊙ ᴠɪsᴀ Closed Sat lunch, Mon eve, Sun.
Stockbrokers and investment bankers who prefer their seafood precisely cooked and without trickery, flock to this fine old fish house in Vieux Montréal. Two long oyster bars with rows of wooden stools funnel diners into the main room in back, where fresh Dover sole and Nova Scotia salmon are high on the list of favorites. It's all cozily Old Guard and Old World.

CHEZ LA MÈRE MICHEL *French*
1209 Guy (Ste-Catherine). Map 9G3
☎934-0473 ▥ ᴀᴇ ⊕ ⊙ ᴠɪsᴀ Closed Sat lunch, Sun.
The bar down below is the staging area for patrons awaiting their tables, and that time can stretch out on weekend nights. Upstairs, the several rooms have

dark wood floors, white plaster walls and scarlet tablecloths. Trendy experimentation is not to be expected. Look instead for solid professionalism at both stove and table, as with the rabbit terrine, lobster soufflé, and salmon and haddock with two sauces.

CLAUDE POSTEL *French*
443 St-Vincent (Notre-Dame). Map 8D5
☎875-5067 ▥ ᴀᴇ ⊕ ⊙ ᴠɪsᴀ Closed Sat lunch, Sun lunch.
Montréalers tend to avoid their old town, dismissing it as a tourist trap. Brokers, government workers, and yes, tourists, know better. Several of the city's most admirable restaurants cast their warm glow along these ancient streets, among them ʟᴀ ᴍᴀʀÉᴇ, **Le Fadeau,** ᴄʜᴇᴢ ᴅᴇʟᴍᴏ, and Claude Postel. This owner-chef used to tend the stove at ʙᴏɴᴀᴘᴀʀᴛᴇ, a few blocks away, and he went on to surpass his former employer. He is a presence in the dining room, always ready to discuss a recipe or recommend a dish, perhaps the legs of duck *confit* crossed atop thin, crisp potato *crêpes*.

The hostesses and captains are cordial to all who cross the threshold, those dressed in jeans and boots as warmly as those in pinstripes or Gucci loafers. No one is made to feel like a cheapskate for ordering the business lunch or dinner *table d'hôte.* If this isn't quite the perfect restaurant, it points the way to that unattainable goal.

LE COMMENSAL *Vegetarian*
2115 St-Denis (Sherbrooke). Map 7C3
☎845-2627 ▥ ᴀᴇ ⊙ ᴠɪsᴀ Open daily.
Vegetarians aren't the only customers, despite the total absence of meat in any form. Most of these dishes are so cleverly assembled, with such scrupulous attention to texture, taste, and color, hardly anyone notices the lack of beef in the chili or the missing chicken in the enchiladas. Serve yourself from the long buffet of tantalizing hot and cold platters and pay by the gram at the end of the line. The below-street-level atmosphere is hardly beguiling, an echoing hall of bare tables and bare floors

seating as many as 200 people. Healthful food at good prices compensate.

This branch is in the Latin Quarter; there is another downtown *(680 Ste-Catherine* ☎*871-1480).*

DUNN'S ✿ *Deli*
892 Ste-Catherine W (McGill). Map 8E4
☎*866-4377* ▢ *to* ▢ ▢ ▢ *Open 24hrs.*
Always included in episodes of the great smoked meat debate, Dunn's can argue that it is the ultimate deli in a town packed with the breed. Its building is cloaked in the gaudiest reds and yellows of the downtown business district, the street-level windows filled with such maddening delectables as huge jars of pickles and garlands of sausage, calculated to stop passers-by in their tracks. All smoked meat is not the same. The Dunn's version is close in texture and flavor to corned beef, in contrast to that at SCHWARTZ'S, which veers toward a darker, very lean pastrami.

Smoked meat is far from the only attraction, even though it features in more dishes than it probably should — would you believe "smoked meat pizzaghetti?" Apart from such evident miscalculations, classic deli sandwiches tower on the plate, joining myriad improbable but delicious components. Full dinners are available, too, along with potato knishes and cheesecake.

ÉLYSÉE MANDARIN *Chinese*
1221 Mackay (Ste-Catherine). Map 9G3
☎*866-5975* ▢ ▢ ▢ ▢ ▢ *Open daily.*
A tasteful display of Chinese ivory figurines and miniature musical instruments is arranged opposite the vestibule service bar. Add the high-ceilinged dining rooms, dark woodwork and European-style service and preparation, and it seems a throwback to the foreign enclave of Shanghai. Admittedly, this is not a lovable environment, for it is too correct for that. But neither is it the garish setting usually associated with Chinese restaurants, and it is serious, not gloomy. There is no sense that the largely Szechuan (not Mandarin, as the name suggests) food is merely scooped from steam tables in

the kitchen, and every indication that much of it is prepared to order. The *table d'hôte* lunch is a bargain, with selections from ten main courses.

Another stylish but younger Chinese restaurant of comparable achievement is **Le Chrysanthème** *(1208 Crescent* ☎*397-1408* ▢*), which features Szechuan and Peking dishes.

L'EXPRESS *French*
3927 St-Denis (Roy). Map 7C2 ☎*845-5333* ▢ ▢ ▢ ▢ *Open daily.*
For a long time, it was *the* white-hot bistro. While that spotlight has moved on, L'Express is still ablaze with shining faces that look to be on the verge of celebrity. It shouldn't be missed by those who wish to be knowledgeable about Montréal dining. The decor is pleasant enough, with the usual palms and mirrors, but everyone is too busy chattering to notice. Surprisingly, for a place so *au courant* it could get away with serving pink bean curd and still be filled from breakfast to midnight, the food is usually pretty good.

All that considered, prices can be deemed moderate. Make note of the address — it's between Roy and Duluth — for the only sign out front is imbedded in the sidewalk. Reservations are usually necessary for the closely-spaced tables, but solitary diners can often get a seat quickly at the bar, which has at least as many diners as drinkers.

LE FESTIN DU GOUVERNEUR
Continental
Old Fort, Île Ste-Hélène ☎*879-1141* ▢ *to* ▢ ▢ ▢ ▢ ▢
An ancient building within the Old Fort complex is the scene of re-creations of 17thC feasts, complete with serving wenches, musicians and jesters. The food is no more than acceptable, but it's the best choice on a day trip to Île Ste-Hélène. The four-course meals are accompanied by a bilingual show from 7–9pm.

FIESTA TAPAS ✿ *Spanish*
479 St-Alexis (Notre-Dame). Map 8E5
☎*844-5700* ▢ ▢ ▢ *Closed Sat lunch, Sun lunch, Mon.*

Lovers of the Spanish bar snacks called *tapas* need look no further than this outpost of Madrid in Vieux Montréal. The cellar setting is so authentic that one half-expects Sancho Panza to belly up to the bar and scarf down a selection of the more than 30 hot and cold tapas available.

People who think Spanish food is either (a) the same as Mexican food, or (b) bland, are in for surprises. For proof, try *patatas bravas* (roast potatoes drenched in spicy tomato sauce), *sardinas a la plancha* (large grilled sardines), or *calamares fritos* (fried squid rings). A common strategy is to order three or four and share with friends. *Tapas* are ideal as a light meal before a show at the nearby Centaur Theatre.

On Friday and Saturday nights, join the large segment of the local Hispanic community that shows up to wax nostalgic over the sound of a live flamenco guitar and dancers of South American salsa.

LES FILLES DU ROY *Continental*
415 Bonsecours (Notre-Dame). Map 8C5
☎ 849-3533 ▥ ▨ ▣ ▥ ▨ *Open daily.*
The name refers to young women sent by Louis XIV to help populate Nouvelle-France. This 18thC building in Vieux Montréal is nearly as old as that migration, its stone interior walls lined with ancestral portraits, gilt-framed mirrors and antique sideboards. Cocktails are served beside a crackling fire or at the marble bar, brought by fetching waitresses in sky-blue folk costumes with ruffled blouses. In such an ingratiating setting, who can be so meanminded as to point out that the food is less than memorable?

GIBBYS *Continental*
298 Pl. d'Youville (St-Pierre). Map 8E5
☎ 282-1837 ▥ ▨ ▣ ▥ ▨ *Open daily.*
It looks like a standard tourist snare, smack in the middle of Place d'Youville, in a 200-year-old stone building in the historical heart of Old Montréal. On the contrary, it is almost as popular with natives as with visitors. The interior is much larger than it looks from outside,

with beamed ceilings and masonry walls. Meals begin with a bowl of pickles and a loaf of warm bread, and go on to hearty portions of beef and seafood. Deviations from steakhouse convention are tiny steps off the beaten path, such as the cold soup, *gazpacho.*

Most preparations are tasty and unpretentious. Lunch is far less expensive than dinner, which is nevertheless more crowded and usually requires reservations.

LES HALLES *French*
1450 Crescent (Ste-Catherine). Map 9F3
☎ 844-2328 ▥ ▨ ▣ ▥ ▨ *Closed Mon lunch, Sat lunch, Sun, 1st 2wks in Aug, Christmas–Jan 6.*
The snug bistro setting is decorated with mock shopfronts intended to recall the lamented Paris market. It is a deceptive *petit-bourgeois* ambience, given the stiff tariffs, but the food is more than competently done, in ample portions. The waiters are pros, who put on a good show of enjoying their work. Game and beef are emphasized, and the kitchen has a gentle hand with seafood, as in the *bouqueterie* of assorted fish. Sauces are light; desserts are huge. The parting gift of a bag of apples softens the shock of the check. These days, not even that figure need be **too** shocking. After a round of menu and price "re-structuring," more options and combinations are available.

HENRI II *French*
1175 Crescent (René-Lévesque). Map 10G4
☎ 395-8730 ▥ *to* ▥ ▨ ▣ ▨ *Closed Sat lunch, Sun.*
This is the sort of unassuming cellar retreat that regulars keep to themselves. At the un-chic end of rue Crescent, it crowds only 13 tables into a room decorated in warm grays and burgundy. Rolled napkins stand alert as rabbit ears in the wineglasses. Dishes arrive with alacrity, but not a rush, and the food is utterly without pretense.

Expect the same three vegetables with every main course. Patrons are mostly satisfied, not transported, yet they return again and again.

LUNA *Mediterranean*
*3435 St-Laurent (Sherbrooke). Map **7D3***
☎844-0616 ▥ ⬤ ▨ *Open daily.*
The rectangular island bar is the center-piece, with working fireplaces on either side, and it fills up quickly after working hours. Crowds are more variegated than they were when this was **Boule-vards**, and their age range is wider. Younger patrons are cloaked in bohemian black. Older, more prosperous men are in shirtsleeves and ties, women in short skirts and long jackets. They divest themselves of expressive Gallic shrugs and tosses of tousled hair, the faintest chuckles ricocheting off moderne marble surfaces. The serviceable food is essentially nouvelle Mediterranean, with *tapenade,* fried *calamari,* pastas, and *cacciucco Livornese* (a seafood stew) among the offerings. No sign is visible out front, so look for the colorful mosaic column at the entrance, near the corner with Sherbrooke.

LE LUTÉTIA *Continental*
1430 de la Montagne (Maisonneuve). Map
9F3 ☎288-5656 ▥ to ▥ ▣ ⬤ ▨
The mezzanine dining room of the hotel DE LA MONTAGNE does full credit to its whimsically iconoclastic surroundings. Profoundly Parisian in appearance and standards, it grabs the eye with arresting late Victorian/Belle Époque details. The happy confusion is abetted by the splash of the lobby fountain and drifting accordion music. The kitchen makes many hits and few misses. One starter is a tasty *carpaccio* of smoked goose. Salmon is gently broiled, and on the side might be a tumble of *haricots verts* and cauliflower florets cupped in a *radicchio* leaf. A top choice for lunch or dinner.

MAISON CAJUN HOUSE *Creole–Cajun*
*1219 Mackay (Ste-Catherine). Map **9G3***
☎871-3898 ▥ ▣ ⬤ ▨ *Closed Sat lunch, Sun lunch, Mon lunch.*
"Bonjour, y'all," greets the picture of an alligator outside. The cookery of Louisiana has a historical connection with Canada, unlikely as that might seem. Long ago, Francophone Acadians from the Maritime Provinces were exiled to the bayous around New Orleans. ("Cajun" is the result of the slurring drawl of "Acadian.") Once there, they set about creating America's most distinctive regional cuisine. It is ably replicated here, in well-spiced renditions that stop short of setting ears afire. Do try gumbo yaya, if it's on the card. It feels like a night on Bourbon Street.

The "Big Easy" memorabilia on display includes a feathered Mardi-Gras headdress and a large pen-and-ink drawing of the Preservation Hall Band. Even those fidgeting over calories and cholesterol can go. The owner has installed a new "Cajun Lite" menu. He's from The Bronx, by the way, but don't hold that against him.

LA MARÉE ⌂ *French*
*404 Pl. Jacques-Cartier (St-Paul). Map **8D5***
☎861-8126 ▥ ▣ ⬤ ⬤ ▨
Fast food and vapid "continental" fare usually dominate in tourist districts. Vieux Montréal runs against that norm, with several admirable mid-priced restaurants and one or two — including this one — that are simply superb. La Marée is less expensive than some, and adds the bonus of a lovely 18thC house. At night, candlelight enhances the inherent romance of the setting; business lunches prevail at midday. French recipes form the core of the menu, with sauces made lighter for contemporary tastes. The staff is well-trained and unobtrusive.

MAZURKA ❀ *Polish*
*64 Prince Arthur (St-Laurent). Map **7D3***
☎844-3539 ▢ ▣ ⬤ ▨
Even among the low prices of rue Prince Arthur, this Polish place stands out. A lunch of barley soup, bread and *pierogis* (ravioli-like dumplings filled with meat or cheese) costs less than a pack of cigarettes. They have offered *two* lobsters for little more than the price of *one* in a fish store. How do they do it? No one cares. Merchants, artists, students and "ladies who lunch" keep swarming back, hoping the management never hires a cost accountant.

LES MIGNARDISES ☖ *French*
2037 St-Denis (Sherbrooke). Map 7C3
☎*842-1151* ▨ ᴁᴇ ᴄᴅ ᵛˢᴬ *Closed Mon lunch, Sun lunch, Sun.*

The exterior isn't prepossessing. Beyond that door, however, lies what many believe to be perfection in dining. Certainly it comes close, from the warm greeting to the seamless service to the dazzling fabrications that issue from behind the kitchen doors. There is a master at work back there, owner-chef Jean-Pierre Monnet. His flawless presentations and artistry with diverse ingredients leave his guests breathless, groping for words to do justice to the experience. The meal can't be hurried, for all is cooked to order. The menu changes daily, according to what was available at market.

The check is as impressive as the dinner. But then, this meal can hardly be bested this side of the Seine.

MOISHES *Steakhouse*
3961 St-Laurent (Duluth). Map 7C2
☎*845-3509* ▨ ᴁᴇ ᴄᴅ ᴄᴅ ᵛˢᴬ *Closed Sun, last 2wks July.*

Those who insist on spending serious money for a chop or steak on otherwise inexpensive Blvd. St-Laurent can take their credit ratings here. Moishes gets the trim new breed of up-and-coming executive as well as those of the older generation who didn't know about such things as triglycerides until it was too late.

All meats are cooked exactly to order; veal chops are memorable. Dills and pickled cabbage come with the bread basket. At lunch, the Junior rib steak with appetizer, soup, dessert and coffee costs substantially less than the same steak alone at dinner.

OGGI *Italian*
108 Laurier W (St-Urbain) ☎*272-9122* ▨ ᴁᴇ ᴄᴅ ᴄᴅ ᵛˢᴬ *Closed Sat lunch, Sun lunch.*

Gentrifying Av. Laurier needed a place that was more than flash. It has it here, in a long room with a basic black-and-white scheme. The decidedly *nuovo Italiano* decor matches the comestibles. Sauces do not drench the pastas,

they dress them, their component fresh herbs strongly in evidence. Restraint is apparent, too, in the salads and crisp vegetables with a mere whisper of extra-virgin olive oil. This spiffy trattoria should play well for years.

L'ORCHIDÉE DE CHINE *Chinese*
2017 Peel (Sherbrooke). Map 9F3
☎*287-1878* ▨ ᴁᴇ ᴄᴅ ᵛˢᴬ *Open daily.*

Not the standard red-and-gold Chinese restaurant, this orchid chooses an understated approach. Black and white and grey, it is, with masks here and there. You don't even get chopsticks unless you ask (although if you do, one waiter advises, the food "tastes more better.") Nothing is likely to improve the cooking, in fact, since it's already as good as it's likely to get. Nominally of the Szechuan and Pekin persuasions, dishes are carefully calibrated balances of hot and cold, sweet and sour, mild and spicy. They don't bother to provide salt, pepper, or soy sauce on the tables, and extra condiments are rarely required. People conditioned to glutinous takeout glop thick with pineapple chunks and fried noodles resent the highish prices. Everyone else will revel in these craftsmanlike expositions of one of the world's great national cuisines.

LA PICHOLETTE ☖ *Eclectic*
1020 St-Denis (Viger). Map 8C4
☎*843-8502* ▨ ᴁᴇ ᴄᴅ ᴄᴅ ᵛˢᴬ *Closed Sat lunch, Sun.*

Civilized dining with touches of wonderment pertain at this mid-Victorian house, built for an English lord in 1867, at the perimeter of the Quartier Latin. The gracious manner in which he lived has been preserved, with bronze figurines holding candelabra aloft in high-ceilinged parlor rooms. He almost certainly didn't eat this well, though, for a woman by the name of van der Berg is in the kitchen fashioning little miracles. She has an enviable knack for all kinds of game — duck, venison, wild boar — with fruit sauces that complement but never cloy. Her amiable *maître d'* is helpful and not the least stuffy. There are only 65 seats, so advance reservation is advisable.

SCHWARTZ'S ♣ *Deli*
3895 Blvd. St-Laurent (Roy). Map 7D3
☎842-4813 ▢ *Open daily.*

The Bill 101 sign outside may read "Chez Schwartz Charcuterie Hébraïque de Montréal," but that doesn't alter what it is and long has been. This is straight Jewish delicatessen, plain and loud and doing business at the same stand for decades. What you want is a small plate of hand-carved smoked meat — listen up, now, small! — with an order of fries, a sausage-shaped pickle and a soft drink. It will feed two teenagers with galloping metabolisms. Or, if you *are* two teenagers, go for the smoked meat and chicken combinations.

You say you want grace and elan? Don't go. A taste sensation? Dash over.

LA SILA *Italian*
2040 St-Denis (Sherbrooke). Map 7C3
☎844-5083 ▥ ▣ ▣ ▣ ▣ *Closed lunch and Sun.*

With such traditional standbys as melon and *prosciutto, fettucini Alfredo* and *saltimbocca*, the owners obviously aren't making a play for the squid-ink-pasta-and-Perrier set. It hasn't a trace of trendiness. No flavor of the week, and the waiters look and act like waiters, not models between shoots. Diners can even hear themselves think. Note particularly the veal dishes. Prices are at the low end of the expensive range, but the special *table d'hôte* comes in below that. A streetside terrace brings diners out into the *brio* of the Latin Quarter night.

LE TAJ *Indian*
2077 Stanley (Sherbrooke). Map 9F3
☎845-9015 ▥ ▣ ▣ ▣

This rue Crescent-area Indian can be packed at lunch and near-empty at dinner. The inexpensive luncheon buffet is one reason. Day or night, this is northern *mughlai* cuisine, prepared in three degrees of hotness. The one in the middle is spicy enough for those who don't think authenticity requires a

seared tongue. The card includes several curries and lamb dishes along with tandoori specialties. Those who admire the attractive temple carvings might like to know that the owner has a shop in the RITZ-CARLTON hotel.

LA TULIPE NOIRE *Eclectic*
2100 Stanley (Sherbrooke). Map 9F3
☎285-1225 ▥ to ▥ ▣ ▥

A wait is inevitable at this, one of the most popular of a hundred variations on the café-tearoom-luncheonette theme. Good-quality soups, omelets and sandwiches make it best for snacks, not full meals. Or, use it just for a late *cappuccino* and a slab of one of the dreamy desserts.

VENT VERT *French*
2105 de la Montagne (Sherbrooke). Map 9F3 ☎842-2482 ▥ to ▥ ▣ ▣ ▣ ▥ *Closed Sun.*

Step down into a room of emerald and apple greens, which half-explains the name ("Green Wind?"). The front room is a glassed, terrace observatory on the street. Adroit waiters bring food that observes modified *nouvelle* conventions but is served in ample, not niggardly, portions.

WITLOOF *Belgian*
3619 St-Denis (Sherbrooke). Map 7C3
☎281-0100 ▥ ▣ ▣ ▣ ▥ *Open Sat lunch, Sun lunch.*

Butcher paper over white tablecloths and the emphasis on mussels and frites mark this as one of the several Belgian-style bistros to gain favor in the city. Veined marble floors and cream walls are the backdrop for the happy bustle, abetted by the congenial staff. Nonsmokers are shunted to a small room in back, beyond the frequent clouds of black tobacco smoke that touch off memories of Left Bank brasseries. Belgian beers go with this food — the *Blanche de Bruges* is a good bet — which tends toward robust stews and sausages and beef tartar. Top off a leisurely repast with apple tart, dense chocolate cake, or one or two of the several sorbets and cheeses.

Montréal: nightlife and entertainment

Montréal after dark

Montréal's reputation as Canada's ultimate party town is deserved. An average slow Tuesday can have a concert by the Montréal Symphony in Place des Arts, a dance recital at Victoria Hall, jazz at a club in the old quarter, heavy metal at the Forum, a Noel Coward play, and a *Folies-Bergères*-style musical revue. That's in winter. By June, Montréal kicks into overdrive. Apart from the scores of cafés and clubs catering to every taste, it brings on one festival after another, devoted, in turn, to Mozart, fireworks, jazz, bilingual comedy and film.

To discover what's on, consult the *Montréal Gazette*, especially the separate *Preview* in Friday editions.

USEFUL TO KNOW
- **Minimum age**: The minimum drinking age in Québec is 18.
- **"Happy hour"**: This is now an institution, usually in effect from 5–7pm, but often longer, when cut-rate drinks and free snacks attract the decompressing after-work crowd. Last call for orders can be as late as 3am.
- **Payment**: As a rule, patrons are expected to pay for drinks when they are served, but the bartender may accept a credit card for imprint, and run a tab that way. Exceptions are sometimes made in quiet places, or for customers with honest faces.
- **Tipping**: A 15-percent tip is customary.
- **Prices**: Wines and liquor are expensive and none-too-generously poured. To cut the cost of imbibing, try domestic wines and beers, which are taxed at lower levels than imports. The former are acceptable, the latter quite good.
- **Cover charges**: A cover or admission charge is often levied at places with live entertainment. It is rarely exorbitant and may include the first drink. At dinner-theaters and in the hotel nightclubs, the show may be included in the price of the meal, but show-only tickets are available.
- **Tickets**: Tickets to major concerts, plays and sports events can be ordered by telephone through **Ticketron** (☎ *288-3651)*. Have a valid credit card handy. For events at **Place des Arts** ☎285-4200 for information or 842-2112 for tickets.

Nightlife

While bars and dance clubs are found in many parts of town, they are in greatest concentration in four distinct areas. Anglophones are most in evidence on **Rue Crescent** and adjacent streets between Ste-Catherine and Sherbrooke. Speakers of French dominate in **Vieux Montréal** and in the **Latin Quarter**, which centers on **St-Denis** from Ontario N to Carré St-Louis. And increasingly active is the **Plateau Mont-Royal** district, incorporating the upper reaches of **St-Denis**, **St-Laurent** and **Avenue du Parc**. As in the city's restaurants, dress codes are rarely in force, but blue jeans are sometimes cause for being turned away.

Policies can change without notice. Always call ahead to determine what is scheduled that night, or, for that matter, whether the club still exists.

BARS

Bars are known less for mere elbow-bending than the proclivities of their habitués, be they jazz buffs, sports fans, or singles on the make. Food is available, but rarely memorable. King of the hill in the **Rue Crescent** district is **Thursday's** *(1430 Crescent ☎ 288-5656)*, prime hunting ground for the yuppie/preppie set. It is connected to **Les Beaux Jeudis** restaurant, a case of tail wagging dog. **Sir Winston Churchill** *(1459 Crescent ☎ 288-0616)* has a sidewalk terrace, open in summer, enclosed in winter, and is great for all-season people-watching. After 5pm, the action shifts to the rambling pub down the stairs. Similar in style is nearby **DJ's Pub** *(1433 Crescent ☎ 287-9354)*, with its own front terrace and a small dance floor where the noon–8pm "happy hour" is very popular.

Cheers *(1260 Mackay)* bests its TV inspiration with one big, square center bar and three satellites at the sides and upstairs. A mixed clientele from barely-drinking-age to grandfatherly enjoy free hot dogs with Monday night football on the tube and karaoke on Wednesday, among other promotions.

Country music bars aren't thick on the ground. The only reliable one is **The Blue Angel** *(1230 Drummond ☎ 866-7146)*. It's been around for over four decades, and has been looking poorly, so fetch over there in one quick hurry. Fans of Irish music can check out **Le Vieux Dublin** *(1219A Université ☎ 861-4448)*.

Piano bars are another variation. The **New York Bar** *(2144 Mackay ☎ 933-8444)* is the downstairs lounge of the **Abacus** restaurant, which means a happy marriage of Chinese bar nibbles and chrome-and-leather Manhattan ambience. **La Porte des Lilas** *(1473 Crescent ☎ 284-0307)* has a Parisian flair, and a piano player too, Thursday to Saturday. **Puzzles** *(☎ 288-6666)*, the lobby bar of the hotel RAMADA RENAISSANCE DU PARC, has a piano player and occasional larger groups every night but Sunday. **Le Purple** *(8387 St-Laurent ☎ 858-7117)* often adds singers. A piano player sits in every night at **L'Île de France** *(801 de Maisonneuve ☎ 849-6331)*. Dinner dancing is added Friday and Saturday. Karaoke hasn't gained a chokehold on the local imagination as it has in Toronto, but exhibitionists have their way at **Shad-O** *(3732 St-Dominique)* and **Beepers** *(1474 Crescent)*.

Over in the Latin Quarter, everyone is drawn to **Le Faubourg St-Denis** *(1660 St-Denis ☎ 843-4814)*. In good weather, tables are set out on the sidewalk, and no part of Montréal so evokes the Parisian Left Bank. The tables are behind glass in winter, and a fire crackles in the downstairs bar. Media types mix with academics at **Le Bistro St-Denis** *(1738 St-Denis ☎ 842-3717)*, while **Les Beaux Esprits** *(2073 St-Denis ☎ 844-0882)* is a refuge for couples more interested in each other than the surroundings. Those who prefer a livelier atmosphere go across the street to **La Côte à Baron** *(2070 St-Denis ☎ 842-6626)*. The food and service are variable, but these glossy folk have other pursuits in mind.

Once a hot after-midnight spot, Lola's Paradise has devolved into **Angel** *(3604 St-Laurent ☎ 282-9944)*, populated by a younger, more homogenized crowd and a grumpy door attendant. Unlike its predecessor, it seems less capable of original thought. In the vicinity is the stylish **DiSalvio** *(3519 St-Laurent ☎ 845-4337)*. Joyous clusters of upper-crust young professionals fill it nightly, intent on cruising or dancing. Easy chairs and a fireplace set the scene. Avowedly a private dance club, some outsiders get through the door if they arrive before 10pm. After that, try to be gorgeous, powerful, or rich. Madonna and Bill Clinton probably wouldn't have trouble.

Otherwise, drop in at the almost as desirable **Zoo Bar** *(3556 St-Laurent ☎ 848-6398)*, where a semi-deconstructivist decor bares heating ducts and intentionally battered supporting columns. The ceiling over the zig-zag bar is painted as a blue sky with clouds. Early on, it's fairly quiet, kicking into action for its casually dressy patrons as the evening slides toward midnight. Next door at **Blue Dog** *(#3550)*, a collegiate crowd sits on stools made of fire hydrants, and dances to the choices of a DJ. **Lux** *(5220 St-Laurent ☎ 271-9272)* looks like a European notion of an American drugstore. Open 24 hours, it doesn't get intriguingly weird until after 2am, when the pale nightbirds start to bop through the doors.

DANCE CLUBS AND DISCOS

At dance clubs and discos, conversation is in competition with thunderously amplified records and live bands. Gaining entrance is rarely a problem before 10pm. After that, lines often form and regulars may be ushered inside ahead of strangers. Sentinels at the door tend to be steroid abusers with tree-trunk necks, so don't expect to push past.

The **Hard Rock Café** *(1458 Crescent ☎ 987-1420)* follows the formula pursued by its siblings in Europe and the US. Two floors of autographed guitars, gold records, costumes, and rock memorabilia from The Beatles to Billy Idol surround the pit dance floor. Barbecued chicken and ten-ounce burgers are the utterly average eats, records the entertainment, tourists the principal clientele. There is a boutique in which to buy the requisite T-shirt for children left at home.

Business *(3510 St-Laurent ☎ 499-9419)* is as warm and welcoming as a prison exercise yard, all raw concrete and steel girders, illuminated by inventive light shows. Such neo-brutalism is "in," obviously, for it is packed with the trendiest young. (It's much easier to get in before midnight, when the grunts at the door don't yet know how great the demand is likely to be.) **Club Balatou** *(4372 Blvd. St-Laurent ☎ 845-5447)* is a steamy, exotic enclave, a refreshing change from prevailing modes. Capable bands explore African and Caribbean roots, and their enthusiastic audiences are given plenty of hip room on the large dance floor.

What was once the electric salsa emporium Club Septembre is now **Ozone** *(2015 de la Montagne ☎ 845-7060)*, a re-decorated disco with four bars. Lively Friday and Saturday, when there may be bands as well as records, it is apt to be all-but-empty the rest of the week. The prominent survivor for Latin American rhythms Wednesday to Sunday is **Salsathèque** *(1220 Peel ☎ 875-0016)*, up the stairs into a large room of mirrors and chase lights. A largely Latino crowd moves exuberantly and proficiently to pounding salsa, merengue, and cha-cha-cha provided by the house band *(after 11pm)*.

Even lambada lives on, at least at the triple-tiered **Alexandre** *(1454 Peel ☎ 288-5105)*. At ground level is a bar-brasserie popular with past-thirty singles (real or temporary). A lot of self-deception goes on, men in gold chains and earrings who comb their hair with buttered toast and women with Ann-Margret perms who never saw a mirror they didn't like. At least they don't have to compare themselves with 20-year-olds. The club downstairs has waitress-dancers in the saucy flounced mini-skirts deemed essential to a dance craze that died everywhere else in North America three months after it was imported.

Nevilles *(2102 de la Montagne ☎ 849-5002)* is an upstairs disco with several bars. It enjoys a surprisingly large number of attractive young women and an unsurprisingly large number of men old enough to be their fathers. Female bartenders are contractually obliged, it would seem, to wear gender-confirming garments. It is dark. Dancers at **Pacha** *(1212 de Maisonneuve ☎ 842-9571)* have a few more miles on them than the patrons of most of these clubs.

L'Esprit *(1234 de la Montagne ☎ 397-1711)*, open Thursday to Saturday, with a Sunday session for youngsters below drinking age, looks like a funeral parlor because it once was. Inside, the only bodies are dressed to kill but very much alive. Most of them have been on this planet 25 to 35 years. The music is unrelenting.

Les Foufones Electriques *(87 Ste-Catherine E ☎ 845-5484 or 845-3040 for concert info)* is as off-the-wall as the breed gets, a *nouvelle vague* outpost in a depressed but not especially dangerous neighborhood s of the main campus of the Université du Québec. It has transient acts by such captivating names as Grimskunk and Blood Sausage. They are augmented by mimes, poets reading their understandably unpublished odes, and whoever else might care to thumb their noses at the straight world.

In the same seedy area is the city's biggest disco, **Metropolis** *(59 Ste-Catherine E ☎ 288-5559, open Thurs–Sat)*, with six bars and a 2,500sq.ft dance floor that is a writhing mass when the customers get their blood up after midnight. The Fritz Lang decor is underscored by an impressive lightshow. Elvis, Buddy Holly and the Big Bopper live on at

Studebakers *(1255 Crescent ☎ 866-1101)*, and this is one dance club that has almost as many receding hairlines as acne cases. The waitresses even dress in cheerleader outfits.

NIGHTCLUBS

A few large hotels have nightclubs with floorshows of the Las Vegas variety, wherein underdressed chorines prance around headliners and other performers. In another category are the **boîtes-à-chansons**, restaurants that showcase folksingers, and vocalists of the Edith Piaf persuasion. **Arthur-Café Baroque** *(900 Blvd. René-Lévesque ☎ 878-9000)* is a splashily elegant room of the REINE ELIZABETH hotel, where the fare is usually frothy, saucy musical revues. There's one show nightly Wednesday to Friday, Sunday, two on Saturday, with dancing after the show. **Le Caf ' Conc'** *(1 Pl. du Canada ☎ 878-9000)* is the gaudy supper club at the hotel CHÂTEAU CHAMPLAIN, a mix of Moulin Rouge and Copacabana. Showgirls and chorus boys do their production numbers around a changing slate of comics, singers, magicians and jugglers. Two shows nightly, three on Saturday; closed Sunday. Reserve ahead; men must wear jackets.

    Au Bistro d'Autrefois *(1229 St-Hubert ☎ 842-2808)* features singers in the French cabaret style (think Jacques Brel), but also might have jazz combos, blues shouters and theatrical groups. Performers come on around 10pm.

COMEDY

Despite the annual **Just for Laughs Festival**, there are only a few places in town that focus entirely on comedy. The two most prominent are **Comedyworks** at **Jimbo's Pub** *(1238 Bishop ☎ 398-9661)* and **Comedy Nest** above **Sir Winston Churchill** *(1459 Crescent ☎ 849-6378)*. There are no guarantees, of course, for one person's guffaw is another's affront. Both have "open mike" amateur nights early in the week. Reserve ahead.

    Vieux Munich *(1170 St-Denis ☎ 288-8011)* comes as close to a replica of a Bavarian beer hall as can be found in North America. Waitresses in *dirndls* weave among the long wooden tables with platters of *wurst* or clutching impossible numbers of foaming mugs. Yodelers yodel, the big brass band oompahs polkas and waltzes with abandon, and in no time everyone is linking arms and singing at the tops of their voices. Weekends are liveliest, and it's so large that reservations are rarely necessary. Often as not, the band casts aside authenticity in favor of country music, or to swing into such non-Teutonic ditties as *Can't Get No Satisfaction*.

JAZZ

Montréal's enthusiasm for jazz predated the creation in 1980 of its 10-day **International Jazz Festival**. All modes are represented — Dixie, swing, blues, be-bop, fusion — in hotel lounges, restaurant cellars and back rooms, and clubs, of course, where the music is supreme. It can be heard every night of the week, although Thursday to Saturday are best. Always inquire ahead.

They're serious about jazz at **L'Air du Temps** *(191 St-Paul E* ☎ *842-2003)*, a longtime Vieux Montréal haunt. A good portion of available floor space is given to a stage for combos that often have five or more members. Lately, it's been spruced up a bit, with a paint job and slightly upgraded furniture. Attractions are changed frequently. Arrive by 9.45pm to get a seat; sets usually begin at 10.30pm. **Claudio's** *(124 St-Paul E* ☎ *866-0845)* is only a few steps away. Live music nightly except Thursday and Sunday, and they often skip the cover charge.

Downtown stalwart **Biddles** *(2060 Aylmer* ☎ *842-8656)* has "jazz and ribs" as its subtitle, and delivers on both counts. The barbecue sauce is of the honey-sweet variety, and the messy job of eating them contributes to the jolly informality, the better to attend to the mellow sounds of the Charles Biddle Trio. **Bijou** *(300 Lemoyne* ☎ *288-5508)* is another choice at the edge of Vieux Montréal, its artists often fudging the line between jazz and soul. The club concentrates on combos, often with singers, but has been known to book comics and magicians. In any case, think of it as a club for grown-ups, with the kinds of acts that rarely pull in twentysomethings. Liza Minnelli, Harry Connick Jr., and headliners of similar magnitude appearing elsewhere in the city sometimes stop in unannounced to jam or just listen. Food is available until late in the adjoining restaurant, **Les Serres** *(* ☎ *288-9788)*.

Le Grand Café *(1720 St-Denis* ☎ *849-6955)* squeezes in large combos and even bands, playing anything from swing to funk. The glass front is opened in summer and there's also a terrace in back. **Upstairs** *(1421 Bishop* ☎ *845-8585)* promotes itself as nightclub, game-room, and restaurant "rolled up into one," but the reason to go is the nightly jazz by skilled trios and quartets. The downstairs **Bar Idéfix** has the obligatory pool table.

ROCK, POP AND FOLK

Montréal is on the North American circuit for every traveling rock and pop superstar group and vocalist. They book the biggest arenas and clubs, as do many Canadian talents. The monster concert hall and mega-bar **Club Soda** *(5420 Av. du Parc* ☎ *270-7878)* defies categories. hosts groups playing funk, soul, reggae, country, metal and blues. Even comedians show up. Most acts only stay around a night or two.

When it isn't sheltering the Canadiens hockey team, the **Montréal Forum** *(2313 Ste-Catherine W* ☎ *932-2582)* is a major venue for rock bands of maximum wattage. **Spectrum** *(318 Ste-Catherine W* ☎ *861-5851)* is a converted movie palace for up to 1,000 music lovers. Groups appearing are not brand names, so ticket prices are usually lower than at Club Soda and the Forum. Still another concert venue is **La Brique** *(32 Ste-Catherine W* ☎ *790-1245 or 861-9516)*. While it has its share of rock nihilists who call themselves things like Napalm Death and Carcass, the menu often drifts toward the mainstream, with reggae groups and bands devoted to "tributes" to The Stones, Guns N' Roses, and other superstars. Also check out **Back Street** *(382 Mayor* ☎ *987-7671)*, with up-and-comers and more tribute bands.

On a more intimate level, Old Montréal has two clubs featuring folk performers, singly and in groups. **Le Pierrot** *(114 St-Paul E* ☎ *861-*

1270, open Wed–Sun) is definitely a party place, with much wiggling, singing and clapping along with the night's soloists and combos. The largely under-thirty be-jeaned crowd pays no mind to the older music lovers in attendance — the first group demonstrating remarkable knowledge of songs recorded before they were born. While the atmosphere skews to a French sensibility, performers usually observe an ecumenical balance between Canada's two contending languages. There is small entrance fee for music almost every night. It is affiliated with **Les Deux Pierrots** *(next door, #104)*, which usually has music only on Friday and Saturday.

Not far away, **Nuit Magique** *(2 St-Paul E* ☎*861-8143)* hosts an earthy crowd for nightly live rock and blues, and pool in the back room. The musical menu changes, with three different bands a week and Saturday and Sunday matinees, but 60s and 70s faves seem to prevail. The surroundings resemble the clubhouse of a messy but non-threatening motorcycle gang. Given the slightest encouragement, the bartender conjures his special house drink, a muscular wonder that involves flames and a straw.

When nothing is happening elsewhere on Sunday, Monday, and an occasional Wednesday, **Charlie's American Pub** *(1204 Bishop* ☎*871-1709)* brings in loud, small rock duos in a cubbyhole within a claustrophobic space that crams in two bars and a pool table. A few steps away is **Deja Vu/Bowser & Blue** *(1224 Bishop* ☎*66-0512)*, a lighthearted denim-and-sneakers place that offers bluesy country-rock much of the time. Crowded even on Sunday. **Char-B-Que** *(1476 Crescent* ☎*289-1943)* books blues artists on an irregular basis when other clubs are closed.

The performing arts

Montréal handily matches Toronto in those performing arts in which language is irrelevant or unimportant. The ever-expanding **Place des Arts**, with its several performing spaces, is augmented by important theaters and concert halls around the city. Homegrown orchestras and dance troupes perform at outdoor venues in warmer months, often at little or no cost, and French-speakers are treated to plays and musicals given by more than a dozen professional companies. Annual festivals celebrating Mozart, modern dance, jazz, and film prompt additional cultural events under private or institutional sponsorship. With all that, visiting Anglophones needn't bemoan the understandable lack of English theater, which has only a couple of regular outlets.

CLASSICAL MUSIC, OPERA AND DANCE
The prime venue for classical music, opera and dance is **Place des Arts** *(map 8 D4* ☎*285-4200 for information, or 842-2112 box office)*. Its two main buildings house three theater-concert halls. The largest, with almost 3,000 seats, is **Salle Wilfrid-Pelletier**, which hosts sym-

phony orchestras, ballet and the opera, while the adaptable **Théâtre Maisonneuve** and **Théâtre Port-Royal** are employed for music and dance recitals, plays (usually in French), and concerts by touring pop and opera singers. Less regularly, performances are held in **Redpath Hall** (☎ *398-4539)* and **Pollack Hall** (☎ *392-8224, closed June–Aug)* at McGill University, where most performances are free.

The winter season is launched by the routinely provocative and often outrageous **Festival International de Nouvelle Danse**, in early October. A rigorous touring schedule has brought acclaim to **Les Grands Ballets Canadiens** (☎ *849-8681)* in cities on five continents. When at home, the company, which explores both classical and contemporary dance forms, appears in the Salle Wilfrid-Pelletier and in summer performs for free in Parc LaFontaine. When it is abroad, the space is filled capably by such admirable troupes as Feld Ballets, the Paul Taylor Company, and, of course, the celebrated National Ballet of Canada (known in these parts as **Le Ballet National du Canada**).

Created in 1980, the **Opéra de Montréal** (☎ *521-5577)* has garnered substantial prestige for such a short period of existence. It presents several productions during the October to May season, sharing Salle Wilfrid-Pelletier with the **Orchestre Symphonique de Montréal** (☎ *842-3402)*. This orchestra, under the direction of Charles Dutoit, has an international reputation and gives free summer concerts in outdoor arenas around the city. **Orchestre Metropolitain du Grand Montréal** (☎ *598-0870)* is the city's junior symphony, appearing in the Théâtre Maisonneuve. Chamber music is supported by the **Société Pro Musica** and performed by the **McGill Chamber Orchestra**, while serious 20thC music is the focus of the **Société de Musique Contemporaine de Québec**.

In dance, look for appearances by **Ballets Jazz de Montréal** and **Les Ballets Classiques de Montréal**. These are the principal companies, and not the full extent of cultural offerings.

CINEMA

Montréalers' enthusiasm for movies of all kinds is manifest in the **World Film Festival**, which takes place from late August to early September. A typical program includes at least 250 feature films, documentaries and shorts from over 50 countries. There is no shortage of cinematic diversion the rest of the year.

All the Hollywood movies appear at the multiple-screen cinemas downtown. Showings usually commence at noon. There are about as many theaters showing movies in French as in English, and some have both, so find out before purchasing tickets. Repertory theaters show less commercial art films and classics.

A few possibilities, some of which alternate between the popular and the obscure:

- **Cinéma de Paris**   896 Ste-Catherine ☎875-7284
- **Cinéma Paradis**   8215 Hochelaga ☎354-3110
- **La Cinémathèque Québécois**   355 de Maisonneuve ☎842-9763
- **Conservatoire d'Art Cinématographique de Montréal**   1400 de Maisonneuve ☎848-3878

- **National Film Board of Canada**   Complexe Guy Favreau, 200 René-Lévesque ☎283-8229
- **Ouimétoscope**   1204 Ste-Catherine ☎525-8600
- **Rialto**   5723 Parc ☎274-3550

THEATER

Over a dozen major Francophone theater companies put on mainstream and avant-garde productions, most notably at the **Théâtre d'Aujourd'hui** *(3900 St-Denis ☎282-3900)*, the **Théâtre de Quat' Sous** *(100 des Pins ☎845-7277)*, and the **Café de la Place** *(Place des Arts ☎842-2112)*.

There are fewer choices for English-speakers. Only the **Centaur Theatre** *(453 St-François-Xavier ☎288-3161, closed Mon and June–Sept)* is a permanent venue of consistent merit. This Greco–Roman building, with its impressive portico, was once a stock exchange. The Centaur mounts both popular and experimental productions, primarily with Canadian themes.

The encompassing menu of the all-purpose **Saidye Bronfman Centre** *(5170 Côte Ste-Catherine ☎ 739-7944 for tickets or 739-2301 for general info)* includes dramas, comedies, and revues in French, English and/or Yiddish, as well as dance, visual arts, opera, jazz, chamber music, and lectures. Despite that somewhat confused identity, it has been on the scene for over 25 years. Call ahead for current attractions.

Dinner-theater is another alternative, usually staging downsized Broadway retreads. One possibility is **Le Stage** at **La Diligence** *(7385 Décarie ☎ 731-7771)*. Consult *The Gazette* for others. Or, call the **English Theatre Hotline** *(☎843-2873)*.

Montréal: shopping

Underground and overground

The workmanship and diversity of Montréal's goods equal or exceed those of any city its size. Furs, designer clothing and leather goods are particularly notable, but few shoppers will be disappointed, whatever they seek.

WHERE TO GO
Rue Ste-Catherine between Crescent and University is the first destination for shoppers. In addition to many independent establishments of varying quality and price level, it runs past the major department stores and retail complexes that surround Christ Church Cathedral in the city center. Boutiques of many local clothing designers are found along upper **St-Laurent** and **Avenue Laurier**. Nearly 30 antique stores take up both sides of **Rue Notre-Dame** between Atwater and Guy. Art galleries cluster along **Sherbrooke**, near the MUSÉE DES BEAUX ARTS.

The UNDERGROUND CITY has over a thousand shops, and the malls stacked beneath such buildings as **Place Bonaventure** and **Place Ville-Marie** add hundreds more. With that abundance of opportunities for acquisition, finding just the right item at the right price requires advance planning and a sacrifice of shoe leather. At least much of the exploration can take place under cover.

Visitors seeking bargains may find the quest unrewarding, in the main, although some good buys can be ferreted out in discount lofts along **Boulevard St-Laurent** and in the **Plateau Mont-Royal** district.

USEFUL TO KNOW
- **Opening hours:** In general, hours are 9.30 or 10am–6pm during the week, but until 9pm Thursday and/or Friday. Most stores close at 5pm on Saturday and remain closed on Sunday. There are exceptions. Many stores in the Underground City stay open until 9pm Monday through Friday, and those in Vieux Montréal are often open Sunday.
- **Refunds of tax:** Federal and provincial sales taxes totaling 15 percent are applied to nearly every purchase, even newspapers. Foreign visitors can obtain refunds of most of the total amounts charged, so save every receipt. See page 29 for refund details.
- **Payment:** Most stores take one or more of the major credit cards. US currency is widely accepted, but nearly always at rates inferior to those offered by banks. Personal checks drawn on out-of-town banks are rarely accepted.

WHAT TO BUY

Fashion and **furs** are paramount, for Montréal has always led the nation in their design and manufacture. Despite high duties, there is an abundance of imported products as well, notably **English china** and **Scottish woolens**. Collectors of art should pay particular attention to **Inuit sculpture**, carved from whalebone, antlers and walrus tusks, as well as the more familiar soapstone. None of it is cheap, but the artistry is commendable.

Antiques and collectibles

Attic Row is the name given to the concentration of shops along rue Notre-Dame. Merchandise is generally cheaper than in the galleries on Sherbrooke. **Antiques Gisela** (*1960 Notre-Dame W* ☎ *937-7695*) trafficks in teddy bears, dolls, trains and other toys dating from the late 19thC. **Antiquitou** (*2475 Notre-Dame W* ☎ *932-3256*) has old duck decoys, country furniture and such offbeat objects as cash registers.

They're used to people "just looking" at **Galerie Archaeologia** (*1486 Sherbrooke W* ☎ *932-7585*), which displays museum-quality artifacts from as early as the 4thC: urns, coins and statuary of Egyptian, Greek and Roman origins. A converted bank is put to appropriate use by **Henrietta Antony** (*4192 Ste-Catherine* ☎ *935-9116*) to showcase chandeliers, period furnishings, ornate mirrors and clocks, and copper and silver objects: three fascinating floors.

In business for three generations now, **Petit Musée** (*1494 Sherbrooke W* ☎ *937-6161*) has four levels of weaponry and armor, Greek and Roman archeological fragments, furniture and jewelry. Both Canadian country furniture and Art Deco are in stock at **Puces Libres Antiques** (*4240 St-Denis* ☎ *842-5931*), along with clocks, chandeliers and duck decoys.

Arts and crafts

For pottery and ceramics by many Québec artisans, try the **Centre du Céramique Poterie Bonsecours** (*444 St-Gabriel* ☎ *866-6581.* The affable staff of the **Eskimo Art Gallery** (*434 Sherbrooke W* ☎ *844-4080*) makes browsing a pleasure, and there are frequent special exhibits.

The **Guilde Canadienne des Métiers d'Art** (*2025 Peel* ☎ *849-6091*) should be the first stop for those interested in blown glass, silver, ceramics, weavings, stained glass and other handcrafted objects of high order, including works by Inuit and Amerindian craftspeople.

Books and magazines

This city of readers has bookstores (*librairies*) everywhere. Many are open 7 days a week, but those dealing in antiquarian books often follow unorthodox schedules.

Bibliomania (*4685 Av. du Parc* ☎ *849-3175*) has new, used and rare books in both French and English. **Double Hook** (*1235a Greene* ☎ *932-5093*) is devoted exclusively to Canadian subjects or books by Canadian authors.

Bright and crisp **Lexis Booksellers** (*2055 Peel* ☎ *848-9763*) purveys only English-language titles, while **Librairie Ulysse** *(560 President-Kennedy ☎ 289-0993)* concentrates on travel books and videos. **Paragraphe** *(2065 Mansfield ☎ 845-5811)* has a refurbished location, with an excellent selection in both French and English. **S.W. Welch** *(5673 Sherbrooke W ☎ 488-5943)* deals in out-of-print books.

Foreign newspapers and periodicals are sold at the many branches of **Maison de la Presse Internationale**. One of the largest is at 550 Ste-Catherine W *(☎ 842-3857)*.

China and crystal

There is really no better source than **Birks et Fils** *(1240 Carré Phillips ☎ 397-2511)*, which presents such extensive selections of china, jewelry and silverware that it almost qualifies as a department store. Smart merchandizing and substantial discounts make **Caplan-Duval** *(6700 Côte des Neiges ☎ 483-4040)* an appealing destination for those looking for Wedgwood and Royal Doulton dinnerware and Lalique and Waterford crystal.

Cadeaux Au Bon Marché *(99 Chabanel W ☎ 388-6564)* discounts china, crystal and silver.

Clothing

While all the top European and American fashion designers are represented, this is an opportunity to check out homegrown clothiers, many of whom have made reputations abroad. One of Canada's most successful designers is **Alfred Sung** *(1455 Peel ☎ 499-0963)*, with moderately-priced and couture lines for both men and women. Chantal Gagnon is featured at **Caboche** *(445 St-Sulpice ☎ 285-1189)*, with clothes for the career woman, and high fashion for those unconcerned with cost.

Fureur *(4391 St-Denis ☎ 844-7467)* sells deceptively simple styles by a Montréal designer, in a modishly bare showroom. The setting is so spare at **Parachute** *(3526 St-Laurent ☎ 845-7865)* it looks as if they aren't selling *anything*. But they are — cutting-edge fashions that get more than their share of attention. **Revenge** *(3852 St-Denis ☎ 843-4379)* has no imports, just garments by important Montréal designers, for both men and women.

Department stores and malls

The Hudson's Bay Company was chartered in 1670 to organize the fur trade, but didn't move into the retail business until the 1880s. Now **La Baie** (The Bay) *(585 Ste-Catherine W ☎ 281-4422)* is one of Canada's most prominent chains of department stores, while retaining an emphasis on furs. **Eaton** *(667 Ste-Catherine W ☎ 284-8411)*, Montréal's biggest store, has undergone updating intended to make it the anchor of an expanded mall along the lines of Toronto's Eaton Centre. It isn't as large as that major tourist attraction, but is similar in design, with several floors and a vaulted skylight. Don't miss the glorious Art Deco lunchroom on the 9th floor.

Holt Renfrew *(1300 Sherbrooke W ☎ 842-5111)* is the upper crust of the chains, signaled by its proximity to the exclusive RITZ-CARLTON; top-of-the-line merchandise at prices to match. **Ogilvy** *(1307 Ste-Catherine W* ☎ *842-7711)* is noted for its merchandizing pizazz, but the Scottish origins of the store are underscored by the noontime skirl of a bagpiper.

The British-owned clothing store **Marks & Spencer** *(McGill and Ste-Catherine* ☎ *499-8558)* is represented by a smaller outlet in Place Montréal Trust.

Food, to take away or eat in or prepare yourself, is the main order of business at **Faubourg Ste-Catherine** *(1616 Ste-Catherine* ☎ *939-3663)*, a block-long, three-story gathering of stalls, cafés, and boutiques. Bins and counters spill over with plump and gleaming produce, the air is filled with the aromas of roasting coffee and just-baked breads and pastries. Non-edible crafts and other items are also on offer.

Finally, even if you have no desire to buy a single thing, don't miss a glance into **Les Cours Mont-Royal** *(Ste-Catherine and Peel)*. A former hotel of *grande dame* elegance and embellishment was restored and restructured to contain an up-to-date retail enterprise with more than 90 pricey shops, among them, the internationally known **Aquascutum**, **Parachute**, and **Giorgio**.

Furs

About 85 percent of Canada's **fur** industry is located in Montréal. Everything from raccoon to sable is sold in department stores and scores of luxurious salons.

Alexandor *(2025 de la Montagne* ☎ *288-1119)* enjoys an excellent reputation, as does **Desjardins** *(325 Blvd. René-Lévesque* ☎ *288-4151)*, which is more than a century old. **Dubarry** *(370 Sherbrooke W* ☎ *844-7483)* and **McComber** *(440 de Maisonneuve W* ☎ *845-1167)* are also highly regarded. Look around first, but if prices are intimidating at other furriers, there may well be something within the budget at **Oslo** *(5149 St-Laurent* ☎ *270-2655)*.

Montréal: recreation

Suggestions for children

Museums and shopping pall quickly for youngsters. Mercifully, Montréal lays out many activities and attractions that are immensely enjoyable for both children and adults, so the need to provide them with diversions to their taste isn't a chore.

For fuller details, see SIGHTS A TO Z, NIGHTLIFE AND THE PERFORMING ARTS and SPORTS; look for the ♣ symbols, for things suitable for children.

AMUSEMENT PARKS AND ZOOS

Île Ste-Hélène is worth an entire day for families. Apart from its three swimming pools and acres of picnic grounds, it has a colonial fort with live "soldiers" and bagpipers, an Aqua-Parc with exhilarating water slides (bring swimsuits), and **LA RONDE AMUSEMENT PARK**. This has 33 rides of varying degrees of adrenalin provocation, from mild to heart-stopping. Frequent firework displays augment live cabaret shows and exhibits.

The city's small zoo and aquarium have been brought together at the new **BIODÔME** beside the Olympic Stadium, which is sufficiently enthralling to disguise its educational intent. Visitors walk through simulated tropical forests and Canadian marshes, and see parrots sitting in the trees and penguins swooshing down ice slides into icy water.

An excursion across the river can lead to the **Granby Zoo** *(Autoroute 10 E, Exits 68 or 74* ☎ *372-9113* ▧ *open end May–Sept 7 10am–5pm)*. Its exhibits harbor over 750 animals of more than 220 species, many of them larger than can be sheltered at the Biodôme, including big cats and elephants. Still more animals are on view at **Parc Safari** *(Autoroute 15 S, Exit 6, then Route 202 W, Hemmingford* ☎ *514-247-2727 or 800-465-8724* ▧ *open mid-May to mid-Sept 10am–5pm)*. Drive through mock savannahs that are summer home to zebra and giraffe, antelope and deer. Some animals can be touched, and there is a small amusement park with gentle rides. Bring swimsuits for the water play area.

BOAT TRIPS

For all but the very young, the jetboat rides over the St Lawrence are thrilling, not frightening. Check with **Lachine Rapids Tours**. 1- to 3-hour cruises of calmer but scenic parts of the river are available from **Montréal Harbor Cruises** *(Victoria Pier* ☎ *842-3871, from May–Oct)*. Sure to please the adventurous child is the amphibious bus of

Amphi Tour *(Old Port ☎ 386-1298, May–end Oct)*. It trundles up the streets of Vieux Montréal, then drives right into the water and pretends it's a boat. These companies all have 1-hour tours, the maximum tolerable length for most children. Even teenagers are apt to bore quickly on longer trips.

EVENTS AND ENTERTAINMENTS
What child doesn't like fireworks, the noisier and more explosive the better? Time a visit, then, for the **International Fireworks Competition** at La Ronde in May–June. A **Winter Carnival** seizes their imagination at several sites in January and early February, with hot-air balloons, a walk-through snow castle, clowns, dog-sled and ice-canoe races, and much more. Held in various locations *(☎ 800-363-0621 for information)*.

PARC ANGRIGNON has a parallel celebration from December 21–late February — a "winter fairyland" with skating rink, slide, and an ice maze. The park is open all year round *(☎ 496-4629 for information)*.

SHOWS AND CONCERTS
The unique **Cirque du Soleil** *(☎ 522-2324)* is a circus without animals, but the acts are so charming and inventive that no one minds. The **Children's Theatre** *(4626 Sherbrooke W ☎ 484-6620)* mounts periodic productions at Victoria Hall. For 2 weeks around Christmas, **Les Grands Ballets Canadiens** *(☎ 849-8681)* perform the evergreen *Nutcracker Suite*.

Stargazers combine knowledge with wonder under the dome of the DOW PLANETARIUM. **Images du Futur**, in the Old Port *(St-Laurent ☎ 849-1612 ⌨ open daily May 15–Sept 20)*, interweaves lasers, holography, computers, interactive devices, and other late-20thC technologies to tell its stories — a new show every summer.

To a generation of jaded TV watchers, the huge screen at the **IMAX Cinema** in the Old Port is a literal eye-opener, with images seven stories high. Another dazzling multi-media show is the one that serves as an introduction to the MUSÉE D'ARCHÉOLOGIE ET D'HISTOIRE, which precedes the descent into just-spooky-enough ancient sewers and graveyards.

OBSERVATION POINTS
Take a horse-drawn *calèche* to the Chalet in **Parc Mont-Royal** for a spectacular view of the city and river that is especially dazzling at dusk. Or, scoot by swift funicular to the top of the tower of OLYMPIC STADIUM for 56-km (30-mile) wraparound vistas.

Sports in Montréal

Language conflicts or not, Montréalers have been known to cheer on Toronto's championship teams if they had none of their own at the moment. They are devoted fans of their professional hockey and baseball clubs, and they play with equal enthusiasm as active participants, especially when the sport is a means to combat the gloom of long Québec winters.

AUTO-RACING

The **Grand Prix Molson du Canada** is one of 16 races in the international Formula One circuit. Île Notre-Dame's refurbished **Gilles Villeneuve Circuit** *(☎ 392-0000)* is the site of the three-day event, held each year in mid-June. More than 130,000 spectators turn out for the spectacle of high-powered cars reaching speeds of almost 200mph.

BASEBALL

After hockey, Montréalers are wild about their Expos. The professional team is one of only two Canadian teams competing in US Major League Baseball. That isn't to say that the city's baseball history is short. Triple A teams, a notch below the major leagues, were in place, on and off, from as early as 1898. Such legendary players as Duke Snider, Don Newcombe, Roy Campanella and Jackie Robinson all once played for the Royals.

The Expos play their home games at **Olympic Stadium** *(season Apr–Sept ☎ 253-3434 for information, or 522-1245 for tickets)*, which is something of a tourist attraction in itself. (Its innovative, retractable roof is proving troublesome, however, and there are plans to replace it with a fixed covering.) Reservations for games may be made by telephone, using a credit card.

BOATING

A huge, rectangular artificial lake was created for the Olympic Games on man-made Île Notre-Dame. It now serves in the summer for windsurfing, pedal-boating and sailing. A sailing school is conducted there by the **Société de l'Île Notre-Dame** *(☎ 872-6093)*, daily from mid-May to early September. In Lachine, between downtown and Dorval Airport, the **École de Voile de Lachine** *(2105 Blvd. St-Joseph ☎ 634-4326)* rents boats and sailboards, and provides group and private lessons. Open mid-May to end September.

CURLING

Played on an ice court by teams of four — curling involves sliding a smooth, rounded, 38-pound granite stone with a handle toward a series of concentric circles 35m (38 yards) away. It is aided on its way (it is believed) by other players who sweep the ice in its path with a broom. The stones stopping nearest the inner circle are given points. The sport was imported by immigrant Scots, where this popular winter sport has been played for at least four centuries.

Curling is played by amateurs, usually the members of clubs. Among these are the **Longue Pointe Curling Club** (☎ *254-2773*), **Montréal West Curling Club** (☎ *486-5831)* and the **Wentworth Curling Club** (☎ *481-6322).* The nation's oldest is the **Royal Montréal Curling Club** (☎ *935-3411).*

CYCLING

Professional cyclists compete in the **Grand Prix Cycliste des Amériques** (☎ *879-1027)* over a challenging 224-km (140-mile) course through the streets and up Mont-Royal. Those who simply wish to ride for fun are pleased to know that the government maintains over 225km (140 miles) of cycling paths on the Island of Montréal (☎ *874-6211).* They include rights-of-way along LACHINE CANAL and the St Lawrence Seaway, in PARC ANGRIGNON, and on rue Rachel between Parc LaFontaine and Parc Maisonneuve.

Solo and tandem bicycles — and even pedal vehicles carrying as many as nine riders — can be rented in the Old Port at the **Jacques-Cartier pier** (☎ *844-9139)* and on **Île Notre-Dame** (☎ *398-0634).* Other rental possibilities are **Cycle Peel** *(6665 St-Jacques* ☎ *486-1148)* and **La Cordée** *(2159 Ste-Catherine E* ☎ *524-1515).*

Guidebooks and brochures on cycling in and around Québec are distributed by the cycling organization **Vélo-Québec** *(3575 St-Laurent, Suite 310* ☎ *847-8356).*

Bicycles are allowed on Metro trains all day Saturday, Sunday, and holidays, and after 7pm Monday to Friday.

FISHING

Promising lakes and rivers for the angler are available within a day trip of the city center. The Québec **Ministry for Leisure, Hunting and Fishing** (☎ *800-665-6527 or (418)-890-6527)* can suggest locations.

FITNESS CENTERS

Many hotels now offer exercise facilities, from simple rooms with a rowing machine and slant board and not much else, to extensively equipped and staffed operations the equal of any private gym to be found. Four of the most complete are in the DELTA MONTRÉAL, HOLIDAY INN CROWNE PLAZA, BONAVENTURE HILTON, and LE CENTRE SHERATON.

For additional possibilities, refer to the hotel listings on pages 163–8.

FOOTBALL

A local team in the Canadian Football League was disbanded years ago. For two seasons, the city had a team called The Machine, in the World League of American Football. That was suspended, possibly never to be reactivated.

The city is contemplating a bid for a future Super Bowl, the championship game of the National Football League of the US. Success in that endeavor seems unlikely, as does hope for an expansion team in that league, also proposed by some boosters. Otherwise, games at the collegiate level are played by McGill University.

GOLF

Most golf clubs are private, but there are a few courses open to non-members. The entrance to **Golf Municipal de Montréal** (☎ 872-1143) is near the Viau Metro station, the only course (9 holes) accessible by subway. It also has a driving range (☎ 252-0419).

Each about 15 minutes from downtown, and requiring a car, are **Brossard Municipal Golf Course** (4705 Lapinière, Brossard, Exit 9 off Rte. 10 E ☎ 676-0201), **Fresh Meadows** (505 Av. du Golf, Beaconsfield, Rte. 20 W ☎ 697-4036), and **Golf Dorval** (2000 Reverchon, Dorval, Rte. 20 W ☎ 631-6624). The Laprairie course has 18 holes, the one in Dorval 36, the others, nine.

HOCKEY

If there is a Canadian faith that crosses all ethnic and linguistic boundaries, it is hockey. Devotions are held in the secular temple, the **Montréal Forum** (2313 Ste-Catherine W ☎ 932-2582) but there is talk of building a new arena downtown. At the Forum, the professional Canadiens periodically raise spirits and break Montréalers' hearts.

The team started before the creation of the National Hockey League, which it has often dominated, winning the Stanley Cup 23 times in 60 years. Its roster of immortals includes Maurice "The Rocket" Richard, "Boom-Boom" Geoffrion, Jean Beliveau and Guy Lafleur.

The fervent followers of the Canadiens buy more than 14,000 season tickets every year, which leaves only 2,500 unpurchased seats. Games are played from October to April, with the playoffs in May.

HORSE-RACING

Hippodrome Blue Bonnets (7440 Blvd. Decarie ☎ 739-2741) is host to trotters and their drivers from around the world. Races are held Monday, Wednesday, Friday, and Saturday. Post time is 7.30pm during the week, 1.30pm on Sunday.

RAFTING

Electrifying white-water rides over the rapids in the St Lawrence river are available from **Lachine Rapids Tours** (☎ 284-9607). Their boats berth at **Victoria Pier** in the Old Port, near Rue Berri. Rain slickers and hats are provided, but expect to get wet anyway. Open from the end of April to the end of September. The trip takes $1\frac{1}{2}$ hours and is not cheap.

RUNNING

More than 10,000 runners, both professional and amateur, participate in the annual **Montréal Marathon** (☎ 879-1027), held in September. Recreational runners train on the trails of Mont-Royal and the several larger parks, such as Parc LaFontaine and riverside Parc René-Lévesque.

ROLLERBLADING

Also known as in-line skating, the fad has caught on with a vengeance. The logical places to indulge are those used by cyclists and runners, which can cause conflicts over use of space. Reason usually prevails, and rollerblading is most visible along the banks of the Lachine Canal, on Île Notre-Dame, and on the paths of the Old Port. Skates can be rented near Place Royale in Vieux Montréal at **Rollerblading** *(117 Commune W ☎ 849-4020, open seven days).*

SKATING

Montréal has about 200 outdoor skating rinks, 30 of them illuminated after dark, and 21 indoor arenas. **Lac aux Castors** (Beaver Lake) in **Parc Mont-Royal** is festive, and PARC LAFONTAINE and **Parc Maison-neuve** are popular. PARC ANGRIGNON has two rinks and a 1-mile ice trail through the trees. Montréal's biggest rink is the former **Olympic Basin** *(☎ 872-6211)* on Île Notre-Dame, and skates are available for rent; but the wind off the river can be piercing.

SKIING

Near **Beaver Lake** in **Parc Mont-Royal** is a modest downhill slope with rope-tow. It is suitable for beginners. Cross-country skiers and snowshoers use the trails of that park and those used for cyclists (see above) around the city. The BOTANICAL GARDEN has what they call an "ecology" trail through the grounds.

Equipment can be rented on **Île Notre-Dame** *(☎ 872-3376)* for cross-country skiing, and at a number of sporting goods shops, including **Ski Dump** *(8366 St-Laurent ☎ 384-1315).* The nearby Laurentian Mountains and the hills of **L'Estrie**, an hour's drive SE of the city, offer some of the best skiing in eastern North America.

NW of Montréal, a center highly regarded by downhill skiers is **Mont Tremblant** *(☎ 514-476-9552 from Montréal or 800-461-8711 from the rest of Canada and the US).*

SNOWSHOEING

Enthusiasts use the same trails as cross-country skiers *(☎ 872-6211 for information).* See SKIING above.

SOCCER

What the rest of the world calls football has had about the same success in Canada as in the States — not much. That doesn't stop entrepreneurs from trying. In 1988, Supra de Montréal became the local entry in the Canadian Soccer League. Matches are played at **Claude-Robillard Centre** *(1000 Émile-Journault ☎ 389-2774).* The season is late May to mid-September, with games on Wednesday and Sunday nights.

SWIMMING

The St Lawrence River has no swimming beaches, but there are many indoor and outdoor pools open to the public, and most of the larger downtown hotels have pools as well. **Olympic Park** *(4545 Pierre-de-Coubertin ☎ 252-4737 ▨)* has five indoor pools open to the public. It's a little far E of downtown to go just for a swim, unless combined with a visit to the nearby JARDIN BOTANIQUE and a ride to the top of the inclined tower that winches up the retractable roof of the adjacent stadium.

Île Ste-Hélène *(☎ 872-6093 ✉)* has three large pools near the island's Metro station. There are neighborhood pools operated by the city *(☎ 872-6211 for information).* Many downtown hotels have pools, and many of these are indoors. See the hotels listings on pages 163–8.

TENNIS

In an unusual arrangement, the annual **Player's International Challenge Tournament** has professional women tennis players competing in even-numbered years, the men in odd-numbered years. It's held at **Parc Jarry** *(☎ 273-1515)* for 2 weeks in August.

Amateurs have an ample number of courts available to them in summer, including those in **Parc LaFontaine** and **Parc Jeanne-Mance**. Further information from the Sports and Leisure line *(☎ 872-6211).*

Québec City

An island of French culture

A more noble setting could not be conceived for a city that was destined to become the very soul of French America. Québec's steeples and turrets rake the sky from the formidable cliffs that rear over the northerly shore of the St Lawrence. The river, silvered by moonlight or high summer sun, makes a majestic sweep past Québec on its way to the ocean, bestowing an exhilarating panorama of sky and water and distant mountains. The treasure that is Québec City was acknowledged when the only walled city north of Mexico was designated "a heritage of the world" by UNESCO in 1985.

It may not seem so to tourists, who spend most of their time in the compact old town and immediate environs, but Québec is a sizeable city, a busy seaport with two universities, and the seat of the provincial government. Today, more than 160,000 people live within the city limits, and a total of 560,000 in the metropolitan area.

Jacques Cartier was the first recorded European to stop at the spot, in 1535. The Algonquin Indians he met there called it "Kebec," meaning "where the river narrows." It was left to Samuel de Champlain to put down roots. He built a small fort there in 1608, at the base of the sheer cliff that rose sharply to the high plateau that is now Vieux Québec. The city's most familiar landmark, the imposing Château Frontenac hotel, has loomed for a hundred years over the constricted streets of gray stone houses, which date from the 17th century.

Québec was the capital of Nouvelle France for more than 150 years, a status it retained despite almost constant conflict with the British, who wanted all of North America for themselves. Finally, in 1759, a decisive battle took place on the Plains of Abraham, southwest of the city. Both the French and British commanders were killed, but New France was subsequently ceded to England in the 1763 Treaty of Paris.

Fortunately for the city and the visitors who now revel in her every summer, colonization quickly moved west to Montréal, then to Toronto and beyond. Québec was left to thrive quietly, an island of French culture in an English sea, its distinctive character and boundless *joie de vivre* delightfully intact.

Québec City: practical information

GETTING THERE

Air: **Québec airport** is only 13km (8 miles) away, to the w of the city, beyond Ste-Foy. While there are a few direct flights to US cities, most air travelers to Québec City, including those from the UK, fly into Montréal's **Mirabel International** airport and make onward connections from there.

Because the distance from the airport is short, a taxi ride isn't too expensive. The airport bus is cheaper and stops at selected downtown hotels, but the wait can be long between departures.

Train: **VIA Rail** has regular trains from Montréal, and the trip takes a little over 3 hours — about the same as it takes by car.

Bus: The **Voyageur** bus line operates a service several times daily between Québec City and Montréal.

GETTING AROUND

Taxi: Much of the city is easily seen on foot, and taxis are useful for the longer distances. Taxis can be hailed in the streets, but most are occupied, so chances are better in front of major hotels. Or, they can be summoned in minutes by telephone.

Car: All the major **car rental** companies have offices at the airport and downtown.

Parking is quite limited; those arriving by private car might prefer simply to leave it in the hotel garage until the time of departure.

Road signs are in French. Explanations of these signs can be obtained from car rental agencies and automobile clubs, or from the Tourism and Convention Bureau (see next page).

Driving in winter is not recommended. Québec is subject to very heavy snows, making driving conditions difficult and even perilous, especially for those not used to driving on ice. Streets can be very narrow and steep in the old town, made more so by banks of snow pushed aside by plows.

Carriages: Horse-drawn carriages, called *calèches*, found also in Montréal, are a romantic and appropriate way to see the old town. Keep *calèches* for sightseeing, however, and not simple transportation, as they are expensive. Most accept credit cards.

Useful addresses

TOURIST INFORMATION
Useful free information on visiting Québec City or Québec province can be obtained from the following addresses.

- **London**   Québec Tourism UK, Québec House, 59, Pall Mall, London SW1Y 5JH ☎(071)930-8314.
- **New York**   Délégation Générale du Québec, Rockefeller Center, 17 W 50th St., New York NY 10020-2201 ☎(212)397-0200.
- **Toronto**   Bureau du Gouvernement du Québec, 20 Queen St. W, Suite 1504, Box 13, Toronto, ONT M5H 3S3 ☎(416)977-6060.
- **Washington, DC**   Bureau du Tourisme du Québec, 1300 19th St NW, Suite 220, Washington, DC 20036 ☎(202)659-8991.
- **By mail**   In Canada or the US, write to the Greater Québec Area Tourism and Convention Bureau *(60 rue d'Auteuil, Québec (Québec) G1R 4C4).*
- **In person**   ☎(418)692-2471 or 651-2882.

   There is a visitor tourist office at the same address (map **14**C4), and, in summer, information booths are found in several locations in the old town, including a kiosk on Terrasse Dufferin in front of the Château Frontenac.

   Also in summer, official bilingual guides on green mopeds can be found in Vieux Québec; they are identifiable by their flag, which sports a question mark. Just hail one and ask away.

TOUR OPERATORS
Baillairgé Cultural Tours   ☎658-4799. Walking tours and "step-on" guides, who use the client's vehicle.
Croisières d'Anty   ☎659-5489. River cruises, May to end October, with daily departures June 24–September 6.
Croisières sur le Fleuve   ☎659-4804. Cruises departing from the wharf near Musée de la Civilisation.
Essor Hélicoptères   ☎872-2222. Sightseeing by helicopter.
Gray Line   ☎622-7420. Several bus tours of city and region, one of which includes a river cruise.
Maple Leaf Sightseeing   ☎ 649-9226. Choice of bus tours.
STEP-ON Guides   ☎654-0310. Guides use client's car.
Tours de Ville   ☎624-0460. Bus and bus/cruise combination.

PUBLICATIONS
Larger hotels and many newsstands carry newspapers from Canadian and US cities; the British *Financial Times* can also be found, but other major UK newspapers are only available in the largest hotels. French-language dailies are *Le Soleil* and *Le Journal de Québec.*

Emergency information

The telephone area code for Québec (City) is **418**.

EMERGENCY SERVICES
Police and Fire   ☎691-6911.
No coins are needed for pay phones.

Dental emergencies   ☎653-5412 Monday to Friday; ☎656-6060
Saturday and Sunday.
Health emergencies   ☎648-2626. 24-hour service. Calls are
answered by nurses.
Pet emergency   ☎647-2000, daily 24 hours.
Pharmacy (late)   Les Galeries Charlesbourg, 1er Av., Charlesbourg
☎623-1571. Open Monday to Saturday 8am–midnight, Sunday 10am–
midnight.

HELP LINES
Alcoholics Anonymous   ☎529-0015, daily 8am–midnight.
Distress Center (personal counseling)   ☎683-2153.

For **Automobile accidents**, **car breakdowns** and **lost travelers
checks**, see EMERGENCY INFORMATION on page 36.

Québec City:
sightseeing

Winter spectacle and summer explosion

The Québec City year is segmented with celebrations and festivals, the most extravagant being the 10-day Winter Carnival in February, with its riotous agenda of costume balls, flashlight parades, ice castles and snow sculpture competitions. Over 200,000 visitors participate every year, more than doubling the population of the city itself.

The Carnival is followed immediately by a series of Olympic-level speedskating and cross-country ski races, hockey tournaments, auto and outdoor shows. In no time it is summer, which explodes with music festivals and street fairs almost weekly into fall.

Only a propensity for bad timing can deny the visitor at least a minor holiday, which is always an excuse for a little festive partying. Even with such misfortune, however, there is enough to this enchanting city to keep anyone occupied for days. Even a little creative café-sitting and people-watching will occupy an afternoon or three. At the very least, a long weekend should be allowed. With day trips along the St Lawrence and into the Laurentian Mountains, a full week is hardly enough.

IN THIS CHAPTER
This chapter on Québec City sightseeing is arranged in three sections:
- A long, first section on **Vieux Québec**, containing a **walk** through the old quarter, followed by an alphabetical list of sights.
- **The Citadel and the defense system** — with entries arranged geographically.
- **Parliament Hill** — with entries arranged geographically.
- At the end of the Québec City section of the book are two suggested **excursions** — a shorter one to the **Île d'Orléans and the Beaupré coast** (page 228) and a longer driving tour of the **Gaspé peninsula** (page 230).

CROSS-REFERENCES
Where a place name appears in SMALL CAPITALS, fuller details can be found in an entry elsewhere in the chapter.

ORIENTATION

Vieux Québec is a twin-level town: the older section down beside the water, the only somewhat less ancient upper quarter running W from the cusp of the sheer escarpment. The CHÂTEAU FRONTENAC and most other hotels and inns are in the upper town. Principal sights are LA CITADELLE, to the S, a fortress completed in 1832 and still an active military post; the BASILIQUE NOTRE-DAME and adjacent **Séminaire**, founded in 1663, with its MUSÉE; the **Musée du Fort**, with a scale model of the city; and the glorious **Terrasse Dufferin**, the broad promenade that runs along the edge of the cliff overlooking the river.

In the lower town, reached by stairs or funicular, are **Place Royale**, a handsome square of restored 18thC buildings; the **Quartier du Petit-Champlain**, similarly refurbished and home to a lively melange of shops and bistros; the new MUSÉE DE LA CIVILISATION; and the **Vieux Port**, a former area of wharfland now recycled into parks, marinas and markets.

Outside the walls bordering the upper town is the HÔTEL DU PARLEMENT of the provincial government, and the PARC DES CHAMPS-DE-BATAILLE.

Along **Grande Allée**, the SW extension of rue St-Louis, is a concentration of bars and restaurants. Most of the larger modern hotels are on this side of the wall, but within easy walking distance of the old town.

Vieux Québec

A WALK IN VIEUX QUÉBEC
See color map 14.

The pleasures of a stroll through Old Québec are precisely those experienced in similar *quartiers* of Europe. The clopping of horses' hooves and the creak of *calèche* wheels echo off the stone facades of tightly-packed houses. Waiters dart among the tables beneath the bright awnings of sidewalk cafés. Darkened streets suddenly emerge upon dappled, sunlit parks and plazas.

Place d'Armes/Château Frontenac

The customary starting point is **Place d'Armes**. In its position at the intersection of rue St-Louis and rue Fort and facing the river, the CHÂTEAU FRONTENAC hotel is on the right. It looms over all, a constant reference point from anywhere in the old town.

Over to the left stands the **Musée du Fort** (*10 Ste-Anne, map 14 C5* ☎ *692-2175, open daily, but times vary by season, so call ahead*). A 37sq.m (400sq. foot) model of the town as it was in 1750 is used in a fast-paced sound-and-light commentary (in French or English) on major episodes in its history. Not surprisingly, the 30-minute show concentrates on the Battle of the Plains of Abraham, and touches on the other sieges suffered by the city. As a bonus, however, newcomers can obtain a notion of the lay of the land, with the upper and lower towns depicted, as well as their relationship to the St Lawrence River and the Île d'Orléans.

On leaving the museum, turn left toward Terrasse Dufferin (◀€), passing a plaque set into a stone plinth, commemorating Vieux Québec's UNESCO designation as a "World Heritage City." Nearby is a monument to Samuel de Champlain, who founded Québec in 1608, only months after the English settled Jamestown, in what is now the State of Virginia.

Bear right along the promenade above the river. Street performers often take advantage of this concentration of tourists. They might include a 5-piece Peruvian band, jugglers, folksingers, magicians. There is even the man who plays *Edelweiss* and the Pachelbel *Canon* on the rims of water-filled brandy snifters.

Québec City skyline, with **Château Frontenac**

Drinking in that fabulous view, continue to the end of the Château Frontenac and turn right up the stairs. Ahead is the **Parc des Gouverneurs**, a leafy enclave bordered on two sides by 19thC row houses. An obelisk honors both General James Wolfe and the Marquis de Montcalm, the victor and loser of the critical battle on the Plains of Abraham.

Take the path that cuts diagonally up through the park to the corner of rue Laporte and Av. Ste-Geneviève. Several of the town's European-style inns are to be seen around the square, a collection with no counterpart in North America. Continue on Ste-Geneviève, which soon merges with Av. St-Denis. Follow it as it bends right.

At the intersection with rue St-Louis, look left. Up there is the **Porte St-Louis**, the main gate in the town wall, which was first built in 1693 and reconstructed in 1878. Next to it is the **Poudrière de l'Esplanade**, a former powder magazine that is now an interpretation center describing the city's fortifications.

Nearby will be found a gathering place of *calèches*. Straight ahead, a block away along rue d'Auteuil, is the main tourist information booth.

Turn right (E) on rue St-Louis, a charming (although admittedly touristy in part) street of shops and appealing restaurants in some of the upper town's oldest houses. Turn left on rue du Parloir. A short block down is the **Chapelle des Ursulines**, the final resting place of General Montcalm. The convent, within whose walls the chapel is situated, was founded in 1642 by nuns dedicated to schooling Amerindian children.

Again, turn right. A few steps along is the entrance to the MUSÉE DES URSULINES, whose most bizarre artifact is Montcalm's skull. Bear left along what is now rue des Jardins. Soon, on the right, is the 1804 HOLY TRINITY ANGLICAN CATHEDRAL. Many of the objects inside, and much of the woodwork were gifts of George III. Artists display their works in the courtyard in summer. The cathedral is undergoing renovations.

As you continue, on the left are the gardens of the **Hôtel de Ville** (City Hall). Turn right on rue Buade. In one block, on the left, is the BASILIQUE NOTRE-DAME. Parts of it, including the bell tower and walls, date to 1647.

Continue past the cathedral on Buade, turning right into the pedestrian alley of rue Trésor. The way is lined with the drawings and prints of numerous artists. Although obviously geared to the tourist trade, some of the work is decently executed and might serve as a suitable memento. At the end of the alley, turn left on Ste-Anne.

This leads back to the Terrasse Dufferin. Look for the staircase on the left. Officially called the **Escalier Frontenac**, locals know it as the **Escalier Casse-Cou (Breakneck Stairs)**. Halfway down, a pedestrian bridge crosses the street called Côte de la Montagne and enters the leafy tranquillity of **Parc Montmorency**. Over on the far side are the first of several batteries of ancient cannon, emplaced in 1711 to protect the upper city from attack from the river.

Return across the bridge and descend Breakneck Stairs to the street, bearing right, and then head right again down another flight of wooden stairs.

Quartier du Petit-Champlain

You have now reached the Quartier du Petit-Champlain, one of the earliest residential neighborhoods of Québec. In summer, the narrow streets swarm with tourists and those who wish to sell them something, but it is a happy, not tawdry, confluence, with many agreeable *boîtes* interspersed with stores selling souvenirs, crafts and clothing.

Continue straight from the bottom of the stairs along rue du Petit-Champlain, noting the entrance, in the house on the right, to the funicular that carries passengers back to the upper town. Note, too, part way along on the left, there are more stairs down — the **Escalier Cul-de-Sac**. Continue to the end of the street, window-shopping or menu-reading, then turn around and take those stairs down to Blvd. Champlain.

Turn left, past still more shops and cafés. Follow the bend to the right, toward the river. On the left is the MAISON CHEVALIER *(60 rue du Marché-Champlain),* a fine 18thC stone structure that is actually three connected buildings. The youngest dates from 1752. After a quick visit, exit left, then turn left again at the next street. Up ahead is a sign marking the entrance to **Place Royale**. Restoration is all but complete of the 3- to 4-story 18thC buildings that define the attractive square. Note the ladders on the steep roofs of some of them, a common device on Québécois houses, meant to aid in fighting fires and in the removal of snow.

The square is dominated by the **ÉGLISE NOTRE-DAME-DES-VICTOIRES**, completed in 1688 and one of the oldest churches in Québec province. A bust of Louis XIV in the center of the square is testimony to the epoch.

Opposite the church is a wine store, in the 1689 **Maison Dumont** *(1 Pl. Royale* ☎ *643-1214, closed Sun, Mon)*. A visit may prove irresistible. At #3A is an **interpretation centre**, with a multi-media show illustrating the history of the square. Exit at the far right corner of the plaza down ruelle de la Place, to the next street, rue St-Pierre.

A few steps down to the right is another **interpretation centre** *(25 St-Pierre* ☎ *643-6631* ◙ *open daily mid-May to end Sept, 10am–noon, 1–5pm),* with exhibits showing the development of the area from the Amerindians forward. Continue in the same direction down St-Pierre.

The next corner, with rue Sous-le-Fort, is an excellent photo opportunity (◀€), taking in both the historic buildings of the lower town and the Chateau Frontenac, up above. Turn left through the gate to reach the **Batterie Royale**, the 1691 fortification with ten cannons that defended the young settlement.

In the converted warehouse across the Place de Paris on the left is an **information centre** *(215 rue du Marché-Finlay* ☎ *643-6631* ◙ *open mid-May to end Sept 10am–6pm)*. Attendants can describe scheduled activities in the area and provide guided and audio tours. Or, from Batterie Royale, walk back to the funicular, visible through the gate just entered.

Vieux Québec sights A to Z

BASILIQUE NOTRE-DAME-DE-QUÉBEC
*16 Buade. Map **14**B4* ☎*692-2533; open daily.*
The cathedral is the central gathering place of the oldest Roman Catholic parish on the continent north of Mexico. Parts of it, including the bell tower and walls, date to 1647, but it has been bombarded or otherwise damaged on several occasions, necessitating extensive repairs.

Now, it is richly embellished in the flamboyant Baroque mode of the decades of its most intensive construction, glinting with flickering candlelight, gilded scrollwork and luminous stained-glass windows. The lamp in the sanctum was a gift of Louis XIV. French bishops and governors are interred in the crypts below.

CHÂTEAU FRONTENAC
*1 Carrières. Map **14**C5.*
Not a visitable castle but a world-famous hotel, the Château Frontenac dominates the Québec City skyline from its vantage point on Terrasse Dufferin in upper old town.

See the entry in WHERE TO STAY on page 217 and the illustration on the previous page.

ÉGLISE NOTRE-DAME-DES-VICTOIRES

Place Royale. Map 14C5 ☎*692-1650* 🔲 *Open daily.*

This church, which dominates Place Royale, was completed in 1688, and is one of the oldest in the province of Québec. Named for battles fought in 1690 and 1711, it has been restored twice — the first time following the English conquest of 1763, the second in 1969.

Within, the high altar takes the form of a castle.

HOLY TRINITY ANGLICAN CATHEDRAL

31 des Jardins. Map 14C4 ☎*692-2193* 🔲 ✗ *available. Open daily May–Aug; Sept–Oct (Thanksgiving Day) Mon–Fri, Sun for services only.*

Said to be patterned after St Martin-in-the-Fields in London, the 1804 cathedral does bear a resemblance to that landmark church's Neo-classical exterior, although it is a good deal smaller in scale. The interior is simple, almost austere, but generously proportioned, with fine woodwork fashioned of oak from a royal forest in England. Many of the objects within were gifts from George III.

In summer, there are weekly organ recitals, and artists display their works in the courtyard.

MAISON CHEVALIER

60 Marché-Champlain. Map 14C5 ☎*643-9689* 🔲 *Open June 15–Sept 30 daily 10am–5pm.*

Three restored late 17th and early 18thC connected houses have become an ethnology exhibition center administered by the MUSÉE DE LA CIVILISATION. The earliest of the houses dates from 1695, the youngest from 1752. Inside are earthy French–Canadian interpretations of furniture styles in vogue in the motherland between 1610 and 1774, during the reigns of Louis XIII, XIV, and XV.

The museum is sometimes unattended, and labels are in French, but there is a guidebook in English available at the front desk.

MUSÉE DE LA CIVILISATION

85 Dalhousie. Map 14B5 ☎*643-2158* 🔳 *(*🔲 *Tues). Open June 24–Sept 6, daily 10am–7pm; rest of year Tues–Sun 10am–5pm.*

Part of the Vieux Port redevelopment, near Place Royale, the new (1988) museum is a striking architectural statement. Early on, it manifested a somewhat uncertain mission, wobbling through metaphysical marshes exemplified by exhibitions with such themes as "How to function in a society based on the visual when we no longer have the use of our eyes" and "An essay on being and seeming."

Things have since taken sharper focus, and it has become one of the most entertaining and enlightening museums in Canada. Grandparents, grandchildren, and everyone in between will find much to engage them. Exhibits are still interdisciplinary in character, following broad themes more often than strict chronology. Every conceivable device and scheme is used to make often subtle points.

Deployed with considerable inventiveness are holographs, computer terminals, video, light, sound, unusual games and even ant farms. Strong doses of natural and social sciences are used, but in ways unintimidating even to those who once found logarithms unfathomable.

The lobby atrium has pools and waterfalls, and slabs of patterned concrete suggesting the spring breakup of ice floes. Through the big glass wall can be seen the restored 1752 **Maison Estèbe**, which now contains the tasteful museum boutique and stands above ancient vaulted cellars.

This is truly a museum for people who think they hate museums.

MUSÉE DU SÉMINAIRE DE QUÉBEC
9 Université. Map 14B4 ☎692-2843. First call at the reception center at 2 Côte de la Fabrique, for tickets and tours ▨ Open June–Sept 30 daily 10am–5.30pm, Oct–May Tues–Sun 10am–5pm.

✗ Tours available in summer (▨) for certain parts of the seminary, including the chapel, the Laval Funeral Chapel, the kitchens and refectory. Call at the reception center.

Sharing a small square with the **Basilique Notre-Dame** is the School of Architecture of Université Laval and a small **reception centre** for this museum. The museum itself is down the hill on another street. The centre has an interesting model of the immediate vicinity. To see the museum itself, walk down bordering rue Sainte-Famille and turn in through the archway on rue de l'Université.

The ground floor is a sampling of the museum's collections, which are, essentially, the bringing together of paintings, relics, scientific devices, and assorted artifacts given to the University over its three centuries of existence. These include, on the upper floors, paintings by European and Québécois artists, rare books and coins, even an Egyptian mummy.

The most important artist represented is Joshua Reynolds, with his portrait of General Wolfe, the commander of the victorious British force in 1759. One gallery is an exhibit of historical stereopticon photographs of Québec from the second half of the last century, using the kinds of coloured 3-D glasses remembered from movies of the 1950s.

MUSÉE DES URSULINES
12 Donnacona. Map 14C4 ☎694-0694 ▨ Open Jan 7–Nov 25 Tues–Sat 9.30am–noon, 1.30–4.45pm; Sun 12.30–5.15pm.
Three nuns of the Ursuline order landed at Québec in 1639 on a mission to convert and teach Amerindian children. One of their number, Mme de La Peltrie, compiled the first dictionaries of Native American languages.

Paintings and engravings, humble household furnishings and embroidery illustrate that arrival and the domestic life of the early years. In upstairs rooms are a few Native objects, overshadowed by a collection of musical instruments, including, need it be said, a harp.

Some of the docents in the museum are nuns of the still-active order, which today has 65 members.

PORT DE QUÉBEC
100 St-André. Map 14B4 ☎648-3300 ▨ ✗ available. Hours vary: call ahead.
This modern exhibition hall on the waterfront of the enclosed Louise

Basin contains four floors of displays illustrating the activities of the port in the 19thC. Shipbuilding and marine trade are emphasized, and audiovisual presentations and lectures are also on offer.

After leaving the centre, regard for a moment the double row of fine houses across the way, topped by the silvery roof and towers of the august **Séminaire de Québec**, part of Université Laval. Then cross rue St-André, go one block, and turn left (E) on rue St-Paul, a street lined for two blocks with restored buildings housing galleries, cafés, antique stores and high-design furniture outlets.

The citadel and defense system

LA CITADELLE ★
*1 Côte de la Citadelle. Map **14D4** ☎648-3563* 🎟 ◁€ 🅇 *available. Open daily Mar–Oct; call to arrange visits Nov–Feb.*

Anticipating future American attacks after the War of 1812, the Duke of Wellington ordered this star-shaped fortress on the E flank of Québec's fortifications to be built in 1820. It took 12 years to complete, and has never heard a shot fired in anger. Still an active military post, and the largest fortified group of buildings in N America, the Citadelle is garrisoned by the Royal 22nd Regiment, the only fully Francophone unit in the Canadian Armed Forces.

The former **powder magazine** (1750) is now a museum, one of 25 buildings in the complex; on display are uniforms, weapons and mementoes from four centuries of Canadian military history. A 40-minute **Changing of the Guard** is held daily *(at 10am, mid-June to Labour Day, except when raining)*. **Tattoos** take place in July and August *(Tues, Thurs, Sat, Sun at 7pm, also except when raining)*. There is also a **Cannon salute** from the Prince-de-Galles bastion daily *(noon and 9.30pm)*.

The only way to get into the Citadelle is to walk up the Côte de la Citadelle from the St-Louis Gate, at the entrance to the old town.

PARC DES CHAMPS-DE-BATAILLE (National Battlefields Park)
*Map **13E3**. Open daily.*

These 235 acres of woods and meadows SW of the CITADELLE were the site of the 1759 battle between the British and French that radically altered the course of North American history.

Declared a public park in 1908, it incorporates the Plains of Abraham, where the blood of Wolfe and Montcalm was spilled, along with that of many of their men. There is no biblical reference in the name: Abraham Martin was the man who was given the land in 1635.

While most of the park is rolling fields and trees, providing unparalleled vistas of the St Lawrence valley, there are a few scattered structures. Included are two round stone **Martello towers**, which were meant to function as 17thC early-warning systems. They are under restoration. According to season, the park is used for picnicking, cycling, running, snowshoeing and cross-country skiing.

NATIONAL BATTLEFIELDS PARK INTERPRETATION CENTRE
Within MUSÉE DU QUÉBEC, 1 Av. Wolfe-Montcalm ☎648-4071; open same hours as museum.

✗ A self-guided, 35-minute audio tour of the center takes visitors through the three centuries of history of New France and Québec. In summer, a shuttle takes them from site to site in the large park.

The new Interpretation Centre has now opened in an old prison building. It was recently incorporated into the MUSÉE DU QUÉBEC, which stands near the monument that marks the spot where Wolfe fell.

MUSÉE DU QUÉBEC
1 Av. Wolfe-Montcalm ☎643-2150. Off map 13F2 ▣ (▣ Wed) ✗ available
▤ Open mid-May (Victoria Day)–early Sept (Labour Day) daily 10am–5.45pm (except Wed until 9.45pm); rest of year open Tues–Sun 10am–5.45pm, closed Mon.

Another praiseworthy addition to Québec's cultural scene, this expanded and upgraded museum complex has three distinctive pavilions and a new INTERPRETATION CENTRE for the Parc des Champs-de-Bataille.

The most visually arresting of the three main structures is the recently completed **Grand Hall**, a soaring pyramidal building with roof and sides sectioned by large expanses of glass. It functions as the reception area, joining and providing access to the original 1933 Neoclassical Gérard-Morisset building, on the W, and the refurbished 1871 Baillairgé building, a former prison, which now contains the interpretation centre.

Fittingly positioned at the edge of the Plains of Abraham, the museum contains painting and sculpture collections that charts the evolution of Québec art from the French colonial period to the vigorous present. These are complemented by works on paper, wood carvings, and objects fashioned of silver and gold. Frequent traveling exhibitions from other parts of Canada and abroad enrich the permanent holdings, as do special film showings and music recitals.

PARC DE L'ARTILLERIE
2 d'Auteuil. Map 13B3 ☎548-4205 ▣ ✗ available. Hours vary: call ahead.

A strategically important French military site dating from the early 17thC, the complex occupies a position at the NW corner of the city walls. Its several buildings served a number of purposes over the years — as a barracks, a foundry, and an armament factory that made bullets for the Canadian Army until 1964.

A program of restoration is underway, and three buildings are now open. Of these, the **Redoute Dauphine**, begun in 1712, has exhibits of uniforms and relics that sketch military life during the French era, while the **interpretation centre** displays a model of Québec in 1808.

THE FORTIFICATIONS
100 St-Louis. Map 14D4 ☎648-7016 ▣ ◀€ ✗ available. Hours vary according to season.

Ramparts almost 5km (three miles) long enclose the old town, the only such intact fortifications north of the Rio Grande River. They grew and evolved over three centuries, according to available manpower and economic means and to dangers perceived by the city's governors and military commanders, first French, then British. Some were erected prior to the Battle on the Plains of Abraham in 1759, but most went up in the 19thC, when invasions by the United States were threats both imagined and realized.

Incorporated into the fortification system were powder magazines, barracks, artillery batteries, and watchtowers, most of them recently restored or undergoing reconstruction. Key components are **Porte St-Louis**, **Poudrière de l'Esplanade**, **Parc Montmorency**, LA CITADELLE, PARC DES CHAMPS-DE-BATAILLE, and PARC DE L'ARTILLERIE.

There are several points at which access to the walls can be gained, including the St-Louis Gate, which separates Parliament Hill from the old town. The most dramatic, however, is the Promenade des Gouverneurs, which runs along the front of the Citadelle, high above the St Lawrence. There is a staircase up to the Promenade from the end of the Terrasse Dufferin, but it is an arduous climb, not to be undertaken by the unfit. Better to reach it by the path that rises from the left side of the Grande Allée, just after walking uphill through the St-Louis Gate from the old town.

Parliament Hill (Colline Parlementaire)

HÔTEL DU PARLEMENT

Map 13D3. Av. Dufferin and Grande Allée E ☎*643-7239* 🎦 *Open daily June 24–Labour Day; Sept–May closed Sat, Sun; closed June 1–23.*

✗ *Frequent 30-minute tours are available. No tours June 1–23. Groups of 10 or more must reserve ahead* ☎*643-7239.*

What prideful Québécois choose to call their "National Assembly" (which it may yet become in actual fact) dominates a hill just N of the St-Louis Gate in the city wall. Completed in 1886, the building had its clear inspiration in the French Renaissance. Its four wings form a wide quadrangle, and the niches in the facade shelter bronze statues of Québec historical figures.

The debating chambers, including the Renaissance-style meeting place for Québec's elected representatives, are open to the public when the Assembly is in session.

GALERIE ANIMA G

1037 La Chevrotière. Map 13D3 ☎*643-6017* 🎦 ◁ƒ *Open Mon–Fri 10am–4pm; Sat, Sun 1–5pm.*

Located behind the HÔTEL DU PARLEMENT, the Complexe G building is an otherwise anonymous concrete tower whose roof bristles with satellite dishes and antennae.

Its 31st floor is an observation deck that provides incomparable vistas of the river, old town, the CITADELLE and the surrounding countryside.

Québec City:
where to stay

Making your choice

There is little reason not to stay inside the walled old town, or at least within walking distance. A felicitous variety of modern high-rise hotels, inns and guesthouses covers every sybaritic desire or budgetary need. At whatever level of luxury (or lack of it), advance reservations are essential, especially in summer and during the Winter Carnival, as Québec's 8,000 rooms can fill up quickly.

Should you have difficulty in finding lodgings, try **Réservation Québec** (☎ *800-363-7372)*, a reservation service for more than 400 hotels throughout the region.

HOW TO USE THIS CHAPTER
* **Symbols**: Full details of all our suggested hotels are given, and symbols show price categories, and give a résumé of available facilities. See the KEY TO SYMBOLS on page 7 for the full explanation. Unless otherwise indicated in the listing below, all are air-conditioned and elevators are available.

   At the smaller, cheaper *auberges* and inns that abound in the old town, don't expect porters, elevators, room service, cable television, nor dining rooms. Given those deficiencies, they are not all that much cheaper than the larger modern hotels, and should be considered primarily for room availability.
* **Prices**: The prices corresponding to our price symbols are based on average charges for two people staying in a double room with bathroom/shower. For this purpose, breakfast and tax are not included. Although actual prices will inevitably increase, our relative price categories are likely to remain the same.

   Prices are given in **Canadian dollars**.

Symbol	Category	Current price
▥	very expensive	more than $180
▥	expensive	$140-180
▥	moderate	$100-140
▥	inexpensive	$80-100
▭	cheap	under $80

Québec City hotels A to Z

AUBERGE DE LA CHOUETTE
71 d'Auteuil, Québec G1R 4C3. Map **14***C4*
☎694-0232 ▢ *10 rms* ➡ ⚏ AE
Location: Near the Information Centre and St-Louis Gate. Those who dine at the ground-floor **Aspara**, arguably the city's best Asian restaurant, may not be aware that this is a true inn, with ten pleasant rooms upstairs. Each has a private bath, color TV, telephone and air conditioning, with antiques adding warmth to the otherwise ordinary furnishings.

AUBERGE SAINT-ANTOINE
10 Saint-Antoine, Québec G1K 4C9. Map **14***B5* ☎692-2211 or 800-267-0525
Fx692-1177 ▢ *28 rms* ➡ AE ⊙ ⊙⊙ VISA ⌂
Location: Lower old town, next to the Musée de la Civilisation. One of the newest hotels (1992) utilizes a 17thC maritime building of stone and heavy timbers for its lobby and breakfast area. The bedrooms, in a modern adjoining structure, are very agreeable, with French–Canadian antiques and reproductions. Few rooms are duplicates, and there are three categories — from good up to memorable, including some with whirlpool baths. Room #31 has a birdcage, and view of the river, #43 has an ornate Gothic bedstead. Rates include breakfast and parking. Apart from its distance from many of the city's most important attractions, there aren't any more satisfactory lodgings to be had.

CHÂTEAU BELLEVUE
16 Laporte, Québec G1R 4M9. Map **14***C5* ☎692-2573 or 800-463-2617 Fx692-4876 ▢ *56 rms* ➡ AE ⊙ ⊙⊙ VISA ⌂ ≛ ☙ ⊰
Location: Upper old town, on Parc des Gouverneurs. Five attached row houses at the top end of the sloping Parc des Gouverneurs were gutted and rebuilt without altering the exterior. They are comfortable rooms, if uninspired, all but one with private bath. No dining room and no charm, but good value for relatively low prices, and a desirable, fairly quiet location. Cable TV. Some rooms have an excellent view, and those without view are a little cheaper. There are modest discounts November to April.

CHÂTEAU FRONTENAC
1 des Carrières, Québec G1R 4P5. Map **14***C5* ☎692-3861 or 800-268-9411 (from Canada), 800-828-7447 (from the US)
Fx692-1751 ▥ *540 rms* ▣ ⚏ AE ⊙ ⊙⊙ VISA ⊰ from many rms ⌂ ⅄ ☙ ☒ ⊟ ♫
Location: On Terrasse Dufferin in upper old town. In appearance, it resembles an outsized Loire Valley château, with its famous turrets, gables and spires dominating the skyline. The lower section was built in 1893, the squared high-rise tower with the green copper roof added three decades later. In recent years, there was a widespread perception that it was coasting on its reputation. Perhaps because of the competition of new luxury hotels in the town beyond the walls, a major overhaul has been undertaken. Bedrooms vary substantially in size, location, and state of cosmetic repair. Ask for one that has been renovated, with a river view. Briskly efficient, impersonal service is the norm. There is, as yet, no health club. A new wing replicating the style of the main building opened in 1993, in commemoration of the hotel's 100th anniversary.

CHÂTEAU DE LA TERRASSE
6 Pl. Terrasse Dufferin, Québec G1R 4N5. Map **14***C5* ☎694-9472 ▢ *to* ▢ *18 rms. Closed late Nov–Winter Carnival. No cards* ➡ ⌂ ☙ ☙ ⊰ *from most rms.*
Location: In upper old town, overlooking river. Ten of the rooms have hypnotic river views and three have balconies in this converted turn-of-the-century house at the edge of the cliffside promenade. All have private baths, and color cable TV with English-language channels. The one suite has a kitchenette, and costs far less than a cramped single in one of the big hotels.

No meals and no air conditioning (a factor only during a few weeks of high summer). At the price, it has very few rivals.

CLARENDON

57 Ste-Anne, Québec G1R 3X4. Map **14***C4* ☎692-2480 *or* 800-361-6162 ᶠᵃˣ692-4652 ▥ *89 rms* ▭ ▤ AE ⊕ ⌀ ⚡ 🏊 ⚰ ♫

Location: Center of old town, near City Hall. While it insists on describing itself as Art Nouveau/Art Deco in style, those decorative details are confined to a few public areas. The building is even older than the Château Frontenac, and the bedrooms remain rather gloomy, despite superficial primping. They aren't air-conditioned, either. The location is good, rates are moderate, and there is a well-regarded restaurant downstairs, next to one of the town's best jazz bars.

LOEWS LE CONCORDE

1225 Pl. Montcalm, Québec G1R 4W6. Map **13***E3* ☎647-2222 *or* 800-235-6397 ᶠᵃˣ647-4710 ▥ *424 rms* ▤ AE ⊕ ⌀ ▥ 《 ☜ 🏊 ⚰ ⌾

Location: Outside the walls, five blocks from St-Louis Gate. It is difficult to forgive a structure of such surpassing ugliness when it blights an otherwise handsome neighborhood of Queen Anne row houses. Get past that esthetic affront and all the expectable first-class comforts and conventions are in place. Those who don't mind eating in a room that moves are treated to spectacular vistas from **L'Astral** rooftop bar/restaurant. Most rooms have excellent views. While it's a 15–20-minute walk from the heart of the old town, the bars and restaurants of the Grande Allée strip are close by. Guests can use a nearby health club, which has a pool and racquet courts.

MANOIR STE-GENEVIÈVE

13 Av. Ste-Geneviève, Québec G1R 4A7. Map **14***C5* ☎694-1666 ᶠᵃˣ694-1666 ▥ *to* ▥ *9 rms. No cards.*

Location: In old town, on Parc Jardin des Gouverneurs. Its nine rooms are small, as is to be expected of a town house that is more than 160 years old. They are immaculate, though, kept so under the watchful eye of a manager who carries on the tradition of her predecessor, who was in charge for more than 30 years. No elevator, no room telephones, no food, and the TV carries only French channels, but all rooms have private baths and most are air-conditioned — and all that Vieux Québec has to offer is right outside the front door. From October 31–May 1, rates are discounted 30 percent.

LE PRIORI

15 Sault-au-Matelot, Québec G1K 3Y7. Map **14***B5* ☎692-3992 ᶠᵃˣ692-0883 ▥ *to* ▥ *26 rms and suites* AE ⊕ ▥ ⌀ ▤

Location: Lower town, near Musée de la Civilisation. The restored 18thC building — two of them, actually — contains rooms that might have been decorated by avant-garde designer Philippe Starck. Not all rooms have bathtubs, but all have shower stalls, as well as remote-controlled cable color TV. Suites are memorable, with such grace notes as grandmother clocks, fireplaces, kitchens equipped with crockery and dishwashers, jacuzzis, CD players, fax and computer ports. No air conditioning, though. The menu of the **Laurie Raphael** restaurant is as fresh and sprightly as the rest of the place.

QUÉBEC HILTON

3 Pl. Québec, Québec G1K 7M9. Map **13***D3* ☎647-2411 *or* 800-268-9275 ᶠᵃˣ647-6488 ▥ *563 rms* ▭ ▤ AE ⊕ ⌀ ▥ 《 ☜ 🏊 ⚰ ♫ ⌾

Location: Outside the walls, near Hôtel du Parlement. Those unwilling to forego modern gadgets and conveniences for Old World charm need look no further. Easily the most desirable of the trio of large, relatively new hotels within walking distance of Vieux Québec, this Hilton scores commendably high on all counts of efficiency and service. Minibars, color cable TV and closed-circuit movies equip every room, with extra goodies available on the *Étages Plus* executive levels. Tour groups and conventioneers throng the brassy, bustling lobby. Non-smoking rooms are available. The health club and outdoor pool are among the few offered in the city. Upper floors have super views.

RADISSON GOUVERNEURS QUÉBEC
690 Blvd. St-Cyrille E, Québec G1R 5A8.
Map **13D3** ☎647-1717 or 800-333-3333
🅵🅰647-2146 ▥ 377 rms ➰ ➡ 🆎 🔘
🔘 ▦ 🔥 ⚓ ♈ ⅄ ☂ 🖭 🎵
Location: Outside the walls, near Hôtel du Parlement. A stark facade encloses

an ungainly and confused modernistic interior. Bedrooms are spacious and well-appointed. With a change in ownership, previous signs of heavy use have been papered over. The in-house restaurant **Le Vignoble** has a tempting and inexpensive luncheon buffet. Non-smoking rooms are available. Exclusive floors promise personalized service, including a separate reception desk and complimentary breakfast. An adequate fitness center and heated year-round pool round out the facilities.

BED AND BREAKFAST

Travelers who enjoy being closer to the natives, and saving money in the process, can arrange accommodations through several bed and breakfast agencies.

Two possibilities in this category are **Bonjour Québec** *(3765 Blvd. de Monaco, Québec G1R 1N4* ☎ *527-1465)* and **Apartments and Bed and Breakfast in Old Québec** *(35 rue des Remparts, Québec G1R 3R6, map 14B4* ☎*655-7685).*

When calling or writing, it is best to be as specific as possible about requirements — location, number and ages of children, bathrooms, personal habits — to avoid disappointments. Many hosts, for example, do not allow young children, or smokers. Advance deposits are typically required, as might be a minimum stay of two nights, and credit cards may not be accepted.

Don't expect all the comforts of a conventional hotel or motel. These are rooms in private homes, after all — no porters, no elevators, and with bathrooms shared or down the hall. The point is to save money and meet some Quebeckers. For cable TV or certain air conditioning or the like, choose a hotel.

Québec City: eating out

Where and what to eat

The Québécois defer to no one in their love of fine food — not to Montréalers, and certainly not to Torontonians. No doubt due to their Gallic heritage, they elevate the act of eating to a plateau far higher than mere need. Visitors profit, and not one meal need be less than gratifying. Some will be memorable, happy marriages of setting, ambience and skill, to be recalled years later.

The several schools of French cooking dominate, not surprisingly — bistros *haute* and *ordinaire,* formal explorations of the classical and *nouvelle,* even the indigenous cooking that had its origins in the challenges of merely surviving in New France. In those days, the need for abundant fare, simply prepared from ingredients easily stored over the long winter, gave rise to much use of pork, potatoes, beans, maple syrup and root vegetables. The resulting pork pies, *ragôuts* and sugar pies are still available, if not as widely as veal wrapped around goat cheese, and sun-dried tomatoes.

After the French variations, Italian restaurants are most evident in Québec City, well ahead of the scattering of Asian, Central European and Mediterranean kitchens. Only a few are truly expensive, and the majority fall into the moderately-priced category and below.

WINE AND FOOD
Imported **wines** are expensive, making the somewhat cheaper Canadian bottlings worth a try. As in Montréal, many restaurants allow or encourage customers to bring their own wine. Ask when booking a table. Wine and beer can easily be purchased at supermarkets and convenience stores *(dépanneurs).* Domestic **beers** are excellent and go well with ethnic and bistro meals. Some brands brewed in Québec are *Belle-Gueule, Boréale,* and *Saint-Ambroise.* For **liquors and premium wines,** an outlet of the government-controlled *Société des Alcools* must be found. There is a *Maison des Vins* on Place Royale in the lower town.

USEFUL TO KNOW
- **Reservations:** Peak summer crowds and the Winter Carnival make reservations essential at the better and/or more popular restaurants and on almost any weekend.
- **Tipping:** A 15 percent tip on the amount before tax is normal, but make certain that a service charge isn't already added.

HOW TO USE THIS CHAPTER

- **Location**: Map references are given for the color maps at the end of the book.
- **Symbols**: See the KEY TO SYMBOLS on page 7 for an explanation of the full list.
- **Prices**: The prices corresponding to our price symbols are based on the average price of a meal for one person, inclusive of house wine, tax and gratuity. Although actual prices will inevitably increase after publication, our relative price categories are likely to remain the same. Prices are given in **Canadian dollars**.

Symbol	Category	Current price
⬜	very expensive	over $70
⬜	expensive	$50–70
⬜	moderate	$30–50
⬜	inexpensive	$15–30
⬜	cheap	under $15

Québec City restaurants A to Z

AUX ANCIENS CANADIENS *Québécois*
34 St-Louis. Map 14C4 ☎*692-1627* ⬜
⬛ ⬛ ⬛ ⬛ *Open daily.*
Very visible, and patronized largely by tourists, but that shouldn't discourage a visit, especially if one is interested in sampling more or less authentic traditional Québécois dishes. The restaurant is in one of the oldest houses in the upper town, the low-ceilinged rooms on two floors hung with antique doodads and farm tools. It's like dinner at Grandma's house, even if she never braised rabbit in beer or baked duckling in maple syrup. And are those meatballs scented with cinnamon and allspice? There is a selection of native cheeses, but a caloric splurge is best saved for the sugar pie floating in heavy cream. This is stick-to-the-ribs stuff, satisfying and not a bit clever. It is swarmed at every meal, so book ahead.

ASPARA *Southeast Asian*
71 d'Auteuil. Map 14C4 ☎*694-0232* ⬜
⬛ ⬛ ⬛ *Closed Sat lunch, Sun lunch.*
They truthfully claim a *cuisine asiatique*, and proceed to skip around the Far East, with culinary stops in Thailand, Vietnam, Cambodia and a quick

side trip to Taiwan. Would that they had stayed put with Thai cooking, which is superior to the others presented. Under this heading are *mou sati* (pork brochettes with marinated cucumbers) and *poulet de Bangkok* (spicy chicken medallions). A 7-course sampler for two persons is appetizing. House wines are cheap, but that's about all that can be said for them. Upholstery and draperies are, incongruously, European, and the Victorian house dates back to 1845. The combination (and the cheap lunch) fills the place with businesspeople, sophisticates, couples, and families, for there is something here for everyone.

BISTRO TASTEVIN *French*
32 St-Louis. Map 14C4 ☎*692-4191* ⬜
⬛ ⬛ ⬛ ⬛ *Open daily.*
Many of the small hotels and guesthouses in the immediate area serve no breakfast, so several places along rue St-Louis fill the void. This is better than most. The *café au lait* is good, the *croissants* fresh. A large copper espresso machine presides over the bar, tables have more space between them than at competitors along this strip. Linger over the morning newspaper, for

no one will silently urge you to be done and gone. It gets more rushed later in the day, as the crowds increase along old town's main drag. Keep it in mind for lunch, dinner, snacks; prices are fair, meals are filling.

Similar, if a trifle more crowded, are the nearby **L'Omelette** (*#66 St-Louis*) and **Buffet St-Louis** (*#44 St-Louis*). Both are open breakfast through dinner and accept credit cards.

CAFÉ DE LA PAIX *French*
44 des Jardins. Map 14C4 ☎692-1430
▥ to ▥ ▣ ▣ ▣ ▥ *Open daily.*
Presumably the sauces are lighter than they were 30 years ago. Otherwise, the dishes on this long menu might well be the same as they were in 1960. Not that this is to be deplored. In an age of the new-new-NEW, what a pleasure to see good old *coquille St-Jacques, escargots de Bourgogne,* lobster thermidor and *châteaubriand garni* (for two, of course). It's a step back from the gastronomic precipice, to let us savor what it was that we loved about French food in the first place. Although meats are featured and game often appears, the kitchen is especially adept with *fruits de mer,* and salmon in particular. The nightly *table d'hôte* is relatively easy on the budget, the light lunch even more so. Reserve ahead, for even with 120 seats, they rarely have room for drop-ins.

LA CARAVELLE *French*
68½ St-Louis. Map 14C4 ☎694-9022 ▥
to ▥ ▣ ▣ ▥ *Open daily.*
The main street of Vieux Québec, rue St-Louis has several essentially interchangeable restaurants, promoting good times, warm feelings, and decent, undistinguished food. This is representative. Four cluttered rooms of no particular school of decor give off a welcoming glow underscored by the attentive staff. The owner is from Spain, so the largely French menu of *pâté* and *gigot d'agneau* is peppered with such specialities of his homeland as *zarzuela* and *paella.* They are sturdy victuals of forthright execution. Jollity is encour-

aged, by the wandering guitarist whose repertoire slides from *La Vie en Rose* to *Nowhere Man* and by showy tableside preparations of after-dinner coffee drinks that involve cascades of blue fire. Upstairs are 24 recently decorated bedrooms whose primary virtue is that they aren't expensive.

CHEZ TEMOREL *Eclectic*
25 Couillard. Map 14B4 ☎694-1813 ▥
No cards. Open daily until late.
Buy no more than an espresso and the table is yours for as long as you want. Those around you, mostly students and professors from the nearby Université Laval, are gossiping and dawdling over books of poetry, and diddling with their laptop computers. Light meals, salads, soups, quiches, *croissants,* sandwiches, plates of wine and cheese with glasses of claret support an enveloping warmth that is just the place to sit out a downpour. Two floors; open for breakfast and snacks until past midnight.

L'ÉCHAUDE *French*
73 Sault-au-Matelot. Map 14B5
☎692-1299 ▥ to ▥ ▣ ▣ ▣ ▥
Closed Sat lunch, Sun lunch. May close Sunday night in winter months.
A *nouvelle* bistro to remember when wandering in the old port area or antiquing along rue St-Paul. A little off the heaviest tourist trails, its custom is primarily local. They use the bistro convention of writing the daily menu on the mirrors — and even uninformed choices are likely to be flavorful and satisfying. You might get skate in browned butter, or rosy aromatic lamb. Evenings, it sheds the businesslike demeanor of the lunch crowd. Wines are pricey.

FLEUR DE LOTUS *Southeast Asian*
50 de la Fabrique. Map 14B4 ☎692-4286
▥ to ▥ ▣ ▣ ▥ *Closed Sat lunch, Sun lunch.*
This tiny, largely unadorned room near City Hall packs them in at both lunch and dinner. They cover the same gastronomic territory as **Aspara**, with a comparable middling-to-good degree

of skill. These Indochinese dishes, more than 20 of them, are about equally divided between the cuisines of three Southeast Asian countries, and again the Thai recipes stand out. Friendly reception by people who remember your face the second time. Top value for just a few dollars. Bring your own wine.

GAMBRINUS *French/Italian*
15 du Fort. Map 14C5 ☎692-5144 ▥
▣ ▣ ▣ ▨ *Closed Sat lunch, Sun lunch.*
A restaurant sharing a building with a commercial museum — the **Musée du Fort** — might not sound too promising. But in fact, this is as agreeable and satisfying as can be found in old town. The menu is competent Continental, borrowings mostly French and Italian, characterized by such staples as garlic snails, rack of lamb, *fettucine Alfredo,* lobster bisque, and pheasant with fruit, all in unfussy presentations. Walls are dark mahogany, lightened by French doors with plants hanging in front. Terrace tables look upon the Chateau Frontenac. A singer with guitar is often on hand. The luncheon *table d'hôte* is good value, with choices of three appetizers, a soup, main course, and dessert.

LE LAPIN SAUTÉ *Eclectic*
52 Petit-Champlain. Map 14C5
☎692-5325 ▢ *to* ▥ ▣ ▣ ▨ *Open daily.*
They do serve rabbit at this bright little bistro in the Quartier du Petit-Champlain, but the featured item is mussels, served many ways. If you like them, one special lunch starts with soup of the day, goes on to a big bowl of the steamed shellfish with a bowl of French fries, in the Belgian manner, and the price includes a glass of wine and coffee. Pastas, mixed grills, lamb chops, chicken kebabs, and sandwiches are also on the card. It looks like a cottage whose owners decided to open their doors to a few close friends. Sheaves of dried grains and bunches of flowers are affixed to beams and walls; tables are set outside on one side, next to a small park. You'll go right past it two or three

times if you spend even a short weekend in town. Breakfast is served Saturday and Sunday, in addition to lunch and dinner daily.

LE MARIE-CLARISSE *French*
12 Petit-Champlain. Map 14C5
☎692-0857 ▥ ▣ ▣ ▨ *Closed Sat lunch, Sun.*
What a pleasure on a warm, spring day to rest on this patio, a cool Chablis at hand, contemplating the passing parade. For that matter, it's as comforting in winter, tucked inside next to the fireplace. It's at the foot of Breakneck Stairs, where three car-less streets meet in the middle of the Quartier du Petit-Champlain. A street performer will almost certainly be situated nearby on good days — an accordionist, perhaps, to add a proper Parisian flavor to the scene. The daily special lunch doesn't cost much more than a couple of Big Macs with Large Fries. And if it's one of the catches-of-the-day, at which they excel, the fish is cooked within seconds of proper doneness and presented without a hint of pretension. Locals like it, despite all the tourists.

PARIS–BREST *French*
590 Grande Allée. Map 13D3 ☎529-2243
▥ ▣ ▣ ▣ ▨ *Open daily.*
Actually, it's hidden around the corner on rue de la Chevrotière, underneath 600 Grande Allée. Make the effort, for this is a most pleasurable dining experience. It has a Thirties look, with a hint of the Right Bank and a touch of Art Moderne. That French tire company that rates restaurants would surely give it a star or two. There's even a flower girl circulating with her basket of blooms. Game is featured, with memorable treatments of rabbit, pheasant, and venison. The dessert table includes a rendition of the eponymous Paris-Brest classic. An observant major-domo makes certain that not even a lone diner is neglected, too often the case in other restaurants. He fills a glass, whisks away empty plates, even smiles genuine smiles. With all that, and considering the high quality of food and

223

service, the *table d'hôte* can be judged the best value in walking distance of the old walls.

PARMESAN *French/Italian*
38 St-Louis. Map 14C4 ☎*692-0341* ▥
▨ ▣ ▣ ▨ *Open daily.*
Flambéed *steak au poivre!* "Surf and turf!" *Duck à l'orange!* It is the 1960s revisited, when restaurants borrowed the same five dishes each from the French and Italian pantheons and called themselves "continental." The kitchen leans toward the Roman way of doing things, with *tortellini in brodo, fettucine Alfredo,* and *manicotti* stuffed with cheese and spinach. As conventional as it sounds, the pasta tastes freshly made, and the veal is of a select grade. Servings are large, and main courses come with vegetables and baked potatoes, so the appetizer and/or dessert can be skipped. An invariably convivial crowd is made more so by the strolling accordionist, whose music prompts certain patrons to leap to their feet and dance between the tables. Yes, it's a mass of dated clichés, but fun, when you're in the right mood. What the heck, you're on vacation.

LE SAINT-AMOUR *French*
48a Ste-Ursule. Map 14C4 ☎*694-0667* ▥ ▨ ▣ ▣ ▨ *Closed Sun lunch, Mon lunch.*
Here's a sophisticated retreat that lives up to its name. Romance breathes by candlelight and Victorian gas fixtures, with lace at the windows in the front room and in the all-weather terrace hung with plants. Two paddle fans whirr up by the roof, which can be retracted on clear nights. The attractive, knowledgeable crowd comes in jeans and polo shirts or dressed to kill. They are there to enjoy themselves. Game is one of chef Jean-Luc Boulay's strong suits, as is boned rabbit stuffed with

chewy wild mushrooms, and the brace of quail, also boned, in a faintly astringent port sauce. The mouthwatering chocolate desserts are a must. Boulay is perfecting a culinary sub-genre — hearty *nouvelle* — pretty as a still-life painting yet lusty with flavor. And they said it couldn't be done.

SERGE BRUYÈRE *French*
1200 St-Jean. Map 14B4 ☎*694-0618* ▥ ▨ ▣ ▣ *Closed Sat lunch, Sun lunch.*
If *everyone* didn't insist that this is the finest restaurant in Québec — some say in *Canada* — it wouldn't be mentioned here. But they do, so we must. Call a respectful three days in advance, don your best clothes, arrive on time. Those who are unknown to the gatekeepers are promptly ushered to a room with the chill of Siberia and the hush of an ecclesiastical experience about to happen. In time, orders are taken. The waiter then disappears, returning much later with the first course. A long time after that, he dashes through with the second. The first is already fully digested. At this rate, the 7-course "discovery" meal can last for hours. It is now apparent why the kitchen prides itself on having only one seating a night: it can't deliver the meal any faster.

The food arrives exquisitely presented and very, very carefully prepared. But for someone who prowls the *nouvelle* frontier, M. Bruyère is remarkably lacking in daring. There are so few surprises even an occasional robust mistake would be welcome. Two good meals can be had elsewhere for the same price, someplace where the patrons aren't afraid to laugh out loud.

For the record, other levels in the complex house a tea salon and *pâtisserie,* a café, **La Petite Table**, and a wine-cellar dining room. They all have different hours than those of the main restaurant, described above.

Québec City:
nightlife and shopping

Québec City by night

As might be expected of a college town — the Université Laval is here — nightlife is vigorous, plentiful, and often raucous. Much of it happens along the **Grande Allée**. The blocks between d'Artigny and Berthelot are bordered with stone houses converted to bars and *boîtes,* most with terraces or balconies on the street side, some with discos or music bars inside. One much-seen libation is a yard-long glass of beer so tall it needs a wooden stand to hold it up and two bottles to fill it. Almost as busily funseeking is the so-called "Latin Quarter," along rue St-Jean, between Côte de la Fabrique and Porte St-Jean. Older revelers tend to move on to less frenetic hideaways in the old town, or down along the gentrifying streets of the port area.

EVENTS AND FESTIVALS
The big summer event, starting in early July, is the **Festival d'été international de Québec**, 10 days of mostly free open-air rock and jazz concerts, dance recitals, and other performance events held in such locations as the grounds of the City Hall, and the park just before the Grande Allée strip. In late June is the **Blue Nights jazz festival**, which can be heard in concert halls, restaurants and on the streets of Vieux Québec. The second week in August ushers in a relatively new celebration, the **Sillery Ancient Music Festival**, with re-creations of the Middle Ages and the Renaissance, in costume, parades, jousts, and recitals. And **Carnavale de Québec**, held from the 1st Thursday through the 2nd Sunday of February, is an excuse to play in the snow, with night parades, an ice palace, and a canoe race across the frozen St Lawrence.

THE PERFORMING ARTS
The principal permanent venue for cultural events is the **Grand Théâtre de Québec** *(269 Blvd. St-Cyrille O ☎ 643-8131),* which contains two concert halls. A modern facility, completed in 1971, it is home to the Québec Symphony Orchestra, the oldest such organization in Canada. Important soloists and ensembles appear in the smaller hall, and there are frequent visits by orchestras and chamber groups from other Canadian and American cities.

At least nine other halls in the metropolitan area lend their stages to music and performances of all persuasions, from rock to jazz to modern dance. Among the most used within the city are the **Palais Montcalm** *(995 place d'Youville* ☎ *670-9011)*, the **Colisée de Québec** *(2205 av. du Colisée* ☎ *691-7211)*, and the **Théâtre de la Bordée** *(1091½ rue St-Jean* ☎ *694-9721)*.

Nearly all theatrical productions are, of course, in the French language

BARS AND CLUBS

Most tastes and proclivities are satisfied. Cover or admission charges are rare. On or near Grande Allée, a pub crawl might take in any of a score of bars. Student-aged clients tend to rule at **Le d'Auteuil** *(35 d'Auteuil* ☎ *692-5308)*, filling the street-level bar (with pool table) and attending to the rock bands upstairs. A sometimes rapacious singles crowd prevails over the indifferent food at **Le Beaugarte** *(2590 Blvd. Laurier* ☎ *659-2442)*, while an older, dressier group with similar intentions gathers at the two bars and pool tables of **Le St Honoré** *(570 Grande Allée E* ☎ *529-7932)*, known to its habitués as "Saint-O." They have a short menu of salads, pizzas, and nachos from which to choose. **Maison du Steak** *(624 Grand Allée)* has live country music Thursday to Saturday, sung in French-accented English or all in French, but with a suitable twang either way.

On rue St-Jean, the **St James** bar in the **Manoir Victoria** *(44 Côte du Palais* ☎ *692-1030)* showcases singers of blues and folk. Hearing a French-Canadian performer announce his next song in his native tongue and then switch to New Orleans English to sing it is an experience not to be missed. Nearby, **Le Pub Saint-Alexandre** *(1087 St-Jean* ☎ *694-0015)* makes its mark with almost 200 beers and ales from just about every country that makes them, with 20 on draught. A few doors away is the raucous and untidy **Le Bistro** *(#1063)*, dominated by an energetic Latino crowd, dancing and drinking to a mix of live and recorded South American rhythms.

Serious jazz fans are courted by the large combos at the reliable **Bar l'Emprise** in the **Hôtel Clarendon** *(57 rue Ste-Anne* ☎ *692-2480)*; people actually go to listen. Nearby, **Le d'Orsay** *(68 rue Buade* ☎ *694-1582)* has a pubby look, with two bars and a small dance floor with a DJ; the mixed crowd can also eat out on the summer terrace in back, serenaded by a singer-guitarist. Young professionals shoot pool and chat each other up at the former workingman's retreat, **La Taverne Belley** *(249 St-Paul* ☎ *692-4595)*. A nightcap can be savored to piano music in the lounge of the CHÂTEAU FRONTENAC.

DISCOS

Discos are the usual youthful bedlam. The tri-leveled **Chez Dagobert** *(9600 Grande Allée E* ☎ *522-0393)* cranks up its sound system to the edge of the pain threshold. On the first floor, live rock is performed, in an arena configuration with raised seating so everyone can see and be seen. The upstairs floors have more bars, a large dance floor, big TV screens, pinball and video games. Go after 11pm. The small disco at **Vogue** *(1170 d'Artigny* ☎ *529-9973)* is less super-charged, and has the **Sherlock Holmes** pub down below, with dart board and pool table. Down in the port area is **Le Tube Hi-Fi** *(139 St-Pierre ☎ 692-0257)*, whose dancers are a couple of years older and started in careers.

Devoted disco darlings must travel to suburban Sainte-Foy to squeeze themselves into the biggest and hottest of them all, **Le Palladium** *(2327 Blvd. Versant N ☎ 682-8783)*.

Shopping in Québec City

Inevitably, there are enclosed malls, most of them in suburban Sainte-Foy and none of them especially noteworthy. For a gift, keepsake, or souvenir that can't be duplicated everywhere, most visitors have more luck (and fun) in the **Quartier du Petit-Champlain**, at the bottom of Breakneck Stairs in the lower town. Local designers and craftsmen offer a variety of handmade goods, including jewelry, leather items, woven cloth, pottery and toys. **Rue du Petit-Champlain** (see WALK on page 209) is the most productive place for making this kind of purchase.

Shoppers with a taste for antique crafts and contemporary native carvings — and the necessary discretionary income — should make a must of **Galerie Aux Multiples** *(70 Dalhousie ☎ 692-4434; smaller branch at 69 rue Ste-Anne)*. Quilts, duck decoys, old game boards, and small furniture pieces are ancillary to the collection of superb Inuit sculptures. For young antiques, folk art, and collectibles, browse nearby **rue St-Paul**.

Foreign newspapers and magazines are available until late at night at the **Maison de la Presse Internationale** *(1050 rue St-Jean ☎ 694-1511)*.

Excursions from Québec City

The Île d'Orléans and the Beaupré coast

Twenty minutes downriver from the Château Frontenac is an island of rural tranquility that has been both refuge and staging point for nearly 400 years of European adventurers, trappers, soldiers, merchants, farmers, and immigrants. The opposite — northern — shore is named after St Anne, the purported savior of numerous shipwreck victims. Along its Avenue Royale is a waterfall more than 100 feet higher than Niagara, and a grand canyon whose spectacular cataracts produced much of the province's hydro-electric power for most of this century. Country inns provide repasts that do nothing to diminish Québec's high gastronomic standards.

While this itinerary could be completed in a day, it should be relished at greater ease with an overnight stay.

Pick up Av. Dufferin, near the St-Louis Gate, as it runs N past the **HÔTEL DU PARLEMENT**. It is also Rte. 440, continuing over the St-Charles River and along the N shore of the St-Laurent. The Île d'Orléans is in view across the water to the right. Soon, cross over to the island on the 1935 Pont de l'Île. Bear right, S, at the other side, on Rte. 368, the Chemin Royal.

Farming is the principal business of the island, which Jacques Cartier first christened Île Bacchus, for the wild grapes he discovered there. With soil and micro-climate thus established as hospitable to fruit cultivation, strawberries and apples became the principal crops, augmented by potatoes, corn, and flowers. An abundance of maple trees ensures a busy, late-winter "sugaring-off" season, when sap is drawn from the trees and boiled down to make maple syrup.

The middle of the 32km x 8km (20-mile x 5-mile) island is all farmland, with its few sparse settlements, or parishes, hugging the 69km (44-mile) perimeter. Stone houses with pitched red roofs are common, some of them preceding The Conquest (as Québécois refer to the British victory in 1759). Less frequently seen are Regency-style (or Late-Georgian) brick homes.

The first parish encountered is **Ste-Pétronille**, the island's smallest. British General Wolfe established his headquarters here in 1759 for his force of 40,000 soldiers and 100 ships. Views of Québec City and of the Montmorency Falls on the Beaupré coast are cause for a short stop. **St-Laurent**, the next parish, has a maritime tradition, evidenced by the island's only marina. A fetching spot for lunch or dinner is **Le Moulin de St-Laurent** (754 Chemin Royal ☎ 829-3888) 🆎 🔘 🆅🆂🅰 closed mid-Oct to early May), a converted 18thC millhouse with a patio beside the stream.

Continuing, the Québec propensity for brightly colored roofs is increasingly apparent. While crimson is the obvious favorite, also seen are green, purple, blue, yellow. Quite by the way, in an attempt to discourage developers, farms on the Île d'Orléans can only be sold to farmers.

Shortly before arriving at the center of **St-Jean** parish, look out for the lovely **Manoir Mauvide-Genest** *(1451 Chemin Royal ☎829-2630 ▨ ✕ available; open June–early Sept daily 10am–5pm; Sept to mid-Oct Tues–Sun 11am–5pm).* A surgeon to the French king Louis XV had it built in 1734. The ground floor has a restaurant, while upstairs is a small museum of French–Canadian domestic life. In the grounds is an active summer theater.

Driving through the center of what was once a parish of seafarers, a number of houses are visibly constructed of Scottish brick. That material was recycled from its first use as ship ballast. The tin roofs much in view were required by British fiat, intended to reduce fire damage.

Not far along, in **St-François** parish, a turn-off leads down to the water's edge and to the **Auberge Chaumont** *(425 Av. Royale ☎829-2735 ▥ ▣ ▨ closed late Oct–early May).* Watch freighters and cruise ships working the river, from the long porch or the terrace around the swimming pool. Most of the food in the restaurant is regional, as with *tourtière* and *pâté de faisan*. The simply furnished guestrooms upstairs are large, quiet, and inexpensive.

On the far side of St-François is a picnic ground with a three-story observation tower. The parish church, also beside the road, dates to 1723. This is the NE end of the island, and the road now bends to the SW. In the next parish, **Ste-Famille**, an unusual dining experience is available (if reservations have been made in advance). Park in the lot for the restaurant **L'Atre** *(4403 Chemin Royal ☎829-2474 ▥ ▨ ▣ ▨ closed mid-Oct to May).* A horse-drawn carriage takes guests to the old stone house down by the water. The staff is appropriately costumed, there is no electricity, and meals are cooked in the fireplace, as they were in the 17thC. Note, however, that 20thC plastic money is acceptable in payment.

The last village, **St-Pierre**, has a church dating from 1718. Cross the Pont de l'Île and turn to the NE. Over on the left are the **Montmorency Falls** *(▣ lower section open May 24–Oct 26, 24 hours).* At 83m (274 feet), they are more than 31m (100 feet) higher than Niagara, but much narrower. The cataract has a yellowish cast, due to the high iron content of the river bed.

Continue NE on Rte. 440, here known as Avenue Royale (a.k.a. Chemin du Roi, or King's Road). It follows the Côte de Beaupré, winding along the edge of the river toward the pilgrimage town of Ste-Anne-de-Beaupré. Along the way, a cozy place for a brief stop is **Chez Marie** *(8706 Av. Royale ☎824-4347 ▥ open daily 8.30am–6.30pm).* Its particular version of comfort food is a slab of fresh bread slathered with a thick coat of maple sugar spread. The bread is baked in the 150-year-old domed brick oven standing outside the door.

Ste-Anne-de-Beaupré could not be described as an attractive nor especially interesting town. Its reason for being is the basilica named after the saint. This is the fifth church built here to honor the grandmother of

Jesus Christ, the earlier versions having fallen victim to flood, fire, and fashion. It is large, lacking in the grace and majesty that might have been wished. But it isn't really about aesthetics. Saint Anne has an unshakable reputation for miracles, and hundreds of thousands of the faithful and the curious come here every year, the former in hopes of casting off disabilities and despair. The discarded crutches and prosthetic devices that festoon the giant pillars in the vestibule are merely symbolic of the thousands left behind by believers.

Proceeding on Av. Royale, turn left on Blvd. Ste-Anne (Rte. 360). Coming into view are the ski runs of **Mont Ste-Anne** (☎ *827-4561)*. Its lifts run to the N side of the mountain, allowing skiing well into May most years. In summer, it has two 18-hole golf courses, and rides to the summit in gondola-style aerial trams.

Not far beyond the resort is a turn-off (right) to **Les Sept-Chutes** *(Saint-Ferréol-les-Neiges* ☎ *826-3139* ◨ *open late May to mid-Oct, 10am–5pm; June 24–Labour Day 9am–7pm)*. From the reception center, seek out the belvedere called "Les Cinq Chutes," which overlooks five of the seven waterfalls that plunge and twist down between high craggy walls.

For a sublime finale to the day, return to Ste-Anne-de-Beaupré and turn E on Blvd. Ste-Anne (Rte. 138). In about 3km (two miles) is **La Camarine** *(10947 Blvd. Ste-Anne* ☎ *827-5703* ⬚ ⬚ ⬚ ⬚ *open for dinner only)*. The name refers to an inedible Arctic berry, a curious choice for a restaurant that is arguably superior to any in the province. The arena is an unpretentious room in a 350-year-old farmhouse with bare wide-board floors; the food is thoroughly contemporary — French, with Asian touches. Almost anything involving salmon or duck should be at the top of the list of choices from the oft-changed menu. A new wing has 31 bedrooms with standard comforts at moderate prices. Less standard is a warm heady drink beside the fireplace in the cellar bar before retiring. Breakfast is available to overnight guests.

Gaspésie

The province of Québec has been the Atlantic gateway to the heart of the continent since the first European explorers and traders sailed its waters in hopes of riches and a passage to Asia. It embraces the St Lawrence (St-Laurent) River all the way from its confluence with the Ottawa River to the ocean, a distance of more than 960km (600 miles).

The Gaspé Peninsula, or Gaspésie, in French, which knuckles into the Atlantic above the Maritime Provinces, is a raw, elemental region entirely of itself, sharing only a language with the urbane citizens of Montréal and Québec City. Over much of its length, ancient blunted mountains fall directly to the shore, their feet laved by combers born off Portugal. In the interior are still higher peaks, traces of snow in their treeless upper reaches even in July. Deer, caribou and bears live there, and the clear tumbling streams are fairly choked with trout and salmon.

The usual starting point for an excursion into Gaspésie is Québec City. People driving from the US, especially from New England, may prefer to make the approach from the s, from Maine via Interstate 95, then N on Route 1 to the New Brunswick border, where it becomes Rte 17. Stay on that road to Campbellton, where there is a bridge to Pointe-à-la-Croix, then drive E on Rte 132. Since this is a circular tour, it can be read backward. See GASPÉSIE map on page 233.

For advance planning, contact the Gaspésie Tourist Information Office, **Tourisme Bas St-Laurent/Gaspésie** *(357 Route de la Mer, Sainte-Flavie, Québec G0J 2L0* ☎ *775-2223)*, or the Québec tourist information offices listed on pages 31 and 204.

From Québec City, a driving tour around the perimeter of the peninsula and back to Québec takes a minimum of 4 days. That's not really enough: 5 or 6 days would be better, and 7 or 8 to allow at least a 2-night stay in the picturesque village of Percé, at the easternmost tip.

This is not a trip to be undertaken from October to late April, when the weather can be fierce, and most motels and restaurants are closed. Even in summer, packing should allow for a sweater or windbreaker, for the nights, and the ocean breezes are cool. Tuck in a French phrasebook, too, preferably one published in Québec, for English is not as widely understood as in Montréal. Remember that use of seat belts is obligatory. Speed limits are given in km (60kph is slightly over 37mph).

Leave Québec City via the Grande Allée (which goes through some name changes), driving W and staying with the Route 175 signs. In about 30 minutes, take the Pont (Bridge) Pierre-Laporte across the river toward **Rivière-du-Loup**. On the other side, pick up Rte 20, driving NE. This is a limited-access highway, passing farms and small towns of pleasant but not compelling aspect. Travelers with extra time available may wish to exit the highway at one of the several intersections, and pick up Rte 132, which runs closer to the southern shore of the St Lawrence. Along that route, the towns of **L'Islet-sur-Mer**, **St-Jean-Port-Joli** and **Kamouraska** invite brief exploration.

Rte 20 merges with 132 just beyond Rivière-du-Loup. That mostly 2-lane road bears the same number for the entire circuit of the peninsula. Heading E, **Rimouski** is the last good-sized city, but it has little of interest to visitors. Continue to the hamlet of **Ste-Flavie**. On the right will be the **Gaspésie Tourist Information Office** *(357 Route de la Mer* ☎ *775-2223)*.

It can't be missed, with its vivid green trim and crimson roof. Brochures, information and advice are available from the bilingual attendants inside. They will surely recommend a stop at the **Jardins de Métis**, about 10km (6 miles) E on 132. Take their word, for these gardens are one of the major attractions of the entire peninsula (☎ *open daily early June to mid-September 8.30am–8pm)*. The entrance is on the left. One Elsie Meighen Reford developed the estate and its formal gardens, a lavish and thoughtfully planned display of more than 500 species of annuals and flowering shrubs. They are laid out in the English manner (more naturalistic than the formal French style), in six distinct settings. A brook runs through the property and past the magnificent rock garden. Ruby-throated hummingbirds whirr through the section called the **Allée Royale**, which is flanked, at least seasonally, by majestic peonies. Ms. Reford's large seaside villa is now a museum and a restaurant, which is good enough, but inevitably crowded.

Matane, about 48km (30 miles) NE, has the last ferry terminal to the N shore of the St-Laurent. The town is best known for its shrimp and salmon fisheries. As many as 3,000 salmon are known to migrate up the Matane River each year. This may be the place to stop for the night.

⚭ ⥤ Among the limited possibilities are the **Motel & Hôtel Belle Plage** *(1310 Matane-sur-Mer* ☎ *562-2323* ▯*)* and the **Hôtel des Gouverneurs** *(250 Av. du Phare E* ☎ *566-2651* ▯ ≋ ⋛ ⋐ *).*

But if time allows, a better stopping-place is **Ste-Anne-des-Monts**, about 85km (53 miles) E, then turn inland on the 299 road. The road slowly rises toward the **Chic-Choc** peaks, the continuation of the Appalachians that are the spine of the peninsula, and into the **Parc de la Gaspésie**, where one of the moose or caribou that roam these slopes might be glimpsed.

⚭ ⥤ In about 40km (25 miles) is **Le Gîte du Mont-Albert** *(P.O. Box 1150, Ste-Anne-des-Monts, Québec G0E 2G0* ☎ *763-2288* ▯*).* The mountain lodge looks up directly at its towering namesake, **Mount Albert**, which is inevitably scored with streaks of snow. Accommodations, which are in the main lodge or outlying bungalows, are decidedly rustic. Cabins have summer camp furniture, painted plywood floors, bathtubs with claw feet, no TV. But there is plenty of hot water, a telephone, a fireplace, and chairs on the porch from which to watch the sun fall and inhale the clean alpine air. (Should a drink be desired along with the sunset, it's best to bring along the necessary supplies, since the bar in the lodge keeps unpredictable hours.) The attractive dining room there comes as a surprise, with its polished floors and crisp napery.

The lodge is part of a training program for young people intent on entering the hospitality trade. Service is by waitresses who are concerned with their clients' welfare, and the food is tasty and easy on the eye. The 5-course dinner is a bargain, and charitable guests will understand the occasional lapses and delays. Reservations for the lodge must be made in advance. Those who stay a full day have their choice of trout-fishing, hikes, helicopter-skiing, and treks to observe the caribou.

When leaving, return to the coast and continue E on 132. Now, the mountains start to crowd the sea and are soon plunging to the rock-strewn shore, and you pass a series of fishing and farming hamlets. At **Mont-St-Pierre**, there may be the startling sight of hang-gliders wheeling in the sky. This is one of the top sites for the sport in eastern Canada, due to the presence of favorable updrafts. Their launching pads are at the top of the mountain for which the town is named.

⚭ ⥤ The **Motel-Restaurant aux Délices** is a lunch possibility, although unexceptional.

A picnic might be preferable, perhaps picking up a loaf of bread at one of the small bakeries and smoked salmon at the *poissonneries* spotted along the way. There is a picnic ground in **Mont-St-Pierre**, another just before **Grande-Vallée** (⋛), a third a little beyond **St-Yvon**.

Drivers and their passengers grow accustomed by now to this juxta-

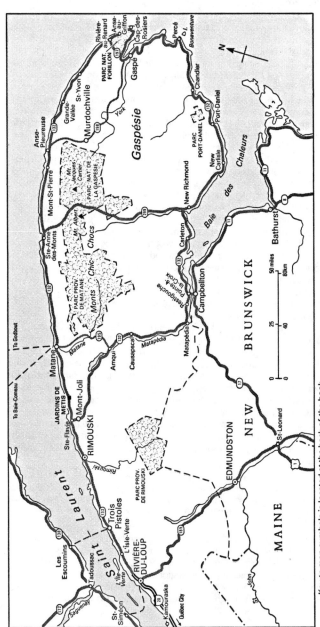

Key to map symbols is located at the back of the book

position of mountains and seascape. Details of Gaspé life become more apparent. The houses, for example, are sunburst yellow, royal blue, lavender, orange, pink or aqua. And these are not pale pastels, but undiluted hues straight from the tube. Perhaps they are painted thus as an expression of individualism. More likely, the colors are antidotes to the long gray winter, or even just a way to find home in a snowstorm.

Watch, too, for the quirky lawn decorations — accumulations, really, that come close to constituting a form of folk art. Here, a shrine to the Virgin composed of driftwood and clam shells; there, a large black cormorant made of mussel shells, with a crab claw for a beak. One homeowner chooses to erect a miniature village of dwarfs, dollhouses, and bridges that go nowhere; another has a gaudy assemblage of pinwheels, cutout cartoon characters and lifesized fantasy animals of painted burlap stretched over wire armatures. Some of the naive displays are quite wonderful.

Ladders are affixed to roofs, to facilitate repair and snow removal. Large Canadian and Québec flags flutter from the ridgepoles. Although fast disappearing, there are still hump-backed ovens in some front lawns, with black iron doors to insert loaves of bread at one end, and a chimney spout at the other to release the wood smoke. Long rows of stacked lobster traps are seen, often next to large drying-racks for cod. Men and boys sell crude ship models at the roadside — even the sails are wood. Logging trucks rumble by, for this is lumbering country, too. Black-and-white dairy cattle graze in rocky pastures, as do goats, sheep and horses. Québec City seems very far away. So does the rest of the world.

The road and the shore start to bend toward the s at **Rivière-au-Renard**, and a small decision must be made. Rte. 197 cuts inland toward the town of **Gaspé**, reducing travel time to the night's destination, **Percé**, by about 45 minutes. The more scenic route is to continue on 132. These are the forested Gaspé headlands, preserved as the **Parc National Forillon**. Apart from the thousands of sea birds that nest in its limestone cliffs each summer, there is the possibility of catching sight of the pelagic whales that pass here, as well as seals basking on offshore rocks.

Boat cruises, hikes, horseback riding, skindiving and fishing trips are offered. Information is available at the **reception center** *(open daily June–Labour Day),* a couple of miles on 132 beyond the Rte 197 intersection.

━━ At **Anse-au-Griffon** is the roadside **Manoir LeBoutillier**, an 1840 house built by a cod merchant, using the cargo of ships wrecked off that coast. Classified as an historic monument, it has a few relics and photos in an upstairs gallery. Its primary function is as a restaurant, with two dining rooms. Service is erratic and the food marginal.

Continuing, the road soon rounds the headland into a deep fjord-like bay. At the end is the town of **Gaspé**. This was where Jacques Cartier first stepped onto the mainland of the New World, in 1534. While the town is important economically to the region, there is not much to interest a tourist, so press on toward Percé. Shortly before reaching the resort village, there is a first sighting of **Percé Rock** and **Bonaventure Island**, sitting in the ocean just off what could be the end of the world. Sky and sea seem to merge, and it is not difficult to imagine that one can make out the curvature of the earth.

Percé is just a few miles farther. The trip from Mont-Albert to Percé Rock will have taken 5–6 hours, a distance of about 350km (220 miles). Perhaps because its development as a resort is fairly recent, Percé does not have the tatty, honky-tonk atmosphere that might be expected. The many motels strung out along the shore are just that: crisp and clean but unremarkable in themselves. What makes them unusual is their views of the most prominent feature of the near seascape — that Rock.

From the near end, it looms like the prow of a beached supertanker, its striated sides dropping straight from its flat top to the water nearly 90m (300 feet) below. At low tide, it can be reached on foot, which everyone does. From the side, the 427m-long (1,400-foot) Rock has a much different aspect: an arched hole pierces straight through the cliff at water level.

Farther out is **Bonaventure Island**, a bird sanctuary. It can be reached by ferry from the central wharf. (Park in the lot with the sign *Parc de l'Île-Bonaventure*.) The ferry leaves about every 20 minutes, and goes first past the Rock, then circles Bonaventure and docks to allow passengers to debark if they wish. (Another ferry will be along soon.)

There are hundreds of thousands of sea birds, and although Bonaventure is known more for its numbers than its varieties, there are enough species to keep dedicated birdwatchers busy for a day. Included among them are double-crested cormorants, razorbills, puffins, kittiwakes, black guillemots, murres, and an estimated 50,000 yellow-headed gannets. To take full advantage of all this, be sure to bring some binoculars and a pair of sturdy shoes.

One of the first motels on the road into Percé is the double-decked **Auberge Les Trois Soeurs** *(Percé, Québec G0C 2L0* ☎ *782-2183 or 800-361-6162* ▯*)*. It has a pleasant staff, a laundry room, and a beach with an unobstructed view of the "prow" end of the Rock. Farther along the road, past the village center, is the **Hôtel La Normandie** *(Percé G0C 2L0* ☎ *782-2112 or 800-463-0820* ▯*)*. Its rooms are only slightly more expensive, and it is more stylish than others in town. A broad lawn leads down to the beach, with its view of the side of the Rock and Island. Both no-meal and Modified American Plan (breakfast and dinner) rates are available. The all-you-can-eat breakfast buffet is a real bargain.

Another breakfast choice might be **Biard Betty's**, near the town center on the main road. This buffet is for those who believe that the first meal of the day is the most important, and the cost is very low. The lunch and dinner buffets are neither as good, nor such a bargain.

Better, take the midday meal — exceptionally well-done for the low price — at the **Maison du Pêcheur** *(Pl. du Quai* ☎ *762-5331)*. A tidy place with a full bar, next to the ferry wharf, it has as pleasant a serving staff as might be asked. A meal might be creamy carrot soup, a whole cold lobster, or mackerel in a delicious tarragon *béarnaise* sauce, followed, of course, by sugar pie. All of it costs little more than the lobster alone purchased in a store. Don't miss it.

The gastronomic event of the entire excursion still awaits. Get directions at the motel for **L'Auberge du Gargantua** *(* ☎ *782-2852* ▯*)*. It's up the road called the Route des Failles, which intersects with 132 at the s end of town, and rises steeply to a peak that overlooks a stunning panorama of the empty fastness of the interior. Ridge follows mountain ridge until they fade into the mists, like a Japanese painting.

Dinner in the restaurant is less tranquil. It is owned and very actively run by an ebullient ferret of a man on the golden side of 70. He brooks no lip from employee or patron. "I'm busy," he says to a man who asks for a drink while waiting for a table, but in due course suggests a "Petit Gargantua." That mild-looking concoction is made with five liqueurs. When a table becomes available, the proprietor sits down with his guests to take their order.

What follows is a wonderment. Plate #1: vegetable and pasta salads, olives, cornichons, pâté and periwinkles (sea snails); #2: tureen of vegetable broth; #3: lobster, fish or beef with side dishes; #4: a dazzle of desserts. All is skillfully wrought, of that delectable order that sends eyes rolling back into heads in pleasure. The bill is high for these parts, especially with wine and after-dinner brandy. It's worth every penny. When they leave, all the children get lollipops.

Those less intent on eating can hike from the inn up the Route des Failles to **La Grande Crevasse** (◊€), although the views from the inn itself will satisfy most people.

The next stretch, from Percé to **Carleton**, is about 273km (170 miles). Very quickly, as the road bends w, the terrain flattens into a broad coastal plain. The mountains, so omnipresent on the northern shore, are no longer visible. After about 48km (30 miles) of contiguous towns and tawdry built-up areas, large dairy farms and neat little rural communities take over. The beaches are more accessible along this coast, and composed more of red sand than of rocks. English place names are frequently seen — Chandler, Newport, Hope Town, New Carlisle — for this part of the peninsula was settled by loyalists to the English Crown who fled the United States during and after the Revolution.

If departure from Percé was made after lunch, **Carleton** is a convenient overnight stop.

There are two good neighboring motels near the center of town: the **Manoir Belle-Plage** (☎364-3388 ⅢⅢ) and the **Baie-Bleue** (☎364-3355 ⅢⅢ). Both have restaurants and ordinary but comfortable rooms. The Belle Plage isn't air-conditioned; the Baie-Bleue is, and has a heated swimming pool, giving it the edge in desirability.

But if it is still early, continue on Rte 132. (Those who wish to go s into the US can turn onto the bridge at **Pointe-à-la-Croix**, picking up Rte 17 traveling s in New Brunswick.) **Restigouche** is the next town and is the center of the Micmac reserve. Some of their handicrafts, including baskets and leather goods, are on sale.

Matapédia, about 72km (45 miles) from Carleton, is a likely place for a lunch break.

Café l'Entracte (Rte 132 ☎865-2734) is the usual choice, featuring home-cooking and a terrace.

Beyond Matapédia, Rte 132 turns inland, following a wide, shallow river of the same name. On the right are the last of the Chic-Choc Mountains, and the tumbling river is known for its salmon fishing. Anglers camp along the banks, amid stands of fir and birch and aspen, to cast dry flies, either in hip waders or from boats. Think twice about wetting a line, though: in addition to a provincial fishing license, every angler must pay a stiff daily fee, and the odds are against even getting a bite in the public access stretches of the river, let alone a fighting salmon. By one estimate, it takes five days of casting to land a single fish.

The prettiest part of the valley starts at **Causapscal**, marked by its two covered bridges. Should it now be time to stop for the night, the town of **Amqui** is only 15 minutes away.

Its **Motel Val-Moni** (340 Blvd. St-Benoît ☎629-2241 ⅢⅢ) has 80 air-conditioned rooms, some with whirlpool baths, a pool and a bar-restaurant.

At **Mont-Joli** (formerly Ste-Flavie Station), 71km (44 miles) on, it is about 338km (210 miles) to Québec City, the last part of the trip on Highway 20.

Index

List of street names

- Listed below are all streets mentioned in the text that fall within the area covered by the full-color maps **1–4** (Toronto), **7–10** (Montréal) and **13–14** (Québec City).
- Map numbers appear in **bold** type. Some smaller streets are not named on the maps, but the reference given will help you locate the correct neighborhood.

Gauchetière, Rue de la, 10F4–8E4
Gosford, Rue, 8D5
Greene, Av., 9H1–10I4
Guy, Rue, 9G3–10G5

Jacques-Cartier, Pl., 8D5
Jeanne-Mance, Rue, 7D3–8E4

Laurier, Av., 000
Laval, Av, 7C1–3
Lemoyne, Rue, 8E5

Mackay, Rue, 9G3
Maisonneuve, Blvd. de, 8A4-9J2
Mansfield, Rue, 9E3–10F4
Marie-Anne, Rue, 7C1–A2
Mayor, Rue, 8E4
McGill, Rue, 8E5–6
Montagne, Rue de la, 9F3–10G6
Mullins, Rue, 10J5–I6

Normand, Rue, 8E5
Notre-Dame, Rue, 9J3–8A5

Ontario, Rue, 8A4–D4

Parc, Av. du, 7D2–E3
Peel, Rue, 9E2–10F6
Phillips, Carré 9E4
Pins, Av. des, 9H1–7C3
Place d'Armes, Côte de la, 8D4
Président-Kennedy, Rue, 7E3–D3
Prince-Arthur, Rue, 7E2–C3

Rachel, Rue, 7B2–D1
René Lévesque, Blvd., 8A5-9J2
Rigaud, Rue, 7C3
Roy, Rue, 7C3
Royale, Pl., 8E5

St-Alexis, Rue, 8E5
St-Amable, Rue, 8D5
St-Antoine, Rue, 9J3–8A5
Ste-Catherine, Côte, 7D1–2
Ste-Catherine, Rue, 9I2–8D5
St-Denis, Rue, 7B1–8C5
St-Dominique, Rue, 7C1–8D5

St-Francois-Xavier, Rue, 8E5
St-Gabriel, Rue, 8D5
St-Hubert, Rue, 7B1–8C5
St-Jacques, Rue, 9J3–8D5
St-Laurent, Blvd., 7C1–8D5
St-Louis, Carré, 7C3
St-Paul, Rue, 8E5–C5
St-Pierre, Rue, 8E5–6
St-Sulpice, Chemin, 9H2
St-Urbain, Rue, 7C1–8D5
Sherbrooke, Rue, 7A3–9J1
Square-Dorchester, Rue du, 10F4
Stanley, Rue, 9F2–10F4

Tupper, Rue, 9H3–G3

Union, Av., 7E3–8E4
University, Rue, 7E2–8F5

Victoria, Rue, 7E3
Victoria, Sq., 8E4
Viger, Av., 8E4–C5
Ville-Marie, Pl., 8E4–5

Youville, Pl. d', 8E5

QUÉBEC CITY

Armes, Pl. d', 14C5
Artigny, Rue d', 000
Auteuil, Rue d', 14C4

Berthelot, Rue, 13D2–E3
Buade, Rue, 14C4–5

Carrières, Rue des, 14C5
Champlain, Blvd., 13F3–14C5
Chevrotière, Rue de la, 13D2–3
Citadelle, Côte de la, 14D4
Couillard, Rue, 14B4

Dalhousie, Rue, 14B5–C5
Donnacona, Rue, 14C4
Dufferin, Av., 13C3–D3
Dufferin, Terrasse, 14C5–D5

Fabrique, Côte de la, 14B4
Fort, Rue du, 14C5

George V, Pl., 13D3
Grande Allée Est, 13F1–14D3

Jardins, Rue des, 14C4–B4

Laporte, Rue, 14C4–5

Marché-Champlain, Rue du, 14C5
Marché-Finlay, Rue du, 14C5
Montagne, Côte de la, 14C5
Montcalm, Pl., 13E3

Palais, Côte du, 13B3–14B4
Paris, Pl. de, 14C5
Parloir, Rue du, 14C4
Petit-Champlain, Rue du, 14C5

Québec, Pl., 13D3

Remparts, Rue des, 14B4
Royale, Pl., 14C5

St-André, Rue, 13B3–14B5
Ste-Anne, Rue, 14C4–5
St-Antoine, Rue, 14B5
St-Augustin, Rue, 13C2–3
St-Cyrille Est, Blvd., 13E1–C3
St-Denis, Av., 14D4–C5
Sainte-Famille, Rue de la, 14B4
Ste-Geneviève, Av., 14D4–C5
St-Jean, Rue, 13D1–14B4
St-Louis, Rue, 14C4–5
St-Paul, Rue, 13B3–14B5
St-Pierre, Rue, 14B5–C5
Ste-Ursule, Rue, 14C4–D4
Sault-au-Matelot, Rue, 14B5
Sous-le-Fort, Rue, 14C5

Terrasse Dufferin, Pl., 14C5
Traversiers, Rue des, 14C5
Trésor, Rue, 14B4

Université, Rue de l', 14B4–5

Clothing sizes chart

LADIES
Suits and dresses

Australia	8	10	12	14	16	18	
France	34	36	38	40	42	44	
Germany	32	34	36	38	40	42	
Italy	38	40	42	44	46		
Japan	7	9	11	13			
UK	6	8	10	12	14	16	18
USA	4	6	8	10	12	14	16

Shoes

USA	6	$6\frac{1}{2}$	7	$7\frac{1}{2}$	8	$8\frac{1}{2}$
UK	$4\frac{1}{2}$	5	$5\frac{1}{2}$	6	$6\frac{1}{2}$	7
Europe	38	38	39	39	40	41

MEN
Shirts

USA, UK	14	$14\frac{1}{2}$	15	$15\frac{1}{2}$	16	$16\frac{1}{2}$	17
Europe, Japan Australia	36	37	38	39.5	41	42	43

Sweaters/T-shirts

Australia, USA, Germany	S		M		L		XL
UK	34		36-38		40		42-44
Italy	44		46-48		50		52
France	1		2-3		4		5
Japan			S-M		L		XL

Suits/Coats

UK, USA	36	38	40	42	44
Australia, Italy, France, Germany	46	48	50	52	54
Japan	S	M	L	XL	

Shoes

UK	7	$7\frac{1}{2}$	$8\frac{1}{2}$	$9\frac{1}{2}$	$10\frac{1}{2}$	11
USA	8	$8\frac{1}{2}$	$9\frac{1}{2}$	$10\frac{1}{2}$	$11\frac{1}{2}$	12
Europe	41	42	43	44	45	46

CHILDREN
Clothing

UK

Height (ins)	43	48	55	60	62	
Age	4-5	6-7	9-10	11	12	13

USA

Age	4	6	8	10	12	14

Europe

Height (cms)	125	135	150	155	160	165
Age	7	9	12	13	14	15

CONVERSION FORMULAE

To convert	Multiply by
Inches to Centimeters	2.540
Centimeters to Inches	0.39370
Feet to Meters	0.3048
Meters to feet	3.2808
Yards to Meters	0.9144
Meters to Yards	1.09361
Miles to Kilometers	1.60934
Kilometers to Miles	0.621371
Sq Meters to Sq Feet	10.7638
Sq Feet to Sq Meters	0.092903
Sq Yards to Sq Meters	0.83612
Sq Meters to Sq Yards	1.19599
Sq Miles to Sq Kilometers	2.5899
Sq Kilometers to Sq Miles	0.386103
Acres to Hectares	0.40468
Hectares to Acres	2.47105
Gallons to Liters	4.545
Liters to Gallons	0.22
Ounces to Grams	28.3495
Grams to Ounces	0.03528
Pounds to Grams	453.592
Grams to Pounds	0.00220
Pounds to Kilograms	0.4536
Kilograms to Pounds	2.2046
Tons (UK) to Kilograms	1016.05
Kilograms to Tons (UK)	0.0009842
Tons (US) to Kilograms	746.483
Kilograms to Tons (US)	0.0013396

Quick conversions

Kilometers to Miles	Divide by 8, multiply by 5
Miles to Kilometers	Divide by 5, multiply by 8
1 meter =	Approximately 3 feet 3 inches
2 centimeters =	Approximately 1 inch
1 pound (weight) =	475 grams (nearly $\frac{1}{2}$ kilogram)
Celsius to Fahrenheit	Divide by 5, multiply by 9, add 32
Fahrenheit to Celsius	Subtract 32, divide by 9, multiply by 5

What the papers say:

• "The expertly edited American Express series has the knack of pin-pointing precisely the details you need to know, and doing it concisely and intelligently." **(*The Washington Post*)**

• "*(Venice)* . . . the best guide book I have ever used." **(*The Standard* — London)**

• "Amid the welter of guides to individual countries, American Express stands out . . . . " **(*Time*)**

• "Possibly the best . . . guides on the market, they come close to the oft-claimed 'all you need to know' comprehensiveness, with much original experience, research and opinions." **(*Sunday Telegraph* — London)**

• "The most useful general guide was *American Express New York* by Herbert Bailey Livesey. It also has the best street and subway maps." **(*Daily Telegraph* — London)**

• " . . . in the flood of travel guides, the *American Express* guides come closest to the needs of traveling managers with little time." **(*Die Zeit* — Germany)**

What the experts say:

• "We only used one guide book, Sheila Hale's *AmEx Venice*, for which she and the editors deserve a Nobel Prize." **(travel writer Eric Newby, London)**

• "Congratulations to you and your staff for putting out the best guide book of *any* size *(Barcelona & Madrid)*. I'm recommending it to everyone." **(travel writer Barnaby Conrad, Santa Barbara, California)**

• "If you're only buying one guide book, we recommend American Express . . . . " **(*Which?* — Britain's leading consumer magazine)**

• "The judges selected *American Express London* as the best guide book of the past decade — it won the competition in 1983. [The guide] was praised for being 'concise, well presented, up-to-date, with unusual information.' " **(News release from the London Tourist Board and Convention Bureau)**

What readers from all over the world say:

• "We could never have had the wonderful time that we did without your guide to *Paris*. The compactness was very convenient, your maps were all we needed, but it was your restaurant guide that truly made our stay special . . . . We have learned first-hand: *American Express — don't leave home without it.*" (A. R., Virginia Beach, Va., USA)

• Of Sheila Hale's *Florence and Tuscany:* "I hope you don't mind my calling you by your first name, but during our recent trip to Florence and Siena [we] said on innumerable occasions, 'What does Sheila say about that?' " (H.G., Buckhurst Hill, Essex, England)

• "I have visited Mexico most years since 1979 . . . Of the many guides I have consulted during this time, by far the best has been James Tickell's *Mexico,* of which I've bought each edition." (J.H., Mexico City)

• "We have heartily recommended these books to all our friends who have plans to travel abroad." (A.S. and J.C., New York, USA)

• "Much of our enjoyment came from the way your book *(Venice)* sent us off scurrying around the interesting streets and off to the right places at the right times". (Lord H., London, England)

• "It *(Paris)* was my constant companion and totally dependable . . . . " (V. N., Johannesburg, South Africa)

• "We found *Amsterdam, Rotterdam & The Hague* invaluable . . . probably the best of its kind we have ever used. It transformed our stay from an ordinary one into something really memorable . . . . " (S.W., Canterbury, England)

• "Despite many previous visits to Italy, I wish I had had your guide *(Florence and Tuscany)* ages ago. I love the author's crisp, literate writing and her devotion to her subject." (M. B-K., Denver, Colorado, USA)

• "We became almost a club as we found people sitting at tables all around, consulting their little blue books!" (F.C., Glasgow, Scotland)

• "I have just concluded a tour . . . using your comprehensive *Cities of Australia* as my personal guide. Thank you for your magnificent, clear and precise book." (Dr. S.G., Singapore)

• "We never made a restaurant reservation without checking your book *(Venice).* The recommendations were excellent, and the historical and artistic text got us through the sights beautifully." (L.S., Boston, Ma., USA)

• "The book *(Hong Kong, Singapore & Bangkok)* was written in such a personal way that I feel as if you were actually writing this book for me." (L.Z., Orange, Conn., USA)

• "I feel as if you have been a silent friend shadowing my time in Tuscany." (T.G., Washington, DC, USA)

American Express Travel Guides

spanning the globe....

EUROPE
Amsterdam, Rotterdam
  & The Hague
Athens and the
  Classical Sites ‡
Barcelona, Madrid &
  Seville
Berlin, Potsdam &
  Dresden ‡
Brussels
Dublin
Florence and Tuscany
London
Moscow &
  St Petersburg ‡
Paris
Prague
Provence and the
  Côte d'Azur ‡
Rome
Venice ‡
Vienna & Budapest

NORTH AMERICA
Boston and New
  England ‡
Florida ‡
Los Angeles & San
  Diego
Mexico
New York
San Francisco and
  the Wine Regions
Toronto, Montréal &
  Québec City
Washington, DC

THE PACIFIC
Australia's
  Major Cities
Hong Kong
  & Taiwan
Singapore &
  Bangkok ‡
Tokyo

‡   Titles in preparation.

*Clarity and quality of information, combined
with outstanding maps — the ultimate in
travelers' guides*

KEY TO MAP PAGES

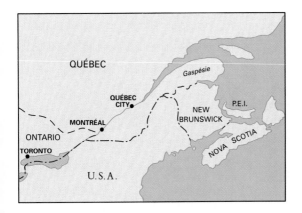

KEY TO MAP SYMBOLS

City Maps

▢	Major Place of Interest
▢	Other Important Building
▢	Built-up Area
▢	Park
▢	Cemetery
†	Church
✡	Synagogue
✚	Hospital
➥	Garage/Parking Lot
i	Information Office
✉	Post Office
✋	Police Station
Ⓢ Ⓜ	Subway, Metro
3	Adjoining Page No.

Environs and Area Maps

■	Place of Interest
▢	Built-up Area
▢	National Park/Woods
▢	Other Land
=O=	Highway (with access point)
▬	Provincial Highway
▬	Other Road
- - -	Ferry
═══	Railway
✈	Airport
✦	Airfield
▬▬	International Boundary
▬▬	Provincial Boundary
_ _	National Park Boundary

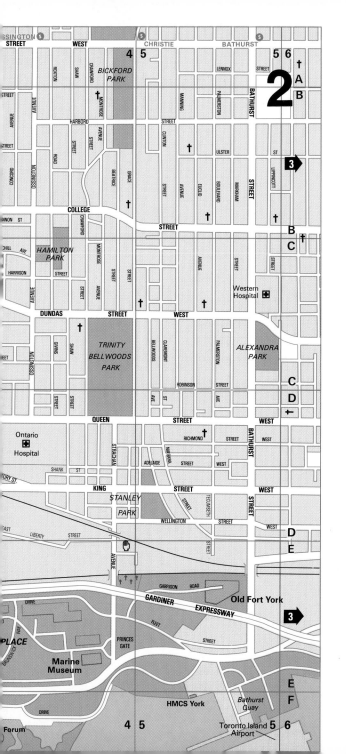

Pickering

Ajax

Fairport

METRO TORONTO ■ ZOO

401

carborough

York

slands

4 5   5 6

TORONTO ENVIRONS 6
A
B

0   5   10 miles
0   5   10   15km

B

C

LAKE   ONTARIO

C
D

Niagara-on-
the-Lake

FORT GEORGE ■   Youngstown

REIF WINERY ■   U.S.A.

D
E

55 **HILLEBRAND
WINERY**

**ST
CATHARINES**

Jordan
Harbour

Queen   Elizabeth   Way

**MUSEUM
AT LOCK 3** ■   **BOTANICAL
GARDENS** ■

Beamsville

406   **NIAGARA
FALLS**   **NIAGARA
FALLS**

20 **HORSESHOE
FALLS**   *Goat I.*

MARINELAND

*Niagara
River*

Queen   Elizabeth   Way

E
F

Bismarck   Pelham   **OLD FORT ERIE**

58

4 5   5 6

WELLAND

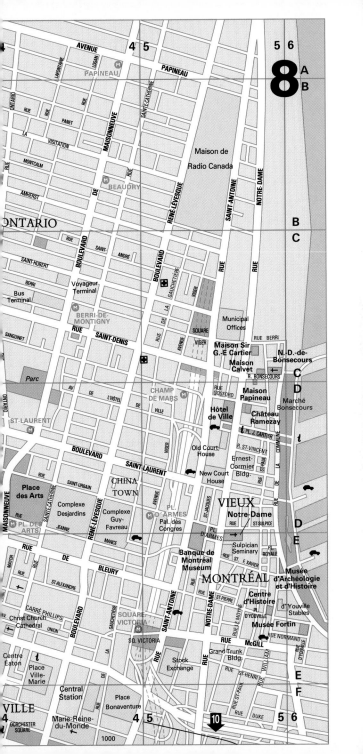

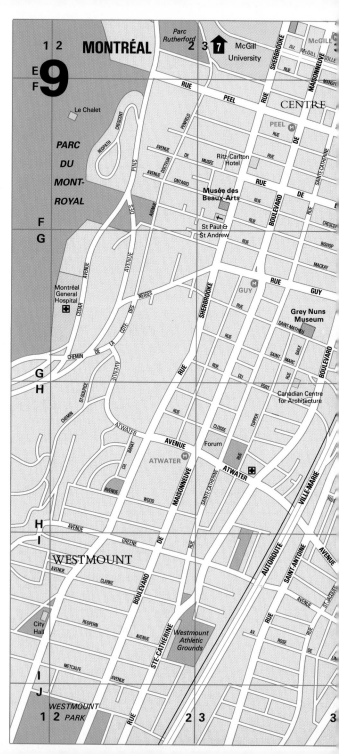

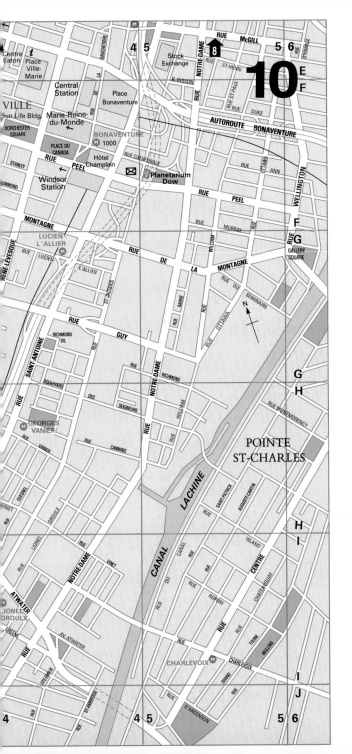

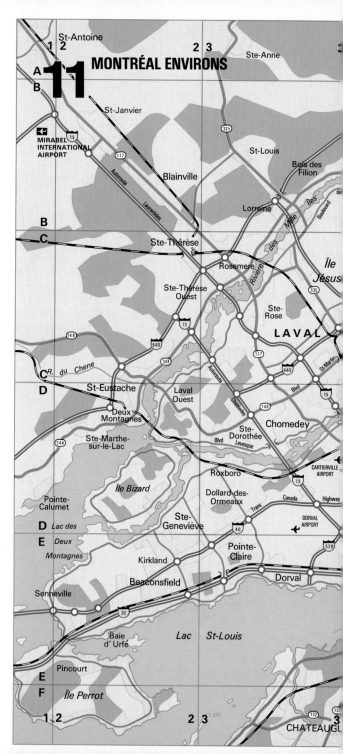

MONTRÉAL ENVIRONS

11

St-Antoine
1 2 · 2 3 · Ste-Anne

A
B

St-Janvier

MIRABEL INTERNATIONAL AIRPORT · 15

335

Autoroute · 117 · Laurentides

St-Louis

Blainville

Bois des Filion

Lorraine · Îles de · Boulevard

B
C · Ste-Thérèse

Rosemere · Rivière · des · Mille

Île Jésus

Ste-Thérèse Ouest · 335

Ste-Rose

148 · 13 · 640

LAVAL

344 · 117 · 440 · St-Martin

C · R. du Chene

St-Eustache · Laval Ouest · Autoroute Chomedey · 148 · Blvd · 15

D

Deux Montagnes · Ste-Dorothée Levesque · Chomedey

Ste-Marthe-sur-le-Lac · 344 · Blvd

Île Bizard · Roxboro · CARTIERVILLE AIRPORT · 13

Pointe-Calumet · Dollard-des-Ormeaux · Canada · Highway

DORVAL AIRPORT

D · Lac des · Ste-Geneviève · Trans · 40

E · Deux

Montagnes · Kirkland · Pointe-Claire · 520

Senneville · Beaconsfield · Dorval

Baie d'Urfé · Lac St-Louis · 20

E · Pincourt

F · Île Perrot

1 2 · 2 3 · 132 · 13

CHATEAUGU

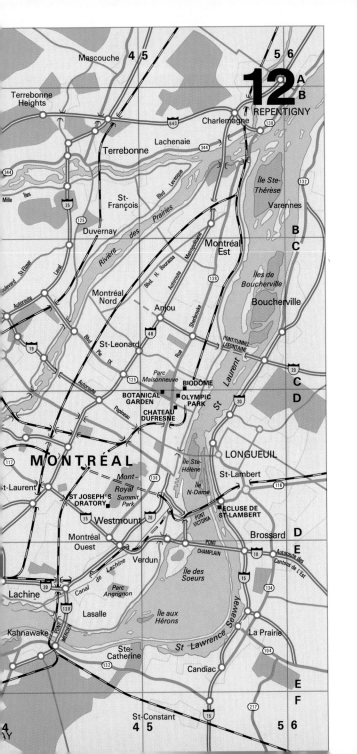

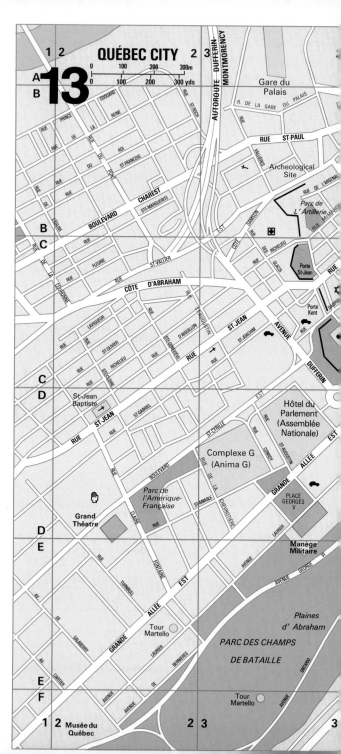